Interfaith Engagement in Milwaukee

A Brief History of Christian–Muslim Dialogue

Interfaith Engagement in Milwaukee

A Brief History of Christian–Muslim Dialogue

Edited by

IRFAN A. OMAR & KAITLYN C. DALY

MARQUETTE
UNIVERSITY
PRESS

Advanced Praise for *Interfaith Engagement in Milwaukee*

"A chorus of voices have come together in this inaugural book to begin telling the story of the greater Milwaukee area's role as a leader in interfaith dialogue, understanding, and relationship building. This is an important effort, one that hopefully will serve as a catalyst to evoke additional perspectives that document the past while inspiring ever greater numbers of people to recognize the value of diversity and transcend the challenges of today."

—Tom Heinen
Executive Director Emeritus
Interfaith Conference of Greater Milwaukee

"The collection of readings documents intentionality and purpose as it takes the reader through a journey of Milwaukee's struggles and successes in understanding the importance of sitting down at the table and engaging in difficult dialogue with those that don't engage in same-religion affiliations. It speaks to all ages and institutions and provokes readers to determine how they can be a participant and more than an observer in the process.

This book is essential reading for those who wish to make a difference."

—Dr. Joan M. Prince,
Vice Chancellor and Clinical Associate Professor
University of Wisconsin–Milwaukee

"Interfaith dialogue has played an extremely important role to overcome negative environment and has provided dignity and respect for all. *Interfaith Engagement in Milwaukee* offers a compelling case for interfaith collaboration."

—Dr. Swarnjit S. Arora,
Member of the Board of Directors, Interfaith Conference
of Greater Milwaukee, Sikh Religious Society of Wisconsin
Professor Emeritus, Department of Economics & Director, Institute for
Survey and Policy Research at the University of Wisconsin–Milwaukee

"A well-conceived, well-documented, and well-executed presentation of the personal, community, and institutional elements that have formed the scope and trajectories of interfaith engagement in Milwaukee, with special emphasis on the Islamic–Christian dialogue that began in 1980 and developed in a number of productive forms of interaction and cooperation in the subsequent decades. . . . A thoughtfully conceived telling, on a number of levels, of locally based and supported efforts to establish and effectively sustain practices of interfaith understanding, friendship, and cooperation attentive to both the local and larger contexts in which such dialogue efforts take place . . . underlines a number of ways in which such local efforts are of fundamental importance for increasing interreligious understanding, especially in a global culture in which the reality of religious plurality has become a pervasive feature of human life and interaction."

—Rev. Philip Rossi, SJ
Emeritus Professor of Theology, Marquette University
Editor, *Theological Studies*

ASSOCIATION
of UNIVERSITY
PRESSES

MARQUETTE UNIVERSITY PRESS
MILWAUKEE

The Association of Jesuit University Presses

Cover image is an adaptation of the logo printed atop official 'Islamic–Christian' dialogue letterhead.

Library of Congress Cataloging-in-Publication Data

Names: Omar, Irfan A., editor. | Daly, Kaitlyn C., editor.
Title: Interfaith engagement in Milwaukee : a brief history of
   Christian-Muslim dialogue / edited by Irfan A. Omar & Kaitlyn C. Daly.
Description: First. | Milwaukee, Wisconsin : Marquette University Press,
   [2019] | Includes bibliographical references and index. | Summary: "This
   book offers a brief history of Christian-Muslim as well as multi-faith
   relations in Milwaukee, Wisconsin. It is in part based on qualitative
   research highlighting the importance of interfaith dialogue and
   documenting the social and communal benefits derived from interfaith
   interactions and partnerships"-- Provided by publisher.
Identifiers: LCCN 2019049184 | ISBN 9781626000568 (paperback)
Subjects: LCSH: Islam--Wisconsin--Milwaukee. |
   Islam--Relations--Christianity. | Christianity and other religions. |
   Christianity and other religions--Islam.
Classification: LCC BP67.U62 W65 2019 | DDC 261.2/70977595--dc23
LC record available at https://lccn.loc.gov/2019049184

The editors gratefully acknowledge the help and financial support from the Marquette University Center for Peacemaking (CfP) and the Center for Urban Research, Teaching & Outreach (CURTO)

Dedicated to all the "people of dialogue" everywhere, and

especially

Dr. Abbas Hamdani
Sr. Jessine Reiss, OSF
Sr. Lucille Walsh, OSF (d. 2013)

CONTENTS

PART 1

CHRISTIAN–MUSLIM RELATIONS IN MILWAUKEE: A BRIEF HISTORY / 47

PART 2

INTERFAITH ENGAGEMENT IN MILWAUKEE: AN OVERVIEW / 179

ACKNOWLEDGMENTS

This book would not have been possible without the ongoing support and encouragement from the Marquette University Center for Peacemaking. We are particularly grateful for a two-year grant from the center to fund the summertime research and writing that allowed the research team (Kaitlyn Daly, Sundus Jaber, Andrew Musgrave, Caroline Redick, and Dianne Rostollan) to produce drafts of their chapters. The grant also allowed us to hire students Jennifer Byrne, Daniel Mueller, and Jashive Quintas, who helped in the preparation of the manuscript. We thank the entire staff, especially Patrick Kennelly, Sherri Walker, Michael McNulty, SJ, and Chris Jeske, for believing in the efficacy of the project, and in the cause of dialogue, as well as for their material support. We are also indebted to Robert Smith, Harry G. John Professor of History and director of the Center for Urban Research, Teaching & Outreach (CURTO) at Marquette University, for his support of the project and for the generous contribution to defray the cost of publication.

Maureen Kondrick, the current director of Marquette University Press, has been enormously helpful in guiding our way through the intricacies of manuscript preparation. We thank her for her generosity in accepting our proposal and for seeing it through the publication process. In addition, Hannah Grubbs-Oechsle, Daniel Mueller, and Caroline Redick contributed by reading through parts of the book, which helped in reorganizing parts of the text to enhance the presentation of the material. We were also fortunate to have Jenn Byrne who gave generously of her time to edit the images for optimal printing. We would especially like to thank Patricia Kot for her exceptionally helpful comments and suggestions in preparing the manuscript for the press.

We thank all the Milwaukeeans who agreed to be interviewed and also provided us with historical and archival materials related to their engagement in interfaith work. These include (in alphabetical order): Huda Alkaff, Naheed Arshad, Intisar Atta, Othman Atta, Rev. Dr. Lisa Bates-Froiland, Inshirah Farhoud, Rev. Reirin Gumbel, Shaykh Ziad Hamdan, Dr. Mushir and Orusa Hassan, Shaykh Noman Hussain, Rev. Alexander (Sandy) Jacobs, Bishop Hee-Soo Jung, Elana Kahn, Rev. Ken Knippel, Cantor Deborah Martin, Rev. Andy Oren, Ahmad Quereshi, Dr. John and Bobbie Schmitt, Imam Ron Shaheed, Kirsten Shead, Bishop Richard Sklba, Lajwanti (Laj) Waghray, Pastor Andrew Warner, and Rabbi Michal Woll. We are also grateful to all the students at various institutions of higher learning, especially Faezh Dalieh, Bradley DeGarmo, Michelle Frederick, Sean Heinritz, Monica Kling, Ruth Lied, Luiz Gabriel Dias Duarte Machado, Wyatt Meyer, Tabitha Miller, Benjamin Pettee, Yuvraj Sandhu, and Nader Shammout. Faculty and staff at Marquette and elsewhere who generously gave of their time to answer questions include, Bernardo Avila-Borunda, Mary Sue Callan-Farley, Dr. Xavier Cole, Dr. Michael Lovell, Dr. Stephanie Russell, and Rev. Jessica Short (Marquette University); Dr. Swarnjit Arora, Thomas Dake, and Rev. Rachel Young Binter (UW–Milwaukee); Dr. Shawnee Daniels-Sykes (Mount Mary University); and Dr. Dan Di Domizio (Cardinal Stritch University).

Many thanks to the two veterans of interfaith dialogue and collaboration, Judi Longdin and Janan Najeeb, for giving their valuable time to speak to the research team, and for their written contributions for this volume. The inclusion of their version of a piece of history of dialogue is crucial in maintaining the weight of the argument that dialogue is transformative. Their chapters offer ample proof of the transformation experienced by these two leaders and subsequently through them by many others. We are also grateful to Tom Heinen, who expressed his wholehearted support of the project from the start. His encouragement for the project is most valuable as he has been and continues to be one of the key actors in promoting interfaith relations in Milwaukee. A special thanks to Dr. Swarnjit Arora, Dr. Joan Prince, and Rev. Philip Rossi, SJ, for reading through the draft and for their invaluable suggestions. Other colleagues at Marquette and elsewhere who inspired the work of dialogue are Gretchen Baumgardt; Serdar Bozdag; Joshua Burns; Kathy Coffee-Gunther; Michael Dante; Deirdre Dempsey; Owen Goldin; Rick Hanson (UW–Whitewater); Rabia Terri Harris (Stony Point Center); Heather Hathaway; Laura Hermann (UW–Milwaukee); Bradford Hinze (Fordham University); Steven Hartman Keiser; Connor Kelly; John Laurance, SJ; James Marten; Jodi Melamed; Gene Merz, SJ (d. 2019); Terry Miller; Susan Mountin; Phillip Naylor; Danielle Nussberger; Carol Ann Smith, SHCJ; James South; Richard Taylor; Madeline Wake; Kate Ward; and William Welburn. We are grateful to all of them for their encouragement, inspiration, and, in some cases, collaboration.

This book is the result of months of research and outreach, interviews, and conversations, none of which would have been possible without the dedication of the research team, which constitutes most of the authors in this volume. We recognize and honor the countless hours they spent in contacting and interviewing, collecting, and documenting artifacts, and producing narratives that provided a platform to share the stories of Milwaukee's interfaith effort.

Finally, this book is dedicated to the pioneering efforts made by the three original founders of the "Islamic Christian Dialogue," Sister Lucille Walsh, OSF; Dr. Abbas Hamdani; and Sister Jessine Reiss, OSF. While Sister Lucille passed away in 2013 at the age of 101, Dr. Hamdani and Sister Jessine have remained in touch. We are particularly pleased to acknowledge the debt we owe to both of them, who despite health issues made themselves available and were very helpful in getting us acquainted with the history behind the formal dialogue. The editors and the research team met with Sister Jessine several times since the spring of 2017. She was always happy to share what she remembered based on the resources at her disposal. She also gave us access to her library of documents, photos, and notes related to the dialogue beginning in 1980 and events that followed. Even though they no longer reside in the same city, the friendship between Sister Jessine and Dr. Hamdani is ongoing and manifests through the exchange of letters. Sister Jessine shared with us a recent letter from Dr. Hamdani, from 2017, which among other things included an update on news regarding other dialogue partners from their circle of dialogue (see fig. I.4 in the Introduction). They seemed to have fulfilled all of the main goals of dialogue, which includes building strong bonds of friendship that transcend whatever separates one from another. These are truly "people of dialogue."

INTRODUCTION

Irfan A. Omar

After his appointment as the new executive director of the Secretariat for Ecumenical and Interreligious Affairs (SEIA) for the United States Conference of Catholic Bishops (USCCB), Father Al Baca wrote an introductory letter, dated July 11, 2017, in which he noted:

> More than ever, the work of dialogue is important for the Church and in the world. Not a day goes by where there isn't some ecumenical and/or interfaith event or initiative happening in Rome or some other part of the world. Following the mandate of the Gospel and guided by the *Decree of Ecumenism* and *Nostra Aetate*, a path of dialogue, understanding and reconciliation has been placed before us. . . .
>
> Interreligious dialogue establishes friendship and cooperation with all religions outside of the Christian family in order to seek the good of every person and of society. And now we look at a new category of people who self-identify simply as spiritual: the "nones." Today, we carry a special burden and a joy in caring for and building up the whole human family.[1]

Furthermore, Father Baca asked the reader to "Pray for all of us in the Secretariat." The research findings in this book are offered here as a form of prayer for the people in SEIA, World Council of Churches (WCC), Islamic Society of North America (ISNA), and hundreds and thousands of other organizations, groups, and individuals—religious or secular—for their continued work toward solidarity across faith, nationality, culture, and ideology, going beyond any personal agendas that may detract from the goal of "caring for and building up the whole human family."

Interfaith relations are not new, and yet there is a considerable lack of familiarity with how communities of faith (and individual members within each community) relate to each other, participate in and contribute to community and social support networks, and collaborate with each other on projects involving social justice issues. There is a dearth of information and of studies

---

1. Father [Alfred] Baca, Welcome Letter, July 11, 2017, http://www.usccb.org/beliefs-and-teachings/ecumenical-and-interreligious/upload/bacawelcomeletterwebsite071117.pdf.

on community interface with an intentional interfaith labeling. Milwaukee, despite having a rich history of such activity, is not known for its pioneering interfaith activism. This work seeks to address that lacuna.

This project grew out of a graduate seminar in theology titled "Christians and Muslims in Dialogue," offered at Marquette University in the spring of 2017. During the course of the semester, and based on participants' interest, it was expanded into a community-wide project to document—even if in an abbreviated version—the practice of interfaith engagement and collaboration in the greater Milwaukee area. Although the project is focused on Christian–Muslim dialogue, it includes an account of the broader contextual framework of interfaith outreach and dialogue in the greater Milwaukee area. Formal dialogues between Jewish and Christian, especially Roman Catholic, groups in Milwaukee began a few years earlier than the Christian–Muslim dialogue. The Catholic–Jewish Conference was officially established in 1975, followed by regular meetings and events aimed at developing personal relationships. This example inspired, at least partially, the effort to bring together a group of Christians and Muslims who formally started their meetings in November 1980. This book goes beyond the original project and includes accounts of other initiatives and programs that have surfaced—some of them ongoing—since the mid-1990s.

The main goals of the research were:

- collecting and documenting programs, meetings, workshops where people of various faith traditions, especially Christians and Muslims, came together to share information about faith and/or to collaborate in faith-related and faith-inspired social, cultural, scholarly, and other activities;
- retrieving and interpreting narratives through personal interviews and preserving artifacts such as flyers, minutes of meetings, event photos, newspaper reports, newsletters, and so on; and
- presenting and organizing these findings based on qualitative data and scholarly research in a book-length study.

Besides the scholarly sources on interfaith—particularly on Christian–Muslim dialogue, data collected through interviews with people involved in dialogue have been an important basis for the narratives in this work. Archival materials obtained from various sources and individual dialogue actors (see Appendices A and B) also informed the writing concerning events, people, application, and impact of dialogue. These materials have been part of the analysis that serves as a window into the history of interfaith activism in Milwaukee. The research findings include an accounting of many previous interactions as well as ongoing engagement between Christians, Muslims, and others at various levels and in a variety of venues. This project constitutes original research because of its reliance on, and the use of, personal interviews and qualitative data. The narratives emerging from this data are further enhanced by the interweaving of scholarly literature on interfaith dialogue, its histories, and its impact on community building as well as on creating greater opportunities for mutual learning and peacemaking. The bibliographic resources created in the process (such as interviews) are a valuable addition to the existing literature on the subject. They will become an important part of the primary sources for any future research on Christian–Muslim as well as multi-faith relations in Milwaukee.

One of the aims of this project is to demonstrate that dialogue creates reliable and sustaining social networks necessary for undertaking mutually beneficial collaborative social and community-oriented projects. The research project is both theoretical as well as praxis oriented. As noted, several authors in this work began their journey as participants in the research project on the topic. The authors' knowledge of the academic literature on dialogue informed the narratives that emerged from their meetings with local dialogue actors whom they interviewed. At the same time, they developed a deeper understanding of the theoretical foundations due to their encounter with real people engaged in dialogue. This process constitutes a form of dialogue in itself. Thus, the project is dialogical both in method as well as in scope.

In the main, the essays are formulated based on the analysis of the scholarly sources that served as an interpretative lens to clarify and elaborate on the principles of dialogue and interactions found within the religious traditions. They offer a perspective that aims to aid the reader in understanding references from textual sources (both quranic and biblical; Muslim and Christian) concerning the call for dialogue and interaction with a religious other. The list of textual sources also includes various religious documents and statements such as those from the World Council of Churches (WCC) and those that came forth as a result of the Second Vatican Council (*Nostra Aetate* and the *Lumen Gentium*), and more recent ones such as "The Makkah Appeal" and "A Common Word" as well as statements from the Wisconsin Council of Churches. All of these sources speak to the imperative of dialogue, providing a theological rationale for engagement with a religious other for the common good. The chapters in this book also sought to draw out specific elements in these sources that speak to the relationship between faith and service within the context of dialogue across religious lines. People from both religious as well as secular backgrounds can find meaning in such connections as their interests often converge on the need to promote social justice. Through exposure to the ideas gleaned from religious texts as well as data from field research, it is hoped that the reader will discover examples of common ground and shared goals. The field research included interview data from activists, academics, scholars, bishops, imams, women religious, community leaders, students at various university campuses, and others involved in the work of dialogue across religious and community lines. These interview meetings focused on recording oral histories as well as locating artifacts related to Christian-Muslim interaction in the past and present. Based on the interviews and other narrative and visual materials, the chapters presented here attempt to tell the stories of the trajectories of interaction going back nearly 40 years.

It is hoped that this book will serve as a useful resource for scholars and students as well as for lay individuals engaged in community dialogues. It is offered in an accessible language and format with an aim to serve the public interest by disseminating key aspects of the record and achievements—somewhat obscured due to the passage of time—regarding the history of the multidimensional and mutually enriching dialogue between Christians, Muslims, and people of other faiths in the greater Milwaukee area.

Summary of Chapters

The Prologue seeks to set the stage by offering an introductory explanation for the *why* and the *how* of interfaith dialogue. Here, Jaber provides a rationale for why dialogue is an imperative in today's world and shares the findings from select theoretical studies that speak to that point. She offers a general definition of dialogue, accompanied with resources necessary for a fruitful and meaningful engagement between people from different faith backgrounds. Using a variety of scholarly perspectives, Jaber lists some of the best practices for initiating and sustaining respectful relationships with a religious "other." Even though interfaith dialogue is not universally accepted, it has been steadily growing in communities, cities, and civic society institutions, even in countries where social and political conditions are not generally conducive for interfaith exchange and collaboration.

One of the main obstacles in dialogue is the spread of misinformation and misunderstanding about the other and their beliefs. Some of it is caused by the media's illiteracy in matters of religion, and some is due to deliberate attempts by groups who seek to divide along religious and ethnic lines. The best antidote to such social ailments is to actively learn about one's own as well as others' religious teachings, while at the same time maintaining regular contact and exchange with them. The goals: peace, mutual understanding, and respect cannot be achieved through theory alone; knowledge should be accompanied by personal interactions. When it comes to building lasting peace, there is really no substitute for personal and open dialogue and respectful interaction with an intention to learn about self and other. The focus of the Prologue is not the Milwaukee dialogue. However, the template for building trust and friendships across religious and cultural lines offered here applies perfectly to Milwaukee's efforts in dialogue as aptly demonstrated in subsequent chapters.

Part I of the book includes six chapters, all connected thematically to the dialogue between Christians and Muslims at various times and involving different people. In chapter 1, Caroline R. Redick tells a remarkable story of interfaith engagement between Christians and Muslims at a time when dialogue was neither popular nor very well understood or accepted by people in many religious communities. The Milwaukee Christian–Muslim dialogue, the "original CM dialogue," began in late 1980 and soon became known as one of a kind in the world.[2] It began due to the efforts by two Catholic, Franciscan nuns and a Muslim professor: Sister Lucille Walsh, OSF (d. 2013), Sister Jessine Reiss, OSF, and Dr. Abbas Hamdani. However, this dialogue did not originate in a vacuum. It was inspired by both the courage on the part of the founders who took inspiration from the teachings of their faith traditions to reach out and meet the other as well as a strong desire to work for "service of faith and the promotion of justice."[3]

Christian and Muslim scriptures and other later texts, such as the Vatican II documents, *Nostra Aetate*, *Lumen Gentium*, and Muslim declarations, most notably, "A Common Word," speak to the need for dialogue in imperative terms.[4] Any religious person with a conscience and a basic understanding of the world today would conclude similarly—that working toward interfaith solidarity is no

---

2. Rembert Weakland, *A Pilgrim in a Pilgrim Church: Memoirs of a Catholic Archbishop* (Grand Rapids, MI: Eerdmans, 2009), 262.

3. Both the Christians and Muslims would wholeheartedly agree to this pairing. The phrase "service of faith and the promotion of justice" comes from Father Peter-Hans Kolvenbach, former superior general for the Society of Jesus. As Pim Valkenberg notes in his recent book, *Renewing Islam by Service: A Christian View of Fethullah Gülen and the Hizmet Movement* (Washington, DC: The Catholic University of America Press, 2015), "'the service of faith' is in fact a form of proclamation of faith," and, when paired with the emphasis on justice, offers a way to express faith in today's world that is both relevant and much needed (253–54).

4. More recently the 34th General Congregation (GC 34) of the Society of Jesus (Rome 1995) informed its readers that the Society "must foster the *fourfold dialogue* recommended by the Church." The dialogue of life, the dialogue of action, the dialogue of religious experience, and the dialogue of theological exchange. For complete text of the decree 5 on "interreligious engagement," visit: https://www.scu.edu/ic/programs/ignatian-worldview/stories/decree-5-gc-34-interreligious-engagement.html.

longer a matter of luxury. The founders of the Milwaukee Muslim–Christian dialogue understood this well; they also benefitted from what went before. As noted above, just a few years earlier, Milwaukee had witnessed the establishment of Catholic–Jewish dialogue.[5] In one of the first letters written by the nuns to the Archbishop they noted that while there is an established dialogue between Catholics and Jews, no such effort exists between Christians and Muslims. Their goal was to see the Church go further by expanding the circle of conversation to include Muslims. They also wished to have an official recognition for their initiative, which they eventually received. The founders and the dialogue group did not stop there. They promoted their group's work by writing to scholars, practitioners, journalists, professors, and pastors, and even the Pope (see Lucille Walsh's letter, fig. I.1). They sought advice, encouragement, and ways to celebrate their work that was rooted in, as they rightly declared, the sacred scriptures they uphold and follow. The letter to the Pope did not go unnoticed. The reply came, first from an assistant to the Pope (fig. I.2) who communicated Pope John Paul II's blessings. After a follow-up letter and a detailed report from Sister Jessine Reiss came the second letter from the Vatican, this time from the President of the "Secretariat for Non-Christians" (now called the Pontifical Council for Interreligious Dialogue), Cardinal Francis Arinze, who thanked Sister Jessine for facilitating this "important activity for today's world . . . and to keep us informed of the fine work of dialogue between Muslims and Christians in Milwaukee" (fig. I.3). This was not insignificant even for today's standards. The dialogue group put Milwaukee on the map, as it were, by drawing attention to the work of bridgebuilding taking place with great enthusiasm. Redick's chapter also includes a discussion regarding the impact of the original dialogue. She summarizes the continuation of dialogue in its various forms and in different periods since the formal structured monthly dialogue ended in early 1990s. Her chapter ends with the brief note on some of the newer groups and dialogue partners, including one that involves Protestant Evangelical Christians and Muslims. This initiative is innovative in its format and style, organizing "peace feasts" and often holding meetings in area restaurants to celebrate their growing bonds and to break bread together.[6]

---

5. The Catholic Jewish Conference, established in 1975, was also partially inspired by the exhortations from the Vatican II documents. In 2015, Milwaukee witnessed the celebration of 50 years of *Nostra Aetate*, while at the same time, the Catholic Jewish Conference turned 40.

6. The topic of the wider dialogue in Milwaukee is the subject of chapter 8, which includes a sampling of the variety of dialogue groups and individuals who make the city of Milwaukee one of the few places where religious communities have and continue to make a difference in bridging the religious divide.

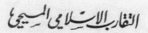

ISLAMIC - CHRISTIAN DIALOGUE

SUBCOMMITTEE OF THE MILWAUKEE ARCHDIOCESAN ECUMENICAL & INTERFAITH COMMISSION

August 21, 1985

His Holiness
Pope John Paul II
Vatican City, Italy

Your Holiness,

Reading of your recent visit with the Muslims in Morocco and in other parts of Africa and hearing your suggestion that more dialogue was needed between Muslims and Christians proved to be very encouraging to a number of us in the United States.

I am a Franciscan Sister who helped to co-found the Islamic-Christian Dialogue group in Milwaukee, Wisconsin. Presently, I am the chairperson for this group which, I am happy to report, has been meeting for the past five years. Our purposes are strictly educational and spiritual. We dialogue about our respective faiths, starting at first with the Vatican Guidelines for Muslim-Christian Dialogues. However, we understand that these wonderful guidelines are now no longer available in the English language.

Our group numbers from 25 to 30 members and includes about a dozen Muslims and about 15 Christians of various denominations. We meet about eight times yearly to discuss such topics as: The Concept of God in Islam and Christianity, Revelation, The Concept of Man in His Relation to God and Islamic and Christian Prayer Life. We also have occasional joint worship services. One beautiful prayer service for peace took place near Christmas time. At this service, the account of the birth of Jesus was read from Luke's Gospel and from the Koran, first in Arabic and then in English.

Our principle aim is educational, i.e. to promote better theological understandings among members of the group through serious dialogue on the respective theologies. Our aims also are to call attention to and correct any misrepresentation of either Christians or Muslims, and to help one another preserve human dignity, as well as to restore to the individual his rightful place in a more just and brotherly society. That is why we also appreciated your words against apartheid in South Africa and your stand for a neutral Jerusalem as a place sacred to all three faiths.

We know that our dialogue is one of few of its kind in the United States. So, we are grateful to our good Archbishop, Rembert Weakland for having encouraged this dialogue in his archdiocese. Unfortunately, we do not get the same support from many of the clergy and religious. That is why, Your Holiness, we appreciated your call for more dialogue. We also ask your blessing on our efforts.

Yours in Christ,

Sister Lucille Walsh, O.S.F.

Sister Lucille Walsh, O.S.F.
MILWAUKEE, WISCONSIN 53217

MAILING ADDRESS: 6801 NORTH YATES ROAD

Figure I.1: Sister Lucille Walsh's letter to Pope John Paul II.[7]

---

7. For a complete list of acknowledgements and credits, see Appendix E.

SECRETARIAT OF STATE

VATICAN CITY

October 11, 1985

Dear Sister Lucille,

　　His Holiness Pope John Paul II has directed me to acknowledge the kind letter which you sent to him on the occasion of his recent Pastoral Visit to Africa.

　　His Holiness appreciates the sentiments which prompted this devoted gesture and he invokes upon you the peace and joy of our Lord Jesus Christ.

Sincerely yours in Christ,

Monsignor G.B. Re
Assessor

Sister Lucille Walsh, O.S.F.
6801 North Yates Road
Milwaukee, WI   53217

Figure I.2: Reply from the Vatican in response to Sister Lucille Walsh's letter.

SECRETARIATUS PRO NON CHRISTIANIS

E Civitate Vaticana, die 30 Dicembre 1985

Prot. N. 19.696

(In responsione fiat mentio huius numeri)

Dear Sister Jessine,

Thank you for your letter of 25 October and for the interesting information which you sent us concerning Islamic-Christian dialogue in Milwaukee. Our Secretariat gives its full support and encouragement to this important activity for today's world. May God bless your efforts abundantly during 1986!

Concerning the Guidelines. The English Guidelines which you are using now are probably the earlier guidelines prepared for our Secretariat by Prof. Gardet, which were translated into English and, as you noted, are out of print. Rather than prepare new guidelines, our Secretariat commissioned Fr. Maurice Borrmans to w write an entirely new set, which is now available in the original French and translation into several other languages. The English translation of the new guidelines will be published by Paulist Press, and Fr. Borrmans has informed us that its publication is imminent. I would suggest that you write directly to Paulist Press, and request the number of copies you need upon its publication.

I take the occasion to thank you for your collaboration and hope that you will continue to keep us informed of the fine work of dialogue between Muslims and Christians carried on in Milwaukee. I believe that in your attention to textbooks, your dialogue group is addressing a major area of religious sensitivity. May you keep up the good work.

Yours in Christ,

Francis Card. Arinze
Pres.

S. Jessine Reiss, o.s.f.
6801 N. Yates Rd.
Milwaukee, Wisconsin 53217
U.S.A.

J. Marcello Zago omi
Secr.

Figure I.3: Cardinal Arinze's response to Sister Jessine Reiss's letter.

Chapter 2, by Andrew Musgrave, discusses dialogue narratives and first-hand accounts of interfaith engagement by founders of two important dialogues: the "original CM dialogue" of 1980, organized by Sister Lucille, Sister Jessine, and Dr. Hamdani (a continuation from chapter 1 but with a different emphasis), and a major initiative of the mid-1990s between Judi Longdin, the then-director of the Archdiocesan Office of Ecumenical and Interfaith Concerns and Janan Najeeb, the founding director of the Milwaukee Muslim Women's Coalition (MMWC). At that time, Longdin invited her to start a Catholic–Muslim Women's Dialogue group. Najeeb and Longdin quickly realized they have similar goals when it comes to community relations and peacebuilding, which made it easier for them to work together and start a formal group in the fall of 1997. Musgrave interviewed each of them in 2007 by which time the original dialogue had already ceased but the Catholic–Muslim Women's Dialogue had been steadily growing. Musgrave's weaving of narratives based on his interviews paints a picture of change and continuity: change in the leadership, style, scope, as well as the reach of the dialogues; and, continuity in terms of maintaining the same core values of seeking to build respectful and (over time) meaningful relationships with members of the other community. Musgrave describes the successes as well as challenges faced by both groups at various times in their journeys. The overlap between the two dialogues[8] in the 1990s was perhaps crucial as it allowed both Janan Najeeb (who first attended the original CM dialogue as a teenager with her parents; see chapter 1, fig. 1.4) and Longdin (who became close to the two Catholic sisters after becoming director of the office of Ecumenical and Interfaith Concerns) to see the lasting value of the effort as well as to learn some of the best practices on how to bring people together in the troubled times of the post 9/11 world. The next four chapters (3–6) offer an in-depth look at how Judi Longdin and Janan Najeeb envisioned, worked toward, and ultimately realized the goals of the women's dialogue through perseverance and hard work. Here, we first read personal accounts from these two well-respected and well-known community leaders, who have been close friends for many years. Longdin (Catholic) and Najeeb (Muslim) inherited the wisdom and the best practices as successors of the earlier participants of dialogue: Sister Jessine Reiss, Sister Lucille Walsh, Dr. Abbas Hamdani, Mahmoud and Intisar Atta, Bishop Richard Sklba, and many others.

---

8. The formal Islamic–Christian dialogue, or the "original CM dialogue," was operational from 1980 to 1991. Informally, many members continued to meet for another few years. The Catholic–Muslim Women's dialogue thrived between 1997 and 2016.

Here, Najeeb and Longdin share their perspectives, struggles, efforts, and the impact of their engagement with each other but also on their city, respective communities, civic, and religious leaders, etc. The two personal accounts are followed by a retelling and comparative analysis of this history by Rostollan and Jaber. Their chapters examine the role of dialogue by lifting up successes, challenges, and experiences faced by the people involved in dialogue in general and the Catholic–Muslim women's dialogue in particular.

Chapter 3, by Judith Longdin, offers a historical overview of the dialogue linking it to the original CM dialogue. She credits the Catholic sisters for inspiring her to become involved in interfaith. Longdin's narrative of the women's dialogue shows a remarkable journey of learning and discovery. She describes the experience of building personal friendships as the most valuable reward of the dialogue. From the start, the dialogue was rooted in "prayer and service" and had three basic goals: to educate, build relationships, and use these to empower the communities—one's own as well as others. Longdin describes the many benefits to members of the larger community in Milwaukee as a result of the collaboration between Muslim and Christian/Catholic women.

One of the most successful projects was the Muslim–Catholic Healthcare Initiative, which enabled many low-income residents to receive care without having to endure a stigma or feel otherwise embarrassed by their economic circumstances. Volunteers included Christian and Muslim nurses, physicians, and others who helped organize and publicize the events. Muslim–Catholic women's dialogue touched the lives of many others who attended their annual events or who participated in the smaller, localized dialogue meetings. Longdin's chapter documents the impact on Milwaukee community through concrete examples, such as the interfaith retreat involving youth from different religions and backgrounds. The news of this dialogue even reached members of the Catholic hierarchy at the United States Conference of Catholic Bishops (USCCB) and the Muslim leadership in the Islamic Society of North America (ISNA) headquarters in Plainfield, Indiana. A special invitation was made for representatives from Milwaukee to join the Midwest Catholic–Muslim dialogue. The first two people to join the dialogue were two women, one Catholic (Judi Longdin) and one Muslim (Naheed Arshad). Later, when Arshad was unable to continue, Inshirah Farhoud replaced her as the Muslim representative, and, as of 2019, both Longdin and Farhoud continue to be part of the official Midwest, as well as the National Catholic Muslim dialogues.

Chapter 4, by Janan Atta Najeeb, is in some ways a mirror account from what Longdin described in her chapter. Najeeb, however, speaks in personal terms and views the dialogue primarily as a journey that transformed her faith perspectives. She has had a long exposure to how dialogue is conducted from her days as young person when she occasionally attended the original CM dialogue with her parents, Mahmoud and Intisar Atta, who were an integral part of that group since the beginning. Najeeb's efforts multiplied as a result of her collaboration with Longdin starting in the mid-1990s. The timing for their joint venture was critical; they were learning about and from the other on how interfaith looks like in action. At the same time, they were learning about themselves and forging a relationship that would endure through time. All this was taking place before the tragic events of September 11, 2001. In fact, the experience of the other, and community engagement efforts in general, had prepared Najeeb and Longdin to face the immense challenges that inevitably arose in the aftermath of the September 11 attacks. Najeeb's chapter is a testimony to the fact that despite challenges faced in dialogue, the relationships built in trust prove to be most valuable in times of crises. In a world that is currently witnessing a sort of valorization of the culture of hate, whether it be in the name of religion, ethnicity, race, immigration status, or caste, such relationships are often instrumental for healing and social cohesion.

Like Longdin, Najeeb also acknowledges a debt of gratitude to the two nuns: Lucille Walsh and Jessine Reiss. Even more than Longdin, Najeeb and her family maintained a close relationship with them, and it has continued to this day with Sister Jessine. Najeeb's chapter ends with the message of hope for the future: that her efforts of all the years of community involvement are finally bearing fruit with the establishment of the Islamic Resource Center (IRC). The IRC along with the Milwaukee Muslim Women's Coalition (MMWC) focuses on education about faith and community-related matters including training young leaders, maintaining professional connections with religious and civic leaders, and disseminating positive and constructive news through their newly registered magazine, *Wisconsin Muslim Journal*.

Chapter 5, by Dianne Rostollan, is a retelling of the story of friendship between Longdin and Najeeb, which resulted in the establishment of the Muslim–Catholic Women's Dialogue (MCWD). Rostollan is reframing some of the key points of the story in light of the scholarly literature on women's activism. Her findings are based on qualitative data collected through interviews and conversations. Based on firsthand accounts, she offers a detailed view of the activities that MCWD undertook over the years and documents the impact these activities have had and continue to have on many groups in Milwaukee and the surrounding areas. One of the themes she focuses on in the chapter is to show

how women's dialogue was uniquely placed to deepen the pathways of dialogue. The women did not have particular ideological and/or political agendas. They met with a deep desire to connect with one another as human beings who were going through similar experiences in life as women. Hence, they were able to relate to each other not merely from a faith perspective, which in a sense separated them into roughly two groups, but they also experienced one another as a single group of women and as being on the same side.

Chapter 6, by Sundus Jaber, continues this narrative but shifts the focus on participants and the themes of the various events MCWD organized over the years. Jaber's chapter heavily relies on qualitative data, but she also cites literature related to women's activism, especially on how it relates to women's roles in society. Women are increasingly taking on leading positions in the field of dialogue and that impacts what themes are discussed and how they are interpreted. Traditional understandings and meanings are being challenged by women actors. Jaber's chapter covers some of the prominent themes that women's dialogue adopted for their public events. There was also a private side to the women's dialogue. This was hidden from the larger community as it consisted of small-group discussions or mini dialogues that mostly women attended. They also met often for planning and organizational purposes, which further helped them to cultivate social bonds that became the bedrock of lasting relationships despite the obvious cultural and religious differences.

The last two chapters, which constitute part II, are linked with the rest of the book in that they provide a wider lens to see Christian–Muslim dialogue within the larger interfaith context. The examples and narratives here are not limited to Christian–Muslim efforts and interactions. The spirit of continuing the tradition of dialogue, which, as we saw in chapter 1, remains strong and is far more dynamic and determined. Interfaith collaborations and programs today include discussions on environmental and ecological concerns, violence prevention, religious literacy, educational and outreach programs aimed to help underserved groups and communities, and much more. Preserving the heritage and continuing the tradition necessitates the retelling of the story that shows the courageous efforts of people in the original CM dialogue, in the Catholic–Muslim women's dialogue, and of the countless others who contributed in various ways. It is imperative that key historical achievements and continuing efforts be documented so as to allow the next generation of leaders—the youth—to learn from and continue the values and traditions of dialogue. These young leaders should be invited to participate in the process of maintaining and transforming the task of building trust between communities that are often pulled apart for political gain.

Chapter 7, by Kaitlyn C. Daly, takes on the topic of the role of educational institutions and youth in promoting interfaith. While the dialogues discussed in part I helped facilitate the training of the youth as an extension of the community dialogues through such events as the organized visits by high school Catholic and Muslims students to each other's schools, sponsored by Islamic Society of Milwaukee and the Catholic Archdiocese, the role of area colleges and universities is paramount in creating a culture where the value of diversity—in this case, religious diversity—is acknowledged, promoted, and celebrated. Part II opens with Daly's chapter, which seeks to do just that. She, like many other authors in this volume, relies primarily on data collected from practitioners and facilitators of dialogue. Her chapter is not limited to Christian–Muslim interactions but aims to reveal general efforts toward creating resources and spaces for discussion and dialogue.

Daly begins with personal experience by describing how she became interested in interfaith. She attributes it to the activities she was exposed to while studying as an undergrad at Marquette University. It is fitting that she tells the story of how and why interfaith matters in today's world and how and why it may be promoted on college campuses. Her personal experience and conclusions are then juxtaposed against the views of many others—some of whom are peers, while others include administrators, academic staff, ministers, and pastors. Daly emphasizes the role of interaction and engagement, arguing that dialogue cannot be effectively done or taught through classroom learning or by way of reading materials. One has to experience the other in various settings and for a sustained period to understand the value of the exercise for oneself and for everyone around. Daly offers many examples of the kinds of activities organized at Marquette, University of Wisconsin–Milwaukee, and Cardinal Stritch University. Even though she did not include all of the institutions of higher learning in the Milwaukee area, the depth demonstrated by her data is sufficient to conclude on the important role universities and colleges play and their potential in creating future leaders who will foster the values of diversity and dialogue in society and in the world.

Moving beyond Christian–Muslim dialogue, it is important to point out that there is a considerable history of interfaith engagement in Milwaukee. Chapter 8, by Omar and Daly, provides an abbreviated account of the variety of interfaith activities in the Milwaukee area during the last three decades. Chapter 8 is a summary version of the story of dialogue, a brief explanation of the many events, initiatives, people, organizations, and institutions that have made Milwaukee a place where religious communities routinely engage with one another as neighbors and collaborators. The chapter opens with an introduction to select dialogue actors—key organizations and individuals. It also includes examples of bilateral dialogues, such as Jewish–Catholic and Jewish–Muslim, but also multireligious dialogues and events. Examples of Christian–Muslim interaction not included in part I are also introduced. These events and activities are mostly recent; however, some earlier initiatives are also noted so as to show the growing interest in and diversity of perspectives and practices. The chapter is not meant to be an exhaustive account of interfaith activities in Milwaukee. To claim that would be to do grave injustice to the rich history of interfaith engagement in Milwaukee. It is, however, meant as a preview to the larger study—yet to be undertaken—that would be more comprehensive in scope covering the work of people and organizations some of which are only briefly covered here. The individuals and organizations selected here represent the past as well as the present. They are deemed as important either because of their commitment and the promise or for their past and ongoing efforts in local peacebuilding. Since peacebuilding is much more than just speaking and writing about peace, interfaith dialogue viewed this way opens the possibility for it to be utilized as a method for maintaining institutions of civil society.

What the men and women discussed in this book have accomplished in the last 40 years should not be taken for granted. However, it is fast becoming part of a forgotten past. This book is a small attempt to prevent that from happening by documenting these stories.[9] It is a modest effort, and the reader will find some stories repeated in more than one chapter. Some of this repetition is necessary in order to stress their historical importance. Although this book has focused on Christian–Muslim dialogue, the larger story of dialogue across faith communities and among people in general also needs to be understood. Many of the events noted in chapter 8 are recent, indicating a rise in people's interest in dialogue; manifesting as part of community activities, religious forums, and organizations belonging to Sikh, Christian, Jewish, Muslim, Buddhist, Hindu, Bahai, and other communities.[10]

In conclusion, I want to share an exemplary statement by Bishop Richard Sklba published recently in the newspaper *Catholic Herald*. It was a joint

---

9. For many of the material examples, we first and foremost thank Sr. Jessine; if it were not for her meticulous record keeping, this book would not have been possible. Many of the photos, articles, news clippings, and personal narratives shared by Sister Jessine constitute one of the primary sources for the ideas expressed in this book.

10. The interest in and the rise of dialogue activities among young people is documented in chapter 7, which examines the role of institutions of higher learning as important places to educate and expose college students to the method and efficacy of interfaith dialogue.

statement by the members of the Catholic–Muslim theological dialogue which began in 2011 and continued for nearly five years. The members included Bishop Sklba (convener), Othman Atta, Barbara Freres, Judith Longdin, Janan Najeeb, Waleed Najeeb, Ahmed Quereshi, Rev. Philip Reifenberg, and Imam Zulfiqar Ali Shah. Their decision to issue this statement is noteworthy because it goes so much further than what is ordinarily approved by officials in the Catholic Church or in Muslim jurist circles for public consumption. In it, Bishop Sklba states that what they offer is "in the hope that it might assist Catholics to understand . . . the complexities and errors of the current conflict" in parts of the Middle East.[11] He wanted to make it plain to Catholic readers that ISIS does not represent Islam, and that it has killed more Muslims in the name of its ideology than any other group or state in recent times. The statement addressed the question of violence and terrorism as "universal issues, not peculiar to one religion, culture, time or place." The statement takes ownership by acknowledging that as Christians and Muslims are responsible for what happens in the world, they must "speak the truth about one another and to act for justice and peace as [their] faiths require" them to do.[12]

Examples such as these ought to be shared widely in communities across the religious and cultural divide. They may be reflected upon by the youth of today who may need to know why faith should matter in their lives, even as many young people seek to abandon it.[13] They ought to know why seeking truth is important and should be sought diligently through diverse sources and with a critical and discerning frame of mind. The following confession by a bishop may give us pause before discounting the value of diversity of faith communities. Bishop Sklba noted: "Ecumenical and interreligious cooperation brings blessings to any community on countless levels. I still find it hard to imagine what life in Milwaukee would have been like without the mutual support of such outstanding religious membership."[14] In the interfaith story of Milwaukee, one will find numerous instances of mutual support and cooperation and even deep bonds of friendship. The ongoing exchange of letters

---

11. Richard Sklba, "Muslims, Catholics Together Bear Witness to Truth," *Catholic Herald*, September 3, 2015, https://catholicherald.org/herald-of-hope/bishop-richard-j-sklba/muslims-catholics-together-bear-witness-to-truth/.

12. Ibid.

13. Pew Research Center, "The Age Gap in Religion Around the World," https://www.pewforum.org/2018/06/13/the-age-gap-in-religion-around-the-world/.

14. Richard Sklba, "Breaking Bread for Kingdom of God," *Catholic Herald*, March 6, 2014, https://catholicherald.org/herald-of-hope/bishop-richard-j-sklba/breaking-bread-for-the-kingdom-of-god/.

between Sister Jessine and Dr. Hamdani represents one such example of how the fruits of dialogue endure through time and space. One such letter, like many others, captures the sense of familial bonds that still exist between these members of dialogue (fig. I.4).

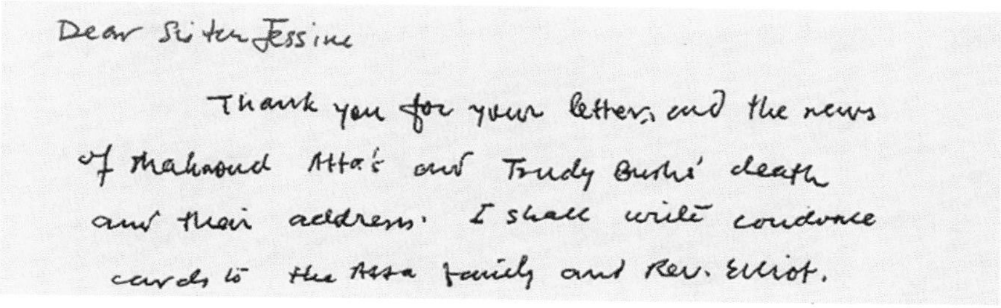
Dear Sister Jessine

Thank you for your letters and the news of Mahmoud Atta's and Trudy Bushi' death and their address. I shall write condolence cards to the Atta family and Rev. Elliot.

Figure I.4: Dr. Hamdani and Sister Jessine continue to exchange letters. Here is an image of part of a letter received by Sister Jessine in 2017. She gave permission to use it as evidence of her ongoing friendship with Dr. Hamdani, rooted in the respectful dialogue that has lasted for several decades.

Bibliography

Baca, [Alfred]. "Welcome Letter." July 11, 2017. http://www.usccb.org/beliefs-and-teachings/ecumenical-and-interreligious/upload/bacawelcomeletterwebsite071117.pdf.

Pew Research Center. "The Age Gap in Religion Around the World." July 8, 2019. https://www.pewforum.org/2018/06/13/the-age-gap-in-religion-around-the-world/.

Sklba, Richard. "Breaking Bread for Kingdom of God." *Catholic Herald*, March 6, 2014. https://catholicherald.org/herald-of-hope/bishop-richard-j-sklba/breaking-bread-for-the-kingdom-of-god/.

———. "Muslims, Catholics Together Bear Witness to Truth." *Catholic Herald*, September 3, 2015. https://catholicherald.org/herald-of-hope/bishop-richard-j-sklba/muslims-catholics-together-bear-witness-to-truth/.

Thirty-Fourth General Congregation of the Society of Jesus. "Decree Five: Our Mission and Interreligious Dialogue." Documents of the Thirty-Fourth General Congregation of the Society of Jesus. Rome: Institute of Jesuit Sources, 1995, https://www.scu.edu/ic/programs/ignatian-worldview/stories/decree-5-gc-34-interreligious-engagement.html.

Valkenberg, Pim. *Renewing Islam by Service: A Christian View of Fethullah Gülen and the Hizmet Movement*. Washington, DC: The Catholic University of America Press, 2015.

Weakland, Rembert. *A Pilgrim in a Pilgrim Church: Memoirs of a Catholic Archbishop*. Grand Rapids, MI: Eerdmans, 2009.

PROLOGUE

The *Why* and *How* of Interfaith Dialogue

Sundus Jaber

There is an increased need for interfaith dialogue due to the perceived involvement of religion in conflicts in many parts of the world. Interfaith dialogue occurs when people from different faiths come together to build understanding, trust, and respect between each other and create a society where they can live and work together peacefully, even if they hold vastly different beliefs.[1] Interfaith dialogue is like air. We cannot always see it, but it is always around us and is necessary for building peace and harmony. The exchange of any type of information will always include social interaction and relationship building (fig. P1). Interfaith dialogue is not limited to peaceful engagement and cooperation between individuals who identify with different faiths but also positive, intentional interaction and sincere collaboration at the institutional and societal level. Interfaith dialogue can sometimes be seen as something limited to theoretical or academic contexts, but this is far from reality. Dialogue takes place between family members, neighbors, classmates, and coworkers often without the label; it is an interaction between individuals in casual as well as formal settings.

In Milwaukee and in many other parts of the world, Muslims and Christians share the same schools, hospitals, parks, and malls. In the most mundane parts of their lives they interact, work with, and learn from each other. Dialogue is not just something reserved for priests and imams, academics and officials, pundits and politicians, but rather it is the thread that binds the fabric of our communities together when members of various groups positively and peacefully interact with each other for the purpose of mutual learning and joint action for the sake of justice and peace for all.

---

1. This short introduction to dialogue is offered here as a prologue to the studies presented in this volume. It is not exhaustive. For a more detailed study, readers may wish to consult the list of works noted in "Further Reading."

What is Interfaith Dialogue?

INTERFAITH DIALOGUE IS...

communication, **conversation, discussion,** interaction, talking, listening, asking questions, a process of learning, mutual sharing of faith, encounter, experience, tool [for], goal [of]

...that is...

open, honest, civil, **respectful,** curious, interested, kind, meaningful, interactive, non-aggressive, non-confrontational, non-judgmental/open minded, non-hostile, more focused on learning than persuading, constructive, directed, sensitive to feelings of other, built on "epistemic humility," "ecumenical" in an Ayoubian sense, intentional

...between...

[People of] two or more faiths / religions / traditions

...as a way of...

building mutual **understanding and respect,** coming to know self as well as other, coming to a higher level of thinking, discovering similarities and differences, finding common ground, building friendship, fostering growth, cultivating concern, enabling appreciation of others and participation in the things meaningful to them, furthering relationships, dispelling prejudice / misconceptions, allowing you to see through the eyes of another culture / walk in the shoes of another, promoting good will, ending ignorance, avoiding violence, discerning truth [about the other] from myths, sharing theological, cultural, and political perspectives, going beyond "diversity" and into "pluralism," celebrating one another / eating together, learning to act together on issues of common concern

and does NOT involve –

forcing agreement, attacking the other faith, an opportunity to promote ideas or agenda of one's faith to those who disagree, a platform for trying to "convert" others, a debate.

Figure P.1: Summary of responses from Irfan Omar's students in an undergraduate course on "Christian-Muslim Dialogue" at Marquette University during the fall of 2015.

Communities across the world are realizing that engagement with the other is the only sure thing to combat bigotry and ignorance that can dominate the info sphere in times of crises, where communities begin to view the other through their fears.[2]

Interfaith Dialogue: A Way Forward

Interfaith dialogue has yet to receive widespread acceptance among many people of faith, including Christians and Muslims.[3] Despite growth in global awareness of the existence of interfaith dialogue, the gap in knowledge about what dialogue truly means and represents remains critical even among those who claim to practice dialogue. In countries where democratic values are not the norm and freedoms of speech and practice are not given, the situation is far grimmer. In places where Christians and Muslims have historically lived together for centuries, dialogue exists as part of their daily life and in social and cultural interactions. One of the main obstacles in advancing interfaith dialogue is the existence of misinformation and misrepresentation about each other in some segments of the population. To counter these, in places such as India, dialogue of religions is being promoted with enthusiasm and openness.[4]

Christian and Muslim leaders recommend a pattern of conduct to facilitate a productive dialogue. These recommendations are beneficial for participants from all backgrounds—not just for Christians and Muslims. According the World Council of Churches' resource document, "Christian Witness in a Multi-Religious World," participants in dialogue should educate themselves on common issues while working with representatives from other religions.

---

2. Cois Tine is a multicultural organization of the Society of African Missions in Ireland, where in 2013, Christian and Muslim leaders launched a "unique resource to assist Muslim-Christian cooperation." See Cois Tine, "A Journey Together: A Resource for Christian Muslim Dialogue," Society of African Missions, https://sma.ie/a-journey-together/.

3. Muhammad Shafiq and Mohammed Abu-Nimer, *Interfaith Dialogue: A Guide for Muslims* (Herndon, VA: International Institute of Islamic Thought, 2007), xi.

4. See the many works by Victor Edwin, S.J. professor of theology at Vidyajyoti College of Theology in Delhi, whose tireless efforts to reach out and engage with members of other faith communities have borne much fruit. Thanks to his activism, there is a vast network of people who are becoming aware of positive stories of outreach, interreligious solidarity and cooperation on a daily basis. Some of Father Edwin's recent scholarly works include: *Windows on Dialogue*, ed. Ambrogio Bongiovanni, Leonard Fernando, SJ, Gaetano Sabetta, and Victor Edwin, S.J. (Delhi: ISPCK, 2012), and *Seeking Communion: A Collection of Conversations*, ed. Joseph Victor Edwin, S.J. (Delhi: ISPCK/Hyderabad: Henry Martyn Institute, 2018).

Each participant should increase her or his understanding of one's own faith as well as seek deeper knowledge of different religions with the assistance of members from within that tradition to avoid distorting their beliefs and practices. Second, as people of faith, they should commit to forming respectful relationships with members of all religions, both at the personal and institutional levels to provide new opportunities for solving problems, reestablishing justice, resolving ill feelings, and making peace.[5] Liyakat Takim elaborates on the latter recommendation with the advice that all dialogue participants need to move beyond complacency in their knowledge of their own tradition and engage in a type of self-criticism while reminding other dialogue participants "that their own traditions are continuously being re-evaluated" if they want to have a more honest and dynamic dialogue.[6] He goes on to say,

> Muslims, for example, need to show that, especially after the events of September 2001, they are engaged in a process of self-critique and are confronted with the challenge of contextual hermeneutics in dealing with the pronouncements of the Qur'ān on issues like warfare, human rights, and freedom of conscience and expression. Muslim scholars and jurists have to engage in hermeneutic and interpretive exercises to provide a coherent re-evaluation of classical formulations and to reassert the Qur'ānic ecumenical and inclusivist vision of peace.[7]

Both Muslims and Christians have a specific mandate in their religions to forge genuine and respectful relationships with others for the betterment of humanity and lasting peace. An example of this can be found in the Qur'an (49:13): "O humankind, We have created you from a male and female, and have made you nations and tribes that you may know one another. Surely, the noblest of you in the sight of God is the best in conduct." This verse outlines the reality and necessity of interacting with and accepting the rich diversity in this world and among human beings and their communities. It challenges humanity to seek God's love and blessings by striving to compete amongst each other to enact what is noble and righteous.

---

5. World Council of Churches, et al., "Christian Witness in a Multi-Religious World: Recommendations for Conduct," June 28, 2011, https://www.oikoumene.org/en/resources/documents/wcc-programmes/interreligious-dialogue-and-cooperation/christian-identity-in-pluralistic-societies/christian-witness-in-a-multi-religious-world.

6. Liyakat Takim, "From Conversion to Conversation: Interfaith Dialogue in Post 9-11 America," *The Muslim World* 94 (July 2004): 353–54.

7. Ibid.

Similarly, Christianity upholds Jesus as a harbinger who gave glad tidings to those who accept others and bring peace between each other. Jesus's words echo this sentiment: "Blessed are the peacemakers" (Matthew 5:9). Additionally, religious communities must take part in interreligious advocacy for the common good. They must build solidarity with those experiencing bias, injustice, and discrimination, and, if necessary, petition governments to safeguard freedom of religion for all, especially in a world where rights of minorities, religious and otherwise, are threatened by the rise of ethno-nationalism.[8] A constructive dialogue occurs where there is a clear understanding that each participant is able to be true to her or his beliefs, while respecting and upholding the rights of others to practice their faith freely.[9]

An important point to remember is that one person's experience as a Muslim does not necessarily reflect the views of other Muslims or of Islam as a whole. The same goes for members of any other religion, including Christians. Therefore, we must learn to understand others in light of their teachings *and* their particular expression of those teachings. The Wisconsin Council of Churches on Interfaith Relations offers a caution in this regard. Their statement reads: "We are not necessarily called to speak for our full tradition, denomination, or even congregation, but only for ourselves."[10] Speaking about one's own personal experience in religion is not the same as attempting to describe the experience of all members of that religion.

Interfaith dialogue does not entail compromising the integrity of the foundations of one's religious beliefs or include partaking in syncretism. The fear of losing one's faith is a legitimate concern for many and can be an obstacle in the path toward dialogue. Often, people do not understand the meaning of interfaith dialogue and view it as an exercise in combining teachings of various religions. Belief in exclusivism in one's faith as superior to other religions also prevents one from engaging with the other. If one believes that one is superior to the other in matters of belief, there is little reason to engage with them in sincere dialogue. This view leads one to believe their mission to be that of seeking to convert the other. Seeking to convert or any form of proselytization is antithetical to very spirit of interfaith dialogue.

---

8. Ibid., 352.

9. World Council of Churches, et al., "Christian Witness in a Multi-Religious World," 5–6.

10. Wisconsin Council of Churches, "Loving our Neighbors: A Statement of the Wisconsin Council of Churches on Interfaith Relations." https://www.wichurches.org/sitecontent/pdf_files/programs/LovingOurNeighbors.pdf.

In a statement on Interfaith Relations, the Wisconsin Council of Churches noted that participants are reminded that dialogue "is not a space for conversion, but a space for witness."[11] Witness is a matter of necessity; if one believes in something, they must share it with others as a motivating and guiding force that leads them to work for peace and justice. Witness is not the same as seeking to convince the other of their supposed incorrect and erroneous ways. Similar to the WiscCC's statement, the Qur'an commands Muslims to be respectful to members of other religions: "There is no coercion in matters of faith" (Qur'an 2:256). For some, unfamiliarity with interfaith ethics leads them to confuse dialogue with *da'wah*, which is often interpreted as "witness" but can also be seen as actions leading to others' conversion. Historically, Muslims also harbor a fear that dialogue may be an "attempt by the Christian majority to convert others."[12]

Interfaith dialogue should be reserved for seeking to increase mutual understanding, respect, trust, and friendship with members of other faiths and is not an exercise to dispute, attack, or invalidate other faiths or the experiences of participants from those faiths. Dialogue is not debate where one offers rational arguments in favor of one's faith to establish superiority. There have been and continue to be "scholars" in both Muslim and Christian communities who engage in such activities; they should not be called dialogues. Any speech that is "aggressive and polemical . . . have nothing to do with interfaith dialogue."[13] The goals of interfaith dialogue, or any type of dialogue, are simple: to create mutual understanding and to recognize the issues that may hinder or jeopardize that understanding in times of crises and confusion. Most often issues related to economic, political, and social matters can be manipulated by those who benefit from discord and conflict by spreading misinformation.[14] The goal is to either preemptively address the most common causes of tension or remedy them once they have been identified through education and trust building. This includes acting in a way to surpass specific barriers to dialogue and address the stereotypes that feed into the creation and normalization of mistrust, prejudice, and intolerance.[15] In *Interfaith Dialogue: A Guide for Muslims*, Shafiq and Abu-Nimer

---

11. Ibid. See also, World Council of Churches, "Issues in Christian-Muslim Relations: Ecumenical Considerations," January 1, 1992, https://www.oikoumene.org/en/resources/documents/wcc-programmes/interreligious-dialogue-and-cooperation/interreligious-trust-and-respect/issues-in-christian-muslim-relations-ecumenical-considerations.

12. Shafiq and Abu-Nimer, *Interfaith Dialogue: A Guide for Muslims*, xvi.

13. Ibid.

14. Cois Tine. "A Journey Together: Introduction."

15. Ibid.

clarify that the goals of interfaith dialogue do not include creating a new religion or calling for anyone to abandon Islam's fundamentals. Rather, interfaith dialogue is meant to create closer ties with each in order to rid the world of fear of the other. By the end of a serious engagement in interfaith dialogue, participants will have become better listeners, have some understanding of theological and philosophical similarities and differences between them and their dialogue partners, and have learned to value other people's experiences and spiritualities, and would be ready to collaborate with others for the sake of justice and peace.[16]

Responding to the Need for Dialogue

Christian–Muslim relations have a complicated history that is marked by conflict but at times also concord. There are many places in the world where Muslims and Christians have lived together peacefully for centuries.[17] Unfortunately, conflicts tend to eclipse the peaceful experiences in human memory. This problem also exists in theological and religious discourse where disagreements and arguments overshadow moments of positive and constructive cooperation.[18] Whether in Milwaukee, Wisconsin, or elsewhere, the relevance and dire need for widespread interfaith interaction between Christians and Muslims is increasing as popular media and global politics help create rifts of misunderstanding and hatred. In the historical document titled the "Declaration on the Relation of the Church with Non-Christian Religions," also known as *Nostra Aetate*, Pope Paul VI and the Second Vatican Council made an important statement advocating that Muslims and Christians must reconcile and work together. It states:

> Since in the course of centuries not a few quarrels and hostilities have arisen between Christians and [Muslims], this sacred synod urges all to forget the past and to work sincerely for mutual understanding and to preserve as well as to promote together for the benefit of all mankind social justice and moral welfare, as well as peace and freedom.[19]

This message has been echoed by many since then. Pope John Paul II in all of his speeches denounced hatred and bigotry in the name of religion. Similarly,

---

16. Shafiq and Abu-Nimer, *Interfaith Dialogue: A Guide for Muslims*, 30.

17. WCC, "Issues in Christian-Muslim Relations: Ecumenical Considerations."

18. Ibid.

19. Pope Paul VI, *Nostra Aetate*, October 28, 1965, http://www.vatican.va/archive/hist_councils/ii_vatican_council/documents/vat-ii_decl_19651028_nostra-aetate_en.html.

Pope Benedict XVI was inspired by the words of the *Nostra Aetate* when he wrote, "Interreligious and intercultural dialogue between Christians and Muslims cannot be reduced to an optional extra. It is, in fact, a vital necessity, on which in large measure our future depends."[20] Pope Benedict also made some remarks that were seen to be offensive, or at least controversial by some in the interfaith community and by Muslims engaged in dialogue. In 2005, Benedict gave a lecture at the University of Regensburg in Germany on the topic of faith and reason. In it he referenced to a medieval author who characterized Prophet Muhammad in a "negative" light, suggesting that Muhammad, instead of advocating reason, encouraged spreading Islam through violence. Pope Benedict later clarified that the negative comments on the part of the medieval Christian author did not in fact represent his own views.[21]

Generally speaking, statements by the Roman Catholic Church that speak of shared heritage were positively received by Muslim scholars, religious leaders, and academics. Muslim groups have been engaged in dialogue with the Vatican scholars for several decades. After Regensburg, there was a new urgency to take the dialogue to a new level. In response to Regensburg comments, 138 Muslim scholars and leaders from around the world sent an open letter to the Pope titled, "A Common Word Between Us and You." In it, they reiterated the need to engage in dialogue and invited him along with leaders from every Christian denomination to begin anew in respectful dialogue.[22] They began the "letter" with the reminder that "Muslims and Christians together make up over half the world's population. Without peace and justice between these two religious communities, there can be no meaningful peace in the world. The future of the world depends on peace between Muslims and Christians."[23] Clearly, one can see the urgency in the need for interfaith dialogue at every level and the consequences it has on future prospects for world peace. Pope Francis has in recent years taken the issue of dialogue to a new level. He repeatedly speaks of dialogue

---

20. Pope Benedict XVI, "Need for Dialogue between Christians and Muslims," September 25, 2006, https://www.catholicculture.org/culture/library/view.cfm?recnum=7177.

21. Jean W. Rioux, "Synopsis of Pope Benedict XVI's 'Regensburg Address,'" https://www.benedictine.edu/press-room/work/regensburg-address.

22. Ghazi bin Muhammad, "On 'A Common Word Between Us and You,'" in *A Common Word: Muslims and Christians on Loving God and Neighbor,* eds. Miroslav Volf, Ghazi bin Muhammad, and Melissa Yarrington (Grand Rapids, MI: Eerdmans, 2010), 3–17. See also the official site of the document with numerous resources for continued conversation at: https://www.acommonword.com/.

23. Ghazi bin Muhammad, "On 'A Common Word,'" 28.

as a means to peace and conflict resolution, and to collaborate on global matters that affect everyone regardless of race, religion, class, or nationality.[24]

Similarly, many mainline Protestant churches have made great strides in outreach to people in other religions. I already noted the efforts by World Council of Churches (WCC), here is an early (c. 1980?) example of a "response to the encounter of religions" from the National Council of Churches (NCC), which sought to educate individuals, churches, and church leaders on Islam and to "assist . . . in those programs and activities which will create better understanding of and promote cooperate with their Muslim neighbors" (fig. P.2).

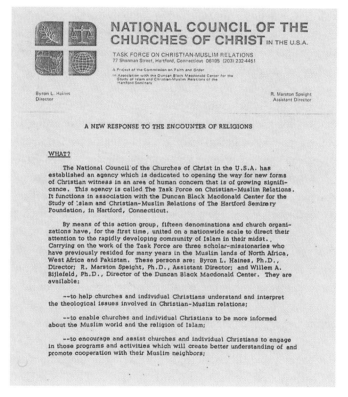

Figure P.2: The letter issued by the "Task Force on Christian-Muslim Relations" established as part of the National Council of Churches' (NCC) efforts to educate their member churches on Islam and dialogue.

---

24. See the recent work on Francis's views on dialogue by Harold Kasimow and Alan Race, eds., *Pope Francis and Interreligious Dialogue: Religious Thinkers Engage with Recent Papal Initiatives* (New York: Palgrave Macmillan, 2018).

Muslim scholars like M. Fethullah Gülen have also stressed the need for Christian–Muslim interfaith dialogue. Gülen's public statements include statements such as: "I believe that interfaith dialogue is a must today, and that the first step in establishing it is forgetting the past, ignoring polemical arguments, and giving precedence to common points, which far outnumber polemical ones."[25] In a sermon titled, "A Call to Bridge the Abrahamic Faiths: Judaism, Christianity and Islam," Imam Feisal Abdul Rauf also reminded the audience of the need for unity between practitioners of different religions stating, "We recognize that all religions have the same relative value with respect to the high goal to be reached, and the same lack of value if they fail to call forth the love of God. This alone is the uniform standard of value in the assessment of religions. Our voices, raised together to proclaim the recognition of the unity of God, serve to bring [humanity] together, while those voices that focus on the differences of our laws cause division and loss."[26]

Both of these scholars have a large following in the United States and around the world. Both have publicly and repeatedly called for interfaith unity and cooperation for the sake of better relations, mutual learning and respect, and discovering common ground. In these scholars, one detects a leaning toward "forgetting" past conflicts; however, others such as Mahmoud Ayoub argue that "learning" might be a better phrasing. We must strive to move forward by understanding the history of Muslim–Christian conflicts, which is necessary to heal the wounds of past violations against the other. He further argues that interfaith dialogue between Muslims and Christians in the West has implications for the state of affairs between the members of the different faiths globally. He notes that a successful interfaith dialogue "is only possible among people enjoying the same standard of security, economic well-being, and social equality in all respects. This ideal cannot be achieved between the rich and technologically advanced West and the Muslims of the so-called Third World." Whereas in some Western countries, especially the United States, Muslims "share the factory workbench, the school, community center, and even the cemetery"[27] with people of all faiths and no faiths. Therefore, Muslims and

---

25. M. Fethullah Gülen, *The Necessity of Interfaith Dialogue: A Muslim Perspective* (Somerset, NJ: The Light, 2004), 3.

26. Feisal Abdul Rauf, "A Call to Bridge the Abrahamic Faiths: Judaism, Christianity and Islam," *The American Muslim*, September 6, 2002, http://www.theamericanmuslim.org/tam.php/features/articles/a_call_to_bridge_the_abrahamic_faiths_judaism_christianity_and_islam.

27. Mahmoud Ayoub, "Roots of Muslim-Christian Conflict," *A Muslim View of Christianity: Essays on Dialogue by Mahmoud Ayoub*, ed. Irfan A. Omar (Maryknoll, NY: Orbis Books, 2007), 58.

Christians, especially in the United States, have to set the example and show positive results for others to emulate. This makes interfaith dialogue in the United States an imperative and not a luxury if we consider the impact it can have in the global context.

Building mutual respect and trust takes time. The dialogue and interaction between communities, religious or otherwise, is already happening. More attention needs to be placed on creating resources that would cater to a variety of people and institutions. Whereas numerous academic studies have emerged in the last four decades covering historical and theological aspects of dialogue, not much is available for lay members in communities of faith who may require some kind of in-house reasoning for why interfaith dialogue is to be considered an important component of the life of faith today. The chapters that follow this prologue will hopefully help the reader see both the academic as well as religious reasoning for understanding and pursuing dialogue.

BIBLIOGRAPHY

Abdul Rauf, Feisal. "A Call to Bridge the Abrahamic Faiths: Judaism, Christianity and Islam." *The American Muslim*, September 6, 2002, http://www.theamerican muslim.org/tam.php/features/articles/a_call_to_bridge_the_abrahamic_faiths_judaism_christianity_and_islam.

Ayoub, Mahmoud. "Roots of Muslim-Christian Conflict." In *A Muslim View of Christianity: Essays on Dialogue by Mahmoud Ayoub*, edited by Irfan A. Omar, 42–63. Maryknoll, NY: Orbis Books, 2007.

Bongiovanni, Ambrogio, et al. *Windows on Dialogue*. Delhi: ISPCK, 2012.

Cois Tine, "A Journey Together: A Resource for Christian Muslim Dialogue." Society of African Missions. Accessed December 1, 2018, https://sma.ie/a-journey-together/.

Edwin, Joseph Victor, SJ. *Seeking Communion: A Collection of Conversations*. Delhi: ISPCK/Hyderabad: Henry Martyn Institute, 2018.

Gülen, M. Fethullah. *The Necessity of Interfaith Dialogue: A Muslim Perspective*. Somerset, NJ: The Light, 2004.

Kasimow, Harold, and Alan Race, eds. *Pope Francis and Interreligious Dialogue: Religious Thinkers Engage with Recent Papal Initiatives*. New York: Palgrave Macmillan, 2018.

Bin Muhammad, Ghazi. "On 'A Common Word Between Us and You.'" In *A Common Word: Muslims and Christians on Loving God and Neighbor*, edited by Miroslav Volf, Ghazi bin Muhammad, and Melissa Yarrington, 3–17. Grand Rapids, MI: Eerdmans, 2010.

Pope Benedict XVI. "Need for Dialogue between Christians and Muslims." September 25, 2006, https://www.catholicculture.org/culture/library/view.cfm?recnum=7177.

Pope Paul VI. *Nostra Aetate*. October 28, 1965, http://www.vatican.va/archive/hist_councils/ii_vatican_council/documents/vat-ii_decl_19651028_nostra-aetate_en.html.

Rioux, Jean W. "Synopsis of Pope Benedict XVI's 'Regensburg Address.'" https://www.benedictine.edu/press-room/work/regensburg-address

Shafiq, Muhammad, and Mohammed Abu-Nimer. *Interfaith dialogue: A Guide for Muslims*. Herndon, VA: International Institute of Islamic Thought, 2007.

Takim, Liyakat. "From Conversion to Conversation: Interfaith Dialogue in Post 9-11 America," *The Muslim World* 94 (July 2004): 343–55.

World Council of Churches, et al. "Christian Witness in a Multi-Religious World: Recommendations for Conduct." June 28, 2011, https://www.oikoumene.org/en/resources/documents/wcc-programmes/interreligious-dialogue-and-cooperation/christian-identity-in-pluralistic-societies/christian-witness-in-a-multi-religious-world.

World Council of Churches. "Issues in Christian-Muslim Relations: Ecumenical Considerations." January 1, 1992, https://www.oikoumene.org/en/resources/documents/wcc-programmes/interreligious-dialogue-and-cooperation/interreligious-trust-and-respect/issues-in-christian-muslim-relations-ecumenical-considerations.

1
PART

Christian–Muslim Relations
in Milwaukee:

A BRIEF HISTORY

A History of Formal Muslim–Christian Dialogue in Milwaukee

Caroline R. Redick

Catherine Orsborn has observed that "the long-term sustainable work to create more inclusive communities is done at the local level."[1] The story of Muslim–Christian relations in Milwaukee is a prime example of a long-term dialogue that has transformed the wider community. The two-decade long dialogue included individuals, men and women, ordained and lay, from several Christian and Muslim denominations. It was one of the first dialogues of its kind in the world[2]—focused on building relationships of trust between individuals of both religions, yet the implications of this local dialogue have yet to be explored in-depth. This chapter will endeavor to tell the story of the dialogue from the perspective of its founders and first participants.

The Background and the "Seeds" of Dialogue

In 1965, Pope Paul VI released a declaration on the relation of the Roman Catholic Church to other religions. *Nostra Aetate* encouraged Catholics to engage in dialogue with persons of other religions, specifically referencing Judaism and Islam. The document calls for Catholics to work for "mutual understanding" with Muslims and urges Catholics to work together with

---

1. Catherine Orsborn, "Shoulder to Shoulder with American Muslims: What the Interreligious Community Is Doing to Combat Anti-Muslim Bigotry in America," *Journal of Ecumenical Studies* 51, no. 2 (2016): 260.

2. Archbishop Jean Jadot identified Milwaukee as one of the only archdioceses in the world with this type of dialogue. As quoted by Rembert G. Weakland, *A Pilgrim in a Pilgrim Church: Memoirs of a Catholic Archbishop* (Grand Rapids, MI: Eerdmans, 2009), 262.

Muslims to promote social justice, peace, and freedom.[3] The spirit of the second Vatican Council, articulated in this document, influenced various dialogue movements, including ecumenical dialogues in Milwaukee, Wisconsin. In response to *Nostra Aetate,* in 1975, the Ecumenical Commission of the Archdiocese of Milwaukee established the Jewish-Catholic Conference in partnership with the Jewish Community Relations Council and the Wisconsin Council of Rabbis.[4] The conference worked toward mutual understanding between Christians and Jews in the Milwaukee area through sponsoring public lectures and hosting educational events, scripture studies, and occasional trips to Israel.[5] In addition to Jewish–Catholic dialogue, the archdiocese also participated in various ecumenical dialogues with Methodists, Lutherans, Orthodox, Polish National church, and Episcopalians.[6] However, no dialogue yet existed between Christians and Muslims despite a growing Muslim presence in Milwaukee since the 1940s.[7]

Following the migration of Arab Christians to Milwaukee in the late 1800s, Arab Muslims began to arrive in the area in the 1940s and 1950s as university students. In the 1960s and 1970s, Palestinian immigrants settled in Milwaukee after becoming displaced from their homeland, as well as Muslims from Pakistan, India, Egypt, and Iraq.[8] Many of them studied at the University of Wisconsin–Milwaukee. Thus, the first organization for Muslims in the area was the Muslim Students' Association at the university, established around 1970. One of the first places for Muslim prayer in the city was across from campus in the basement of Kenwood United Methodist Church, becoming the first religious space intentionally shared by Christians and Muslims in Milwaukee.[9] However, the two congregations did not interact with one another besides sharing this space. The story of intentional Muslim–Christian dialogue in Milwaukee begins with the vision of two sisters of Saint Francis of Assisi and one professor of history at the University of Wisconsin–Milwaukee (UWM).

---

3. Pope Paul VI, *Nostra Aetate,* October 28, 1965, 3.

4. Milwaukee Jewish Federation, "Catholic-Jewish Conference Mission Statement," www.milwaukeejewish.org.

5. Ibid. For a list of past events see, Archdiocese of Milwaukee, "Catholic-Jewish Conference," https://www.archmil.org/offices/ecumenical/Catholic-Jewish-Conference.htm.

6. Most. Rev. Richard Sklba, interview by Caroline Redick, February 17, 2017.

7. Islamic Society of Milwaukee, "Muslims in Milwaukee: A Brief History," *Islamic Society of Milwaukee: 25 Years of Service* (2007): 1.

8. Ibid.

9. Ibid., 3. Cf. Alexander (Sandy) Jacobs, interview by Irfan Omar, May 23, 2017.

Sister Lucille Walsh, OSF

Sister Lucille Walsh was the first to notice the absence of Muslim–Christian dialogue in Milwaukee and attempted to promote it. Born in Alberta, Canada, Lucille moved with her family to North Dakota, where she met the Sisters of St. Francis at Sacred Heart boarding school. When she turned 19, she moved to Milwaukee to join the congregation of The Sisters of St. Francis of Assisi—a religious order that held the worldview that all creatures are brothers and sisters.[10] There, she trained to become a dentist for the congregation, becoming the first woman religious (nun) to graduate from Marquette University with a Doctorate in Surgical Dentistry.[11] Although she practiced dentistry for twenty years, her true passion was the study of religion. Her fellow religious sister and close friend, Sister Jessine Reiss, remembers that Lucille would often discuss religion while performing dental operations, so "every time you'd get your tooth filled, you'd be filled with some philosophy."[12]

After back pain prevented her from continuing to practice dentistry, Lucille returned to Marquette University to pursue a master's degree in religious studies. She then served as a professor of theology at Cardinal Stritch University in Milwaukee, where she became interested in Eastern religions.[13] Inspired by the namesake of her order, St. Francis, who dialogued with a Muslim Sultan, Sister Lucille was drawn to learn about Islam and other traditions beyond the Western hemisphere.[14]

Reflecting on her personal journey toward dialogue with Muslims, Sister Lucille imagined a "seed" that needs proper soil and environment to grow.[15]

---

10. Amy Merrick, "Sr. Lucille Celebrates 100th Birthday," *Catholic Herald*, February 14, 2013, http://catholicherald.org/special-sections/mature-lifestyles/sr-lucille-celebrates-100th-birthday/.

11. Anonymous Author, "Nun Will Get M.U. Degree of Doctor of Dental Surgery," *Milwaukee Journal Sentinel*, June 25, 1944. See also, Guy Boulton, "Obituary for Lucille Walsh," *Milwaukee Journal Sentinel*, April 24, 2013. She was also voted the "most popular student in her class."

12. Jessine Reiss, OSF, interview by Irfan Omar and Caroline Redick, March 25, 2017.

13. Boulton, "Obituary for Lucille Walsh," 2013. Walsh taught at Stritch from 1967–1988.

14. Reiss, interview by Irfan Omar and Caroline Redick. Reiss comments, "St. Francis, as you know, went out to proselytize the Sultan. It worked the other way around. He was fascinated with the Sultan. He admired him deeply, and the Sultan apparently felt the same about Francis. . . . And that has been something that has permeated our community." For the story of Francis and the Sultan, and its implications for Muslim–Christian dialogue, see George Dardess and Marvin L. Krier Mich, *In the Spirit of St. Francis & the Sultan: Catholics and Muslims Working Together for the Common Good* (Maryknoll, NY: Orbis Books, 2011).

15. Lucille Walsh, OSF, "The Genesis of an Islamic-Christian Dialogue," *New Catholic World*, November/December 1988, 282.

Vatican II's admonition for hospitality toward world religions, coupled with her own curiosity, became the soil for Sister Lucille's interest in interreligious dialogue, leading her to study Buddhism, Hinduism, and Taoism. She remembers feeling particularly "at home" with her Buddhist friends, but initially feeling averse to Islam, its legalism, and the "shadowy figure of Muhammad."[16] Despite these initial impressions, as she studied Islam, she realized that Muslims and Christians shared a monotheistic religion and a common religious lineage from Abraham. In addition to this formal academic study, she also informally interacted with Muslims. While teaching college courses at Stritch University, she met students from Sunni and Shi'ite traditions who corrected many of her previous stereotypes. This informal dialogue with her students led her to see the possibility for dialogue beyond the classroom.

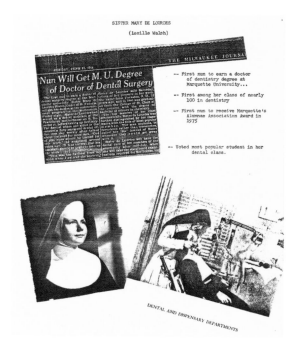

Figure 1.1: Collage of images and newspaper clippings regarding Lucille Walsh's background in dentistry, the first woman religious (nun) to graduate from Marquette Dental School.[17]

---

16. Ibid.

17. Unless otherwise noted, all photos and images in this chapter are supplied by and used with permission of Sister Jessine Reiss, OSF. The research team met with Sister Reiss in the spring of 2017 (fig. 1.8).

Sister Jessine Reiss, OSF

As Sister Lucille was becoming interested in the study of Islam, one of her colleagues and a fellow member of the order, Sister Jessine, was teaching literature at Cardinal Stritch. Like Sister Lucille, Sister Jessine was interested in studying Eastern culture, particularly literature. After a college review board recommended that Cardinal Stritch expand its curriculum to include classes about the non-Western world, both sisters received scholarships to continue their education abroad. They moved to Sophia University in Japan to study Eastern religion and literature. In addition, the sisters attended courses at Hamline University for African literature and mythology. Sister Lucille then went to San Francisco State University for courses in Islam, while Sister Jessine studied literature at Seton Hall University in New Jersey. When they returned to Stritch, they applied their expanded knowledge by teaching courses that highlighted Eastern religions and "world literature."[18] Finally, together the sisters attended a course in Islam at the University of Wisconsin–Milwaukee. Through this class, they met Dr. Abbas Hamdani, a professor of history, who would partner with them to initiate the first Muslim–Christian dialogue in Milwaukee.

Figure 1.2: Dr. Abbas Hamdani, Sister Jessine Reiss, and Sister Lucille Walsh.

Dr. Abbas Hamdani

Abbas Hamdani was born in Surat, India, and taught Islamic history at UWM beginning in 1969. Like the sisters, he had traveled globally, studying at Bombay

---

18. Reiss, interview by Irfan Omar and Caroline Redick.

University and the University of London where he received his PhD in Arabic and Islamic studies. A recipient of a Fulbright Commission Fellowship, Dr. Hamdani focused on medieval Islamic philosophy, the conflicts between Abbasid and Fatimid caliphates, and 12th-century heresiological literature.[19] He taught at the University of Karachi as well as the American University in Cairo before coming to Wisconsin to join the UWM faculty in 1971.[20] There, he met Sister Lucille and Sister Jessine as students in his courses.

The two sisters were enthused by the study of Islam and dismayed by other students' ignorance about the religion. As voracious learners, the pair would often stay after class to speak with Dr. Hamdani further about the history of Islam. During one of these informal meetings, Sister Lucille vocalized her frustration with the ignorance regarding Islam that she sensed in her classmates. Seeking a solution to this problem, she asked Dr. Hamdani if there was anything they could do to help the situation. Believing that education was the best solution, Dr. Hamdani proposed that a group meet together occasionally to educate themselves. Sister Lucille enthusiastically agreed, and with Sister Jessine's help, the pair asked the archdiocese for permission to begin a Catholic–Islamic dialogue. With the support of archbishop Rembert Weakland, the sisters proceeded with the blessing of the Church. Dr. Hamdani invited Muslim participants, including his wife, Zubeda, as well as Mahmoud and Intisar Atta, a Palestinian couple. Sister Lucille sent letters to Christians, such as Rev. Elliot Bush, a Methodist minister, and Rev. Humphrey Walz, a Presbyterian minister who had previously worked in New York re-settling Holocaust refugees.[21]

The Formal Dialogue

In 1980, with the archdiocese's approval, the sisters hosted the first official Islamic–Christian dialogue in Milwaukee.[22] Sister Lucille and Dr. Hamdani envisioned the goal of the dialogue would be to "create an atmosphere of

---

19. The Institute of Ismaili Studies, "Biography: Professor Abbas Hamdani," https://iis.ac.uk/people/prof-abbas-hamdani.

20. Ibid.

21. Abbas Hamdani, interview (via email) by Irfan Omar and Caroline Redick, April 23, 2017.

22. Reiss, interview by Irfan Omar and Caroline Redick. Sister Lucille continued to receive approval from the Ecumenical and Interfaith Commission. The sisters always followed official policy in planning their dialogue and worked closely with the archdiocese Ecumenical and Interfaith Commission, as evidenced by Bert C. Mulroy (Coordinator of Ecumenical & Interfaith Commission) letter to Sr. Jessine and Sr. Lucille, February 19, 1990.

mutual understanding, trust and cooperation between Christians and Muslims" in the Milwaukee area.[23] The meetings followed the Vatican *Guidelines for Dialogue Between Muslims and Christians*, issued by the Secretariat for non-Christians in 1969, which aimed at creating a hospitable space for dialogue for everyone.[24] Thus, the guidelines, followed scrupulously by the sisters, reminded participants that "dialogue takes place between human beings; not between systems."[25] In order to foster relationships, the guidelines, written for Catholics engaged in dialogue, encouraged participants to "show real friendship for the other person" and to accept each person for who he or she is. The attitude of someone entering dialogue should be "truth and love," proposing that "only truth can overcome divisions between men and truth's victory is love."[26] The document also prompted Christian participants to view Islam as a faith: "we must consider the Muslim as a man of faith, who, like us, is striving to live in the sight of God, and to accept his holy will in all things. In this way we shall discover a brother in this believer."[27]

Figure 1.3: Members of the dialogue in meeting (left to right): Zubeda Hamdani, Trudy and Rev. Elliot Bush, Mrs. and Rev. Walz, Gloria Luenberg, Dr. Sethi, Gloria Ropella, and Rev. Parrish.

Along with this vision for the purpose of dialogue, the sisters also followed the practical advice provided by the Church guidelines. For example, the document warned against unwittingly taking sides in intra-Islamic controversies,

---

23. Walsh, "The Genesis of an Islamic-Christian Dialogue," 282.

24. Ibid., 283.

25. Secretariat for Non-Christians, *Guidelines for Dialogue Between Muslims and Christians*, copy supplied by Sister Jessine Reiss.

26. Ibid.

27. Ibid.

such as by referring to "Sunnis" as a "sect" of Islam, which would be offensive to Sunni Muslims. In addition, Christian participants were encouraged to become aware of cultural differences among Muslims. These practical instructions were delivered in the hope of forming a "true dialogue" that remains constantly aware of the interlocutor as a person.[28]

While the sisters knew some Christians who would be interested in dialogue, it was more difficult to find Muslims interested in participating, since many were weary of dialogue as a cover for proselytization or did not see the need for dialogue with another religion.[29] However, with Dr. Hamdani's assistance, the sisters sent out letters of invitation to particular persons in the Muslim community. Fifteen Muslims and 15 Christians, of various denominations, attended the first meeting.[30] Many of the Christians present were ordained ministers or members of religious orders, but the Muslim participants were all laypersons.[31] Since the Islamic community in Milwaukee did not have an imam until 1995, many of the Muslim participants were not formally educated in Islamic theology.[32] Thus, the dialoguers had to be aware of different perspectives and types of familiarity with the faiths. While it was officially called the "Catholic–Islamic dialogue," the group was interdenominational from the beginning, and soon changed its title to "Islamic–Christian dialogue" to better represent the diversity of the group. After asking the group what they would like to discuss, the members of the first meeting dialogued about "the concept of God in the Qur'an and in the Bible."[33]

Subsequent dialogues, held six or seven times a year, followed the pattern of choosing and discussing theological topics such as Jesus, the family, Abraham, and the Church and the *ummah* (global Muslims).[34] Other meetings focused on the personal impact of interfaith engagement. For example, at a meeting on February 17, 1989, the participants were each asked to share their experiences of encountering persons of other faiths. Christians and Muslims shared what most surprised them when they met others of a different religion,

---

28. Ibid.

29. Walsh, "The Genesis of an Islamic-Christian Dialogue," 283.

30. Ibid. See also "Muslim-Christian Dialogue in Milwaukee," *The Presbyterian Outlook* 163, no. 1, January 5, 1981. Participants at the first meeting included Abbas Hamdani, Vali Kiaie, Father Robert Lambeck, SJ, Father Melvin Michalski, and Rev. Humphrey Walz.

31. For a list of the participants in the original dialogue, see Appendix A.

32. Islamic Society of Milwaukee, "Muslims in Milwaukee," 6.

33. Reiss, interview by Irfan Omar and Caroline Redick.

34. Walsh, "The Genesis of an Islamic-Christian Dialogue," 283.

and what this encounter taught them about their own faith.[35] Thus, the dialogues centered around theological and personal topics but intentionally avoided political issues.[36]

Figure 1.4: Sister Lucille Walsh, Tayyibah Sethi, Janan Atta, and an unidentified participant at one of the dialogue meetings.

Whenever politics became a topic of discussion, it led to disagreements, which some viewed as impediments to dialogue and mutual understanding. Others, however, believed that political issues, such as the state of Israel, were inseparably bound up in Christian–Muslim relations. Some argued that the avoidance of political conversation stemmed from the American belief in the separation of church and state.[37] This disagreement became a challenge for the group, which eventually agreed to focus exclusively on theological issues. It is an example of challenges that such dialogues will inevitably face.

While the group was joined at times by new members, a core membership developed over the years, which sustained an atmosphere of trust in the dialogue. The longevity of this group also ensured that they could discuss deeper

---

35. Jessine Reiss, letter to the Members of the Islamic Christian Dialogue, January 31, 1989.

36. Reiss, interview by Irfan Omar and Caroline Redick.

37. Anonymous Author, "Politics Hinders Dialog, Interfaith Committee Finds," *The Milwaukee Journal*, April 30, 1983.

issues since they had already developed basic understandings of one another's faiths.[38] John Renard, a scholar of Islamic studies, observes that this familiarity allowed a "catechism like exchange" to become a "more personal reflection on how each member" internalized the beliefs of his or her religion.[39] The members self-identified as "a group of men and women of the Islamic and Christian faith traditions" who met on a regular basis to "discover, appreciate and promote those values found in our respective religious traditions which will foster mutual understanding, truth, justice and peaceful interdependence."[40] At first, meetings rotated between various locations, such as St. Rita's parish, the United Methodist Church, Marquette University library, and St. Francis Seminary, before finding a permanent host at Cardinal Stritch University.[41]

Community Engagement

The members of the dialogue did not remain sequestered at Cardinal Stritch, but they often put on events for the community to educate others in Milwaukee about Islam. For example, following a dialogue session on war and peace, the group hosted a public prayer service in which a Christian read the nativity narrative from the Gospel of Luke and a Muslim read the Qur'an's account of Jesus's birth. Following these readings, Rev. Matthew Gottschalk delivered a homily on "The Meaning of Peace," and Muslims and Christians took turns leading prayer.[42] While the Muslim group prayed in Arabic facing Mecca, non-Muslims were given an English translation of the prayers so that they could participate.[43]

Another public event was a conference at Cardinal Stritch on *Islam: Faith of 800 Million People*. Sister Jessine wrote a proposal for the National

38. Walsh, "The Genesis of an Islamic-Christian Dialogue," 283.

39. John Renard, *101 Questions and Answers on Islam* (New York: Paulist Press, 1998), 115.

40. Committee of the Milwaukee Archdiocesan Ecumenical and Interfaith Commission, "Statement of Identity," revised April 12, 1983.

41. Reiss, interview by Irfan Omar and Caroline Redick. The meeting minutes show that the group met at Memorial Library at Marquette University for the group's second meeting in January 1981, as well as a subsequent meeting in April.

42. Archdiocese of Milwaukee Ecumenical and Interfaith Commission, "Islamic-Christian Group Sponsors Peace Prayer Service," December 1, 1982. Also, Walsh, "The Genesis of an Islamic-Christian Dialogue," 283.

43. Walsh, "The Genesis of an Islamic-Christian Dialogue," 283. Also, Anonymous Author, "Peace, Prayers," *Milwaukee Journal Sentinel*, December 11, 1983. The prayer service was held at the McFetridge Auditorium of the Deaconess Campus of Good Samaritan Medical Center.

Endowment for the Humanities and received a substantial grant for the conference.[44] Dr. Hamdani was one of the keynote speakers at this public program, along with John Renard, SJ, from St. Louis University; Ghada Talhami, from University of Illinois; and Farouk Sankari, from University of Wisconsin (Oshkosh).[45] The one-day conference drew 300 people and featured lectures such as those on media stereotyping, St. Francis, and Jerusalem.[46] Dr. Hamdani introduced the conference attendees to Islam as the religion of "one-fifth of the human race." He explained that Islam shares many beliefs with Christianity and Judaism, such as the belief in One God, spiritual practices of prayer, fasting, and pilgrimage, and concepts such as the Day of Judgment.[47] In another lecture, Father Renard attempted to correct stereotypes and caricatures of Islam. For example, he explained that Islam does not worship Muhammad, only God. Mecca is a central place of worship because Muhammad was born there, but the focus of worship remains the Creator.[48]

In addition, the dialogue sponsored a number of public lectures aimed at education about Islam and tolerance. On May 5, 1983, the dialogue supported an event at the United Methodist Church in Milwaukee, at which Byron L. Haines, the director of the National Council of Churches, and Dr. Ahmad H. Sakr spoke about "the conditions of our life together," namely, "right disposition, right understanding, and right effort."[49] Haines pointed out pitfalls in dialogue, such as the tendency to perceive the interaction as between "the ideal me versus the real you." In this case, the dialoguer contrasts the best of his or her religion to the perceived reality of the other's religion, instead of allowing the other person to represent himself or herself. He warned against judging Islam as a religion based upon the actions of individual Muslims, just as many Christians do not exemplify Christ. Events, such as this one, introduced churches in Milwaukee to the idea of dialogue with Islam and promoted tolerance in the community.

44. Reiss, interview by Irfan Omar and Caroline Redick.

45. Cardinal Stritch College, *Islam: Faith of 800 Million People*, pamphlet, supplied by Dan Di Domizio.

46. Ibid.

47. Abbas Hamdani, "Islam" presentation at *Islam: Faith of 800 Million People*, Cardinal Stritch College, Milwaukee, WI, March 20, 1982.

48. Thomas J. Smith, "Islam Plays a Role in Religious History," *Catholic Herald*, April 1, 1982.

49. Pat Windsor, "Respect, Tolerance Key Elements in Fruitful Christian, Muslim Dialogue," *Catholic Herald*, May 5, 1983.

Recognition of the Dialogue

In 1985, Sister Lucille wrote a letter to the Vatican thanking Pope John Paul II for his statement during his visit to Morocco in which he promoted the idea of dialogue between Catholics and Muslims. She informed the Vatican about the work in Milwaukee and requested an English translation of the Vatican guidelines for Muslim–Christian dialogue, since the current version was out of print.[50] She quickly received a response from the Vatican acknowledging her letter. Later, in response to Sister Jessine's letter, which provided more detail of the work the dialogue group had undertaken in their first few years, Cardinal Francis Arinze, president of the Secretariat for Non-Christians, wrote a letter encouraging the dialogue and lending his full support. In addition, Cardinal Arinze's letter referred her to the new translation of the guidelines for dialogue that was to become available in English shortly thereafter.[51] This correspondence depicts the dialogue's close relationship with the highest offices in the Catholic Church.

This relationship of respect cultivated a reputation for the dialogue in Rome. When Archbishop Rembert Weakland left Milwaukee to travel to Rome for his *ad limina* visit to report to the Vatican on the diocese, he was surprised to be greeted with the comment, "You're the archbishop from Milwaukee where they have that Muslim–Christian dialogue!"[52] In addition to this comment, Archbishop Jadot, head of the office for the promotion of dialogue with Muslims, informed Archbishop Weakland that Milwaukee was one of the only archdioceses in the world with a comparable dialogue (involving people from the local parish or community). Archbishop Jadot encouraged him to support the dialogue, foreseeing that "it is going to be very important in the future."[53] This

---

50. Lucille Walsh, letter to Pope John Paul II, August 21, 1985.

51. Cardinal Francis Arinze, letter to Sr. Jessine, December 30, 1985. Arinze, a Nigerian Cardinal, was highly regarded by Pope John Paul II and received the gold medallion from the International Council of Christians and Jews for his work in interfaith relations in 1999. For an overview of Cardinal Arinze's life and work, see Yussuf J. Simmonds, "Cardinal Francis Arinze," *Los Angeles Sentinel*, September 23, 2009. "Secretariat for Non-Christians" was later renamed Pontifical Council of Interreligious Dialogue (PCID) in 1988.

52. Reiss, interview by Irfan Omar and Caroline Redick. See the images (in the "Introduction") of the letters exchanged between Sr. Lucille Walsh and Monsignor G. B. (Pope John Paul II's representative) and a letter from Cardinal Francis Arinze, then president of the "Secretariat for Non-Christians" at the Vatican sent to Sister Jessine. Cardinal Arinze's words are particularly interesting as they are as relevant today as they were in 1985: "I take the occasion to thank you for your collaboration and hope that you will continue to keep us informed of the fine work of dialogue between Muslims and Christians carried on in Milwaukee . . . may you keep up the good work."

53. Weakland, *A Pilgrim in a Pilgrim Church*, 262.

Figure 1.5: Sister Lucille Walsh, OSF, is presented with the Vatican II award by Archbishop Rembert Weakland in 1999.

demonstrated that knowledge and impact of the dialogue was spreading, and the sisters were encouraged to learn that the dialogue was recognized in Rome.[54]

In 1999, Sister Lucille's and Sister Jessine's efforts were again recognized by the archdiocese as the archbishop presented each of the sisters with the Milwaukee archdiocese's Vatican II award.[55]

Impact of the Dialogue

Throughout the years of dialogue, there have been multiple discernible impacts on the Muslim community in Milwaukee, the wider Milwaukee community, and the individuals involved in the dialogue. One attendee of the first dialogue, Reverend Melvin Michalski, was inspired to write a letter to then president-elect Ronald Reagan, on behalf of the group, recommending that an invitation to the presidential inaugural ceremonies be extended to an Islamic religious leader.[56] While Christian pastors and leaders of other faiths had been traditionally invited to give an invocation at the ceremony, the invitation had yet to be extended to an imam. In his letter, Rev. Michalski cited *Nostra Aetate* as well as the Arab contribution to civilization as reasons to include a Muslim representative. In addition, he argued that this gesture would "provide an opportunity to recognize indirectly the contributions of Black Muslims to American society" and that the invocation would "promote respect and mutual understanding among Jews, Christians, and Muslims."[57] Although Michalski never received a response from the president-elect, his letter exemplified the future

54. Reiss, interview by Irfan Omar and Caroline Redick.

55. Anonymous Author, "13 to be Honored with Vatican II Award," *Catholic Herald*, July 15, 1999.

56. Cathy Geyso, "Dear Mr. Prez . . ." *The Challenger* 3, no. 4, December 1980. The letter was also sent to the chairman of the Inaugural Arrangement Committee.

57. Melvin Michalski, letter to President-Elect Ronald Reagan, November 25, 1980.

trajectory of the dialogue, which worked toward societal change through various strategies.

The first notable impact on the Muslim community was the extension of hospitality by the Christian community and reciprocal hospitality extended by Muslims in the community toward Christians. For example, one group of Muslim university students, looking for a place for Friday prayers, requested to use space in a Catholic parish. Sister Lucille sought advice from the Secretariat for Non-Christians in Rome, who responded that although there was no official Catholic position, it was an "opportunity to extend Christian hospitality" that could serve as a sign "of what Christianity is really about."[58] In this way, the particular church embodied the "moral duty to relate to one another as good neighbors."[59] Similarly, Sister Lucille viewed the dialogues as a "means of sowing seeds of trusting relationships in the Milwaukee area."[60]

As another example of neighborly hospitality, the archbishop of Milwaukee, on behalf of the Islamic–Christian dialogue, donated $500 to the construction of a new Islamic Center on 13th Street and Layton Avenue. The letter accompanying the gift specified that it was "a symbol of mutual friendship, and a tangible complement to our united prayers to God for peace—peace among all peoples, peace between nations, peace between faith communities."[61] Sister Lucille presented the donation to Mahmoud Atta, another member of the dialogue, on behalf of the archdiocese. In this tangible way, the members of the dialogue worked to build trust between their communities.

The educational impact of the dialogue extended beyond public forums and into Milwaukee classrooms. As a group, the participants decided to conduct evaluations of social studies and history textbooks used in Milwaukee public schools, seeking to discover any biases or misinformation about Islam and Christianity. The group gathered various texts and worked together to read them thoroughly before sending their evaluations to the textbook publishers.[62] Hearing of the dialogue's endeavor, Harvard University's Center for Middle Eastern Studies requested a copy of the group's evaluations to assist in

---

58. Walsh, "The Genesis of an Islamic-Christian Dialogue," 285.

59. Committee of the Milwaukee Archdiocesan Ecumenical and Interfaith Commission, "Some Principles and Proposed Goals for Christians and Muslims Living Together as Good Neighbors," revised April 12, 1983.

60. Walsh, "The Genesis of an Islamic-Christian Dialogue," 285.

61. Anonymous Author, letter to Mr. Mahmoud Atta, no date. See also the receipt of the donation from the Islamic organization, fig. 1.6.

62. Ibid.

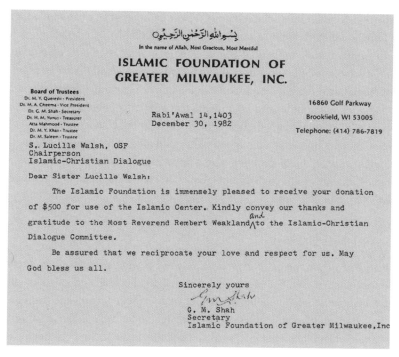

Figure 1.6: Receipt for the donation from the archdiocese to the newly established Islamic Center in Milwaukee addressed here to Sister Lucille.

the center's own evaluation of American textbooks.[63] Other requests for copies of the group's evaluations came from as far as Africa.[64] Thus, the dialogue impacted the education of future generations through its service to the Milwaukee public schools.

Another important impact of the dialogue was the creation of a network of interfaith relationships throughout Milwaukee. This network became important in moments of need, such as when a ship captain, off the shore of Sheboygan in Lake Michigan, contacted the archdiocese because a Muslim member of his crew had died. The ship was from India, with a mostly Hindu crew, but the Hindu captain was aware that Muslims practice a unique burial rite.[65] The

---

63. Harvard University Center for Middle Eastern Studies, letter to Islamic-Christian Dialogue of Milwaukee, June 19, 1986.

64. Walsh, "The Genesis of an Islamic-Christian Dialogue," 283. Requests also came from Madison, WI, Bloomington, IN, and the College of the Holy Cross in Worcester, MA.

65. Othman Atta, interview by Dianne Marshall, Sundus Jaber, and Caroline Redick, March 24, 2017.

archdiocese forwarded the message to Sister Lucille, who then contacted the Atta family. Since no one in the small Milwaukee Muslim population knew how to perform the traditional burial rituals, Intisar Atta read about how to properly wash the body and prepare it for burial. She bought the proper fabric for burial and taught her son the burial rite. He then prepared the body of the man so that he could be buried according to Islamic custom. Intisar reflects that the preexisting connection between the communities resulted in the ability to properly care for another Muslim. This whole process took place within a matter of days—a feat that would have been impossible if the Muslim–Christian network did not exist.[66] In this way, the dialogue impacted the lives of particular persons.

Personal Reflections

In addition to these broader impacts upon the community, many participants experienced personal transformation through the dialogue. Sister Jessine reflected on her time of dialogue as one of the most important moments in her life. "Personally, it did everything for me," she explained in an interview. "As a result of our involvement with the Muslims, we learned to become better Christians in a way . . . their life is in sync with their religion. They give the priority to prayer that should be given to it. . . . They've taught us many things."[67] These lessons took place in the context of deep friendships that formed through the dialogue. In light of this experience, Sister Jessine comments, "we see the Muslims as our brothers and sisters. I couldn't have a brother or sister that is kinder or more wonderful."[68] Similarly, Sister Lucille reflected, "outstanding among my experiences are the friendships I have formed and the gratitude I felt for my Muslim friends who visited me in the hospital to tell me they were praying for me."[69]

Through dialogue, the sisters formed lifelong relationships with Muslims. Sister Jessine fondly recalls when she and Sister Lucille were at home by themselves during the Christmas holidays. They received a call from Intisar Atta, one of the dialogue members, wishing them a Merry Christmas and asking about their day. After telling her that they were simply at home watching television, Intisar

---

66. Intisar Atta, interview by Dianne Marshall, Sundus Jaber, and Caroline Redick, March 24, 2017.

67. Reiss, interview by Irfan Omar and Caroline Redick.

68. Ibid.

69. Walsh, "The Genesis of an Islamic-Christian Dialogue," 284.

promptly invited them to her house for dinner so that they would not spend Christmas alone. Sending her son to pick them up, Mrs. Atta prepared a beautiful meal for the sisters. Sister Jessine warmly remembers, "she was the only one who thought of us."[70] Through the dialogue, they formed a lasting friendship.

Intisar also recalls her invitation to the sisters and feels like they are her long-lost friends or "older sisters."[71] Mahmoud Atta, Intisar's husband and another original member of the dialogue, looked forward to the discussions as a way to socialize with others. As an engine technician with a challenging job and a family man, the dialogues were one of the main spaces in which he developed friendships. He also enjoyed the opportunity to explain his religion to other people, finding that the members were genuinely interested in learning and interacting.[72] In this way, the dialogues formed bonds of friendship that enriched the lives of those who participated. Their son, Othman Atta, remarks that the "success of interfaith action was that it developed a good, strong, relationship between people of different faiths. And it has obviously impacted the next generations."[73]

Two other participants in the dialogue, Trudy and Elliot Bush (former pastor of the United Methodist church in Fox Point, Milwaukee), also emphasize the importance of friendship in dialogue. They reflect that their participation in the group gave them an opportunity to learn more about Islam and enabled them to become friends with Muslims. Although the couple had previously lived in Algeria with Muslim colleagues, students, and neighbors, they did not have the opportunity to develop friendships with Muslims and discuss faith until becoming involved in the Milwaukee dialogue. Based upon their experience, they believe that "the greatest value of the dialogue is that it makes people of both faiths aware of their common values and aspirations: the desire for holiness, the quest for justice, and the love of peace."[74] These values unite Muslims and Christians "in brotherhood and sisterhood" with one another.[75] Thus, the Bushes, like Intisar Atta, use familial language to describe their experience of dialogue.

In light of these experiences, we may wonder how to initiate a similar project, and what lessons to take from the story of the original Milwaukee dialogue.

---

70. Reiss, interview by Irfan Omar and Caroline Redick.

71. Intisar Atta, interview by Dianne Marshall, Sundus Jaber, and Caroline Redick.

72. Othman Atta, interview by Dianne Marshall, Sundus Jaber, and Caroline Redick. In this interview, Othman recounted his father's experience of the dialogue.

73. Ibid.

74. Elliot and Trudy Bush, "What the Islamic-Christian Dialogue Has Meant to Me," *New Catholic World*, November/December 1988, 285–86.

75. Ibid.

In an article she wrote for *New Catholic World* in 1988, Sister Lucille offered several suggestions for Christians engaging Islam that continue to be helpful today. For example, she suggests that Christian colleges and seminaries offer courses on Islam with qualified professors.[76] Her advice echoes Dr. Hamdani's observation that education is the solution to ignorance or misperceptions of the faith.[77] Universities, in particular, provide the resources necessary to discover another faith with the guidance of experts. In addition, colleges may promote community education through hosting public forums and lectures on Islam.

Beyond the classroom, Sister Lucille suggests that Christians invite their Muslim neighbors to become members in social and civic organizations.[78] In these social spaces, Christians and Muslims may build relationships of mutual understanding and work together toward the common good. For Sister Jessine and Sister Lucille, the greatest fruit of the dialogue was the development of life-long friendships. Thus, building sustained relationships is not only a means to dialogue but one of its principal goals.

In addition to these insights, Sister Lucille advises that Christians should denounce any stereotypes that degrade Muslims.[79] This practical suggestion is, perhaps, even more pertinent in our own time—in which media often portrays Muslims in negative ways. Finally, she urges Christians to offer hospitality to Muslim neighbors.[80] Lucille's own experience of being invited to a Christmas dinner at Intisar Atta's home provides a model for hospitable dialogue.

As an act of hospitality, dialogue involves personal risk, requiring vulnerability to others. John Renard, a speaker at the *Islam: Faith of 800 Million People* conference, observes,

> [In dialogue] one finds acknowledgment of the importance of simply meeting one another in breaking down stereotypes, of the need for patience and persistence, of letting go the desire to see the other change, of willingness to risk one's putting one's fears on the table, of willingness to be misunderstood and be told one does not understand. All such matters demand a considerable level of personal security, maturity, and freedom, since they touch on issues potentially very threatening.[81]

---

76. Walsh, "The Genesis of an Islamic-Christian Dialogue," 285.

77. Reiss, interview by Irfan Omar and Caroline Redick.

78. Walsh, "The Genesis of an Islamic-Christian Dialogue," 285.

79. Ibid.

80. Ibid.

81. Renard, *101 Questions and Answers on Islam*, 115.

The Milwaukee dialogue required maturity and vulnerability on the part of its participants—since their views of each other's faiths, and of their own faith, were often challenged. Yet, this risk resulted not only in a deeper understanding of the other's faith but also growth in their own faith. Thus, confident maturity in one's own faith allows hospitable vulnerability to the faith of another.

The Spread of Dialogue[82]

The Milwaukee Islamic–Christian dialogue began as a "seed" in the mind of Sister Lucille Walsh. Along with her co-visionaries Sister Jessine Reiss and Dr. Abbas Hamdani, this vision grew into a reality with discernable impacts on the wider community over two decades. As the members aged, the dialogue eventually came to a close in the late 1990s, but many of the members continued the work by joining various dialogues and organizations.[83] In this way, branches formed from the seed of the original dialogue—creating new spaces and opportunities for Muslim–Christian relations in Milwaukee.

Many members of the first formal dialogue later joined the Milwaukee Association for Interfaith Relations (MAIR), which began in 1982 as a local branch of the national Catholic–Jewish dialogue. Michael and Silvia Weber, a Jewish couple, partnered with Richard Lux, a Roman Catholic, to create MAIR.[84] Most of the members of the group were Christians and Jews through the 1990s, but they gradually decided to open the organization to persons of other faiths. Participation in MAIR declined in the early 2000s, but after September 11, 2001, the remaining members of the group reorganized into the Committee for Interfaith Understanding, which fosters understanding in the community through public educational events.[85] Currently, this committee has a diverse membership, including Muslim and Sikh participants.[86]

---

82. This concluding section offers an abbreviated version of other dialogues that emerged around the time when the "original" Islamic–Christian dialogue was slowing down. The last chapter in this volume "the overview" provides a more detail account of the spawning of dialogue in Milwaukee.

83. Dan Di Domizio, interview by Kaitlyn Daly, Milwaukee, March 1, 2017.

84. Richard Lux was a professor of scripture studies at Sacred Heart Seminary. In addition to cofounding MAIR, he also worked to found the Lux Center for Catholic-Jewish Studies at Sacred Heart. For more on the Lux Center, see https://www.shsst.edu/theluxcenter/.

85. For example, on April 27, 2016, the committee sponsored a panel at Crossroads Presbyterian Church in Mequon featuring Rev. Scott Hauser (Crossroads pastor), Janan Najeeb, and Rabbi Ronald Shapiro. Interfaith Conference of Greater Milwaukee, *Exploring Islam: Addressing Difficult Questions*, flyer.

86. Di Domizio, interview by Kaitlyn Daly.

The Committee for Interfaith Understanding functions as the educational unit of the Interfaith Conference of Greater Milwaukee (ICGM).[87] Founded in 1970 to advocate for low-income families in Milwaukee, the original members of the ICGM also intended it to "create awareness of and advocacy between different faith communities."[88] Today, the Interfaith Conference works to foster mutual understanding between persons of different faiths through various programs, including Amazing Faiths Dinner Dialogues, in which participants share a vegetarian meal and engage in a moderated conversation.[89] This provides attendees with the opportunity to "learn about the beliefs and traditions of others within an atmosphere of respect and understanding" and to be "empowered to stand as witnesses for tolerance."[90] Along with these dinners, the interfaith conference also runs the Interfaith Earth Network and, in the past, initiated a program called Beyond Racism, which designed educational resources for children to recognize common bonds and to talk about "common problems that cause conflict," and "affirm themselves and others."[91]

In addition to these dialogue initiatives, a number of specifically Muslim–Christian dialogues have emerged in Milwaukee. Bishop Richard Sklba initiated a new dialogue by inviting some of the Muslim clergy and leaders to participate in a theological conversation. This dialogue group aims to build relationships and establish freedom to speak honestly about theological topics. It is composed of nine Catholic and Muslim participants: Othman Atta, Barbara Freres, Judith Longdin, Janan Najeeb, Waleed Najeeb, Ahmed Quereshi, Philip Reifenberg, Zulfiqar Ali Shah, and Bishop Sklba. They have met once every four to six weeks since 2011 as a closed group in order to foster long-term relationships of trust and honesty. This model resonates with Bishop Sklba's conviction that "nothing happens except through friendship."[92]

---

87. Ibid.

88. Tom Heinen, "The Interfaith Conference of Greater Milwaukee," March 22, 2017, http://pluralism.org/. Currently, the conference is the largest organization of its kind in southeastern Wisconsin.

89. Interfaith Conference of Greater Milwaukee, "History of Amazing Faiths Dinner Dialogues," http://interfaithconference.org/cms-view-page.php?page=afdd-history.

90. Interfaith Conference of Greater Milwaukee, *Amazing Faiths: Seeking Hosts for Dinner Dialogues 2017*, virtual flyer, provided by Tom Heinen.

91. Ibid. See also, Interfaith Conference of Greater Milwaukee, "Interfaith Earth Network," http://www.interfaithconference.org/cms-view-page.php?page=earth-network and Interfaith Conference of Greater Milwaukee, "Alike and Different," http://interfaithconference.org/cms-view-page.php?page=alike-different.

92. Sklba, interview by Caroline Redick.

Another organization, Peace Catalyst International, works to involve evangelicals in Muslim–Christian dialogue.[93] It aims to create partnerships between Christians and Muslims in the pursuit of peace in a way that does not dissolve the distinct faiths into "an imaginary 'One World Religion'" but draws upon the resources inherent in each faith tradition to create relationships of love and respect.[94] For this reason, members of Peace Catalyst agree to "seek to be accurate" when speaking about each other's faiths and respect how each faith community interprets itself.[95] Steve Lied, program coordinator for the organization in Milwaukee, hosts "quick to listen" sessions in evangelical churches that explore the biblical foundations for loving neighbor, refugee, and enemy. Most of these events take place at Brew City Church, a nondenominational congregation in downtown Milwaukee. For example, in April 2016, Peace Catalyst International partnered with the Milwaukee Muslim Women's Coalition (MMWC) and Brew City Church to host a panel on "breaking down barriers and building trust" between Muslims and Evangelicals.[96] Panelists included Janan Najeeb, the president of MMWC; Fatih Harpci, an assistant professor of religion at Carthage College; Jenny Heckman, a professional counselor; and Randie Knie, the lead pastor of Brew City Church.[97] In addition to these events, Peace Catalyst International has developed discussion groups based on the virtues of "faith, hope and love." Each group includes 12 to 15 participants who alternate between homes and discuss their faith journeys together. The objective of the group is not to "preach to the choir" of regular interfaith attendees but to impact people who would otherwise not be involved in dialogue. Thus, the organization focuses primarily on fostering dialogue with the evangelical community, particularly young adults and families.[98]

One participant in the dinner discussions, Bob Turner, experienced a personal transformation through his encounter with Muslims at the table. Before

---

93. See www.peacecatalyst.org. The organization works to create "safe spaces and foster authentic relationships between Christians and Muslims. We also partner with Muslims to work for peace."

94. Peace Catalyst, "Seven Resolutions Against Prejudice, Hatred and Discrimination," document provided by Steve Lied.

95. Ibid.

96. Brew City Church, Milwaukee Muslim Women's Coalition, and Peace Catalyst International, *Muslims & Evangelicals: Breaking Down Barriers & Building Trust*, flyer, provided by Steve Lied.

97. Ibid.

98. Steve Lied, interview by Irfan Omar and Caroline Redick, May 25, 2017.

attending a dinner, Bob did not personally know any Muslims and was suspicious of Islam.[99] Desiring to better imitate Christ's love for others, he decided to participate in the program. Through developing friendships with Muslims through the dinner dialogues (or "peace feasts," fig. 1.7), Turner explains that he has "come to see Muslims as 'regular' people—that is, good, bad, saintly and evil, fascinating, or average; in other words, the same as any Christians I have ever known."[100] Turner's story is one example of personal transformation that continues to occur in Milwaukee through Muslim–Christian dialogue.

Figure 1.7: A gathering of Muslims and Christians for a "peace feast" at Ramallah restaurant.

Conclusion

Since the first formal dialogue of 1980, Muslim–Christian relations in Milwaukee continue to develop as the legacy of the dialogue is embodied in the next generation. For example, two of the youngest participants in the original dialogue, Othman Atta and Janan Najeeb, the children of Intisar and Mahmoud Atta, attended the dialogue with their parents as teenagers. Since

---

99. Lied, interview by Irfan Omar and Caroline Redick.

100. Bob Turner, as quoted in Anonymous Author, "Disarming Ignorance with many Canons," *Summer Carthagian*, September 2016, 36.

then, they have become deeply involved with Muslim–Christian relations in Milwaukee.[101] Othman now leads the Islamic Center of Milwaukee and frequently gives public talks on Islam.[102] Janan cofounded the Milwaukee Muslim Women's Coalition and advocates for Muslims in Milwaukee, frequently participating in dialogues such as the Interfaith Conference dinner dialogues, the Muslim–Christian women's dialogue, and the Catholic–Muslim dialogue initiated by Bishop Sklba. Their work points to the long-term impact of the original dialogue, reflecting "precisely what [the original dialogue members] hoped would happen"—that the dialogue would grow, branch out into new outlets, and create a culture of respect in Milwaukee.[103] Thus, the next generation carries the vision of mutual understanding, friendship, and cooperation toward the common good, forward in new directions.

Figure 1.8: The research group met with Sister Jessine Reiss (left) in the spring of 2017. The researchers present were Sundus Jaber, Dianne Rostollan, Caroline Redick, and Kaitlyn Daly.

101. Reiss, interview by Irfan Omar and Caroline Redick. Also, Othman Atta, interview by Dianne Marshall, Sundus Jaber, and Caroline Redick.

102. For example, Othman presented on the history of Muslims in Milwaukee at the *Christian-Muslim Relations in America Symposium*, Marquette University, Milwaukee WI, March 29, 2017.

103. Reiss, interview by Irfan Omar and Caroline Redick.

Bibliography

Archdiocese of Milwaukee. "Catholic-Jewish Conference." https://www.archmil.org/offices/ecumenical/Catholic-Jewish-Conference.htm.

Archdiocese of Milwaukee Ecumenical and Interfaith Commission. "Islamic-Christian Group Sponsors Peace Prayer Service." December 1, 1982.

Anonymous Author. "13 to be Honored with Vatican II Award." *Catholic Herald*, July 15, 1999.

Anonymous Author. "Disarming Ignorance with Many Canons." *Summer Carthagian*, September 2016, 34–6.

Anonymous Author. Letter to Mr. Mahmoud Atta. No date.

Anonymous Author. "Muslim-Christian Dialogue in Milwaukee." *The Presbyterian Outlook* 163, no. 1, January 5, 1981.

Anonymous Author. "Peace Prayers." *Milwaukee Journal Sentinel*, December 11, 1983.

Anonymous Author. "Politics Hinders Dialog, Interfaith Committee Finds." *The Milwaukee Journal*, April 30, 1983.

Arinze, Cardinal Francis. Letter to Sister Jessine. December 30, 1985.

Bush, Elliot and Trudy Bush. "What the Islamic-Christian Dialogue Has Meant to Me." *New Catholic World,* November/December 1988, 285–86.

Boulton, Guy. "Obituary for Lucille Walsh." *Milwaukee Journal Sentinel*, April 24, 2013.

Brew City Church, Milwaukee Muslim Women's Coalition, and Peace Catalyst International. *Muslims & Evangelicals: Breaking Down Barriers & Building Trust.* Flyer provided by Steve Lied.

Cardinal Stritch College. *Islam: Faith of 800 Million People.* Pamphlet provided by Dan Di Domizio.

Committee of the Milwaukee Archdiocesan Ecumenical and Interfaith Commission. "Some Principles and Proposed Goals for Christians and Muslims living Together as Good Neighbors." Revised April 12, 1983.

Committee of the Milwaukee Archdiocesan Ecumenical and Interfaith Commission. "Statement of Identity." Revised April 12, 1983.

Dardess, George, and Marvin L. Krier Mich. *In the Spirit of St. Francis & the Sultan: Catholics and Muslims Working Together for the Common Good.* Maryknoll, NY: Orbis Books, 2011.

Geyso, Cathy. "Dear Mr. Prez..." *The Challenger* 3, December 4, 1980.

Hamdani, Abbas. "Islam." Presentation at Islam: Faith of 800 Million People. Cardinal Stritch College, Milwaukee, WI, March 20, 1982.

Harvard University Center for Middle Eastern Studies. Letter to Islamic-Christian Dialogue of Milwaukee. June 19, 1986.

Heinen, Tom. "The Interfaith Conference of Greater Milwaukee." March 22, 2017. http://pluralism.org/.

The Institute of Ismaili Studies. "Biography: Professor Abbas Hamdani." http://iis.ac.uk/people/abbas-hamdani.

Interfaith Conference of Greater Milwaukee. "Alike and Different." http://interfaith conference.org/cms-view-page.php?page=alike-different.

———. *Amazing Faiths: Seeking Hosts for Dinner Dialogues 2017.* Virtual flyer provided by Tom Heinen.

———. "History of Amazing Faiths Dinner Dialogues." http://interfaithconference. org/cms-view-page.php?page=afdd-history.

———. "Interfaith Earth Network." http://www.interfaithconference.org/cms-view-page.php?page=earth-network.

———. *Exploring Islam: Addressing Difficult Questions.* Flyer.

Islamic Society of Milwaukee. "Muslims in Milwaukee: A Brief History." In *Islamic Society of Milwaukee: 25 Years of Service.* 2007.

Merrick, Amy. "Sr. Lucille Celebrates 100th Birthday." *Catholic Herald*, February 14, 2013. http://catholicherald.org/special-sections/mature-lifestyles/sr-lucille-celebrates-100th-birthday/.

Michalski, Melvin. Letter to President-Elect Ronald Reagan. November 25, 1980.

Milwaukee Jewish Federation. "Catholic-Jewish Conference Mission Statement." http://www.milwaukeejewish.org.

Mulroy, Bert C. Letter to Sister Jessine and Sister Lucille. February 19, 1990.

Orsborn, Catherine. "Shoulder to Shoulder with American Muslims: What the Interreligious Community Is Doing to Combat Anti-Muslim Bigotry in America." *Journal of Ecumenical Studies* 51, no. 2 (2016): 257–63.

Peace Catalyst. "Seven Resolutions Against Prejudice, Hatred and Discrimination." Document provided by Steve Lied.

Pope Paul VI. *Nostra Aetate.* 28 October 1965. Papal Archive. The Holy See. http://www.vatican.va/archive/hist_councils/ii_vatican_council/documents/vat-ii_decl_19651028_nostra-aetate_en.html.

Reiss, Jessine. Letter to the Members of the Islamic Christian Dialogue. January 31, 1989.

Renard, John. *101 Questions and Answers on Islam.* New York: Paulist Press, 1998.

Secretariat for Non-Christians. *Guidelines for Dialogue Between Muslims and Christians.* Unpublished copy.

Simmonds, Yussuf J. "Cardinal Francis Arinze." *Los Angeles Sentinel*, September 23, 2009.

Smith, Thomas J. "Islam Plays a Role in Religious History." *Catholic Herald,* April 1, 1982.

Walsh, Lucille, OSF. "The Genesis of an Islamic-Christian Dialogue." *New Catholic World,* November/December 1988, 282–86.

———. Letter to Pope John Paul II. August 21, 1985.

Weakland, Rembert G. *A Pilgrim in a Pilgrim Church: Memoirs of a Catholic Archbishop.* Grand Rapids, MI: Eerdmans, 2009.

Windsor, Pat. "Respect, Tolerance Key Elements in Fruitful Christian, Muslim Dialogue." *Catholic Herald*, May 5, 1983.

INTERVIEWS

1. Atta, Intisar. Interview by Dianne Marshall, Sundus Jaber, and Caroline Redick. March 24, 2017.

2. Atta, Othman. Interview by Dianne Marshall, Sundus Jaber, and Caroline Redick. March 24, 2017.

3. Di Domizio, Dan. Interview by Kaitlyn Daly. March 1, 2017.

4. Hamdani, Abbas. Interview via email by Irfan Omar and Caroline Redick. April 23, 2017.

5. Lied, Steve. Interview by Irfan Omar and Caroline Redick. May 25, 2017.

6. Reiss, Jessine. Interview by Irfan Omar and Caroline Redick. March 25, 2017.

7. Sklba, Richard. Interview by Caroline Redick. February 17, 2017.

Dialogue Narratives from the Perspective of the Practitioners:

Muslim–Christian Encounters in Milwaukee: 1980–2007

Andrew Musgrave

Editors' Note: *This chapter is based on firsthand accounts of and discussions with the founders of the original Christian–Muslim dialogue in Milwaukee. The author met with key figures in the dialogue in the fall of 2007, some years after the original dialogue had ended. However, as will become evident, the three original founders of the Milwaukee Christian–Muslim dialogue were very satisfied with what they had achieved. Even though the original dialogue had ceased, they felt it had been picked up by others and was continuing on in different forms. They expressed gratitude for having accomplished something valuable; they also empha-sized how much they cherished the friendships they built over the years and how it has impacted their personal lives. All quotes from the founders of the original dia-logue and other participants are derived from author's interviews with them that took place between October and December 2007.*

The Context

The story begins in the 1950s with two professors at what was then the Car-dinal Stritch College. Sister Jessine was teaching in the English department, and Sister Lucille was teaching in the Religious Studies department. Cardinal Stritch was undergoing accreditation process, and the accreditors believed that it would be beneficial to expand the offerings to include studies of "Eastern cultures." Therefore, one of the deans approached the sisters and asked them to embark on an educational journey to prepare themselves to introduce a non-Western dimension to the university. Thus, over the next decade and a half, they took summer classes at various institutions of higher learning, including San Francisco State University (where they studied Hinduism, Buddhism, and Daoism), Hamline University, and Seton Hall University. They also attended a study abroad program in Japan and took classes after returning to Milwaukee at the University of Wisconsin–Milwaukee (UWM). It was at UWM (1980) that the sisters enrolled in an Islamic studies class taught by Professor Abbas Hamdani. After class one day, Sister Lucille and Dr. Hamdani discussed the role of faith in society and how little is known about the faith of Islam. They concluded that something needed to happen in Milwaukee to educate Christians about Islam, and vice versa. They were motivated by the shared desire to build trust and harmony between the communities. Sister Lucille later wrote in her 1988 article for *New Catholic World*, "the goal of our dialogue (was) to create an atmosphere of mutual understanding, trust and cooperation between Christians and Muslims in our area"[1] and

> to work at knowing, trusting and understanding our global neighbors, to help build a mutually sound and peaceful foundation for our lives together as neighbors and as fellow citizens of our global community.[2]

Both the sisters, Lucille and Jessine, had entered the Sisters of St. Francis of Assisi at an early age. Neither of the sisters had received any training or education during their formation that encouraged or even mentioned dialogue with members of other faiths. Academically speaking, Sister Jessine was trained to be an English teacher; and Sister Lucille was a newly minted Religion teacher after spending her first 20-plus years in the order as a dentist. Sister Lucille believed that it is for a simple reason that dialogue must be pursued. She said, addressing a mostly Christian audience, that it is "important to remember that Muslims are real people, living in our midst, struggling as we are with eternal and human problems." She believed that our common humanity is itself a sufficient reason for us to move toward mutual learning and respect.[3]

The Milwaukee Christian–Muslim dialogue began not due to any outside pressure from anyone, and it was not an outgrowth from previous learning. The nuns did not learn about dialogue in their formational training. Dr. Hamdani,

---

1. Lucille Walsh, OSF, "The Genesis of an Islamic-Christian Dialogue," *New Catholic World*, November/December 1988, 282.

2. Lucille Walsh, OSF, interview by Andrew Musgrave, circa October 2007.

3. Ibid.

a historian, was not trained specifically to engage in interfaith dialogue either. Sister Jessine recalls Prof. Hamdani's assertion that, "It started with us. Before us, it didn't exist."[4] The dialogue founders learned as they began to think of solutions to the widespread ignorance on the part of Christians and Muslims about each other's faith. After several meetings and discussions, Sister Lucille and Dr. Hamdani agreed that further action needed to be taken. The first step in developing a dialogue was to let people know that this possibility existed and garner interest from the wider community. They started organizing, with Sister Lucille giving many talks for churches and other groups.

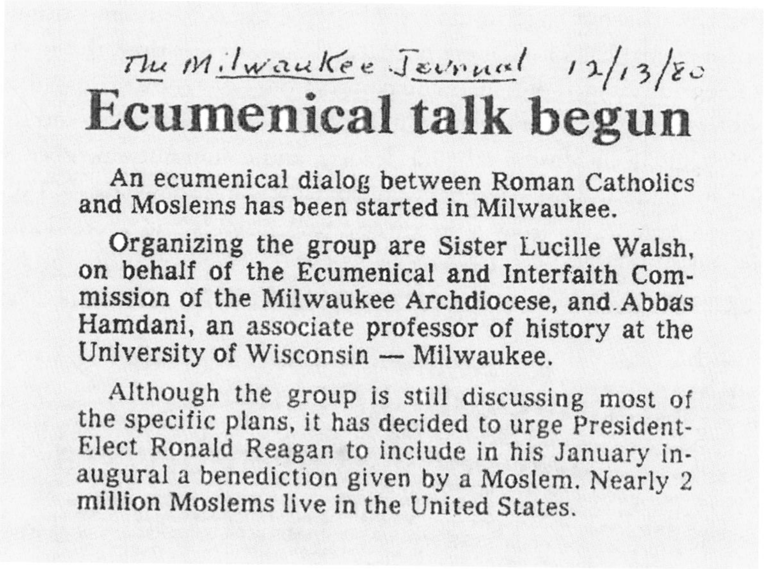

The Milwaukee Journal 12/13/80

Ecumenical talk begun

An ecumenical dialog between Roman Catholics and Moslems has been started in Milwaukee.

Organizing the group are Sister Lucille Walsh, on behalf of the Ecumenical and Interfaith Commission of the Milwaukee Archdiocese, and Abbas Hamdani, an associate professor of history at the University of Wisconsin — Milwaukee.

Although the group is still discussing most of the specific plans, it has decided to urge President-Elect Ronald Reagan to include in his January inaugural a benediction given by a Moslem. Nearly 2 million Moslems live in the United States.

Figure 2.1: The Milwaukee Journal report from December 13, 1980, on the launch of the dialogue.

One particularly significant talk occurred at a United Methodist Church which at the time was led by Rev. Elliott Bush, who was very supportive of these talks and lectures about other religions. Because the word had spread within the Muslim community that there was a Roman Catholic nun giving talks on Islam at Christian churches, Mr. Mahmoud Atta, one of the founders of the Islamic Center in Milwaukee, came with a Qur'an in hand to hear her talk. Mahmoud was an immigrant to the United States. Having served in the US military, he

---

4. Jessine Reiss, OSF, interview by Andrew Musgrave, circa October 2007.

became a naturalized citizen and settled in Milwaukee. He was not a religious cleric but was a practicing Muslim. At the talk given by Sister Lucille, Atta was quite impressed with her knowledge and had no objections to how she presented the basics of Islam.[5] Soon thereafter, both Atta and his wife, Intisar, became a part of the dialogue. Over time, the sisters and the Attas became fast friends; they often spent time in each other's homes, talking over meals. Mrs. Atta said of the sisters, "I respect them like I respect my mother; I love them from the bottom of my heart."[6] They had become close as a family. As a token of affection, Lucille and Jessine made an afghan for the birth of the Attas's first grandchild.

These information sharing events, talks, and lectures continued for several years which attracted larger numbers. However, the core group continued to meet on a regular basis for a more formal dialogue. At one time, the group had 40 people and included preachers and pastors from different Christian denominations (including representatives from Baptist, United Methodist, and Roman Catholic churches), Muslim religious leaders, and community members interested in dialogue and the news of the dialogue was spreading (figs. 2.1 & 2.2). The participants came from quite diverse backgrounds and professions; two such members were Father Robert Lambeck, SJ, a theology professor at Marquette University, and a Pakistani-American physician, Dr. Mohammed Sethi.

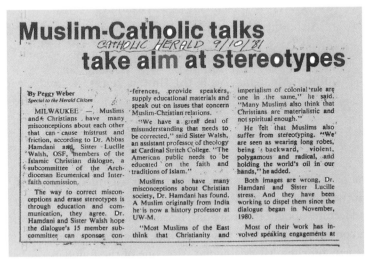

Figure 2.2: The Catholic Herald's September 10, 1981, report on the ongoing dialogue.

---

5. Ibid.

6. Intisar Atta, interview by Andrew Musgrave, circa November 2007.

The Dialogue

At first the group called itself the "Islamic-Christian Dialogue." They acknowledged their differences but agreed that "we anchor our faith in the One, Same, and Only God . . . we recognize our obligation to bring it (our faith) to bear on human issues, trusting that God has the power to lead peoples on the way of transcending the differences that divide and the power to lead us all toward peace and unity."[7] Based on the document produced at the behest of the Vatican's Secretariat for Non-Christians *Guidelines* for dialogue, they established the following ground rules to guide their dialogue:[8]

1. To seek to understand "the other" as "the other" wishes to be understood;
2. To approach dialogue in the spirit of willingness—to receive, to learn, and to listen, as well as to give, to teach, and to talk;
3. To share what we have learned from our dialogue with our co-religionists and to assist them in developing positive, trustful and fraternal attitudes and policies towards members of the Islamic and Christian faith traditions;
4. To help others preserve their human dignity and to accord to individuals their rightful place in society;
5. To engage in a variety of educational programs, designed to give accurate information and to correct damaging stereotypes of the Muslim and/or Christian wherever found; and
6. To avoid using the dialogue as a tool for proselytizing or for political gain.

The meetings were simple and informal; there were no attempts at proselytizing. They were held once a month, two hours each, followed by refreshments. The first meetings were held on the Cardinal Stritch University campus, then at St. Rita's on 60th Street, and then at various area churches (with Stritch remaining as the home base). A few were also held on Marquette University campus, no doubt hosted by Rev. Lambeck, SJ who was a core member from the beginning (fig. 2.3). As Sister Lucille said, "A long journey starts with one step. This was the first step."[9]

From the perspective of the Attas, this dialogue was a logical step. In Palestine, Christians and Muslims have lived in relative peace, side-by-side, for

---

7. Walsh, "The Genesis of an Islamic-Christian Dialogue," 282.

8. Reproduced from Walsh, "The Genesis of an Islamic-Christian Dialogue," 283.

9. Walsh, interview by Musgrave.

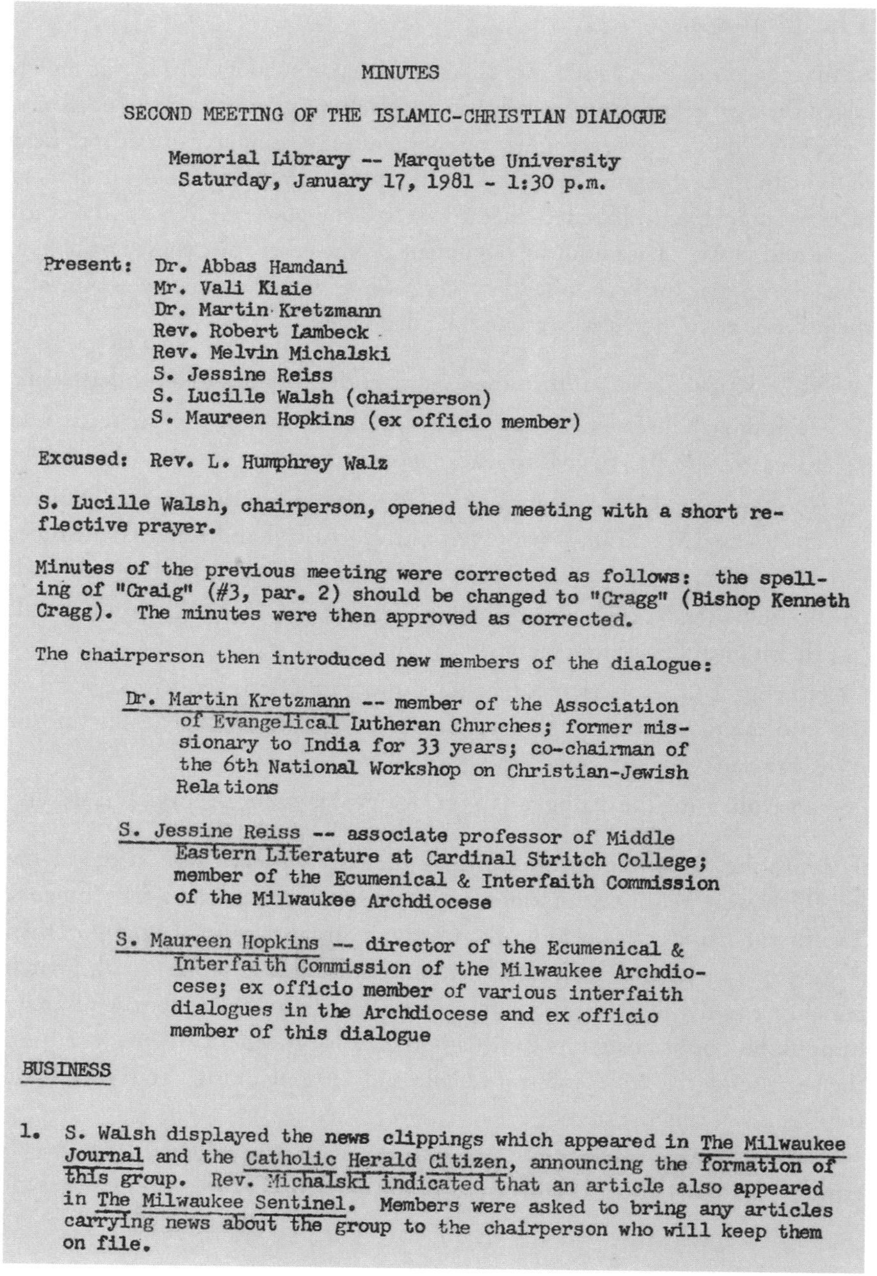

MINUTES

SECOND MEETING OF THE ISLAMIC-CHRISTIAN DIALOGUE

Memorial Library -- Marquette University
Saturday, January 17, 1981 - 1:30 p.m.

Present: Dr. Abbas Hamdani
          Mr. Vali Kiaie
          Dr. Martin Kretzmann
          Rev. Robert Lambeck
          Rev. Melvin Michalski
          S. Jessine Reiss
          S. Lucille Walsh (chairperson)
          S. Maureen Hopkins (ex officio member)

Excused: Rev. L. Humphrey Walz

S. Lucille Walsh, chairperson, opened the meeting with a short re-
flective prayer.

Minutes of the previous meeting were corrected as follows: the spell-
ing of "Craig" (#3, par. 2) should be changed to "Cragg" (Bishop Kenneth
Cragg). The minutes were then approved as corrected.

The chairperson then introduced new members of the dialogue:

          Dr. Martin Kretzmann -- member of the Association
              of Evangelical Lutheran Churches; former mis-
              sionary to India for 33 years; co-chairman of
              the 6th National Workshop on Christian-Jewish
              Relations

          S. Jessine Reiss -- associate professor of Middle
              Eastern Literature at Cardinal Stritch College;
              member of the Ecumenical & Interfaith Commission
              of the Milwaukee Archdiocese

          S. Maureen Hopkins -- director of the Ecumenical &
              Interfaith Commission of the Milwaukee Archdio-
              cese; ex officio member of various interfaith
              dialogues in the Archdiocese and ex officio
              member of this dialogue

BUSINESS

1. S. Walsh displayed the news clippings which appeared in The Milwaukee
    Journal and the Catholic Herald Citizen, announcing the formation of
    this group. Rev. Michalski indicated that an article also appeared
    in The Milwaukee Sentinel. Members were asked to bring any articles
    carrying news about the group to the chairperson who will keep them
    on file.

Figure 2.3: Minutes of the second meeting in early 1981 which was held in the Memorial Library on the campus of Marquette University.

several centuries. It was not out of the ordinary for the Attas to engage with Christians in this kind of dialogue. The reasons for doing so here in the United States were even more important because it was not just interfaith, it was also intercultural dialogue. Three other reasons necessitated dialogue for the Muslims. The first was the political turmoil and state violence taking place in parts of the Middle East. The Muslim community wanted to communicate to their Christian neighbors who they were and wanted to share their perspective on the events. Second, Muslims wanted to ensure that Christians have access to accurate information about Islam, including the authentic translations of the Qur'an in order to minimize misinformation and misinterpretation. The third reason was simply humanistic. Mrs. Intisar Atta remembers thinking that there were smart people in the United States, and she was glad to speak to them and build relationships with them. She says, "It doesn't matter if they're Christians or Muslims or Jews. There are good people everywhere . . . how you treat people, this is the religion, the true religion. We are brothers and sisters, created by the same God."[10]

The dialogue group made remarkable strides in a very short period. In June 1981, they sponsored an adult education series at the United Methodist Church in Whitefish Bay on "Christian-Muslim Relations." In November of the same year, the group organized an event which the sisters recall with great pride. A fire at a Muslim mosque outside of Milwaukee led the Muslims in the community to ask a priest in Kenosha for permission to meet in his parish. The priest, unsure as to what to do, asked Sisters Jessine and Lucille and their group for their thoughts on the matter. They believed that it was okay to do so but thought it best to ask the Vatican. The response came and was written by Father Thomas Michel, SJ, who at the time was working at the Secretariat for Non-Christians:[11]

> There is no official stance of the Vatican on this matter . . . (how-ever) . . . it is an opportunity to extend Christian hospitality. St. Paul said, 'Let hospitality be your special care.' Especially in countries like the United States, where Muslims are relative newcomers, Christians should extend support and welcome them. Thus, offering our facilities to the Muslim (group) could be a deeper sign than any words of what Christianity is really about.[12]

---

10. Intisar Atta, interview by Musgrave.

11. Rev. Thomas Michel, SJ, visited Milwaukee for dialogue-related events organized at Marquette University, first in 2007 and again in 2012.

12. Quoted in Walsh, "The Genesis of an Islamic-Christian Dialogue," 285.

Another significant milestone was when the Archbishop of Milwaukee, Rembert Weakland, became interested in the dialogue. At first, the archbishop was invited to be present at one of the meetings. He could not attend because he was summoned to the Vatican during that time and he was going to return to Milwaukee to a full schedule. However, while in Rome, he met with a certain cardinal who said (paraphrase), "Oh, you're from Milwaukee, the city that has that Muslim–Christian dialogue." This opened his eyes. His return flight happened to be the same day as the meeting. So, when he arrived back in Milwaukee, he went directly to the meeting. Sister Jessine remembers a knock at the door, and, upon opening the door, she found the archbishop standing there, asking if he could join the meeting. He brought greetings from Archbishop Jean Jadot (the prefect of the Secretariat for Non-Christians) and was very generous to the group. Later, the archdiocese contributed to the Muslim building campaign to construct their first mosque and Islamic Center in Milwaukee.

In the spring of 1982, Sister Jessine was able to obtain a grant from the National Endowment for the Humanities and directed a conference, *Islam: Faith of 800 Million People*, at Cardinal Stritch College (thanks, in part, to the appointment of Sister Lucille to the Islam/Christian Dialogue Committee by the archbishop on behalf of the Ecumenical and Interfaith Commission). The event drew around 300 participants and greatly helped in raising awareness of the dialogue in the area. In the winter of 1982, another of the group's rewarding accomplishments happened; they managed to hold an interfaith prayer service. A United Church of Christ minister agreed to facilitate the organizing of this event at the Deaconess Hospital where he served as chaplain. By the numbers, it was a successful event, with over a hundred in attendance. A Muslim read the account of the nativity of Christ from the Qur'an, and a Christian read the account from the Bible. There were Muslim and Christian prayers and Christian songs. It was well-received and demonstrated that cooperation was possible between members of these two faiths and that there was interest in these kinds of events.

In 1985, the group undertook one of its most intensive projects. They obtained copies of the textbooks distributed to and used by the Milwaukee Public Schools (MPS) for the purpose of combing through them to search for stereotypes, gross exaggerations, or omissions. Upon completion, the report was submitted to MPS, the book publishers, and others who requested it. A report was also sent to Cardinal Arinze, the Vatican's cardinal in charge of non-Western affairs. After the word spread about the report, they received requests from all over the world, including one from Prof. John Esposito, who at the time was a professor at the Holy Cross College in Massachusetts, already a world-renowned Catholic scholar of Islam and Christian–Muslim relations. In 1987, a public lecture was held at the Cousins Center, the headquarters for the Milwaukee Catholic Archdiocese. In 1988, Sister Lucille was asked to write an article for a national Catholic magazine, *New Catholic World*.[13] In 1989, a public lecture was held at Cardinal Stritch College on "Perspectives on the Middle East Situation." Also, in 1989, a public lecture was held at University of Wisconsin–Milwaukee on "Intifadah: Is Non-Violence a Solution?," with Palestinian and Jewish speakers presenting. In 1990, they organized their biggest event to date, a symposium, "The Role of Religious Leaders in the Middle East Peace Process."[14]

While all of these special events were happening, their regular monthly meetings continued. These meeting covered all manner of topics, both theological and social in nature. Theologically, they did not go too deep nor rely too heavily on written resources to inform the other. They spoke from their experiences on topics including their understandings of God, Jesus, and Mary. They started with the concept of God according to the Bible and to the Qur'an. When the group tackled the Trinity, each group of Christians had their own version of understanding. The Muslims sat back and chuckled at this, amused that the Christians could not, even within their own faith, come to a consensus (which goes to prove what Sister Jessine says—that you must be knowledgeable in your own faith tradition before entering into dialogue with another faith tradition). The group also discussed their understandings of the Church and the global Muslim community, major holidays of both faiths, Sufism and Christian mysticism, Islamic poetry, and art in both traditions. They also addressed social issues, such as living in a pluralistic society and war/peace, but did not delve too deeply into violence, crime, poverty, or politics because they did not want to be controversial or to give people a reason to not continue. After meeting for many years, they came to realize what the group members were and were not willing to discuss, and this helped guide the dialogue in becoming productive and a growing reality. They also sponsored several evening lectures. Topics included "Christians and Muslims: Conditions of Our Life Together," "St. Francis and

---

13. This article is one of the foundational documentary pieces of evidence for the success of the Islamic–Christian dialogue in Milwaukee. The article is cited throughout this chapter.

14. This event was held at Marquette University because it was too big for conference facilities at Cardinal Stritch University at the time. Board members from several different universities and religious leaders from various denominations attended, as did a representative from the Vatican.

the Muslim World," "The Media and Stereotyping," and "Jerusalem: Its Importance to Three Faiths." The dialogue continued to meet informally for 20 years and most of the members stayed very active, both within the dialogue setting as well as out in the community, organizing, speaking, and communicating with others what they were doing in the dialogue (fig. 2.4). By the mid-1990s, the meetings became irregular. This was partly because many of the original members had become older and had difficulty finding ways to travel to the meeting places; others had moved away from Milwaukee area.

Figure 2.4: Dr. Abbas Hamdani and Sister Lucille Walsh, OSF, are seen here long after the 1980 dialogue had ceased. Many members of the dialogue continued to meet informally.

Even as the original dialogue was ending, the impact was becoming visible. Sister Lucille recalls Professor Hamdani saying that "our dialogue, grass rooted as it was, has changed the mentality of Muslims in Milwaukee toward Christians."[15] This was a great commendation. Sister Lucille also insisted that "Muslims are perhaps the most God-conscious people I have ever associated with both socially and religiously."[16] She also believes that their dialogue worked because there was a good core group of people committed to "building rapport and developing a basic understanding of each other's beliefs." Because of this

---

15. Walsh, interview by Musgrave.

16. As quoted in the Jack Wintz, OFM, "Lucille Walsh, OSF – Building Bridges Between Christians and Muslims," *St. Anthony Messenger* 98, no. 7 (December 1990): 8.

solid core, "we did not lose valuable discussion time, backtracking in response to elementary questions, sometimes posed by casual observers."[17] Mr. and Mrs. Atta were encouraged to continue as they realized there were Christians who were kind and were willing to listen to followers of other religions.

The Next Generation of Leaders

Gradually, new branches of dialogue emerged, taking on different directions in order to bring the fruits of the dialogue to others. One person who played a major role is Judith Longdin. Judi became involved in interfaith dialogue in 1993 when she was appointed the director of the Office of Ecumenical and Interfaith Concerns at the Archdiocese of Milwaukee. Before she came to that vocation, she worked with United Farm Workers and low-income African Americans on community organizing. In these and other roles, she observed that people of different faith traditions wanted to work together but could not quite connect because of a lack of self-understanding. She came to believe that people cannot know themselves independent of knowing others. Her graduate studies were in philosophy, but she remained interested in communication and how people misunderstand each other. She then became the director of social ministry for Gesu Parish; it was here that she had an idea of coming together of experiences to address both social justice and ecumenical/interreligious understanding. As part of the official Catholic efforts to engage in dialogue, she was limited and yet committed to doing as much as can be done to bridge the gap in knowledge.[18]

In her work, Judi emphasized that people ought to know where they are coming from and what they hope to get from it. They must also discern what they are bringing to this dialogue that they are not acknowledging that could limit how far they can move forward in dialogue. In addition, one must make these inquiries: What are your influences? How am I changed by this (positively and negatively)? How am I changing the other? When speaking of the two faiths' involvement in dialogue, she believes that we cannot fulfill our mission as the Church until we find a way to create greater unity. Those involved must view the dialogue also as a spiritual journey and discover what the spiritual element of this dialogue is and how it will affect us as spiritual people. The participants must see themselves as engaging in God's work, working for peace

---

17. Walsh, "The Genesis of an Islamic-Christian Dialogue," 283.

18. For more on her journey in dialogue, see Judi Longdin's chapter in this volume.

as a people. Further, she believes that the Milwaukee version of Muslim–Catholic dialogue is special because it goes back and forth between dialogue and action, not just sticking to one element.

Talking Together in Milwaukee

In 1980 Lucille Walsh, O.S.F., a professor who teaches courses in Islam and other religions at Cardinal Stritch College in Milwaukee, organized the Islamic-Christian Dialogue of the Diocese of Milwaukee, with the assistance of Dr. Abbas Hamdani, a Muslim university professor. Roman Catholics, Protestants and Muslims (Milwaukee's Muslim community mumbers almost 4,000 persons) have been meeting several times a year in ongoing discussions. Talking together here are Janan (Atta) Waleed Najeed, Sister Lucille Walsh and Trudy Bush. In the boxes on pages 107, 109 and 111 are comments from some participants in the Dialogue. Photo courtesy of Lucille Walsh, and statements from her article, "The Genesis of an Islamic-Christian Dialogue," *New Catholic World*, Nov.-Dec. 1988. Used by permission.

Figure 2.5: Janan Najeeb, Lucille Walsh, OSF, and Trudy Bush are seen here with a description of the Milwaukee dialogue published in a book on Islam by R. Marston Speight, God Is One (1989). Speight's narrative was based on Lucille Walsh's 1988 article.

In 1994, Judi connected with the head of the Milwaukee Muslim Women's Coalition, Janan Najeeb, the daughter of Mahmoud Atta. Judi spoke with Janan, who was familiar with many aspects of dialogue because of the involvement of her parents and had even attended a few of the meetings while in high school (fig. 2.5).[19] Judi discussed with her the possibility of starting a women's dialogue similar to one in Canada at the time. Janan responded positively and was eager to collaborate. She viewed interfaith dialogue as a natural part of being Muslim, with the injunction to be in relationship with one's neighbors

---

19. A picture of Milwaukee dialogue participants with Janan in the frame was published in a book on Islam by R. Marston Speight. The book was an introduction to the faith of Islam and also included exemplary forms of Christian–Muslim dialogue from around the country. See R. Marston Speight, *God Is One: The Way of Islam* (New York: Friendship Press, 1989), 106–9.

and people of other faiths. In fact, dialogue is central to creating a society that takes issues of social justice seriously and views it as integral to their faith. Furthermore, she saw that, over the years, there had been so much misinformation and mistrust. With the tremendous amount of misinformation out there, she realized that some type of forum or network was needed where they could work together to disseminate correct information. If people are not in dialogue, they may be too ready to hear what they want to hear, not necessarily what the truth is.

They met several times to organize the dialogue parameters. Beginning in 1995, a small group of Christian and Muslim women met to discuss the basic issues of the faith, such as the sacraments and the pillars of faith. Their goal was to build a good base community. One strength this dialogue had over the earlier dialogue is that this group was created with the idea of creating a level playing field. When the dialogue began 15 years earlier in 1981, the Muslim community was much smaller, and that meant there were fewer people who were informed enough and available to effectively engage in and attend regular dialogue. Conversely, the Christian community was large and well developed. The participants, mostly clergy and ordained religious, were well versed in Christian theology and, thus, were more prepared to share their faith with others. By 1995, the Muslim community had grown, with many more informed members who were available for dialogue. Like the founding dialogue, the women's dialogue had rules of engagement, many of them reminiscent of those set by their predecessors. As Najeeb recalled, "If you came to proselytize, thank you very much, but we don't want you. If you think you know more about the other than the other and you are here to talk on their behalf, that's not acceptable. Some former Catholics who are now Muslims came early on and wanted to attack, to distribute their materials; they were told that is not what this dialogue is about."[20] They made sure to let everyone know what the goals of the dialogue were and what would and would not be permitted. Originally, the dialogue was all "politically correct." But as they have gotten to know each other, they have been able to ask each other about anything. They have been very comfortable talking about all issues, even the difficult ones.

When the Catholic priest scandal erupted, they talked about the celibacy issue (i.e., the requirement for ordained persons). September 11, 2001, brought a new level of interest in engaging in dialogue to learn about each other; the difficult issue there was clearly religiously inspired violence and the

---

20. Janan Najeeb, interview by Andrew Musgrave, circa November 2007.

misunderstood notion of Jihad. The women, especially Judi and Janan, spoke frequently at public gatherings during that time and made tremendous efforts to educate the public about Islamic teachings against violence and terrorism. This effort helped prevent any major attack against Muslims. The Islamic Society of Milwaukee received threats and abusive calls. However, the larger Milwaukee community rallied against any attempt to create divisions. There were several forums and programs to address the misinformation regarding whether Islam encourages extremist behavior, which were also opportunities to discuss Islam's teachings on peace.[21]

Over time, Janan and Judi became ambassadors for each other, and they continue to be so. They dispelled rumors and addressed misinformation about each other. If someone spoke erroneously, they took it upon themselves to defend, clarify, educate, and point him or her in the right direction. Because they have this relationship, they do not speak *for* each other but *with* each other, usually after consultation. They do not assume truths or believe rumors but ask for clarification. Getting to this point was not easy and it did not happen overnight. The group built a relationship of trust where they have come to know the other as the other wants to be known.

While they felt comfortable delving into these deeper issues as a steering committee, they did not do so as a wider group. The original group had the experience of meeting for years, but the community at large did not have such exposure, and they were, therefore, not equipped to address the deeper, more controversial issues. Experience taught them that steps must be taken with precautions with this type of dialogue so as to engender understanding and respect and not raise defensiveness and anger. As Janan said, "People stand up for justice, stand up for what is right. But it has to be an educated understanding."[22]

In addition to their regular meetings, the dialogue took place in public venues, such as community forums and churches. The most visible forum for several years was their annual public event. At one point, they decided that they must find a way to develop and expand the dialogue. There were many issues that had to be considered: people's interest and level of understanding about a particular topic and the availability of materials that would supplement the dialogue event for ongoing learning. After addressing these questions, the

---

21. The Milwaukee Association for Interfaith Relations (MAIR, of which Judi was the chair at the time), which has members from all faith traditions, organized forums to discuss terrorism in Christianity, Islam, Judaism, and one other (Sikh, Hindu, Bahai, etc.) so as to view the topic comparatively.

22. Janan Najeeb, interview by Musgrave.

group began to hold a large public forum every year, bringing in a well-known representative from each faith to speak on a particular issue. The dialogue was not necessarily on women's issues, but it was a dialogue between women for the benefit of all.[23]

Fruits of Sustained Engagement

The women's dialogue created a number of projects that contributed greatly to the Milwaukee community because, as Janan Najeeb put it, "We (had) been meeting for several years and just doing one annual event wasn't enough."[24] The first project arose because of the background and expertise of the participants. A large number of the women involved had medical and social concerns and had the sense that they did not want to be just about dialogue; they wanted to serve the community. Before these meetings began, the Muslim community had been concerned about the large number of uninsured or underinsured persons in Milwaukee. They thought about opening up a clinic at the Islamic Center, but it was deemed too difficult logistically and legally. The idea was brought to the dialogue group, and soon the Muslim–Catholic Healthcare Initiative came into being. The project only lasted a few years, but it had a great impact. The participants would set up a makeshift clinic in a church on Saturday mornings where groups of nurses performed health care assessments for low-income and uninsured people. Eventually, a group of 30 Muslim physicians with varied specialties agreed to help out. The patients were given a kind of insurance card to use at local medical offices, which gave them the opportunity to be like every other person—they could set up an appointment and then be treated. It was less like a free clinic and more like a regular doctor's appointment. For those people who remained in a neighborhood, the doctor and patient had the opportunity to build a real relationship. Unfortunately, it is no longer functioning because it became hard to maintain administratively, and the nature of the homeless community made it nearly impossible for the patients to navigate the system effectively. It did prove to be a good learning opportunity, and the Islamic Society of Milwaukee continues to offer periodic medical screenings.

Another significant project dealt with Wisconsin's repeated attempts to reinstate the death penalty. The state legislature keeps reintroducing the issue of the death penalty. While it is defeated each time, there is always the fear

---

23. For more on this, see the chapter by Sundus Jaber in this volume.

24. Janan Najeeb, interview by Musgrave.

that one day it will pass. Therefore, a large coalition of religious leaders came together and expressed a collective opposition to death penalty. This may not have been possible 10 years ago, but because of dialogue and collaboration across religious lines, it became possible. The group crafted a statement suggesting that while they do not necessarily have the same reasons for opposition to the death penalty as some of the secular groups, they agree that it is wrong, and it should not be made legal in Wisconsin. Judi believed that this was yet another proof that interfaith dialogue is effective. It is no longer true "that if you do not agree with me completely, we have nothing to talk about." Instead, the faith communities can come together on a mutually agreeable position and make a unified stand, regardless of whether their reasons are exactly the same. The coalition may not be together exactly theologically, pragmatically, or practically, but we can come to agreement (and speak about it publicly; see fig. 2.6).

Figure 2.6: Tonen O'Connor, Zen Buddhist leader, speaking at a press conference opposing the death penalty. It was organized by the Interfaith Conference of Greater Milwaukee and held on the Marquette University campus in 2006. Janan Najeeb was among the faith leaders invited to speak.

One project that Judi is particularly proud of was a youth forum. The youth director of the archdiocese came to Judi after the dialogues that took place post-9/11 and suggested doing a youth forum involving Christian, Jewish, and Muslim youth, led by the youth. Eighteen teenagers were trained to be facilitators, and the other young men and women were invited to the forum (run by the newly trained facilitators). Over 100 young people met, talked, and learned about the basics and practices of the three faith traditions. Parents had many trust issues and were apprehensive not only about the safety of their children, but also about the format, not knowing if there was some secret agenda to proselytize or convert. Fortunately, many parents put these fears aside, and the forum turned out to be a great success. The youth present were able to address issues of prejudice and gained an understanding and appreciation that will certainly last for years to come.[25]

A lighter interfaith meeting occurred when Archbishop Weakland was asked to come and bless the newly constructed baseball stadium, Miller Park. After some consideration, he suggested doing the dedication with members of the Muslim community present as well. Judith asked the Muslims in the group if they were interested in taking part in the dedication, and they agreed to join. This simple thought of the larger community raised yet another instance of awareness and recognition. One year the group set up a table at both the Summerfest and Arab World Fest. According to Judi, the best part of having the booth is that people pass by the sign and stop to ask what they are all about, thereby raising awareness of their work. Both Janan and Judi expressed faith in the future by saying that other possibilities will emerge and when they do, the group will evaluate them and figure out how to address them with a spirit of cooperation and understanding.

Challenges

For all of the successes achieved and positive strides made by the Milwaukee Muslim–Christian dialogue, there have been some significant challenges that have arisen over time. Some of these barriers have come from within the group of participants. For Sister Lucille, she came to the table with some stereotypes from her childhood and her earlier education (e.g., thinking of the Crusades), so it had not always been in her head and heart to engage in this endeavor. Fortunately, she noted, "if my life was worth anything, then this was one of them, something God gave me the grace to do."[26] Sometimes the sisters wondered if they should continue the work because of the concerns raised by conservative Catholics. But their own religious superiors always supported them. Some

---

25. Another unexpected benefit of this event came not from the youth but from the parents. The parents were able to learn from their children, and many have subsequently been willing to be involved with dialogue in other aspects.

26. Walsh, interview by Musgrave.

other nuns in their own religious order did not understand their work. They wanted to know why the sisters had not been successful in converting any Muslims to Christianity. Some thought even worse, that Muslims are trying to convert the nuns. This opposition was especially strong from other members of the faculty at Cardinal Stritch University, where the two sisters taught. While some agreed it was necessary, others did not. They wondered about the motivations of Muslims who visited the campus for dialogue and other events. Additionally, the Christians initially sensed an apprehension from the Muslim members of the community as to their real intentions. Some Muslims seemed fearful that it was a threat to their Muslim identity. Sister Lucille noted, "One Muslim, who felt no need for dialogue, explained, 'Islam is a simple faith. You can either take it or leave it.'"[27] However, these feelings were not shared by other Muslims who eventually became part of the established dialogue.

Many Muslims were skeptical of engaging with Christians because they feared that Christians may be critical of them after learning about their stories. This fear was born out of some the experiences they previously had. But for Mr. Atta at least, it was important to not generalize about Christians even if the media often portrays Muslims and Islam negatively. Sister Lucille mentioned something from her earlier writing that there "seems to be a real reluctance, and even a refusal on the part of our citizenry in the United States to understand the Arab and the Muslim, and to give them a place of respect within our society."[28] Other Muslims were wary of the true intention of the dialogue: was it understanding or proselytizing? Some saw the dialogue as a waste of time because they believed Christians come to the dialogue with less than honorable intentions: they wish to "study" the average Muslim to facilitate their work as missionaries and to figure out best ways to entice Muslims to convert to Christian faith. Indeed, some Christian missionaries in parts of the world have participated in dialogue with other motives, displaying a bit of dishonesty.

The quality and commitment of participants were also problematic. Judi insists that members must be not only informed but also open to the other, putting their presuppositions aside. People can easily forget their commitment to listen to the other when their presuppositions are questioned or contradicted in a dialogue. They begin to translate what they actually hear into what they want to hear. Therefore, a deeper commitment to being open is important. The participants must also have self-knowledge and awareness. In dialogue there

---

27. Walsh, "The Genesis of an Islamic-Christian Dialogue," 283.

28. Walsh, interview by Musgrave.

are different types of people. Some are sincerely and deeply committed to their faith, can defend and articulate it, and are not intimidated by other persons' beliefs. Such a person is able to bracket his or her own beliefs and really hear the voice of the other, while not misinterpreting the other's beliefs through an exclusive personal lens. Unfortunately, this type of person is rare at the local level. Some people are genuinely interested but do not know enough about themselves or the other to really engage in meaningful dialogue. A significant barrier arises when these uninformed people attempt to speak for the whole community. People are not (but should be) very clear that they are speaking for themselves and not for the entire religion. It is better to say "this is my belief" or "this is what I understand from the teachings" without claiming that everyone in the religion believes or understands things that way. Or one could say, "I do not know the official position, but I'll find out for you." There is no easy solution to this problem. As some members noted, if we only speak for oneself, then the group cannot respond to questions that are about general beliefs such as five pillars for Muslims or centrality of Christ for Christians.

The reality of the life of the church is also challenging. Churches and mosques are dealing with their own issues such as the increase in the number of youths who are deciding to skip attending religious services and in general appear to be disillusioned by religious institutions and its leadership. While this can be fodder for dialogue (i.e., we are dealing with similar issues), it can also keep dialogue from happening. The communities may feel they must first deal with their internal issues before they have the resources to deal with external issues. To be specific, some Catholics seem to have the view that Muslim–Christian dialogue or other social concerns are things they will get to when they have time, after they teach others the basics of their faith. Judi argues that this *is* essential to the faith. It is part of the responsibility, the core identity of a person of the faith, for Christians and Muslims. It is not something the church gets to later; you do it now.

This raises another issue that Janan also noted, that Muslims are very active on many social justice issues and have strong views on certain issues such as Palestinians' rights over Jerusalem or the problems caused by America's wars. But several of the members of the steering committee for the women's dialogue, who happened to be representatives of the archdiocese, were sensitive to these issues and felt differently. The members may individually have positions that aligned with views held by Muslims in the group, but they were not willing to state these publicly. Janan stated that, "We as a group will discuss anything but can't always make public statements." This difficulty also applied to discussing issues noted in the documents of the Second Vatican Council. Some Christians will openly question it, but others refuse to do so, feeling that they must remain aligned with their institutional position. Janan thought there is no Muslim leader who is beyond criticism, but that is not the case with some Catholics in the group who could not see themselves criticizing officials in the Church.

A final issue that challenged the women's dialogue was that it had become too big and too popular. The volunteer group could not keep up with the demand for more and bigger events. The desire of the women involved to expand their operation threatened the dialogue itself because it would necessitate everyone to take on several roles—attending, participating, organizing, being on the steering committee, program committee, facilitator, and more—all of which can be exhausting. It also limits the time one can actually dialogue. Janan believed that the members needed to temper their enthusiasm with practicality.

Two specific instances were particularly challenging for the dialogue. The first arose with the conference that was held at Marquette in 1990. The organizers of the event received very strong letters of opposition from the Jewish community. They felt that none of the speakers fairly represented the American Jewish community. There were several Jewish speakers there, including Dr. Marc Ellis, but none were viewed to be sufficiently representative. Consequently, members of the Wisconsin Council of Rabbis declined to attend because of what they perceived to be the lack of balance. One speaker in particular, Rabbi Michael Lerner, a well-known Jewish peace activist and scholar, was scheduled to present. Before he went on, he received a call from his wife saying that she had received a death threat that may be carried out if he spoke at this program. Additionally, three Jewish men arrived, unannounced and without tickets, and demanded entry. Despite their disruptive presence, Rabbi Lerner did speak but gave only part of his previously prepared talk. This incident caused Sister Jessine to be questioned by the president of Stritch College regarding her role and that of Stritch's Religious Studies Department in the planning of the MU Conference. By association, the entire Stritch College had been labeled as supporter of an "anti-Jewish" program. Letters from members of the Jewish community kept coming to the Stritch administration in protest.

The second incident involved a theology professor and priest Father Robert Lambeck, SJ, at Marquette. Every year, the Muslim community leaders would hear from Muslim students at Marquette that he (Father Lambeck) was presenting false information in his lectures (e.g., the Prophet was a womanizer). One student finally recorded what was said (on paper and electronically) and shared it with the Muslim community leaders. The community then went to the administration and questioned the credentials of the professor as an expert on Islam. After numerous complaints over the years, Father Lambeck was still teaching Islam and, according to Muslim students, was continuing to disseminate misinformation. The Muslim leaders considered this to be quite tragic that over the years so many students were adversely affected and misinformed by Father Lambeck.[29] Finally, after the tragic events of September 11, 2001, the administration became convinced that someone with a degree in Islamic studies should be teaching the course on Islam. In late 2001, the search was instituted for a position in "Christianity and World Religions," which was apparently a cover for seeking an expert in Islam.[30]

Conclusion

Milwaukee has a long and rich history of Muslim–Christian dialogue. It came to be through the efforts of individuals who collectively had the desire to engage their neighbors and were willing to take the community-wide initiative. Several passionate and motivated people have taken part in the dialogue and have made it into what it is today. The dialogue between people of different faiths is thriving and with the number of people impacted by the efforts discussed above, it will continue to grow.

The future for Muslim–Christian dialogue is generally bright and has the potential to become a world-class example in building community relations and intercultural, interreligious, and international cooperation. For the momentum to continue, the efforts of the pioneers must be documented, recreated for each era, and implemented for the new generation of passionate and open-minded people committed to the values of mutual learning and mutual respect.

Bibliography

Speight, R. Marston. *God Is One: The Way of Islam*. New York: Friendship Press, 1989.
Walsh, Lucille, OSF. "The Genesis of an Islamic-Christian Dialogue." *New Catholic World*, November/December 1988, 282–86.

---

29. Ironically, as noted above, Father Lambeck was part of the original Christian–Muslim dialogue group and hosted a number of monthly meetings on the campus of Marquette University. He was, however, not averse to controversies.

30. Eventually this search resulted in the 2002 hiring of the current professor of Islam, Irfan Omar.

Wintz, Jack, OFM. "Lucille Walsh, OSF – Building Bridges Between Christians and Muslims." *St. Anthony Messenger* 98, no. 7 (December 1990): 8.

Interviews

1. Atta, Intisar. Interview by Andrew Musgrave. Circa November 2007.
2. Hamdani, Abbas. Interview by Andrew Musgrave. Circa October 2007.
3. Najeeb, Janan. Interview by Andrew Musgrave. Circa November 2007.
4. Reiss, Jessine, OSF. Interview by Andrew Musgrave. Circa October 2007.
5. Walsh, Lucille, OSF. Interview by Andrew Musgrave. Circa October 2007.

History and Development of the Muslim–Catholic Women's Dialogue in Milwaukee

Judith Longdin

The world in which we are now living is a very different world from the world of 1997, the year the Muslim–Catholic Women's Dialogue of Milwaukee began. While we were concerned at that time to learn more about one another, to continue to counter stereotypes, and to educate the community, the ugly specter of Islamophobia as it is now being experienced was a mere blip on the radar screen. In this chapter, I propose to tell this story in four parts. First, I look at the foundation on which the dialogue was established. Second, I consider a history of the dialogue itself. Third, I relate some of the effects of the dialogue on interfaith encounter in the greater Milwaukee area and beyond. The final section includes a discussion of what we learned along the way and what might be gleaned for the future.

It is not possible to talk about the women's dialogue without first acknowledging the contributions of Sister Lucille Walsh, OSF, and her colleague Sister Jessine Reiss, OSF, to the first Muslim–Christian dialogue in Milwaukee and what was very likely one of the first Muslim-Christian dialogues in the country. Sister Lucille, a sister of St. Francis of Assisi, who died at the age of 100 in 2013, was a member of the theology faculty of Cardinal Stritch University, where she founded the religious studies department. Her background was in Asian studies, but at Stritch she encountered Muslim students and began to learn from them about the Muslim faith. Her curiosity, openness, and desire to learn led to the founding with Dr. Abbas Hamdani, a professor at the University of Wisconsin–Milwaukee, of the Muslim–Christian Dialogue, which took place under the auspices of the Archdiocesan Ecumenical Commission with the blessing of then-Archbishop Rembert Weakland. The initial conversations began in 1980, and the first formal dialogue was held in November of that year. The dialogue went on for over twelve years and covered many topics on working toward overcoming stereotypes about Muslims and Islam, which Sister Lucille was quick to admit had been instilled in her from an early age. Sister Lucille's is a long and interesting story, some elements of which may be echoed in other chapters in this volume. What is important to remember is that Sister Lucille, Sister Jessine, Dr. Hamdani, and other members of that original dialogue set the stage for all future Muslim–Christian engagements, clearing away a good deal of the underbrush of suspicion and stereotyping that both Muslims and Catholics held for one another, thereby making the path easier for those who followed.

In 1997, when I contacted Janan Najeeb, director of the then-fledgling Milwaukee Muslim Women's Coalition (MMWC), I did so out of a concern that the archdiocese was no longer involved in an active Muslim–Catholic dialogue. Contemporary Catholic teaching about Islam and interreligious relations, beginning with the documents of Vatican Council II, the growth of the Muslim community in Milwaukee, the involvement of the Milwaukee Muslim Women's Coalition in many community events, and the desire of Catholics to learn more about Islam were all factors in my reaching out to the MMWC. At the time, I was not aware that Janan and her brother Othman had been involved in the earlier dialogue through their parents, Mr. and Mrs. Mahmoud Atta. Based on the success of the ear-

Figure 3.1: Janan Najeeb, director of the Milwaukee Muslim Women's Coalition (MMWC) and a longtime dialogue partner.

lier dialogue, you may wonder why we chose to establish a women's dialogue. The simple answer is that I had been reading about the success of a similar dialogue in Canada, and I was aware that the MMWC had a strong interest in educating about Islam. Given that we had established women's groups in both communities with an interest in dialogue, it seemed like a natural fit.

Roots of Dialogue in Prayer and Service

The dialogue began with the modest intention of bringing together a small group of women from both communities who would be well versed in their faith and be willing to meet in an open and honest environment where they could be free to share their faith with one another. From the start, we agreed that the dialogue would be informal and would have some orientation toward action. The dialogue had three loosely articulated goals: to educate, to build relationships, and to relate the work of the dialogue to the real life and work of our respective communities. We started with a small group of about 10 women and agreed to meet on a regular basis. The first topic for discussion was the "Pillars of Faith in Islam." The original plan was for the group to meet on a monthly basis to discuss a selected topic.

A number of things happened at the first meeting that further shaped the future of the dialogue. In addition to learning about the pillars of faith in Islam, which include the profession of faith in God and Muhammad as his prophet, prayer, fasting, almsgiving, and pilgrimage to Mecca, the Catholic members of the group had the opportunity to "witness" faith in action. Nothing could have made it clearer to the Catholic participants that these Muslim women took their faith seriously than the fact that they halted our meeting in order to pray. As I was writing this and remembering that moment, I felt the same sense of awe that I felt in that moment—a realization that these women's lives were guided by prayer. I had a Muslim friend say to me once that it is difficult to contemplate doing evil when you are always coming from or headed to prayer. The second interesting thing we realized was that the flow of our meetings would always encompass prayer. The act of prayer was not a radical halt in the movement of the conversation, rather it was its integral part. While we might not "pray together," we would be "in prayer together." The final thing that we learned was that almost all of the women in the dialogue were either in the medical field or had a history of involvement in social service. This led to a very early discussion of how those skills could be used in service to the community.

Thus, even in those early stages, the dialogue began to move in two directions: sharing of faith and service to the community. Had it not been for the strange coincidence of professions, it is unlikely that the group would have moved so quickly to a focus on service or that service would have taken such a concrete form. In fact, the primary focus of the first several meetings was to determine what project the women would undertake. By this stage, the women's group became aware that a number of Muslim doctors were eager to donate their services to uninsured and underinsured individuals in the community. This led the group to the decision to launch the Muslim–Catholic Healthcare Initiative. While the sharing of faith did not stop, it did slow down during this phase. There were some clear assumptions in the group that both Catholics and Muslims should be engaged in service to the community, and there was never a doubt that this project would be acceptable to both communities. In many ways, this approach tipped the ordinary approach to dialogue on its head. Rather than starting with a dialogue about the nature of and call to service in our respective faith traditions, we started with service and somewhere much further down the line began to talk about the theological rationale.

In 1998, the Muslim–Catholic Healthcare Initiative was launched. The founding members initiated a collaboration with the Women and Children's Project—a collaboration of communities of Catholic women religious and service agencies, working together to meet the spiritual and material needs of women and children. Several Muslim doctors also joined the initiative. The project was unique in that we did not set up a clinic in one location. Rather, the group traveled from one place to another; often it was set up in a church basement in an underserved area of the city. Publicity was done primarily through church bulletins and neighborhood groups. Individuals who attended the clinics received basic health care screenings and were then referred to a doctor either in their neighborhood or another location which was easily accessible on a bus line. Each individual received a replica insurance card that they would present at the doctor's office in the same manner as any other patient. The doctors would then provide as much service as possible at no cost and continue to see the patient for as long as needed. Patients were responsible for making their own appointments; the clinic would make the follow-up calls to determine if anyone was in need of further assistance. Social workers on site also made referrals to social service agencies when needed.

These services were open to all. In fact, the first clients were a Hindu family of five who had recently arrived from India—a father, a mother, grandmother, and two children. They came to us because they were afraid to go to a public clinic for fear that their reliance on the service would prevent them from being able to purchase a home one day. In addition to alleviating their health concerns, the clinic staff was also able to help them better understand how the social service system worked. This initiative lasted for several years but is no longer operative primarily due to lack of sufficient administrative support. Sometimes passion is not enough to keep a project going. It is heartening to know that some of the patients involved in the initiative are still being seen by the same doctors who were part of the program. The Islamic Society of Milwaukee (ISM) has now established a health care clinic where the underinsured can be sure of compassionate care.[1]

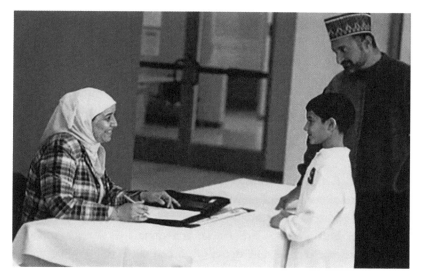

Figure 3.2: Inshirah Farhoud, MSN, RN, CPNP, attending to a young patient at the free clinic run by the Islamic Society of Milwaukee.

There were a couple of unanticipated outcomes from the health care initiative. First, the simple act of being together for several hours, caring for people, sharing stories during downtimes, and learning about one another's lives strengthened the bonds of the group. The Catholic Church promotes four types of dialogue: the dialogue of life, the dialogue of action, theological dialogue, and the dialogue of spirituality. The dialogue of life is made up of all those times when we encounter others, engage with them, learn about their lives, eat together, laugh together—in short, all of the activities of our daily life that bring us into contact with others. So here we were sharing our lives, engaging in the dialogue of life, building relationships, and solidifying bonds of

---

1. Photo published as part of the profile by Schinka Fitch, "A Caregiver for the Community: Children's Hospital Nurse Reaches Those Who Need Care the Most," *Children's Nurse: A Magazine of the Children's Hospital in Milwaukee*, Winter 2009, 2.

friendship. Another unanticipated outcome of the dialogue was the realization that being together could be as significant as what we were doing together. As part of the project the group created a large banner emblazoned with "Muslim–Catholic Healthcare Initiative." One year we brought it to Arab Fest along with stethoscopes, blood pressure cuffs, and brochures. We were amazed by the number of people who stopped and wanted to know how and why we came together. Thus, the word "witness" entered our vocabulary.

Alongside the health care initiative, there were dialogue meetings covering numerous topics. As we met, the need to continue snipping away at misperceptions was evident. Just as Catholics were learning that Islam is not monolithic, Muslims were learning that not all Christians hold the same beliefs, especially regarding issues such as who can be saved. Work was being done to rid our language of phrases such as "all Catholics believe" or "all Muslims believe." As noted earlier, the dialogue began with a discussion of the Pillars of Islam and moved on to other fundamental beliefs in each tradition: Catholic Creeds; life cycle events: birth, death, marriage, sacraments; holydays and holidays; a closer look at prayer, fasting, and almsgiving in light of Ramadan and Lent; angels and saints; the importance of names and naming; clergy; celibacy; judgment; scripture and revelation; *da'wa*; and Catholic Social teaching. Through these conversations, Muslim and Catholic women came to a deeper understanding of one another and became better equipped to serve as ambassadors for one another, speaking up when the beliefs of one or the other tradition were misrepresented.

The friendships and relationships that developed within the group served us well through the years and were a source of great comfort when we were confronted with the events of September 11, 2001. It was evident almost immediately that there would be backlash against the Muslim community. The archdiocese was able to reach out to the Muslim community right away to offer our support, and, in a testament to the strength of the dialogue, our Catholic schools office reached out to me. They wanted to send a fact sheet on Islam out to our Catholic schools but also wanted to make sure that it accurately represented the beliefs of the Muslim community. We were able to send a copy of the fact sheet to Janan Najeeb so that the Islamic Society could view and amend it if necessary before it went out to the schools.

I do not want to think of dialogue in terms of before and after September 11, but many things did change after that fateful year. Among them was an increased desire on the part of our schools and congregations to learn more about Islam and a renewed or deepened sense of the need to expand the boundaries of the dialogue. Additionally, the topic of our conversations changed. Suddenly, we were talking about the Patriot Act and hateful email chains in our meetings. The women in our small group were probably among the few Americans who actually read the entire Patriot Act. The events of September 11, 2001, and the days and months that followed hinted at a question that was not directly addressed by the group: Should we be engaged in political advocacy?

As our dialogue group continued to meet, we turned to the issue of community outreach. What, we asked, could we do in order to expand our reach, to inform more people, and to do it in a manner that would encourage dialogue and relationship building? We decided that the group should hold an annual event. Such an event would focus on a single topic with a Muslim and a Catholic speaker, followed by questions and answers and dialogue in small groups. The annual dialogues began and were intentionally held at area colleges to encourage student involvement and to reach into various geographic areas. The hope was that we might bring together roughly equal numbers of Catholics and Muslims so that various perspectives on the topic could be shared around the tables. One real difficulty in trying to bring together Catholics and Muslims for dialogue was and continues to be the size of our communities. What we wanted to avoid was a situation where seven Catholics and one Muslim would be at a table together, or worse yet, Muslims and Catholics would choose to sit with members of their own faith traditions. Such a situation would clearly diminish the educational and relational value of these gatherings.

The first annual dialogue was held in 2004 and focused on Muslim and Catholic perspectives on Mary/Maryam. The event was held at Alverno College, and the turnout for the program was excellent with a good balance of Muslims and Catholics and participation from some other faith traditions as well. Many Catholics realized for the first time that Muslims recognize Mary as an important person of faith.[2] These annual events were open to all—women, men, people of all faiths or no faith. Programs in the following years included Peace through Submission (2005; Cardinal Stritch University), Muslim and Catholic Perspectives on Jesus (2006; Mount Mary University, see figs. 3.4 & 3.5), and Muslim and Catholic Perspectives on Prophets (2007; Islamic Society of Milwaukee). In each case, the majority of participants were Muslim and Catholic women.

---

2. See the recent study on Mary that looks at the subject through a comparative lens. Rita George-Tvrtkovitch, *Christians, Muslims and Mary: A History* (Mahwah, NJ: Paulist Press, 2018).

Interspersed with these larger public programs, the dialogue hosted smaller sessions on a variety of topics: repentance and creeds; styles of prayer (2006); religious requirements for modesty; the holiest places on earth; and the role of women (2008). These sessions took place at different congregations. Some involved careful research on the part of participants or the sharing of expertise in a particular area. For example, a member of the original dialogue group had extensive experience in leading retreats and the use of centering prayers, and she was able to bring that expertise to the group. The sessions held in 2008 were different in kind (fig. 3.3): They involved bringing people together in small groups to reflect on a set of common questions out of their own experience. The question related to the holiest places on earth revealed a deep spiritual connection between many of the women. Jerusalem, Mecca, Rome, mosques, and churches were rarely mentioned in these small groups. The number one holy place for both Muslim and Catholic women turned out to be "nature."

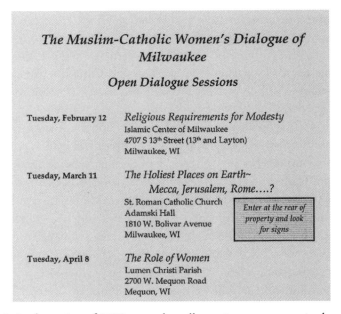

Figure 3.3: In the spring of 2008, several small meetings were organized at different places of worship.

In 2009 and 2010, the dialogue took a different turn and cosponsored programs featuring representatives of the Midwest Regional Muslim-Catholic Dialogue, "A Common Word Between Us and You" in 2009 and "Islam, Muslims,

College Hosts Muslim-Catholic Dialogue

An interfaith discussion, "Jesus: Muslim and Catholic Perspectives," drew more than 130 visitors to the College campus on September 9. The event was co-sponsored by the Mount Mary College Theology Department and the Muslim-Catholic Women's Dialogue, which is a collaborative effort of the Milwaukee Muslim Women's Coalition and the Office of Ecumenical and Interfaith Concerns of the Archdiocese of Milwaukee. The Muslim-Catholic group is in its third year of offering programming aimed at fostering interfaith understanding among its members and within the community.

The opening welcome, delivered in both Arabic and English, was given by Dr. Don Rappé, chair of the College's theology department. Visiting speaker Aisha Sobh, Ph.D. candidate in history at the University of Illinois, discussed the Muslim perspective on Jesus. She was followed by Constance Popp, Ed.D., director of campus ministry at Alverno College, who addressed the Catholic perspective. The day also included a recitation from the Qur'an and a scripture reading, educational exhibits, an opportunity to converse with the speakers and continuing dialogue over lunch. The event was facilitated by the women of the Dialogue, among whose members is Wendy Rappé, director of adult and family ministry at St.

Mary's Parish in Hales Corners, Wis. and adjunct faculty member in Mount Mary's theology department.

"Muslims honor Jesus as a great prophet, while Christians view him as the Messiah. This event examined how each tradition understands the person and mission of Jesus," said Wendy Rappé. "The Catholic tradition is supportive of dialogue, respect, and understanding of other faiths. The Milwaukee Muslim community is very interested in sharing from their tradition as well."

The group sees events like this as a way to provide accurate information, diffuse stereotypes and promote unity. "The question and answer session at this event could have gone on and on," said Wendy Rappé. "People wanted a better understanding of the theological, the political and the practical aspects of both faiths."

The group's next event will be a series of dialogues structured around small groups. The first two sessions will focus on prayer, and will involve visits to Muslim and Catholic worship spaces and an examination of questions such as: Where and when do we pray? How and why do we pray? What do our prayers have in common? Sessions will be held November 2, January 9, March 6, and May 15. For more information, please contact the Office of Ecumenical and Interfaith Concerns at 414-769-3425.

"Give me, O Lord,

The courage to live in dialogue

In the midst of divisions and conflicts

And to build peace with all people of

Sincere hearts and who believe

In your love and compassion. Amen"

*Excerpt from the closing prayer
at the September 9 event*

Figures. 3.4 and 3.5: Events organized by the Women's Dialogue were often not reported in the broader media. The news of this event in 2006 reached the readers of the magazine of Mount Mary College.

and the Current Global Context: What US Catholics Need to Know" in 2010. These programs brought in larger groups with greater gender balance than previous programs. They also addressed significant developments in the Muslim–Catholic conversation on the international and national level and raised the question of how positive developments in dialogue as well as continued distortions about Islam should or could be addressed by a local dialogue.[3]

The Impact of Women's Dialogue on the Larger Community

I have already noted that the Archdiocesan Office of Schools placed and continues to place a high value on their relationship with the Muslim community. Their trust was based in large part on the visibility and success of the Muslim–Catholic Women's Dialogue. As a result of the dialogue, Muslims have been invited to speak in our classrooms and congregations, to address our religious education congresses, and to address staff and clergy of the archdiocese. Because of the dialogue, the relationship between the Archdiocese of Milwaukee and the Islamic Society was strengthened. This bond and institutional collaboration played an important role in planning and organizing events that followed the September 11 tragedy. Due to the network of relations in place, the Interfaith Conference of Greater Milwaukee (ICGM),[4] a nonprofit organization representing 13 member denominations committed to the solidarity of the human community and the dignity of every person, was able to quickly gather religious leaders, including members of the Muslim community, for an interfaith prayer service. Perhaps, more significantly, the Interfaith Conference was able to put together a community-wide response to the fears that people harbored about religion and its association with violence. In the weeks following September 11, 2001, the Interfaith Conference hosted four sessions on religion and violence. Each included a speaker from the Islamic tradition and representatives of three other faith traditions and addressed how their faith traditions viewed violence and terrorism. The goal was to take the attention away from Islam and to initiate a wider conversation about the issues.

---

3. I should note that expanding the table and bringing more people into the dialogue did not come without concerns, most often discovered in the process, among them proselytizing and sharing one's opinions as though they were doctrine, a reality that made it clear that we needed to have an unambiguous set of principles of dialogue.

4. Interfaith Conference is a multifaceted organization with a rich history of initiatives and innovative programs responsible for introducing and informing thousands of people in the greater Milwaukee area about religious and cultural diversity of peoples and viewpoints. For more information, visit its website at: https://interfaithconference.org/.

A significant by-product of these events was the launching of a program for Jewish, Muslim, and Catholic high school youth called the "Sons and Daughters of Abraham." The seed for the program was planted at one of the Interfaith Conference forums when a Muslim and a Catholic, both of whom worked with youth, wondered why there could not be a similar event for youth. Because of our strong ties with the Muslim community, Lisa Calderone, youth director for the archdiocese, and I were able to bring together leaders from the Catholic, Jewish, and Muslim communities to launch the project. Over the course of close to a year, under Calderone's guidance, 18 young people, six from each tradition, committed to learning leadership skills, designing a day-long program for their peers and creating power point presentations explaining the highlights of their faith. These young people ultimately took full responsibility for guiding a hundred of their peers through a day of dialogue designed by youth for youth.[5] None of this would have been possible if we did not already have strong relationships in place. The event led to other projects including a day-long interfaith retreat which, at the request of the young people involved in the "Sons and Daughters of Abraham" project, included representatives from a number of other faith traditions. This, in turn, led to the establishment of the Interfaith Youth Cafes, a multiyear project bringing together youth from various denominations in a small, café-like setting to share their faith and to learn from and with one another.

Another outcome of the women's dialogue was the invitation to participate in the regional Muslim–Catholic dialogue, mentioned earlier, sponsored by the United States Conference of Catholic Bishops (USCCB) and the Islamic Society of North America (ISNA). The regional Catholic–Muslim dialogues, one on the East Coast, one on the West Coast, and one in the Midwest, were originally designed to bring together scholars and practitioners to engage around issues of common concern. Cities throughout the Midwest with established Muslim–Catholic relationships were invited to send paired partners to the Midwest dialogue. For the most part these were imams and priests. Scholars were sometimes invited based on the topic chosen for the dialogue. When the invitation was extended to me, I reached out to the Muslim–Catholic Women's Dialogue for a Muslim partner. Initially, I went to the meetings with Naheed

---

5. This program, the "Sons and Daughters of Abraham," was recorded and was made available on video soon after the event. Jasive Quintas, "Video Summary of Sons and Daughters of Abraham," unpublished, February 28, 2018.

Arshad, an active community organizer, and in later years with Inshirah Farhoud, a member of the Milwaukee Muslim Women's Coalition (MMWC)
and one of the founding members of the Muslim–Catholic Women's Dialogue. I suspect we came as something of a shock to the dialogue members.
While there were a few female scholars in the dialogue at that time, we were
the first and only female partnership that came from the same city and had a
history of involvement in the dialogue together. Inshirah and I were later also
invited to represent the Midwest Regional Dialogue on the National Muslim Catholic Dialogue, established in 2016. None of this would have happened without the Muslim–Catholic Women's Dialogue, which sowed the
seeds for dialogue long ago. These invitations to become part of the regional
and national dialogues are significant because they come at a time when we
are grappling with how to bring together theology and practice. We cannot
address practice if we exclude the voices of women and of local practitioners
from the conversation.

Figure 3.6: Judi Longdin and Inshirah Farhoud in 2017.

Conclusion

These are but a few brief reflections on how the Women's Dialogue has expanded its reach and made a difference. These stories give way to learning from the past and visions for the future. On a personal level, I have been enriched in numerous ways by the dialogue. My own prayer and spirituality have been enhanced; my practice and piety have taken on new and richer dimensions. My understanding of God and revelation has been expanded. These are all gifts that I have been given through the dialogue. Although I studied Islam as a philosophy and religious studies major, explored the relationship between religions and justice in my graduate studies, and have taken advantage of opportunities offered by the United States Conference of Catholic Bishops (USCCB) and the Catholic Association of Diocesan Ecumenical and Interreligious Officers to deepen my understanding of Islam, it has been my association with Muslims and the opportunity to learn together that has both enhanced my understanding of the faith and also made me acutely aware of how much more I have to learn.

In retrospect, it is clear that the dialogue has had a lasting, positive impact on Muslim–Catholic relations in Milwaukee. Members of the dialogue and participants in its programs have become advocates and ambassadors for one another. It is equally clear that the nature and purpose of the dialogue has always been in flux. A tension has always existed between, on the one hand, dialogue and education about beliefs and, on the other, social action and outreach. At times action was clearly defined, as in the healthcare initiative. At other times, action was seen more as outreach to larger audiences, bringing more people into conversations around specific topics. It is possible to extract four strands of dialogue from the experience of the Muslim–Catholic Dialogue: (1) semi-formal dialogue, (2) educational programs with a dialogue component, (3) small-group dialogue (it appears that bringing people together under these conditions enhances understanding on both an intellectual and experiential level; we also know that there are inherent risks, lack of deep understanding of the faith, expressing opinion as fact, even proselytizing), and (4) common service, such as the healthcare initiative. All of these activities had merit and based on anecdotal evidence continue to bear fruit. However, the desire on the part of the original dialogue group to engage in action and to find ways to reach a larger audience thrust the group into the dual role of dialogue group and steering committee, limiting in some ways the ability of the group to continue to engage in dialogue and thrusting the members into roles for which they were not necessarily prepared. The healthcare initiative is one example. Taking someone's blood pressure is easy for an experienced nurse, and doing a social service intake is easy for a social worker. Dealing with paperwork, forms, follow-up, finding locations, and doing publicity are quite another. This suggests that while Muslim and Catholic communities should be encouraged to work together whenever possible, such an ambitious project should be put into the hands of individuals who have strong administrative skills.

For various reasons, the Women's Dialogue has not been active over the last several years. On a positive note, the Milwaukee Muslim Women's Coalition has expanded its programming and community outreach over the years and increased its ability to educate the public. As new programs are added, there are greater demands on staff and less time to devote to the dialogue. At the same time, the archdiocese has seen cutbacks in staff. While the role of volunteers in any dialogue is invaluable, we have learned that dedicated staff is necessary to keep the wheels turning. It remains to be seen whether there will be a role for the dialogue in the future or whether it will serve as a steppingstone to new forms of dialogue.

A local scholarly dialogue that includes female and male participants, clergy and laity, has been in place for a number of years. The group has discussed many topical issues and has focused often on the connection between our shared values and the requirement to serve the common good. The tension between theory and practice is as palpable here as it was in the Women's Dialogue. In 2015 the group published a common statement, *Muslims and Catholics Together Bear Witness to Truth*. The text asserts our need to speak the truth about one another and to work together for peace and justice but leaves open what it means to work for peace and justice and how that end might be accomplished. Is our role to increase our educational outreach, to enhance our understanding of one another, and to encourage action for justice. Or should we be directly involved in action? Should this involve direct service programs like the Muslim–Catholic Healthcare Initiative or advocacy for social change or some combination of both?

Our local dialogue is not alone in trying to balance theology and practice. The regional and national dialogues face the same issue. In the charged political reality in which we find ourselves, Muslims and Catholics agree that we must work to restore civility and to ensure that all persons are treated with dignity and respect; however, the devil as they say is in the details. One of the problems that we face with respect to advocacy for social change is our institutional structure. Given the hierarchal structure of the Catholic Church we are not always as nimble as Muslim organizations. While the giving of charity and programs such as the Muslim–Catholic Healthcare Initiative are not generally an issue for either community, assuming that staff and funds are available to keep them going, advocacy and action for social change can be more difficult. Given the Catholic institutional structure, Catholics are often not able to respond to issues as quickly or in the manner that Muslims might expect, especially given the body of Catholic Social Teaching that is so well known in the interfaith community. While Muslims may look to national Muslim organizations for guidance, they do not need to wait for these bodies to take a position before acting on a local issue. It would be fair to say that our institutional structures can at times make it difficult or even impossible to take a united stand even on issues that may seem clear cut to individuals. In such instances, the question that demands our attention is how we act as models of civility and demonstrate that it is possible to maintain a healthy relationship despite obstacles, misunderstandings, and potential disagreements.

The Muslim–Catholic dialogue in the United States is a relatively new dialogue and, unlike other dialogues, has developed in large part from the bottom up rather than from the top down. In that sense, we are in a unique place to inform how the national conversation unfolds. At the same time, understanding our history will help us to discern next steps in order to maintain a healthy and robust dialogue on the local level. As we move forward it will be necessary for our institutions at the local, regional, and national levels to identify and empower women's leadership and to provide the administrative and financial support necessary to insure the viability and continued growth of our relationships.

BIBLIOGRAPHY

Fitch, Schinka. "A Caregiver for the Community: Children's Hospital Nurse Reaches Those Who Need Care the Most." *Children's Nurse: A Magazine of the Children's Hospital in Milwaukee*, Winter 2009.

George-Tvrtkovitch, Rita. *Christians, Muslims and Mary: A History*. Mahwah, NJ: Paulist Press 2018.

Quintas, Jasive. "Video Summary of Sons and Daughters of Abraham." Unpublished, February 28, 2018.

Christian–Muslim Relations:

A PERSONAL JOURNEY OF DIALOGUE AND MUTUAL LEARNING

Janan Atta Najeeb

I am always a bit amused when asked about my history and extensive involvement in Christian–Muslim dialogue (as well as other interfaith dialogue), as if it is akin to people from different planets meeting for the first time, completely forgetting that we are fellow human beings who may very well be neighbors, classmates, colleagues, soccer moms, and a host of other things. We just happen to be of different faiths, and we most probably have many more commonalities than differences. In fact, there are often members of the same family who choose different spiritual paths, yet when they get together no one views it as an interfaith dialogue.

Cultural Common Ground

Born in Jerusalem of Palestinian heritage, I grew up in Milwaukee, having left Palestine when I was four years old. My parents, Mahmoud and Intisar Atta, were among a small number of Muslims in the area at that time. They were as comfortable with their Arabic-speaking Palestinian Christian friends as they were with their Muslim friends. In fact, I often felt there was a sense of familiarity with the Palestinian Christians as one would find among family members. This was particularly evident as they reminisced about their olive groves, the delicious smell and taste of fruits and vegetables "back home" (we would now call organically grown), family outings to the Mediterranean and the Dead Sea, village weddings where everyone attended, and the sense of community from a people that never needed to call before dropping in for a visit.

The Palestinian Christians used the words "Allah" for God, "insha'Allah" for God willing, "alhamdulillah" for all praise to God," and when they walked in the door they always said "masha'Allah" or as God has willed, as they patted me or my siblings on the head and exclaimed how much we had grown in the week or two that they had not seen us. All of these terms were part of our daily language as Muslims as well. Our parents never discussed theology with their Christian friends but often spoke about how much they missed hearing the church bells and the *'adhan*, or call to prayer, as well as all of the religious shrines that decorated Palestine. My parents were very familiar with the inside of the Church of the Nativity and the Church of the Holy Sepulcher, and our Palestinian Christian friends were just as familiar with Al-Aqsa Mosque and the Dome of the Rock. There was a palpable pride not only in each family's own place of worship but also in those that belonged to others. We never defined our Christian friends by their faith. Rather, in accordance with Arab culture, they were always thought of as "khalto" (auntie) and "ammo" (uncle). This was a relational co-existence, not particularly encumbered by dogmatic assertions that are sometimes used to define religious traditions and divide their followers. Our Christian neighbors were culturally sensitive and avoided alcoholic beverages when they entertained Muslims in their homes, although they were free to do so. During Christmas and Eid, our families would visit each other and bring a variety of Palestinian pastries to share. The Christmas pastries were nearly identical to the Eid pastries, and you never served them without Arabic coffee. What left a lasting impression on me is how my parents would talk to each other about our Christian neighbors; to them, the cultural common ground was so important that they felt they were part of the same family.[1]

My family lived on Milwaukee's North side, and my siblings and I attended Milwaukee Public Schools. My parents greatly stressed the importance of faith and education; all of us children excelled and were always at the top of our class. We were very social and had many friends both in school and outside. Yes, there were things that we did differently, but our classmates were nonjudgmental. We

---

1. This idea is certainly echoed in the Qur'an. Thus, religiously speaking, the Qur'an refers to Christians and Jews as *ahl al-kitab*. Mahmoud Ayoub interprets this to mean "family of the book," implying there is a familial relationship based on the shared heritage that includes monotheism but also the ensuing ethical precepts. Mahmoud Ayoub, "The Need for Harmony and Collaboration between Muslims and Christians," in *A Muslim View of Christianity: Essays on Dialogue by Mahmoud Ayoub*, ed. Irfan A. Omar (Maryknoll, NY: Orbis Books, 2007), 13.

did not eat pork or celebrate Christmas, although we learned all of the Christmas songs in school and many of our classrooms would be decorated during Christmas. Our parents also insisted we give Christmas gifts to our teachers, friends, and our neighbors, and we shared Eid cookies during our holiday. During Ramadan, we sat in the cafeteria and entertained our friends as they ate lunch. We were the only Muslim family in the school. Almost all of our friends were either Catholic or Lutheran. I was in high school when I met Jewish classmates for the first time.

I was still young, when in 1979, the Iranian revolution took place and the CIA-installed Shah of Iran was removed from power. Ayatollah Khomeini returned to Iran after a long exile, and 52 Americans were held hostage for 444 days. This was the first time I felt targeted as a Muslim and became aware that we were viewed as outsiders. This was also the beginning of a lifelong journey of self-education and research in order to explain Islam and clear misconceptions. After graduating from high school and entering UW–Milwaukee, I would join the students for Friday prayer across the street from the Student Union in the basement of the Kenwood Methodist Church, which Muslims had rented for this purpose. The rhetoric against Muslims, particularly Iranians, increased gradually. For years, the Methodist Church had to fend off people who were opposed to them renting space to Muslims. They even received hate mail and angry calls and encountered some vandalism. However, the church administration and clergy refused to back down. They responded by saying that they had never seen anything except good will from Muslims. This was one of the first instances that I recall that represented an interfaith alliance, cooperation, and support when the Muslim community was targeted.

The second opportunity for me to witness interfaith action was learning about the Christian–Muslim dialogue that my parents were involved with at Cardinal Stritch University. Two Catholic nuns, who taught at the university, began the dialogue. The lead architect of the dialogue was the late Sister Lucille Walsh, and Sister Jessine Reiss, her friend and longtime roommate, was also deeply involved. I would drop in on occasion and find a large and very impressive group of Christian theologians, priests, and ministers representing a wide range of Christian denominations interacting with a handful of Muslims. One was a professor of Middle East history who was quite secular; two were physicians. There were a couple of foreign graduate students from UW–Milwaukee who were studying engineering, and two were housewives, one a convert to Islam. The Muslim community was quite small and there were no scholars among them.

Figure 4.1: Mr. Mahmoud Atta and Sister Jessine at one of the dialogue meetings in the late 1990s.

This dialogue continued for almost two decades, meeting on a regular basis. What I soon realized was that this group was as much a dialogue between Christian denominations as it was between Christianity and Islam. As I watched the dynamics, it was very clear that some denominations had more of an affinity and regard toward Muslims, while others may have been there for nondialogical reasons. I found all of this fascinating. The two individuals that were deeply committed to their relationship with Muslims were Sisters Lucille and Jessine. Over the years, the relationship and love with these two Catholic nuns remained strong. My parents often invited them to our home to share meals, and they were among the first to give a

Figure 4.2: Sister Jessine (standing) and Sister Lucille sometime after their retirement from Cardinal Stritch University.

donation to the Islamic Society of Milwaukee when the building was first bought. They stayed in touch with me after I got married and moved to New York and remained genuinely interested in my life. When I came home for a visit with my newborn daughter, one of the first stops I made was to Cardinal Stritch University, where both nuns were excitedly waiting to see the baby. They gifted her a beautiful crocheted blanket. After Sister Lucille retired, my parents and I were invited to an award ceremony at the archdiocese, where she was recognized by then-Archbishop Rembert Weakland for her work in interfaith dialogue with the Muslim community. At the program, Archbishop Weakland said Milwaukee's Christian–Muslim dialogue was believed to be the first in the country. When Sister Lucille passed in 2013 (may she rest in peace), I offered a reflection at her funeral. I occasionally stop in and visit Sister Jessine at the retirement home, and she has invited me to give talks to the retired nuns. Over the years, she has kept up on my work with the Milwaukee Muslim Women's Coalition, and when she is particularly excited about a project, she will tuck a $100 or $50 bill in an envelope and mail it as a donation toward the program.

Personal Involvement in Formal Dialogue

My husband and I moved our young family back to Milwaukee in 1991, where he began his medical practice so we could be closer to family. A few years later, a handful of Muslim women and I organized an Islamic study and discussion group in English that met monthly. The group grew to about 20 women, many of them highly professional. As we studied and talked, there was a common complaint amongst the women that the majority of people they worked with or interacted with had a very erroneous view of Islam and especially regarding the position of Muslim women, in spite of the fact that these women were physicians, teachers, and engineers. In 1996, we decided to form an informal group that would have a speaker's bureau as part of its mission. We scheduled a day to meet, specifically to outline the goals of this group, and to come up with a name. Everyone felt it was important to remain under the umbrella of the Islamic Society of Milwaukee, but it was also important to form a women's organization that included the word "women" in the name because part of the mission was to dispel the stereotype that Muslim women were second-class citizens in their faith and in their homes. Thus, the Milwaukee Muslim Women's Coalition (MMWC) was founded. We began by reaching out to schools, women's clubs, and churches. Most of the initial responses came from women's clubs, where we found a very receptive audience. Members of these clubs would then invite us to speak to their adult education groups at their churches, and soon the word spread about our presence in Milwaukee.

About a year later, in 1997, I was contacted by Judi Longdin from the Ecumenical and Interfaith office of the Catholic Archdiocese. She wanted to meet with me to discuss the possibility of creating a dialogue group. When I presented this to the women in the MMWC, some were excited and saw it as a wonderful opportunity. There were others who could not see what benefit there was in this since Muslims were already knowledgeable about Christians and Jesus because "the Qur'an had everything we needed to know." Some members warned us that this was simply a front for Catholic missionary efforts. A handful of enthusiasts decided we would go ahead and meet. The Muslim–Catholic Women's Dialogue became one of the most enriching endeavors the MMWC took on.[2]

The initial Muslim–Catholic Women's Dialogue was successful for a number of reasons. Both groups were enthusiastic participants and wanted to learn. The participants were all women, which created a level of comfort and sisterhood, particularly when the meetings were held in homes. It was also clear that both groups of women were knowledgeable about their respective faiths. Dialogue covered a multitude of topics, beginning with basic beliefs. Each month, one Catholic member and one Muslim member of the dialogue group prepared remarks on a selected topic, which was followed by a discussion. This monthly gathering was limited to the original group of women. Over the years, we felt comfortable enough to ask each other about aspects of each other's faith that seemed puzzling to us, gaining a real understanding of what a true practitioner of the faith believed. We shared family events, happy occasions as well as sad, and we became friends. Most importantly, we referred to each other as "ambassadors" for each other's faith, working to dispel stereotypes and build community. Less than a year after the dialogue group formed, there was uneasiness among the Muslim members who felt it was important to do more than just meet as a small group.[3] The Muslim participants mentioned a discussion

---

2. It is not uncommon to have reservations and concerns among groups belonging to different religions regarding interfaith dialogue. There are several fears that can arise from an opportunity to engage with people different from ourselves: Will they try to convert me? Will my own beliefs change? Is there a hidden agenda? These questions are frequent—whether thought internally or spoken out loud—and their presence and persistence can deter people from new engagement opportunities. This exemplifies purpose and need for guidelines for dialogue. It is also important to share the results of that dialogue with the general public so people can see formal and informal varieties of dialogue and their intention and impact.

3. These Muslims may have been speaking as social and moral agents, but many also knew that in the Qur'an, faith (*iman*) is seldom mentioned by itself—it is always tied to "doing good deeds."

that had been going on with a group of Muslim physicians who wanted to find a way to give back to the broader community. This was during a time when the numbers of uninsured and underinsured families in Milwaukee were skyrocketing. Many of the Catholic participants and some of the Muslim participants were nurses. The Catholics also had a number of parish nurses that they could involve as well. The Muslim–Catholic Healthcare Initiative was launched. The physicians decided that rather than having them come to parishes or other facilities where they may not have the equipment they needed at their disposal, the nurses would set up at a given parish or on occasion at the Islamic Center; they would take vitals and then assess the patient and determine what specialty the patient needed and set up an appointment with that particular physician. It was important to find a way where patients are able to maintain their dignity. For that reason, the group created personalized insurance cards, which did not make the patient look any different than other visitors to the clinic. They would show their insurance card like any other patient, except for them the services were free of charge. This project was incredibly successful, and as the group went to various locations around the city, more and more people learned about the dialogue group.[4] Despite the success of the project, which matched hundreds of uninsured patients with about 30 Muslim physicians who volunteered their time, we had to end the project. It became bigger than we ever anticipated, and we realized we needed paid personnel to handle the administrative side of things. The program was becoming overwhelming for the volunteer nurses.

The dialogue continued for many more years. Due to Judi Longdin's position at the archdiocese and her efforts to promote understanding of Muslims in the Catholic community, there were ongoing requests for a Muslim speaker from Catholic parishes and schools. Judi directed these to the MMWC. The MMWC was also receiving an increasing number of requests from other non-Catholic groups due to our original outreach efforts. We became very busy giving presentations, participating in panel discussions and workshops for schools, universities, libraries, hospitals, women's social clubs, and a wide range of other groups and institutions. Although the focus of this chapter is mainly

---

4. I remember on one occasion, there was a snowstorm and it was going to be very difficult if not dangerous for the nurses to drive down to the church, especially since the patients, who many times did not own vehicles, would probably not show up. So, we decided to cancel, and we contacted the various news agencies to inform them that the Muslim–Catholic Health Care Initiative was canceled for that day. We were so excited when we saw the name of the Muslim–Catholic Healthcare Initiative on the television screen and when we heard the name mentioned on the radio.

on Muslim–Catholic dialogue and collaboration, I would like to note that the MMWC worked with a number of other Christian denominations and faith groups, particularly those with strong social justice leanings such as the ELCA Churches and the Unitarian Universalist Churches. More recently, MMWC has also engaged with the Evangelical Christian groups (fig. 4.3).

The Muslim–Catholic Women's Dialogue group began discussing how to bring our experience to a broader audience so that this type of dialogue can expand; we did not want it to be "a best-kept secret." Over the years, we held large open events on the Muslim and Catholic perspective on Mary, Abraham, Jesus, the concept of prophethood, and a number of other topics. The large events were well attended and people, mainly women, were eager to be part of our dialogue. We decided to open up our dialogue and meet in churches or the Islamic Center to accommodate the large groups. We soon realized that we had not thought this out very well. Our original dialogue group had been meeting for years.

It was an intimate group that learned to listen to each other with genuine interest. We had developed a dialogue etiquette that created a safe space for sharing, and we were very far along in our understanding of each other's beliefs and practices. Furthermore, each of us had a relatively good knowledge of our faith. With the new groups, we were suddenly referees needing to lay down ground rules for dialogue: not to interrupt others while they speak, not to monopolize the discussion, not to try and represent the faith of others, not to tell others what they believe, and, of course, not to proselytize. Since the original dialogue was made up of only Catholic women, we suddenly had individuals from a variety of Christian denominations who were irritated that the Catholic perspective was the dominating view representing Christianity. In addition, we did not know how to implement our dialogue model with those who were coming as "seekers," people that had left their faith tradition and were searching, or those who came with no coherent understanding of their own faith, and others that had no faith at all. We realized we needed to regroup, set down ground rules, and plan differently.

Some of the events and programs that stand out during the years the dialogue group met were the programs organized to respond to the horrific attacks on September 11, 2001. The first call that I received on the morning of September 11 was from Judi Longdin; she wanted to know if I was all right and what she could do. I will never forget that call. We immediately began brainstorming and decided to discuss this with the Interfaith Conference of Greater Milwaukee. Both Judi and I were active committee members of the Interfaith Conference. The discussion led to the organizing of a citywide interfaith prayer service and four community forums on religion and violence, with representatives of different faith groups discussing the difference between faith and politically motivated acts of violence. The second call I received was from my husband, who was concerned because I was pregnant. He encouraged me to stay home that day, but I told him "that's not an option." The third call was from my daughter; she had just started ninth grade at her new high school. Less than a week earlier she had decided to begin wearing the hijab. I could sense the fear in her voice. She said she did not feel well and wanted to come home. I immediately went and brought her home with me.

The events of September 11, 2001 led to a monumental jump in speaking requests about Islam. In addition to Muslim beliefs and practices, we were now being asked to address political issues as well. The request for speakers came from every imaginable institution, organization, and even businesses. Interfaith organizations, social justice groups, and religious parishes that were horrified at the broad generalizations targeting Muslims and the efforts by some to link Islam with violence and terror were very deliberate in including a Muslim representative in every prayer service, panel discussion, photo opportunity, or anything else that would indicate unity. The number of requests for speaking to community and religious groups continued to rise for several years.

Another program that launched as a result of the dialogue was for high school youth from the Abrahamic traditions called the "Sons and Daughters of Abraham." We were able to draw on the women in the dialogue to help recruit students. My daughter was one of them. The project lasted for many months, eventually leading to the creation of a video that was shared in several places around the country. For a number of years afterwards, members of the original youth group were involved in interfaith cafes and similar projects that they then started at their respective schools.

In the 1990s, the US Catholic Conference of Bishops (USCCB) and the Islamic Society of North America (ISNA) had convened a Midwest Catholic–Muslim dialogue. Since the Muslim–Catholic Women's Dialogue was the only formal and ongoing Muslim–Catholic dialogue in Wisconsin, Judi Longdin asked if we would be interested in representing Wisconsin in the regional Midwest Catholic–Muslim Dialogue organized by the USCCB and ISNA. It was a great opportunity to showcase the work of MMWC. This was important on many levels because it highlighted to the Midwest Dialogue, which consisted mainly of male clergy, academics, and other leaders, the work that the women of dialogue were doing in Milwaukee. It also showed the power of a grassroots initiative that was women-led. In addition, Wisconsin was the only place that

Figure 4.3: Flyer for a recent Christian–Muslim dialogue event organized by Brew City Church in collaboration with MMWC.

had two female representatives among the permanent members of the dialogue, and both of whom were practitioners of their faith and also experienced and active partners in interfaith conversations locally. When the Midwest Dialogue was invited to meet in Milwaukee in 2009, the members benefitted from the groundwork that the Muslim–Catholic Women's Dialogue had been doing for years. Their experience also helped the hosting of the regional dialogue, which was a great success and had record attendance. The Midwest Dialogue met in Milwaukee again in 2010 and became the occasion for many national and local players in the interfaith movement to interact and socialize (fig 4.4).

Figure 4.4: In October 2010, the second Midwest Catholic–Muslim Dialogue was held in Milwaukee. Gathering hosted by Inshirah Farhoud, VP of MMWC and member of the Midwest Catholic–Muslim Dialogue. From left: Dr. Sayyid Syeed (former Secretary-General of the Islamic Society of Milwaukee), Dr. Zeki Saritoprak (John Carroll University), Dr. Scott Alexander (Catholic Theological Union), and Katie and Tom Heinen (Interfaith Conference of Greater Milwaukee).

As the work of the MMWC expanded, we realized we needed to change our model. A lot of our work was related to interfaith dialogue and building bridges of understanding in the broader community, but our mission was greater than that. We had robust programming for women and children, which included job training, leadership training, and even cultural programming. In 2010, the MMWC applied for and acquired the 501(c)3 designation, and in 2011 the Islamic Resource Center (IRC) was inaugurated. IRC is a cultural center that houses Wisconsin's first Islamic public lending library. This move helped us take our work to an entirely new level. We could now hire staff and fundraise for the programming that we felt was needed. Instead of constantly being on the road and hauling brochures, books, and materials, there was now a resource center that people and groups could come to.

As our work at the Islamic Resource Center expanded, our monthly Muslim–Christian women's dialogue sessions ceased. However, our broader interfaith work continued with increasing requests for presentations and various collaborations. In addition, there was a convening of a Muslim–Catholic leaders dialogue that met almost monthly and included Judi and I, as well as Catholic and Muslim leaders in the community. These meetings involved in-depth theological discussions on a variety of topics and were often held at the Islamic Resource Center. Judi and I were also members of the Committee for Interfaith Understanding, a committee of the Interfaith Conference of Greater Milwaukee. In that capacity, we continued a lot of our interfaith work in the form of public programs. This committee, which represents over a dozen faiths, met regularly at the IRC.[5]

The MMWC continued to expand in the area of interfaith programming and found interesting ways to engage the broader community in dialogue. This included programs such as the IMAX film, *Journey to Mecca*, shown at the Milwaukee Public Museum's IMAX Theater, resulting in four sold-out shows and talk backs, art exhibitions, and other informative displays at ethnic festivals, universities, and the Holiday Folk Fair. MMWC invited the Interfaith Conference of Greater Milwaukee to participate in a program on "Giving Thanks" in conjunction with a three-week photo exhibition on Ramadan, held in the Milwaukee City Hall rotunda.

Figure 4.5: Students from UW–Madison who are studying South Asian languages visit the IRC to experience "a day of language and cultural immersion" on September 14, 2018.[6]

5. The IRC is also known for catering to a variety of groups who visit to dialogue, learn, and to browse the impressive collection of books on Islam and Muslims (fig. 4.5).

6. Photo courtesy of the online *Wisconsin Muslim Journal* available at: https://wisconsin-muslimjournal.org/safli-students-from-uw-madison-experience-a-day-of-language-and-cultural-immersion/.

In 2015, the MMWC launched the Milwaukee Muslim Film Festival, a citywide film festival that is intended to use film as a means for presenting topics and issues that are timely, relevant, and generate meaningful discussion about Muslims and the Muslim world. Every show is followed by a talk back or panel discussion to engage the audience in dialogue. In February 2018, the MMWC began publishing the *Wisconsin Muslim Journal*, an independent online news service that recognizes the Muslim community as an integral part of American society. The publication serves as Wisconsin's Muslim community newspaper, with a mission to connect the Muslim population of Wisconsin as well as those of other faiths and spiritual groups. The *Wisconsin Muslim Journal* is the first media organization that reports news and information about the Muslim community in the state of Wisconsin. Its aim is to highlight the American Muslim experience as well as offer Muslim voices an opportunity to be heard.

Conclusion

While the Muslim–Catholic Women's Dialogue and interfaith dialogue in general have been incredibly enriching, they also presented us with some challenges. Several issues of justice that are obvious to many in the Muslim community are not similarly viewed by others. When the terrorist attacks took place on September 11, 2001, Muslim leaders were quick to condemn those actions. Yet, Muslims were often puzzled when Catholic or interfaith leaders did not make similar gestures and did not voice their concerns against the violence committed by other groups and even state actors such as the Israeli bombardment of Palestinian civilians and the American use of the drones in Afghanistan and other places that has killed civilians in large numbers.[7]

Whereas Muslim religious leaders share the same views as their parishioners and are willing to vocalize those views, this was not always the case among our Christian, especially Catholic, counterparts. At times, this cast a cloud over some of our meetings. We realized that part of it was due to the hierarchy in the Catholic Church and how decisions are made. Muslim groups involved in

---

7. It is ironic that while the American interfaith and religious leaders more or less remain silent, many secular groups take huge risks and speak out against injustices wherever they see them. Consider the huge show of support against the first "Muslim" ban by Americans of all backgrounds and ethnicities covered widely in the mainstream media. See the long list of protests worldwide against Trump's Executive Order 13769: https://en.wikipedia.org/wiki/List_of_protests_against_Executive_Order_13769.

dialogue felt it was a political decision to cater to more conservative voices and donors in the Church. Although we knew we had built strong friendships and allies and we often shared similar views on issues of social justice, there were instances where there appeared to be a disconnect between the professed values and actions by leadership among Catholics and the laity. I imagine this will continue to be a challenge.

Another issue that I consider to be a challenge, and which may very well influence the future trajectory of Muslim–Catholic relations, is how each community truly views the other. This is probably best explained by an event held to commemorate the 50th anniversary of *Nostra Aetate*, when the Second Vatican Council outlined for Catholics a new approach and understanding for interfaith relationships, particularly toward Jews and Muslims. I was invited by Bishop Richard Sklba to give a Muslim response to his remarks. I noted that while Catholics were given instruction on interfaith relations 50 years ago, for Muslims that relationship was revealed in detail in the Holy Qur'an over 1,400 years ago. I explained that in the Qur'an, Jews and Christians are referred to by an honorific title, "People of Scripture" in recognition that they believe in the same God, the God of Abraham, they are honored by God, they received scripture from God, and share a common moral code with Muslims. The Qur'an commands Muslims to honor the Virgin Mary. An entire chapter in the Qur'an is named after her. Muslims also honor Jesus as a great prophet. Muslims cannot claim a monopoly on God's mercy or deny it to other faith communities. The issue that has become apparent to those of us involved in dialogue over the years is that the extent and scale of programs and potential decisions that impact Catholic–Muslim discussions and collaborations is very dependent on the views of the reigning archbishop, where he stands on Muslim–Christian relations, and how he interprets *Nostra Aetate*. While top Muslim scholars and leaders in Greater Milwaukee have easily come to the table whenever they have been called on to dialogue or collaborate with Catholics or other faith communities, where they can make quick decisions on a particular call to action, this has not necessarily been the case with our Catholic friends. Since 2002, we have requested a couple of meetings a year between Muslim leaders and the archbishop. However, neither the previous archbishop, Timothy Dolan nor the current archbishop, Jerome Listecki, accepted our offer. I personally think that the Catholic–Muslim Dialogue would have had an even greater impact in educating the wider community if the archbishops representing Southeastern Wisconsin were less conservative and were more welcoming of Muslims. There is no doubt that the dialogue and collaboration will continue, but it will most likely be as a grassroots collaboration between Muslims and Catholic laity who see faith as a call to action and work independent of leadership. If the collaboration is a more formal or "official" in nature, the impact of any encounter and discussion will mostly be dependent on the Catholic hierarchal establishment and their efforts. In spite of these challenges at the hierarchal level, my life has been forever enriched by the meaningful friendships that have been built with wonderful people who share a love for God, a love for justice, a love for humanity, a love for God's creatures, and for the earth we all co-habit. The time we spent together has deepened my faith, increased my knowledge and awareness, and given me tremendous hope in the goodness of humanity. For that, I will forever be grateful.

I will end this chapter with two significant passages from the Qur'an that have guided me to pursue dialogue and cooperation with people of other faiths.

> Oh people, you have been created from a single male and a female and made into nations and tribes so that you may come to know and cherish one another, not despise each other. Truly the best of you in the sight of God is the one who is most righteous (Qur'an 49:13).

> And of God's signs is the creation of the heavens and the earth and the diversity of your languages and your colors. Indeed, in that are signs for those of knowledge (Qur'an 30:22).

BIBLIOGRAPHY

Anonymous. "List of Protests against Executive Order 13769." https://en.wikipedia.org/wiki/List_of_protests_against_Executive_Order_13769.

Ayoub, Mahmoud. "The Need for Harmony and Collaboration between Muslims and Christians." *A Muslim View of Christianity: Essays on Dialogue by Mahmoud Ayoub*, edited by Irfan A. Omar, 9–16. Maryknoll, NY: Orbis Books, 2007.

Wisconsin Muslim Journal. "SAFLI Students from UW-Madison Experience a Day of Language and Cultural Immersion." September 14, 2018, https://wisconsinmuslimjournal.org/safli-students-from-uw-madison-experience-a-day-of-language-and-cultural-immersion/.

Catholic–Muslim Women's Dialogue:

Stronger Together in Faith and in Friendship

Dianne Rostollan

The greater Milwaukee metropolitan area has had a rich history of interfaith dialogue—particularly Christian–Muslim dialogue, which has ebbed and flowed involving different groups over the past four decades. By 1999, the original Christian–Muslim dialogue had ceased, but the legacy and success of that dialogue was not completely forgotten. Judi Longdin began as the director of the Office of Ecumenical and Interfaith Concerns for the Archdiocese of Milwaukee in 1993 and started the process of reviewing previous initiatives in the area. In her inquiry, she found a reference to the idea of starting a Catholic–Muslim Women's Dialogue. She was intrigued by the idea and in 1996 contacted Janan Najeeb, the president of the Milwaukee Muslim Women's Coalition (MMWC) for initial conversation. The MMWC was started by a group of professional Muslim women who, witnessing the rampant misunderstanding of the Muslim faith, wished to educate the public on Islam. Not only was Najeeb a leader in the Muslim community, she had participated in the Muslim–Christian conversations in the area as a teenager with her parents, Mahmoud and Intisar Atta. Her previous experience showed her the value of interfaith dialogue. This experience, coupled with the coalition's desire to educate, led Najeeb to collaborate with Longdin in starting a dialogue for women of the two faiths in the Milwaukee area.[1]

---

1. Intisar Atta, interview by Dianne Rostollan, Sundus Jaber, and Caroline Redick, March 24, 2017.

The Women of Dialogue

In my interview with Janan Najeeb, she said that because she had attended dialogues with her family at a young age, interfaith work became a norm in her life and was viewed as important from the faith perspective. Having been a part of founding the Milwaukee Muslim Women's Coalition and being contacted by Longdin, she believed this would be a perfect opportunity to partner and begin dialoguing. Her belief was that this would be an excellent opportunity to partner with the Archdiocese of Milwaukee for the good of the community as well as support the mission of the MMWC.[2] Initially, the group had no stated objective except to bring women from the two faiths together and explore their interests. The first meetings allowed the participants to break down barriers, and they began to challenge their misconceptions of one another. Although these initial meetings were successful, the women quickly realized the need to do more. The group was specifically interested in action-oriented effort; they wanted it to be something that will involve service to others. It so happened that many of the women in the group were involved in the health care field, therefore, a natural direction for the group was to think about a health care initiative. In 1998, they formed the Milwaukee Muslim–Catholic Healthcare Initiative to help provide health care screenings and access to physicians for those who might otherwise not be able to afford it.[3]

The initiative may seem to have distracted them from formal "table" dialogue, but ultimately it allowed the women to create something more meaningful without even realizing it. Spending hours in church basements on the weekend allowed these women to strengthen friendships. There they discussed their families and their lives. They shared their joys and struggles. These discussions, without the women realizing it, constituted a sort of informal dialogue. It was not a formal dialogue but rather something that occurred organically when the women gathered to serve together. This informal dialogue created a sense of trust and familiarity that developed bonds perhaps no formal dialogue could have. It was informal because it was not planned, there was no agenda, no list of discussion questions. Rather, the women naturally shared about their lives, and over time, these discussions became more personal and allowed them to truly know each other on a deeper level. Previous studies have found that when women of different faith backgrounds gather, even when they are there specifically to represent

---

2. Janan Najeeb, interview by Sundus Jaber, April 18, 2017.

3. Judi Longdin, "Muslim-Catholic Women's Dialogue: Lessons from the Past and Future Prospects" (lecture, Marquette University, Milwaukee, WI, March 28, 2017).

their faith tradition, they tend to "talk" more than "dialogue." That is, they prefer to get to know the other as a whole person rather than simply a representative of a particular religious tradition.[4] These women became friends, and friendship allows a level of intimacy and honesty that cannot be falsely manufactured in a formal setting. The health care initiative, besides what it did for the many people who still see these doctors nearly 20 years later, had a lasting impact on the future of interfaith relations in general and for the women's dialogue in particular.[5] The

Figure 5.1: At a networking brunch put on by MMWC, Kirsten Shead, an evangelical Christian and program director of the Interfaith Earth Network, presented on cultivating tools necessary for collaborating with others to address divisions and conflicts.

---

4. Martha Frederiks, "The Women's Interfaith Journey: Journeying as a Method in Interfaith Relations," *Missiology: An International Review* 4 (October 2012): 470.

5. Judi Longdin, interview by Dianne Rostollan, March 14, 2017.

women could be more open and felt greater levels of trust, feeling they could be more vulnerable and honest. The more individuals can be vulnerable, the more transparent and impactful a dialogue will become.

The health care initiative ended in 2005, but many of the women continued to meet and share their faith with one another, slowly dismantling misconceptions and even evoking a desire to defend one another in the public sphere. Participants in the group had created a strong bond, and, at times, it seemed difficult to incorporate others into this already established group. In a personal interview, Najeeb and Longdin both spoke of experiences where women came trying to proselytize or convert members of the other faith. But any such efforts were not successful because both Muslims and Christians in the group reiterated that this was not the purpose of the group. The leadership in the group and its members rejected attempts from members of their own tradition who wished to engage in preaching or propagandizing. Women who joined hoping to convert others quickly found that they were in the wrong place. Some members of other Christian denominations felt uncomfortable joining because the Catholic view seemed to them to be overrepresented. Some Christian women were reluctant to enter in dialogue or engage with Muslim women altogether.[6]

Nevertheless, the group members benefitted from their own personal encounters by developing lasting friendships and growing to appreciate one another, not just as a Muslim or Christian but as individuals. Their understanding and appreciation of the other faith continued to grow. Especially, following the events of September 11, 2001, the women felt a strong desire to impress a deeper appreciation of the "other" upon the wider Milwaukee community. They decided to develop a community outreach program in the form of holding annual events often on or near the anniversary of September 11. Each event had a theme that allowed attendees to learn how both religions viewed the same topic. They would invite a knowledgeable speaker to present on a topic and had dialogue tables for participants to share. The events were open to everyone, but the majority of those who attended were women. Starting in 1996, some of the early events were extremely successful, drawing hundreds of people to area colleges where the programs were held. These events helped participants break down many misconceptions and fears of Islam.[7] As the Milwaukee Muslim Women's Coalition (MMWC) grew, the Muslim women involved in the dialogue found it necessary to refocus on issues that required greater attention

---

6. Najeeb, interview by Jaber.

7. Longdin, "Muslim-Catholic Women's Dialogue."

and were important for the Muslim community. The MMWC began to shift its focus to becoming an advocacy group for Muslim community and Muslim women. While this brought an end to perhaps more of the formal dialogues and public events, a permanent organizational partnership was already established between the MMWC and the Archdiocese of Milwaukee.

Longdin and Najeeb continued to work together on a variety of initiatives that tended to be more focused on the good of the city and the wider community (see fig. 5.1), rather than benefitting individual groups.[8] They built and

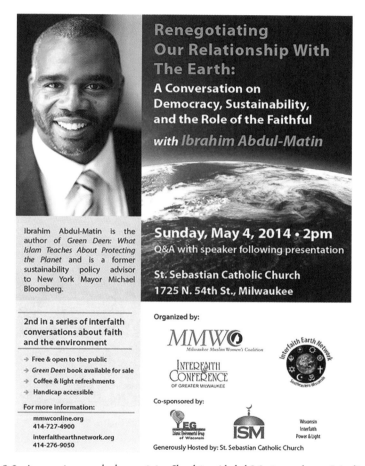

Figure 5.2: A prominent scholar-activist, Ibrahim Abdul-Matin spoke on Muslim environmental movement at an area Catholic Church, highlighting the strong interfaith cooperation between various religious and community groups.

---

8. Najeeb, interview by Jaber.

expanded their networking efforts to include women and other groups who previously did not join them at the table because the earlier configuration of the dialogue was limited to Muslim and Catholic women. Today, MMWC routinely partners with other religious and secular organizations to organize events and build solidarity for social causes (fig. 5.2).

In 2009, the public face of the women's involvement in dialogue evolved in another direction. Two women (Judi Longdin and Naheed Arshad) who have been part of the Milwaukee women's dialogue were invited to attend (and later to become members of) the regional Midwest Catholic–Muslim Dialogue sponsored by the USCCB and ISNA. These were important national initiatives. The Midwest dialogue met in different cities each year. In 2009 and 2010, it met in Milwaukee and was jointly sponsored by local Catholic and Muslim institutions, after Longdin had been a member of the Midwest dialogue for some years. After Naheed Arshad withdrew from attending the regional dialogue due to personal family reasons, Inshirah Farhoud, vice president of the MMWC, and a nurse practitioner, joined as the Muslim participant. Since then, these two women have been regular participants of the Midwest dialogue.[9] Farhoud notes that she and Longdin were the first active women participants and currently are the only regular attendees who are faith practitioners rather than scholars or clergy members.[10]

Figure 5.3: At the meeting of the National Catholic–Muslim Dialogue in March 2018, held at Mundelein Seminary in Illinois. Milwaukee members pictured include.: Judi Longdin (back row) and Inshirah Farhoud (middle row, second from right). Judi and Inshirah were two of the five women present.

9. Longdin, "Muslim-Catholic Women's Dialogue."

10. Inshirah Farhoud, interview by Sundus Jaber, March 14, 2017.

Even as the local women's dialogue was becoming inactive, some of the core members of that dialogue were becoming prominent in the regional and national Catholic–Muslim dialogue activities. Since 2015, Judi Longdin and Inshirah Farhoud have also become part of the newly formed National Catholic–Muslim Dialogue. It is significant that of the 20 or so Muslim members on that committee, three come from Milwaukee (the third member is Dr. Irfan Omar; see fig. 5.3).

Figures 5.4 and 5.5: Bobbie and John Schmitt, longtime residents of Milwaukee and active members of various dialogue groups in the community. The Shalom/Al-Salam artwork (right) they displayed in their home represents their deep interest in dialogue and peace (courtesy of Bobbie and John Schmitt).

Why Women?

The dialogue that was first envisioned and organized by Judi Longdin and Janan Najeeb bore much fruit over two decades. But a significant question that might be raised is, "Why just women?" According to Longdin, it might not be for the reasons we expect. One might assume that the common link between Muslim and Catholic women would be their perceived "oppression" in their faith traditions. However, this was not an issue that the women seemed overly concerned about. In fact, many things that outsiders to the faith may see as oppressive can be seen as liberating and fulfilling to the practitioners who understand the truth of the faith practice.[11] One of the influential factors in pursuing a women-only dialogue was the success of a similar dialogue in Canada. This gave them the idea that perhaps women in Milwaukee should give it a

---

11. Maura O'Neill, *Mending a Torn World: Women in Interreligious Dialogue* (Maryknoll: NY: Orbis Books, 2007), 115.

try. The presence of a Muslim women's group from which to draw participants also played a role. Women who have participated in the dialogue expressed a feeling of ease being around other women with whom they could discuss issues more freely. They thought that dialogue meetings organized and designed by men were largely academic. The women's dialogue allowed the participants to be more down to earth, allowing them to share their own personal experiences and beliefs rather than simply speaking in abstract, academic style. Bobbie Schmitt, a long-time participant in the dialogue, said that it felt more informal and relaxed with just women rather than the formality of men and women together. Women are also more comfortable talking about subjects that might be deemed not central to dialogue. They felt more relaxed and able to open up about all sorts of life issues.[12]

Historically, women have not been a part of interfaith dialogue meetings due to a variety of reasons. Women have not been religious leaders in their faith tradition; also, they have not had the required education. Women were not seen as an authority on faith matters. However, women bring a unique perspective to the interfaith discussion because of their particular way to see and experience the world.[13] As Jeanine Fletcher observes, while men's interfaith dialogue may focus more on intellectual and academic issues, women's dialogue is more organic, as their spiritual experiences tend to be rooted in their daily living.[14] Women have (by choice) tended not to focus so much on theologies, dogmas, or definitions but on what it means to live the faith. They share stories of their faith as a part of their lives, showing that for them, faith is something living and embodied. Women tend to feel the presence of the divine, which encounters humanity in and through lived experiences. In this way, the dialogues themselves become sacred spaces.[15]

Reflecting upon women's dialogue, Fletcher argues that religion is not meant to be separated from life, as narrated by a theologian distanced from the world; rather, it is set within the messiness of life.[16] The Milwaukee Women's Dialogue, as well as other women's dialogues, have shown that women engage

---

12. Bobbie Schmitt, interview by Diane Rostollan, February 28, 2017. Bobbie and her husband John Schmitt have been some of the most ardent supporters of dialogue and engagement between people of different faiths and cultures. See also figs. 5.4 & 5.5.

13. Jeannine Hill Fletcher, *Motherhood as a Metaphor: Engendering Interreligious Dialogue* (New York: Fordham University Press, 2013), 177.

14. Fredriks, "Women's Interfaith Journey," 474.

15. Fletcher, *Motherhood as a Metaphor*, 159.

16. Ibid., 149–50.

in a way where they remain connected to real-life issues. Women tend to be oriented toward relationships, and the nurturing of these relationships, making conversation, and getting to know the individual and their lived experience are important aspects.[17] Maura O'Neill notes that men and women also tend to have different communication styles. Men have been taught to use reason and intellect and to speak objectively—an approach that appears in many interfaith dialogues in which women are not present. It is not that women cannot speak with reason and use intellect, but more often than not, a woman's approach is to be subjective and self-disclosing.[18] They are more comfortable talking about their personal experience of their faith because many women believe that they do not know enough to speak about doctrinal and/or dogmatic issues in a dialogue. These perceptions are gradually changing as more women have risen to leadership positions. Hurdles remain in matters of their serving as clergy, but the pace of change may be on their side.

Women have been historically denied access to the same kind of education and leadership roles that men have; systematic exclusion has caused them to feel as though they cannot speak authoritatively about their faith.[19] Many times, among academic or faith leaders, women have been treated as objects of dialogue rather than equal partners, moved about as pawns to come to some agreement about their role in religion rather than be included in foundational discussion themselves.[20] Women's knowledge of the faith as lived is sometimes discarded as mundane or unimportant to the realm of religious thought.[21] Among other women, what may seem mundane to the academic world is steeped with meaning because it is where these women encounter the divine. Women speak of the passing on and living of their faith in the family. Their faith is not knowledge that can be separated from life but instead has been woven into the very fabric of their lives. Fletcher describes it as a nonrational, embodied, and emotive production of knowledge that is shared through bodies, lives, and practices.[22] It is a living, breathing organism, which takes from the knowledge held within a particular tradition and makes it alive as a part

---

17. Maura O'Neill, *Women Speaking, Women Listening: Women in Interreligious Dialogue* (Maryknoll, NY: Orbis Books, 1990), 23.

18. Ibid., 44.

19. Fletcher, *Motherhood as a Metaphor*, 171–75.

20. Catherine Cornille, *Women and Interreligious Dialogue* (Eugene, OR: Cascade Books, 2013), 4.

21. Fletcher, *Motherhood as a Metaphor*, 181.

22. Ibid., 184.

of the world around them. It does not compromise religious truth but makes it applicable. Women's dialogue tends to be more personal and interpersonal, and it could be valuable to the academics in providing a holistic understanding of the faith.[23] Women often feel comfortable sharing about their emotions and their lives because they are taught that it is normal. Thus, their interactions are more personal and their dialogue is more practical.[24] O'Neill notes that through practical dialogue women have the ability to see the world and themselves through the eyes of the other and this brings about new dimensions to religious convictions, dramatically deepening the sense of self and the experience of the sacred.[25]

Many successful women's dialogues have focused on the sharing of the spiritual journey, where women describe their faith as it is experienced and lived. O'Neill includes a story of one woman who participated in a women's interfaith dialogue in Philadelphia and said, "Women bring all of who they are to the monthly meetings—sharing their beliefs, their faith, their stories, and their lives."[26] Storytelling allows women to show the faith as embodied and living. It allows the sharing of a faith in a way that women can relate to, by the sharing of their encounter with or discovery of the divine in the course of their lives and in their experiences. This storytelling experience is important for several reasons. First, it helps create an atmosphere of trust. It is easier to trust someone whose story you know—who you have seen share their desires, fears, and joys. Trust is needed so that individuals can speak openly and honestly. Second, it clarifies diverse perspectives, as not every Muslim or Catholic believes exactly the same things. Each woman has her own perspective, her own ways of knowing and experiencing the divine, which deepens the experience of the divine for others. Sharing also allows individuals to discover points of commonality and distinction.[27]

Third, the idea of storytelling is comfortable and familiar for women; it opens up diverse experiences and understandings. Inshirah Farhoud, a Muslim participant, noted that when just women are present, "we are able to become more ourselves."[28] The comfort that women feel around one another and

---

23. Cornille, *Women and Interreligious Dialogue*, 5.

24. O'Neill, *Mending a Torn World*, xiv.

25. Ibid., 108–9.

26. Ibid., 149.

27. Ibid., 57.

28. Farhoud, interview by Jaber.

among their peers leads to a deeper level of authenticity as well as discovery. Fourth, dialogue itself is a part of life and ultimately shapes the experience of faith. Women come to dialogue not just to share but to be changed. It is a sacred experience that is transformative for many. Finally, dialogue cannot simply be a recitation of propositions, because that is not what true faith is. Rather, faith is lived, and dialogue becomes a part of that living. Dialogue ultimately should become an experience of faith, something that increases faith and deepens one's experience of the divine. Thus, O'Neill argues, "dialogue is not so much a process of sharing truth as it is of discovering it. . . . The most significant way in which truth is discovered in dialogue is when I and my dialogue partner together discover something neither of us had known before."[29]

Goals of Dialogue

The dialogues between the Muslim and Catholic women profoundly impacted the women who participated but also affected the wider community. These effects can be summed up into five general categories: fellowship, advocacy, education, faith-building, and social justice–oriented actions. These five themes were present throughout the entirety of the dialogue but also trace the general development of the purpose of the dialogue over the years.

Fellowship

Frederiks holds that there are four categories or levels of interfaith dialogue: intellectual, ethical, life, and heart.[30] While the women's dialogue began as any typical interfaith dialogue might have, it shifted as the women began engaging in the dialogue of life and the dialogue of the heart. As they began the Muslim–Catholic Healthcare Initiative, they spent hours planning and carrying out these free health screenings. During these weekends, they would find ample time to get to know one another as "neighbors" and not simply "that Muslim woman" or "that Catholic lady."[31] Rather, they became people with stories, families, careers, and friends. They discussed their similarities—many were wives and mothers. They shared the joys and the pains of their lives and became friends.

---

29. O'Neill, *Women Speaking*, 106.

30. Frederiks, "Women's Interfaith Journey," 473.

31. Longdin, interview by Rostollan.

Fellowship involves being present with one another; it develops bonds and a familiarity that breaks down all sorts of barriers. Friends are more capable of being honest with one another and have the implicit permission to ask difficult or even sensitive questions for the sake of deeper understanding of the other. Friendship allows true dialogue, but in order to be friends, we must first recognize the humanity and dignity in one another. The Milwaukee women's informal dialogue allowed their group to flourish into a community. Though their formal dialogue during this time period seemed to fizzle out, the effect this period had on the success of the dialogue and the hearts of the participants was monumental. The power of this shared humanity was an unbreakable bond. These friendships still exist today. For example, when Farhoud and Longdin met with this author, they needed to greet each other and talk about the gloves that one had left in the other's car. The relationship between these women had ceased to be simply one of being a dialogue partner in a formal sense; they were now sisters.

There has been discussion in the interfaith community about dialogue through the "journeying method." This method allows individuals, particularly women, to have a shared journey or experience. According to Martha Frederiks, who writes about a series of these journeying encounters, "The unvoiced implication of this stance is that interfaith dialogue happens naturally, as a part of the interpersonal relationships; no specific time needs to be allocated for discussing religious issues."[32] It would have been very easy for any sort of dialogue to die off completely as the Muslim–Catholic Women's Healthcare Initiative took off, but the women were doing dialogue without even realizing it. The women, through their informal conversations, did not learn about "dogmatic truth" of faith but rather about what it feels like to be a Muslim or a Catholic in the world and in Milwaukee. Their interactions focused on experiential aspects of faith more so than its cognitive dimensions.[33] The women became bound to one another through their humanity and not just through their institutional or faith identity.

Advocacy

Both Catholics and Muslims can relate to having their faith misunderstood and slandered in the media. Both have fallen under extreme scrutiny, especially during the time of the Muslim–Catholic Women's Dialogue in Milwaukee. The Catholic Church was in the midst of dealing with the priest sexual abuse

---

32. Frederiks, "Women's Interfaith Journey," 475.

33. Ibid.

scandal, and Islamophobia was running rampant, especially in the aftermath of September 11, 2001. Both groups were subject to harsh criticism, but since they had formed these bonds of friendship by the early 2000s, they were able to advocate for one another. Longdin told the journal, *US Catholic*, "We aim to create advocates and ambassadors."[34] Following the events of September 11, 2001, the majority of Americans did not actually know any Muslim personally. As a result, the Catholic women in the dialogue could tell their friends, neighbors, and fellow parishioners that Islam does not support terrorism. Similarly, as the story of Catholic priest sexual abuse scandal hit the media, the Muslim women could tell others that not all priests are pedophiles and the Church does not condone such behavior. As Farhoud shared, "One person does not represent the whole faith."[35] Because these women had come to know each other prior to the media attacks, they had already learned the hearts of the other believers and the intrinsic good that existed in each of the faith traditions. They knew that the actions of a few did not represent the true belief and teachings of the religion but rather the failures of those individuals. They became a voice for those who perhaps felt helpless to defend their own religion in the face of the negative media. They spread truth and goodness in the midst of heartbreak and despair.

This advocacy reached far deeper than simply discounting media rumors in casual conversation. From the dialogue, a growing connection developed between the Archdiocese of Milwaukee and the Milwaukee Muslim community, particularly the Milwaukee Muslim Women's Coalition, through the friendship and work of Longdin and Najeeb. As soon as the news of the September 11 terrorist attacks hit Milwaukee, Longdin knew the ramifications this could have on the city and on the Muslim community. She knew that it was the responsibility of the Catholic Church to educate its parishioners and most especially, its children. Following the attack, the archdiocese, in collaboration with Janan Najeeb and other Muslims, created a fact sheet about Islam.[36] This sheet was then distributed to each of the parishes and schools in the archdiocese, but not before each and every word was approved by the Muslims that the sheet claimed to represent. Without the prior relationship, such collaboration and quick response would not have been possible. This advocacy impacted over 200 parishes and over 100 Catholic schools in the Archdiocese of Milwaukee, which includes hundreds of thousands of Catholics, from the Illinois border to Sheboygan and west to Ripon, Wisconsin.

---

34. Megan Sweas, "Won't You Be My Neighbor?" *US Catholic*, February 2007, 26.

35. Ibid.

36. Longdin, "Muslim-Catholic Women's Dialogue."

Education

The terrorist attacks on September 11 and the resulting Islamophobia also called the group to act. They saw what an impact these discussions had on them as individuals but knew that a small group of women could not have the large-scale impact that was needed in the area. As a result, they decided to hold community education events. These events, as discussed before, were open to the public and held at local universities. They sought to allow participants to learn about each faith in regard to a certain topic and then participate in table discussions with members of different faith traditions. The events were very successful; if one is to judge success by the numbers, having several hundred people at some of these events would certainly qualify. One of the most fondly remembered events was on the topic of Mary or Maryam, the mother of Jesus in both Islam and Christianity. It was a shock for many Christian women in attendance to learn about the high regard Muslims have for Mary.[37] The event provided a way to witness the common ground between Muslims and Catholics, at least in regard to the importance of Mary. It also showed the intimate links between the two faiths, which happen to have many important things in common. Other topics that were discussed were "Jesus in Islam and Christianity," the concept of "submission in faith," and "prophethood."[38] These dialogue meetings highlighted the importance of common respect and understanding of the other in a time when hate-filled sentiments of Islamophobia were on the rise.

While the large speaker-oriented dialogues were held annually, other, smaller dialogue meetings were organized throughout the year. The success of the annual day-long dialogues indicated a need, and individuals from both faith groups expressed a desire to meet more frequently to learn about one another. These smaller meetings happened in a more informal atmosphere "where relationships can be established and nurtured, where inquiry and openness to one another is seen as a path to knowledge."[39]

Faith-Building

When Judi Longdin, Janan Najeeb, and other members of the original dialogue began meeting, their only goal was to get together as a group of women to discuss faith. From the very first meeting, it became obvious to the participants,

---

37. Schmitt, interview by Rostollan.

38. Longdin, interview by Rostollan.

39. Muslim Catholic Women's Dialogue, *Open Dialogue: The Role of Women,* flyer.

especially the Catholic women, that they had much to learn about each other. Judi Longdin recalls that in the middle of the meeting, the Muslim women stopped and said that it was time to pray. Given that Catholic laity typically do not exercise regular, scheduled prayers throughout the course of the day, this was a bit shocking at first. At a specific time, Muslim women gathered in one corner of the room briefly where they performed one of their regularly pre-scribed prayers and then returned to the discussion. Longdin shared that this action on their part had an impact on her personal view of prayer. She recalled what one Muslim woman had shared that having the regular habit of prayers throughout the day meant that you were always coming from and going to prayer. With this mindset, it made it more difficult to do something wrong because you knew that you were close to the presence of God.[40]

One of the many challenges that individuals face when trying to facilitate interfaith dialogue is the temptation to proselytize. This is often because of the lack of a clear understanding about the purpose of dialogue. People who are passionate about their faith want to share it and want others to believe what they do. In and of itself, that is fine. However, this goes against the ultimate goal of interfaith dialogue, which is to share your faith with others and learn about theirs as well without being concerned about convincing others of one's perspective. Though the Muslim–Catholic Women's Dialogue has had indi-viduals who initially came to proselytize and sought to convert others to their own faith, they quickly learned that this was not the purpose of dialogue. Some believers were resistant to dialogue because they feared it would challenge their faith and cause unnecessary doubt. But women in the group all testified that the interfaith dialogues actually made them better Muslims or better Catholics. Longdin, as mentioned above, said that it changed her view on prayer because of the Muslim devotion to the regular habit of prayer. Najeeb noted in her interview that participation in the dialogue over the years has made her a bet-ter Muslim because it forced her to learn more about her faith and to become better at articulating it. When someone asked questions about what Muslims believed and why, she sometimes had to go and do research, which caused her knowledge to grow.[41] Bobbie Schmitt, another Catholic member of the group, said that learning the beliefs that Muslims had about Mary and other parts of their faith helped her to better appreciate her own faith.[42] Inshirah Farhoud,

---

40. Longdin, interview by Rostollan.

41. Najeeb, interview by Jaber.

42. Schmitt, interview by Rostollan.

a Muslim, believes that there is wisdom in the diversity and perhaps God did not will everyone to be a Muslim for a reason as the diversity helps to challenge individuals to think outside the box in their understanding of the divine.[43] Thelma Walker, another participant, told the *US Catholic* in 2007 that, "Everybody has wisdom. The more we interact with other people, the more we learn from their wisdom and they learn from ours."[44] Instead of challenging their faith and making them feel the need to convert, the women's own faith was enriched by listening to the perspectives of the other. They delved deeper into their own spiritual traditions and learned more about themselves as well as allowing the beliefs and traditions of the other faith to enrich their understanding and devotion to the one true God.

Social Justice–Oriented Actions

The women of the Milwaukee Catholic–Muslim Women's Dialogue were not provided with any agenda. They did not have to "do" anything, and yet early on it became very clear that the women from both faiths had a strong desire to serve and help those who were unable to help themselves. Often, dialogue groups are very cautious when deciding to act. Careful steps are taken to discuss theology and motivation, to dissect sacred texts. However, the women's dialogue did just the opposite: they acted first and discussed theology later. Some members noted that this was a far more effective way of actually getting things done. Everyone understood that their faith called them to serve and to care for others, and since many of the women involved in the group were involved in the medical field, a health care initiative seemed to be a perfect idea. Perhaps had it not been for this circumstantial similarity, the move to action might have taken more time. It has been noted that women have a desire to discuss the practical and social aspects of religion, including the impact their faith should have on others and the way they should live.[45] When deciding to serve the underprivileged, theology came second, while the needs of the individual and the desire to serve came first. This made this a more practitioner-level rather than scholar-level dialogue, where the purpose of faith is to apply the teachings rather than debate them. The women knew they were called to serve others, and the depth of the theology did not matter at the outset. This approach clearly was very beneficial to the people they served.

---

43. Farhoud, interview by Jaber.

44. Sweas, "Neighbor," 25.

45. O'Neill, *Women Speaking*, 53.

The way the Milwaukee Muslim–Catholic Healthcare Initiative approached the issue providing health care to low-income individuals was unique. It showed respect for the dignity of the individual, which is central to both faith traditions. The women organized health screenings in make-shift clinics set up in the basements of churches around the city. Everyone was welcome to come for a basic health care screening to have an assessment of their health care needs. A number of Muslim doctors had volunteered in the program. However, it was important for these doctors that the patients come to see them in their offices, develop relationships, and have ongoing health care visits. The patients who came in for an initial screening could subsequently be referred to any physician in the area of the patient's choice because each patient was issued an insurance card that would be acceptable in other places. This was to make sure they would not seem out of place, and no one would know they could not afford their own health care. According to Najeeb, this was to provide each of the individuals with dignity. Just because they lacked the means did not make them any less worthy of respect.[46] The results of the Healthcare Initiative, though it ended well over a decade ago in 2005, are still evident in the city today as some of those people are still seeing the very same physicians they were referred to years ago, still maintaining that relationship and seeking ongoing medical care.

The dignity of each human being, the idea that every individual has innate worth requiring that they receive respect and just treatment, is an important part of both the Muslim and Catholic faiths. A recent Catholic–Muslim Forum, held in Rome in November 2008, focused on the theme "Love of God, Love of Neighbour: The Dignity of the Human Person and Mutual Respect." There, Pope Benedict XVI gave a speech about the centrality of the dignity of the human person as something common to both religions. The participants at the meeting were able to "adopt a common position on the need to worship God totally and to love our fellow men and women disinterestedly, especially those in distress and need."[47] The forum, recognizing that the new relativistic society has devalued the individual and led to selfishness and greed, expressed the desire common to both faiths to recognize the goodness in all of God's creation, particularly in each person. Both faiths hold in common an explanation of the Golden Rule, the idea that we should treat others as we ourselves wish to be treated. Service to others is linked to the very core of both traditions. To

---

46. Najeeb, interview by Jaber.

47. Pope Benedict XVI, "Address to the Catholic–Muslim Forum," speech at Vatican's Clementine Hall, November 6, 2006.

serve means to believe in God and follow God, to deny those in needs means to deny God or to be condemned to hell. In Islam, this is present in the Qur'an:

> Have you seen one who denies the Day of Judgment?
>
> Who turns away the orphan,
>
> And who does not urge the feeding of the poor?
>
> So woe to those who pray,
>
> But whose hearts are not in their prayer.
>
> Those who do things only to be seen by others.
>
> Who are uncharitable even over very small things.
>
> (Qur'an 107: 1–7)[48]

For Christians, a very similar sentiment is present in Matthew 25, where Jesus separates people between those who would either enter heaven or hell. Those go to heaven, he says, fed "Him when He was hungry and gave Him drink when He was thirsty." Those going to eternal punishment did just the opposite. When they asked Jesus when they did these things, Jesus responded, "Whatever you did for one of these least brothers of mine, you did for me" (Matt. 25:40). The sacred texts in both religions impress the idea that helping those in need is integral to following God.

Inshirah Farhoud said, "I think . . . Allah orders us to be servants and he didn't say servant to Muslims, but servant to mankind."[49] The women of the dialogue understood the centrality of serving all those in need because it was a part of their lives. They felt a desire to serve and a desire to make others feel as though they had equal worth. They cared about the feelings and the insecurities of those they served because they deserve the same love, care, and sense of security that the more fortunate already enjoy. It has been suggested perhaps that women's greatest sin is being too selfless and giving too much. While that subject is certainly debatable, the women of the Muslim–Catholic Women's Dialogue in Milwaukee put those in need of health care ahead of their own desire to be heard and understood. They felt their role to serve others had more value than their need to be heard. They did not realize the unintended consequence of fellowship, which ultimately resulted in a tremendous service to the practice of dialogue as well as to the wider Milwaukee community.

---

48. Wahiduddin Khan, trans. *The Qur'an* (New Delhi: Goodword Books, 2009).

49. Farhoud, interview by Jaber.

Conclusion

It is impossible to fully grasp the impact of any group on an entire community, especially one that has evolved in so many ways as is the case with the Milwaukee Catholic–Muslim Women's Dialogue. What is clear is that thousands of people reaped the benefits of the work this group of women undertook, who had simply gathered to talk about their faith. Hundreds of people were exposed to the teachings of faith and had an opportunity to encounter a religious other and even to meet a person of different viewpoint within one's own faith tradition. The efforts of this group undoubtedly had a profound impact on the women involved. It changed their minds, their hearts, and their view of their faith and that of the other, and in turn some say that it changed their families' hearts as well.

AWARD RECIPIENTS

Frank Zeidler Award
Judith Longdin

For exceptional service since 1993 as an Interfaith Conference Cabinet member and officer, and as director of the Office of Ecumenical and Interfaith Concerns for the Archdiocese of Milwaukee – including assisting with the Conference's various educational and social programs, co-chairing the Catholic-Jewish Conference, co-founding the Muslim-Catholic Women's Dialogue and promoting dialogue and relationship building on the local, regional and national levels.

Figures 5.6 & 5.7: Judi Longdin at the 47th Annual ICGM Luncheon where she received the 2017 Frank Zeidler Award for her "exceptional service" in the interfaith community.

Women have a great deal to offer to interfaith dialogue based on their individual perspectives and approaches to life issues. Their life experiences give them a different vantage point, and their focus on relationships and care for the other makes their voice in faith invaluable, not to mention their theological and scholarly contributions that have historically been ignored. For the reasons discussed above, I believe there should be more dialogues that lift the voice of women. They may be women-only events or ones with a strong female presence. Women's ideas and approaches to faith must be accepted as integral and important, because the faith as found in holy texts is nothing if it is not lived and practiced and if it did not include the input from all of the faithful. Women's views and voices have an important place in interfaith dialogue. The Milwaukee Catholic–Muslim Women's Dialogue has shown the way of building relationships through friendship and service, which can have a deep and lasting impact upon individuals and the wider community.[50]

BIBLIOGRAPHY

Catholic–Muslim Women's Dialogue. *Open Dialogue: The Role of Women*. Flyer.

Cornille, Catherine. *Women and Interreligious Dialogue*. Eugene, OR: Cascade Books, 2013.

Fletcher, Jeannine Hill. *Motherhood as a Metaphor: Engendering Interreligious Dialogue*. New York: Fordham University Press, 2013.

Frederiks, Martha. "The Women's Interfaith Journey: Journeying as a Method in Interfaith Relations." *Missiology: An International Review* 4 (October 2012): 467–79.

Longdin, Judi. "Muslim-Catholic Women's Dialogue: Lessons from the Past and Future Prospects." Lecture presented at Marquette University, Milwaukee, WI, March 28, 2017.

---

50. The impact of the work of these women is fairly evident from the foregoing, however, it has not been acknowledged as generously and widely as it should. Nevertheless, Janan Najeeb and Judi Longdin have received numerous honors and awards for their leadership and service. Here I will mention one that is significant in light of the discussion thus far. Judi Longdin was recognized and honored with the 2017 "Frank Zeidler Award" by the Interfaith Conference of Greater Milwaukee (ICGM) at the 47th Annual Luncheon for her "exceptional service" in the interfaith community. See figs. 5.6 & 5.7.

Editors' Note: As this book is being prepared for the press, the Interfaith Conference announced that at their 49th Annual Luncheon on December 5th, the 2019 "Frank Zeidler Award" will be given to Janan Najeeb for being "one of the best known and most active advocates for interreligious understanding, tolerance, and friendship in Southeast Wisconsin" (from the invitation card). The journeys of these two women seem to mirror each other. They have been promoting mutual respect and interreligious cooperation for most of their professional lives; both have become influential leaders, and both have been recognized for their work by the interfaith community.

O'Neill, Maura. *Mending a Torn World: Women in Interreligious Dialogue.* Maryknoll: NY: Orbis Books, 2007.

———. *Women Speaking, Women Listening: Women in Interreligious Dialogue.* Maryknoll, NY: Orbis Books, 1990.

Pope Benedict XVI. "Address to the Catholic–Muslim Forum." Vatican's Clementine Hall, November 6, 2006.

The Qur'an. English translation by Wahiduddin Khan. New Delhi: Goodword Books, 2009.

Sweas, Megan. "Won't You Be My Neighbor?" *US Catholic*, February 2007.

Interviews

1. Atta, Intisar. Interview by Dianne Rostollan, Sundus Jaber, and Caroline Redick. March 24, 2017.

2. Farhoud, Inshirah. Interview by Sundus Jaber. March 14, 2017.

3. Longdin, Judi. Interview by Dianne Rostollan. March 14, 2017.

4. Najeeb, Janan. Interview by Sundus Jaber. April 18, 2017.

5. Schmitt, Bobbie. Interview by Dianne Rostollan. February 28, 2017.

Catholic–Muslim Women's Dialogue:

NOBLE THEMES, DIVERSE PARTICIPANTS

Sundus Jaber

Milwaukee, Wisconsin, is one of the few places in the United States with a history of Christian–Muslim dialogue. Additionally, it is one of the few places in which women from these Abrahamic faith traditions have participated in a sustained dialogue. It has been argued that there is a greater need for women's voices in interfaith dialogue to be recognized. In most of the early organized dialogues between Christians and Muslims, women's voices were noticeably absent.[1] The situation changed considerably in the 1990s and especially after the terrorist attacks in the United States in September 2001. After this event, both Christian and Muslim women activists began a serious conversation on matters of faith as well as social issues they faced. Despite an increase in numbers of women participating, their voices have rarely been allowed to be disseminated widely with respect to the role and impact of dialogue in their lives. Thus, this chapter seeks to showcase the Milwaukee women's dialogue in order to amplify the voices of these women.

The main purpose of this research is to document and call attention to the unique strengths and important contributions of these women to the field of interfaith dialogue. A secondary purpose of this research is to document the themes that were featured in the dialogues. The themes present in the dialogues include: *Social Justice, Faith-Building, Mary, Fellowship, "A Common Word,"* and *Youth Education*. The themes are an important component to consider in the history of dialogue, but the fact that the dialogue and interaction took place between Catholic and Muslim women is ever more significant. The

---

1. Ursula King, "Gender and Interreligious Dialogue," *East Asian Pastoral Review* 44, no. 1 (2007), http://www.eapi.org.ph/resources/eapr/east-asian-pastoral-review-2007/volume-44-2007-number-1/gender-and-interreligious-dialogue/.

women in this dialogue were drawn for reasons beyond the appeal of the theme. However, themes are important because they show what is relevant to these women practitioners. The dialogical models presented here as well as themes may be improved and replicated elsewhere. Writing about the history of women's dialogue will hopefully lead to a greater awareness of and balanced narratives regarding women's interfaith engagement and interactions that are more frequent and more cordial than we are led to believe through the usual channels of reporting. The dialogues covered here represent the voices of women, their religious experiences, and issues that they found to be important and relevant.

Recognizing Women's Voices

Academic literature, conference proceedings, and media regarding interfaith dialogue at first glance presents a reader with a plethora of the different interfaith experiences and points of view. However, upon closer investigation, a troubling trend becomes clear: the systematic "marginalization, invisibility, and exclusion of women wherever interreligious dialogue is happening at the official level."[2] This gap in the literature illustrates a failure to appreciate the experiences of women involved in interreligious dialogue and the chance to recognize the valuable implications of their contributions. According to the Columban Interreligious Dialogue, "The reality is that women are active in the whole of interreligious dialogue, probably more so than men, and probably more effectively than men! However, their voice and their participation are often screened out by patriarchal blinkering!"[3] Most, if not all, mainstream books and historical examples documenting interfaith dialogue and other related topics fail to include or mention women's contributions.[4] Ursula King similarly notes that "few writers on religious pluralism and interfaith dialogue refer to women at all."[5]

In addition, interfaith dialogue is often discussed and explored with an androcentric and patriarchal focus.[6] King states, "most dialogue practitioners, whether male or female, are unaware of the fact that interfaith dialogue still remains strongly embedded in the patriarchal structures of existing religions

---

2. Ibid.

3. Columban Interreligious Dialogue, "Interreligious Dialogue," 2015, http://columbanird. org/interreligious-dialogue/.

4. King, "Gender and Interreligious Dialogue."

5. Ibid.

6. Androcentrism is a practice where male examples and practices are understood as the norm.

and includes many exclusive sexist practices and deeply androcentric, male-centered ways of thinking."[7] However, we ought to separate sociocultural contexts from the "original" inclusive messages of religions, which may have been adulterated with androcentric practices that predated the religions themselves. It seems to be the case with Islam and Christianity as evidenced by the new readings of the sacred texts by scholars with an eye for inclusivism. Unfortunately, the limited representation of women in formal interfaith dialogues also contributes to the lack of topics related to women being explored in these discussions. Kate McCarthy notes how gender can often be a "regulating mechanism" in interfaith dialogue council and organization membership.[8] She cites how some religious groups may refuse to join any interfaith groups where female religious leaders or clergy are seen as legitimate.[9] In addition, women cannot be ordained leaders in some religious traditions, such as Roman Catholicism. So, positions on interfaith councils or boards reserved for clergy would not include women from those religions.[10] Thus, the problematic gender imbalance remains unchanged in those circumstances. Even when women do participate in these dialogues, it is still marginal in relation to the coverage that traditionally male religious leaders receive.[11]

Women's involvement in religious practices and interreligious dialogue is overshadowed by male religious leaders who perform most, if not all, public roles within the religious institution and who make up the majority of the representation of the religion.[12] Although women of faith often have active and strong connections between each other, the lack of public visibility, society's unquestioning adherence to cultural gender roles, and "theological collusion"[13] all contribute to the preservation of this status quo.[14] This lack of participation

---

7. King, "Gender and Interreligious Dialogue."

8. Kate McCarthy, *Interfaith Encounters in America* (New Brunswick, NJ: Rutgers University Press, 2007), 89.

9. Ibid., 90.

10. Ibid., 91.

11. Maura O'Neill, *Mending a Torn World: Women in Interreligious Dialogue* (Maryknoll, NY: Orbis Books, 2007).

12. Miriam Thérèse Winter, "Doing Effective Dialogue—and Loving It," *Journal of Ecumenical Studies* 43, no. 2 (2008): 31–32.

13. Theological collusion is the secret cooperation or conspiracy between religious figures toward a certain agenda.

14. Marshall, Katherine, et al., *Women in Religious Peacebuilding* (Washington, DC: United States Institute of Peace, 2011), http://www.usip.org/publications/women-in-religious-peacebuilding.

is unfortunate since women are usually the unofficial bearers of religious tradition, forming the majority of religious congregations. They also influence religious continuity by passing traditions onto the next generation. In addition, women pass down practices and values such as community service, peacemaking, and teaching. Furthermore, women are more likely than men to participate in forming relationships and friendships with women from other religious traditions.[15]

Many of the women involved in the Milwaukee Muslim–Catholic Women's Dialogue, such as Bobbie Schmitt, Naheed Arshad, and Sister Jessine Reiss, were not deeply cognizant of an inequality between male and female participation. They did not fully recognize the manifestation and impact of marginalization of women in interfaith dialogue and public representation of religion. This may have hindered them from fully appreciating the value of their narratives as women of faith in dialogue. The trend was to devalue the interfaith contributions made by women by referring to their meetings as merely social and casual exchanges. For example, Arshad in her comments implied that dialogue should include men.[16] Perhaps Arshad needs to recognize that men have historically dominated the field of interfaith dialogue and that the women's dialogue is trying to offer opportunities for women's voices to be documented. Farhoud seems to have been one of the only participants who understood the negative consequences of gender imbalance in any dialogue. She noted that often at more formal dialogues, which consisted of male academics, clergy, and theologians, she and Judi Longdin were the only women practitioners of the faiths present.[17] This was the extent of the participants' recognition of their unique contributions to a more gender-balanced representation in interfaith dialogue. These observations highlight the need to recognize women's unique impact on interfaith relations and create more avenues for participation in formal dialogue settings.

The Public Face of the Women's Dialogue

As noted in the chapter by Dianne Rostollan, the larger institutional dialogue set the stage for the present discussion. In this chapter, I will move beyond looking at institutions and focus on the participants in the Muslim–Catholic dialogue in Milwaukee and their unique contributions. Select Muslim women

---

15. Winter, "Doing Effective Dialogue—and Loving It," 30–31.

16. Naheed Arshad, interview by Sundus Jaber and Caroline Redick, May 24, 2017.

17. Inshirah Farhoud, interview by Dianne Rostollan and Sundus Jaber, March 14, 2017.

involved in the Muslim–Catholic dialogue included Janan Najeeb, Inshirah Farhoud, and Naheed Arshad. Select Catholic participants in the dialogue included Judi Longdin, Sister Jessine Reiss, Bobbie Schmitt, and Dr. Shawnee Daniels-Sykes. Together, Najeeb and Longdin helped found the Muslim–Catholic Women's Dialogue group that met once a month to discuss a topic of interest and to develop social bonds.

Participants

Janan Najeeb is a speaker, educator, business leader, activist, and the founder of a nonprofit, the Islamic Resource Center (IRC) in Milwaukee, Wisconsin. She became a pivotal member of the Muslim–Catholic Women's Dialogues after being raised in a family that involved itself in interreligious dialogues and relationships. Her mother, Intisar Atta, participated in the original Islamic–Christian dialogue in Milwaukee.[18]

Inshirah Farhoud has been an important Muslim member of the Women's Dialogue group. Her expertise as a pediatric primary care mental health specialist and a pediatric nurse practitioner helped guide the creation of the health care initiative that was mentioned in other chapters. Farhoud's deep involvement in the greater Milwaukee area includes her services to the Department of Health and Human Services' Minority Health Leadership Council, Wisconsin Public Health Council's State Health Plan Quality Improvement Committee, and the board of the Milwaukee Muslim Women's Coalition (MMWC), where she serves as vice president.[19]

Naheed Arshad is an accountant by training and has served the Milwaukee Muslim community by being a Sunday school administrator at the Salam Muslim school for 20 years. She was a participant in some of the Muslim–Catholic Women's Dialogues as well as in Muslim–Christian dialogues.[20]

Judi Longdin was a pivotal member and also worked closely with members of many other religious communities. Longdin became involved in dialogue while working at Gesu parish as the director of Social Ministry.[21] As she networked with others regarding social justice, she realized that while

---

18. Intisar Atta, interview by Dianne Rostollan, Sundus Jaber, and Caroline Redick, March 24, 2017.

19. Milwaukee Muslim Women's Coalition (MMWC) website: www.mmwconline.org/.

20. Arshad, interview by Sundus Jaber and Caroline Redick.

21. Judi Longdin, interview by Sundus Jaber, Dianne Rostollan, and Caroline Redick, March 14, 2017.

members of different religious groups could come together as allies for a short period to address social problems, it would be more beneficial for the whole community if these short-term alliances evolved into stable relationships. Since 1993, this realization continued to motivate her work as the director for the Office of Ecumenical and Interfaith Concerns for the Archdiocese of Milwaukee[22] and as a member of the board of directors for the Interfaith Conference of Greater Milwaukee.[23] This is how she began her involvement in the Muslim–Catholic dialogue.

Another important member, Sister Jessine, is a nun who worked for Cardinal Stritch University for 60 years[24] and, along with Sister Lucille Walsh, was also a founding member of the original Islamic–Christian dialogue in Milwaukee. While she was not involved in the establishment of the Women's Dialogue, she did occasionally participate in the events.[25]

Bobbie Schmitt, a writer and editor, frequently took part in the Muslim–Catholic Women's Dialogue fairly regularly.[26] She along with her husband, John Schmitt, have been ardent supporters and promoters of interfaith friendships and collaboration.

Dr. Shawnee Daniels-Sykes, a professor of theological ethics at Mount Mary University, has also attended a number of meetings. Thus, she described herself as an occasional participant in order to keep in touch with other women regarding outside interfaith opportunities and integrating lessons on interfaith understanding into her courses.[27]

These women came from different religious, ethnic, cultural, and professional backgrounds and found a common thread in their belief systems, which propelled them to work in teaching, advocacy, and health care for the benefit of the community at large. Along with the connections they built within the city, they also formed lasting relationships and friendships which truly model the dialogue of life.

---

22. Ibid.

23. Ibid.

24. Jean Merry, "18 Sisters Celebrate Jubilees of Profession," Sisters of St. Francis of Assisi, July 26, 2016. http://www.lakeosfs.org/news/18-sisters-celebrate-jubilees-of-profession/.

25. Scott Rudie, "Peacing Pioneers," *Stritch News*, October 8, 2012, https://www.stritch.edu/News/Stritch-Magazine/Sisters-of-St-Francis-of-Assisi/Peacing-Pioneers/; Jessine Reiss, interview by Irfan Omar and Caroline Redick, March 25, 2017.

26. John and Bobbie Schmitt, interview by Dianne Rostollan and Sundus Jaber, February 28, 2017.

27. Shawnee Daniels-Sykes, interview by Caroline Redick, May 16, 2017.

Events and Dialogues

The initial success of this dialogue became a catalyst for the women to organize public programs in the general community on similar topics. Najeeb cited how she and her parents' close relationships with the Catholic women, especially Judi Longdin, Sister Jessine, and Sister Lucille, allowed them to reach out to each other in the wake of 9/11 and organize programs to teach the community about Islam and combat the rise of Islamophobia (her main motivation for her public interfaith work).[28]

This small Muslim–Catholic Women's Dialogue group further evolved into a steering committee that collaborated with various colleges to host events with speakers and dialogue opportunities. One of their small-group formation sessions took place on April 14, 2005. Within this session, they discussed their goals as a dialogue group and their future plans (fig. 6.1). The Women's Dialogue group hosted events at several locations including Cardinal Stritch University, Alverno College, Marquette University, Islamic Society of Milwaukee, Lumen Christi Catholic Church, Sacred Heart Seminary, and Mount Mary College. These events, open to

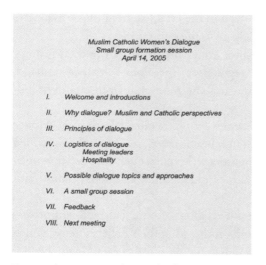

Figure 6.1: A typical agenda for small-group meetings.

men and women, began with a presentation by an expert and ended with round table discussions. In addition to these formal events, the Women's Dialogue group continued to organize informal meetings that were topically focused.

A major event titled, "A Time for Sisterhood," was hosted by the Sacred Heart School of Theology in 2007. The description was as follows:

> Throughout the centuries, in all cultures and religious traditions, great and holy women have modeled a profound spirituality characterized by grace and wisdom that has influenced generations after them. Come and hear about

---

28. Ibid.

these two women who, while from different cultures and different religious traditions, possessed the same gift . . . wisdom (fig. 6.2).

The event discussed the lives and contributions of Rabia Basri and Teresa of Avila through presentations by Janan Najeeb and Sister Mary C. Caroll, SSSF, a professor at the Sacred Heart School of Theology.

Sacred Heart School of Theology Presents

A Time for Sisterhood

Sunday, March 25, 2007
2:00 p.m.
Sacred Heart School of Theology

Throughout the centuries, in all cultures and religious traditions, great and holy women have modeled a profound spirituality characterized by grace and wisdom that has influenced generations after them. Come and hear about two of these women who, while from different cultures and different religious traditions, possessed the same gift...wisdom.

Wisdom Women

Rabia Basri   Teresa of Avila

Presenters
Janan Najeeb
Director of the Milwaukee Muslim Women's Coalition
Sr. Mary C. Caroll, SSSF
Professor of Systematics
Associate Director of Human and Spiritual Formation
Sacred Heart School of Theology

Sacred Heart School of Theology
7335 South Highway 100
Franklin, Wisconsin 53132
(Highway 100 and Rawson Avenue)

For reservations, contact Peg Boyles, director of public relations at Sacred Heart School of Theology.

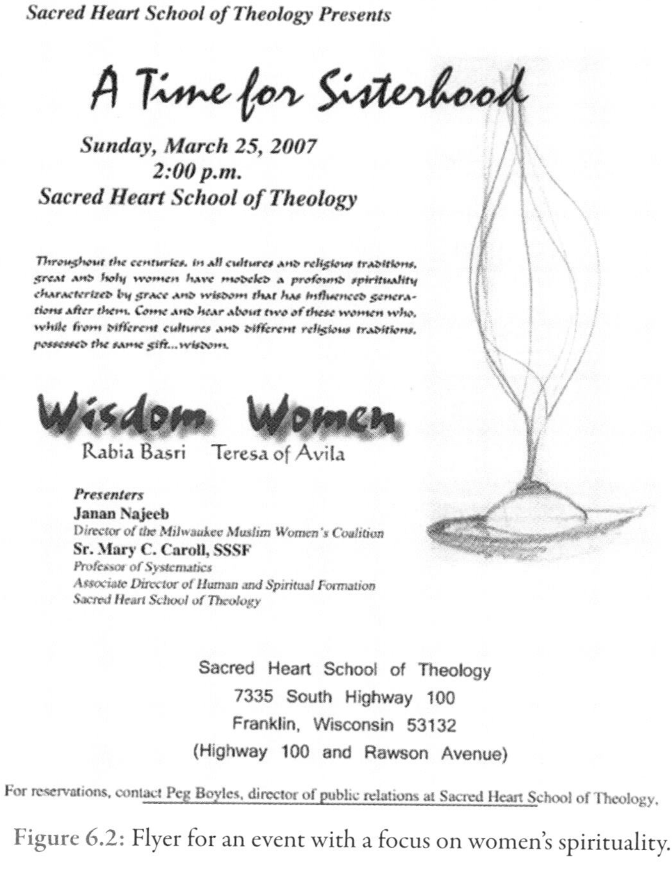

Figure 6.2: Flyer for an event with a focus on women's spirituality.

Another large event took place in the Archbishop Cousins Catholic Center on February 28, 2007, and was titled, "Muslim Catholic Relations: Local and Global Perspectives." It featured Rev. Thomas Michel, SJ, who spoke about the "current state of Muslim/Catholic affairs at the universal level," and Janan Najeeb, who presented on relations between Muslims and Christians in the local community. She shared some of the beliefs and practices of Muslims that

Christians ought to know about and also identified resources to foster greater understanding.

In 2007, an event titled "The Prophets: Muslim and Catholic Perspectives" was hosted by the dialogue at the Islamic Society of Milwaukee. In addition, smaller gatherings took place in 2007 and 2008 on topics deemed important to women in the dialogue. They explored roles and values of women of faith. The 2008 flyer reads:

> These sessions have been designed as a response to the desires expressed by members of both faiths to meet and learn more about one another in an informal atmosphere where relationships can be established and nurtured, where inquiry and openness to one another is seen as a path to knowledge (fig. 6.3).

This excerpt sets the tone for the kind of environment that was desirable for the women who participated in the smaller, open dialogue sessions. The topics for these smaller events included, "Religious Requirements for Modesty" and "The Holiest Places on Earth: Mecca, Jerusalem, Rome . . . ?" with alternating locations between a Catholic church and the Islamic Society of Milwaukee. These events were free and open to the public and were structured to include a brief overview of the topic by a host from each faith, followed by an opportunity for open dialogue.

These sessions have been designed as a response to the desires expressed by members of both faiths to meet and learn more about one another in an informal atmosphere where relationships can be established and nurtured, where inquiry and openness to one another is seen as a path to knowledge.

Each session will be held from 6:30PM-8:00PM. A brief overview of the topic, including Muslim and Catholic perspectives on the issue, will be offered followed by an opportunity for participants to engage in dialogue around the specified topic.

All events are free and open to the public. Pre-registration via email, longdinj@archmil.org, or phone, (414) 769-3483, will assist us in making appropriate room arrangements.

Figure 6.3: Flyers for smaller events or "open dialogue sessions" often included a rationale to help new participants become acquainted with the overall goals.

A similar event, "Understanding the Islamic Faith: Commonalities with Christianity and the Role of Women," was hosted by the School Sisters of St. Francis and was led by Janan Najeeb. In 2009, the group organized a panel and discussion titled, "A Common Word between Us and You," at the Islamic

The Muslim-Catholic Women's Dialogue Presents

"A Common Word between Us and You"

Thursday, May 21, 2009
Islamic Society of Milwaukee School
815 W. Layton Avenue
Milwaukee, WI
(Please note address: This is the new ISM Building, 5 blocks east of the ISM Center)

7:00-8:30PM

In 2007, 138 Muslim scholars representing every Muslim denomination and school of thought and every major Islamic country and region came together to sign an historic document: *A Common Word between Us and You*. The document is a statement from the Muslim community calling for interreligious dialogue around shared scriptural principles of love of God and love of neighbor.

Join with us as we explore the origins of the document, its significance from the Catholic and Muslim perspectives and the joys, challenges, and necessity of dialogue between Muslims and Christians.

Scott Alexander, Ph.D. **is Associate Professor of Islam and Director of the Catholic-Muslim Studies program at Catholic Theological Union in Chicago.**
His academic career has been dedicated to the study of Islam in the context of his broader training as an historian of religions. His teaching and research interests include medieval Muslim sectarianism, the mystical traditions of Muslim spirituality, Quranic studies, and the history and future of Muslim-Christian relations and interfaith dialogue. He is currently working on two projects, one as the co-editor of the *Cambridge Dictionary of Christian-Muslim Relations*, and the other as the author of a monograph entitled, "The Race to Goodness: an End to Triumphalism in Christian-Muslim Relations." Scott is a frequent speaker on Islam and Muslim-Catholic relations and a member of and contributor to numerous local, national and international interreligious dialogues and conversations.

Irfan A. Omar, Ph.D. **is Assistant Professor of Islam and World Religions in the Department of Theology at Marquette University in Milwaukee.** He received his Ph.D. in Religious studies from Temple University in 2001. He specializes in Islamic thought with a special focus on inter-religious connections between Islam and other religions. His secondary areas of interest are Islamic mysticism and South Asian Studies. He is the editor of *A Muslim View of Christianity: Essays on Dialogue by Mahmoud Ayoub* (Orbis, 2007) and *Islam and Other Religions: Pathways to Dialogue* (Routledge, 2006), and is currently working on a book on Islamic revivalism in India. In 2006, he received the US Fulbright Senior Scholar Award for lecturing in Indonesia. He is an Associate Editor of the Journal of Ecumenical Studies.

The event is free and open to the public and will take place in the new ISM School Building. The building is set back off the road. You will enter through a parking lot shared with a small strip mall. Drive behind the shops and you will see the larger building that houses the School.

The Muslim-Catholic Women's Dialogue is a program of the Milwaukee Muslim Women's Coalition and the Office of Ecumenical and Interfaith Concerns of the Archdiocese of Milwaukee. We seek to promote religious understanding and to build interfaith relationships. Programs are open to all women and men of good will. For more information call 414-769-3483, email: icepdej@archmil.org, or call the MMWC at 262-241-9522

Figure 6.4: Flyer for the event on "A Common Word."

Society of Milwaukee. The discussion was led by Scott Alexander, professor of Islam and the director of the Muslim–Catholic studies program at Catholic Theological Union in Chicago, and Irfan Omar, a professor of Islam and Interfaith studies at Marquette University (fig. 6.4). This program was designed to be educational for the community at large (Muslims and people from other backgrounds) as it included the history, meaning, and mission of this historic letter—an emphatic call for dialogue—issued by a group of Muslim religious leaders from around the world. Programs like this show that the Women's Dialogue group made a concerted effort to move the discussion from something between scholars to becoming more accessible to the general public.

The evidence for the group's continued efforts teaching the community about interfaith relations can be found in their event titled, "Islam, Muslims and the current Global Context: What US Catholics Need to Know," co-sponsored by Cardinal Stritch University, which also featured Dr. Scott Alexander. The goal of the event was "to address the current context of widespread misunderstanding and divisiveness, while presenting a framework for understanding Islam and Muslims within the current global and domestic context."[29] The event highlighted the fact that Catholic institutions of higher learning have a special role in helping "the Church fulfill her mission of dialogue, hope, and reconciliation within the human family."[30]

Later, the Milwaukee Muslim Women's Coalition collaborated with the Catholic–Muslim Women's Dialogue and Marquette University to present a program in 2012 titled, "A Catholic Priest Among Muslims: What I Have Learned and How One Man's Story Can Build Bridges." This event consisted of a keynote with Rev. Thomas Michel, SJ, followed by small-group dialogue sessions (fig. 6.5). The theme of the event was "Building Bridges Locally," and it was held at the Islamic Society of Milwaukee.

More than a decade after 9/11, the women continued to facilitate the coming together of two communities through interfaith dialogue, positive interactions, and lively discussions. It is interesting to note the timing of these events. These events among others took place before and increased after 9/11, which shows their actions were not just a reaction to one of the most notable tragedies in the United States, but they came from a sustained belief and increasing commitment to the importance for working toward interfaith relationships rooted

---

29. Muslim–Catholic Women's Dialogue and Cardinal Stitch University, *Islam, Muslims and the Current Global Context: What US Catholics Need to Know*, flyer supplied by Judi Longdin.

30. Ibid. For more on the role of education, see Daly's chapter in this volume.

The Milwaukee Muslim Women's Coalition is pleased to present a program of
The Muslim-Catholic Women's Dialogue in Collaboration with Marquette University

A Catholic Priest Among Muslims: What I have Learned
How One Man's Story Can Build Bridges
Lecture and Dialogue Session
Thursday, November 8, 2012
7:00pm – 9:00pm
Islamic Society of Milwaukee
4707 S. 13th Street

With Keynote Speaker
Rev. Thomas Michel, S.J., Ph.D.
Rev. Francis C. Wade Chair, Marquette University
Senior Research Fellow of Georgetown University
Woodstock Theological Center

Building Bridges Locally
Program will include responses from members
Of the Midwest Muslim-Catholic Dialogue Sponsored by
the Islamic Society of North America
And the United States Conference of Catholic Bishops
Followed by the Muslim evening prayer and small group dialogue

Reverend Thomas Michel, S.J., was ordained a Catholic priest of the St. Louis Archdiocese in 1967. He entered the Society of Jesus in Indonesia in 1969. Following Arabic and Islamic studies in Egypt and Lebanon, Fr. Michel received a doctorate in Islamic theology at the University of Chicago. In 1981 he was appointed to the Asia Desk of the Vatican Pontifical Council for Interreligious Dialogue, and in 1988 he became Head of the Office for Islam in the same Vatican department where he served for 13 years. Fr. Michel has also served as Secretary for Interreligious Dialogue for the Jesuits, based in Rome and as Ecumenical Secretary for the Federation of Asian Bishops conferences, based in Bangkok, Thailand. Following his time as an International Visiting Fellow at Woodstock in 2008-9, Fr. Michel left Georgetown to work together with the Jesuit community in Ankara, Turkey, the only Catholic community working in that city.

Fr. Michel serves in many national and international institutions and organizations. He has lived and worked with Muslims in many countries including Indonesia, Malaysia, the Philippines, and Turkey and is teaching in the theology department at Marquette in the fall, 2012, semester.

The Muslim-Catholic Women's' Dialogue, a program of the Milwaukee Muslim Women's Coalition and the Office of Ecumenical and Interfaith Concerns of the Archdiocese of Milwaukee was founded in 1997 to encourage joint dialogue and action. Programs are open to all.

MARQUETTE
UNIVERSITY
Be The Difference.

Milwaukee Muslim Women's Coalition

For More Information
Contact the MMWC
Phone # 414-727-4900

Figure 6.5: Flyer for a lecture by a renowned Jesuit scholar of Islam, Father Thomas Michel, SJ.

in love, understanding, and peace. They also collaborated to address Islamophobia in their events, speaking engagements, and workshops for educators, elected officials, religious leaders, and journalists. In this way, the participants of the Catholic–Muslim Women's Dialogue not only benefited and enriched their own lives through participating in interfaith conversations but used their experience to plan thought-provoking and necessary gatherings with speakers who would be viewed as credible, engaging, and relatable to both the Christian and Muslim audience members. The next section will highlight the specific themes that the Women's Dialogue explored and embodied during their development: *Social Justice, Faith-Building, Mary, Fellowship, "A Common Word,"* and *Youth Education.*

Themes Reflected in the Women's Dialogue

Social Justice: Faith through Compassionate Action

The women who were part of the Women's Dialogue were involved in community-building efforts—utilizing their specialized skills and connections to their respective community. As already noted, beginning in 1996, one of the main projects of the Women's Dialogue was the Islamic-Catholic Healthcare Initiative. It was described by Longdin, Farhoud, and others as a program in which basic health care screenings were conducted in church basements for any individuals in need within the surrounding area. A March 2000 press release by Najeeb and Longdin titled, "Free Health Care Screening and Wellness Lecture on Hypertension for Milwaukee County Residents" first announced this initiative. The invitation was open to all those in need, without preconditions, to come to public places like the Bay View Community Center and the Holy Trinity Church for free health screenings. The press release noted that these services were "offered by the Islamic–Catholic Health Care Initiative, a group of Muslim and Catholic women working together in the service of the community" (fig. 6.6). After the screenings, patients would be referred to further services from local Muslim doctors, with a replica insurance card valid for six months from their initial health screening. This was done to protect patients from feeling the stigma of being uninsured. Some of these patients continued to see these same doctors for many years even after the official program was discontinued.[31]

---

31. The official initiative was later discontinued because of logistical issues. Longdin, interview by Jaber, Rostollan, and Redick.

MEDIA RELEASE

CONTACT:
Janan Najeeb, Milwaukee Muslim Women's Coalition
241-9862 (home)
Judith Longdin, Ecumenical/Interfaith Office
769-3483

FOR IMMEDIATE RELEASE

March, 2000

FREE HEALTH CARE SCREENING AND WELLNESS LECTURE ON HYPERTENSION FOR MILWAUKEE COUNTY RESIDENTS

MILWAUKEE--A free health care screening and lecture on handling hypertension will be held on Saturday, April 1, at BayView Community Center, 1320 E. Oklahoma Avenue, Bayview. Screenings will be held from 10:00am-2:00pm. No appointment is necessary. The lecture will be held at noon. The screening and lecture are free and open to the public.

Health screenings, offered by the Islamic-Catholic Health Care Initiative, a group of Muslim and Catholic women working together in service to the community, will include a health history and a blood pressure check. No medical treatment will be available on site but physician referrals will be made for those who need medical follow-up and have no access to medical resources. Doctors cooperating with the Initiative will see uninsured and underinsured patients free for a six-month period.

Future screenings for the first Saturday of each month from 10a.m. to 2:00 p.m. are scheduled at the following locations:

May 6	The Women and Children Project, 4th & Brown
June 3	Holy Trinity-Our Lady of Guadalupe, 613 S. 4th Street
July 1	St. Mary Czestochowa, 3055 N. Fratney Street

Please contact the Ecumenical/Interfaith Office of the Archdiocese of Milwaukee at 769-3483 or the Milwaukee Muslim Women's Coalition at 964-6692 for more information. Health care professionals who are interested in volunteering should also call one of the above numbers.

Figure 6.6: Press release announcing the launch of the Islamic–Catholic Healthcare Initiative.

Farhoud recalled her work for the Healthcare Initiative as one of her best memories of the Women's Dialogue. She reminisced, "I really enjoyed [the health care initiative] a lot and I was a public health nurse, so I was really familiar with the community needs. . . . I felt comfortable doing it no matter where we went and my purpose was to get people healthier and to help people learn better health and do it in collaboration with the Catholic sisters."[32] Farhoud

---

32. Farhoud, interview by Rostollan and Jaber.

displays a similar attitude when she states, "I think from my experience, even with the Catholic sisters, is that the sisters get the work done . . . so the goal [of the women's interfaith dialogue] is really to have women involved and to be seen as active participants in the community."[33] Additionally, the participants agreed that their focus on compassionate action and social justice, specifically preserving lives and health, is a mandate in both Islam and Christianity.[34] These women deliberately linked their religious teachings of social justice with their actions. This was not only helpful to them in educating themselves and each other, but it also demonstrated to the general public that there are shared values between religions and that collaboration brings out the best in everyone. As compassionate practitioners of the religions, instead of simply discussing their respective religion's value for life at a conference, the women were committed to action and pooled their local resources because they saw a need in their communities. Farhoud adds, "I think the most is that Allah orders us to be servants and he didn't say servants to Muslims, but servant to mankind, so that's really my role to help in any way I can."[35]

Faith-Building

The interreligious cooperation and relationships mentioned here assisted the women in learning how to become better practitioners of their respective faiths. In the words of Sister Jessine, "As a result of our involvement with the Muslims, we learned to become better Christians in a way . . . I think with Muslims; their life is in sync with their religion. They give the priority to prayer that should be given to it."[36] Daniels-Sykes reiterated this when asked if interfaith dialogue had a personal impact on her. She stated, "Definitely . . . I like the intentionality of prayer. Here at the college we have two chapels and they're hardly ever filled. Our Muslim students are a real role model."[37] Farhoud's

---

33. Ibid.

34. This mandate is summarized in the Qur'an within the verse, "If anyone saved a life, it would be as if he saved the life of all mankind" (Qur'an 5:32) (*The Meaning of the Glorious Qur'an*, trans. M. M. Pickthall [Amana Publications, 1996]). The same message can be seen in Matthew 25:39-40, "When did we see you sick or in prison and go to visit you?' The King will reply, 'Truly I tell you, whatever you did for one of the least of these brothers and sisters of mine, you did for me" (NIV).

35. Farhoud, interview by Dianne Rostollan and Sundus Jaber.

36. Sister Jessine Reiss, OSF, interview by Irfan Omar and Caroline Redick, March 25, 2017.

37. Daniels-Sykes, interview by Redick.

experience was similar, "The more I learned about Catholicism, the more I went back and said: what does Islam say and how can I apply that? So really, it's nice to learn what the other faith tradition teaches about the same issues."[38] Najeeb also mentioned having similar feelings in her interview, describing how exploring Christianity with her Catholic sisters helped renew her curiosity and made her feel more responsible to learn more about her own tradition as well as other traditions. When asked about how her involvement in these dialogues had impacted her personally, Najeeb stated that it has made her a stronger and more capable Muslim. She said, "It's easy to live unchallenged in your faith by not interacting with others, but you gain so much by meeting with others and answering their questions and going out to find answers when they ask you about stuff you don't know."[39] None of the women mentioned any negative aspect of participating in the dialogues. There was only a collective feeling of love and appreciation from the women toward their partners in dialogue that only develops after years of intentional cooperation, shared values, and deep friendships.

Mary: A Role Model for the Women in Dialogue

One theme throughout the dialogues was a common role model found in Mary, the mother of Jesus. Mary is seen as a "hermeneutical tool for Catholic Muslim dialogue"[40] in general because of her value for both Christians and Muslims. The Catholic document from the Vatican II council, *Nostra Aetate*, emphasizes what both religions share: "The Church regards with esteem also the Moslems . . . They also honor Mary, [Christ's] virgin Mother; at times they even call on her with devotion."[41] Mary was a common unifier in the history of the Women's Dialogues in Milwaukee. For example, Janan Najeeb recalls a dialogue that took place regarding the Virgin Mary that attracted several hundred people.[42] The event, "Mary/Mariam . . . A Woman for All Times: Catholic and Islamic Perspectives," was sponsored by Alverno College Campus Ministry and the Muslim–Catholic Women's Dialogue and took place on September 11, 2004 (fig. 6.7). She observed, "The Muslim view of Mary surprised most Christians in attendance. Many did not know how close Muslims were to

---

38. Farhoud, interview by Dianne Rostollan and Sundus Jaber.

39. Janan Najeeb, interview by Sundus Jaber, April 18, 2017.

40. Bahar Davary, "Mary in Islam," *New Theology Review* 23, no. 3 (2010): 26–27.

41. Pope Paul VI, *Nostra Aetate*, October 28, 1965, 3.

42. Najeeb, interview by Sundus Jaber.

Mary, that Islam embraces the Virgin Birth, and the fact that there is an entire chapter devoted to her in the Quran. It was a tremendous eye opener for so many people because of the close emotional ties [both faiths] have to Mary."[43] Naheed Arshad also iterates this point, discussing how Catholic participants and audiences were consistently surprised by the honor and respect Islam and Muslims have toward Mary and Jesus whenever they were a topic of discussion during the dialogue.[44]

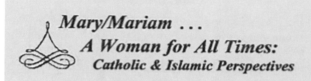

Mary/Mariam ...
A Woman for All Times:
Catholic & Islamic Perspectives

Alverno College
Teaching, Learning and Technology Center
3400 South 43rd Street
Milwaukee, WI 53234
Saturday
September 11, 2004
9:30am–2:00pm

Sponsored by
the Muslim-Catholic Women's Dialogue of
Milwaukee
And Alverno College Campus Ministry

The Muslim-Catholic Women's dialogue is sponsored by the Milwaukee Muslim Women's Coalition and the Office of Ecumenical and Interfaith Concerns of the Archdiocese of Milwaukee. Founded in 1997, the dialogue seeks to bring Muslim and Catholic women together to promote interfaith awareness and action.

Figure 6.7: Flyer for one of the most well-attended and well-liked events on Mary/Maryam, held at Alverno College.

---

43. Rudie, "Peacing Pioneers."

44. Arshad, interview by Sundus Jaber and Caroline Redick.

One event that discussed the overlap between the religious traditions' views of Mary in her relationship to Jesus was sponsored by the Women's Dialogue and Mount Mary College, titled "Jesus: Muslim and Catholic Perspectives," and took place on September 9, 2006. While a precursor to the Muslim–Catholic Women's Dialogue, a popular prayer service took place at Deaconess Hospital in Wisconsin on December 10, 1982.[45] According to Sister Jessine, both Christians and Muslims participated; she went on to say, "We drew a hundred outside members at that point. And we had one of the Muslims . . . who read the story of the birth of Jesus from the Qur'an. First, it was the birth of Jesus from Luke, and then from the Qur'an. So, it was first read in Arabic, and then in English. And we had other prayers that went along with that."[46]

A cross-generational and cultural connection formed between many of the women when they spoke about Mary, which shows the timeless value of her as a unifier between women of faith. With the common theme of respect toward Mary and other figures and sages from these Abrahamic religions, the women began to draw many parallels between their beliefs and grew more comfortable and trusting toward each other in the process.

Fellowship: The Bonds of Sisterhood

Based on their shared vision of Mary and other later meetings and discussions on their common values, these women built a sisterly bond. This is unique in that the majority of their interactions were not formal dialogues; they were informal gatherings that took place in homes and small offices. This supports the idea that "women, different from men, prefer an existential and experiential approach to interfaith relations rather than a cognitive one."[47] These small and more casual meetings allowed for the women to get to know each other on a personal level. For example, Longdin happily recalled the occasion where she invited a group of Muslim women to dinner at her house during the Advent season. After being asked about her missing Christmas tree by a Muslim friend, she realized how "authentic dialogue gives people license to ask questions" and then went ahead to describe the meaning of Advent season. In her opinion,

---

45. Reiss, interview by Irfan Omar and Caroline Redick.

46. Ibid.

47. Martha Frederiks, "The Women's Interfaith Journey: Journeying as a Method in Interfaith Relations," *Missiology: An International Review* 40 (October 1, 2012): 469. Frederiks is citing Diane d'Souza, "Some Reflections on Women Doing Interfaith," *Jahrbuch für Kontextuelle Theologien* (2000): 101–9.

when it comes to interfaith dialogue it is "the small things" that makes a difference and helps to reshape opinions.[48]

Sister Jessine and Intisar Atta would agree, since one intimate moment they both cherish is when the Attas hosted the Catholic sisters, Jessine and Lucille, for Christmas dinner by surprise one year when they did not have any plans on Christmas.[49] Intisar Atta also related how the regularity of exchanging holiday cards alerted her to check on her friends one year when she did not receive a card—to behold that her friend was seriously ill.[50] Besides Christmas and Easter, the women would also socialize on different occasions, such as when the Catholic sisters celebrated the birth of Najeeb's children with her family.[51] There is significant value to the Catholic and Muslim women's sharing of personal stories and experiences with each other, which is often not found in formal, "academic"-style interfaith dialogues. As a method of interfaith encounter, "this avoids the pitfall of making unfounded generalizations about another religion as a whole and helps to ground the discussion in lived reality."[52] This helped women become more comfortable with one another and consequently motivated them to continue to cooperate with each other for the common good.

"A Common Word"

A practical theme of the Women's Dialogue was the common agreement that no one was there to proselytize. This allowed the women to speak freely, not feel defensive over their beliefs, and be open to the ideas of others. Sister Jessine recalled how one should "never attempt to proselytize. Listen. Listen and the outcome should be respect for whoever is discussing."[53] Inshirah Farhoud spoke along the same vein, saying, "I'm not there to convert them, they are not there to convert me. We are really there to find a mutual benefit to the community."[54]

---

48. Longdin, interview by Jaber, Rostollan, and Redick.

49. Reiss, interview by Omar and Redick; Atta, interview by Rostollan, Jaber, and Redick.

50. Atta, interview by Rostollan, Jaber, and Redick.

51. Najeeb, interview by Jaber.

52. Ruth N. M. Tetlow, "The Missing Dimension: Women and Inter Faith Encounter in Birmingham" (Ph.D. diss., University of Birmingham, 2004), 1–5.

53. Reiss, interview by Omar and Redick.

54. Farhoud, interview by Rostollan and Jaber.

The notion of mutual respect was a theme parallel to ideas that guided the conversation around the letter, "A Common Word." In 2007, initially, 138 Muslim scholars and leaders signed an open letter to the Pope titled, "A Common Word," which called for a respectful dialogue between members of the two religions and the world at large.[55] It reminded its readers of the common ground that members of both faiths share as stated in their respective scriptures: love of God, and love of neighbor.[56] Lastly, it encouraged readers to forget all "hatred and strife" and take this common ground to use as a foundation for future interfaith relationship building.[57] The letter called for a shift from interfaith dialogue being characterized as "a polite ecumenical dialogue between selected religious leaders" and instead advised members and leaders from every level of the community to work together and strengthen the relations between Christians and Muslims in their locality.[58] While this is a tremendous task, the letter reminded readers that it is the responsibility of all to make every effort for peace because the future of the world is dependent on it.[59]

The women involved in the Muslim–Catholic dialogues are a shining example of interactions embodying the mission of the document "A Common Word." They not only created relationships between each other grounded in love of God and love of neighbor, but they encouraged their greater communities to do this as well. The connection between accepting each other and building strong relationships to then beginning to work together for the common good became apparent to these women which helped nurture their relationships far beyond any specific projects.

Youth Education

As mentioned in earlier chapters, the original dialogue efforts included the work of writing to school textbook editors regarding misconceptions, inaccuracies, and omissions of Islam and Christianity in school textbooks for children. One of the most important next steps in the future progress of Muslim–Christian

---

55. Ghazi bin Muhammad, "On 'A Common Word between Us and You,'" in *A Common Word: Muslims and Christians on Loving God and Neighbor*, eds. Miroslav Volf, Ghazi bin Muhammad, and Melissa Yarrington (Grand Rapids, MI: Eerdmans, 2010), 3.

56. Ibid., 8.

57. Miroslav Volf, et al., "Loving God and Neighbor Together: A Christian Response to 'A Common Word Between Us and You," in *A Common Word*, 55.

58. Ibid.

59. Ibid., 55–56.

dialogue work is to make sure that textbooks, especially those intended for religious instruction, do not carry "material that is unacceptable to either."[60] This helps ensure children grow up without misinformation and bias against members of other faiths.

The Muslim–Catholic Women's Dialogue also contributed to education through a more direct approach toward increasing interfaith understanding between high school and university-age youth. Arshad mentions how, as an Islamic Sunday school administrator, she focused on making the children literate in their own religious beliefs and placed a focus on current events in the curriculum so that the children would feel more comfortable and secure in their identities when among people of other faiths. She continued:

> For example, my children weren't part of the dialogue, they still made their presence felt at the schools they went, whether it's during the month of fasting or celebrating a holiday. They are always called upon to give opinions related to our religion (Islam). So even if they were not part of a titled dialogue, I think that for the kids who were well informed and went to the Sunday school or who had parents that were involved [for such children], the dialogue has been ongoing in their schools [without a label].[61]

Farhoud had been involved with the Milwaukee Area Interfaith Youth Café hosted by the Cardinal Stritch University Leadership Center and Tomorrow's Present. It started in 2011 and has expanded since then to include involvement of St. Boniface Episcopal Church, First Unitarian Society, Islamic Society of Milwaukee, Beth El Tamid Synagogue, and support from the Milwaukee Muslim Women's Coalition. The intention behind these events was described in the mission for the program:

> To give young people from different religious traditions an opportunity to gather together and share their faith, talk about issues important to youth and to develop relationships. By fostering dialogue and mutual understanding we hope to reduce conflict, eliminate stereotypes and promote peaceful relationships among all people (fig. 6.8).

In addition, the Milwaukee Muslim Women's Coalition partnered with Alverno Women's College to regularly bring students into the Islamic Resource

---

60. Stuart E. Brown, *Meeting in Faith: Twenty Years of Christian-Muslim Conversations Sponsored by the World Council of Churches* (Geneva, World Council of Churches, 1989), 89.

61. Arshad, interview by Jaber and Redick.

Center to learn about Islam, Muslims in Milwaukee, and socialize with Muslim women and girls. With the direction of Janan Najeeb and Inshirah Farhoud, similar events including both high school age boys and girls from Muslim and majority Christian backgrounds are conducted at the Islamic Society of Milwaukee since it has a larger capacity than the Islamic Resource Center.

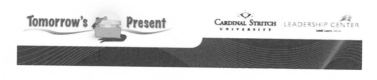

Milwaukee Area Interfaith Youth Café 2011-2012

All Café events take place on Sunday afternoons from 12:30 – 3:30 PM.

Our Mission
To give young people from different religious traditions an opportunity to gather together and share their faith, talk about issues important to youth and to develop relationships. By fostering dialogue and mutual understanding we hope to reduce conflict, eliminate stereotypes and promote peaceful relationships among all people.

To Register
Because space is limited, please register by contacting Sean Lansing, Director of Tomorrow's Present at (414) 410-4583.

2011-2012 Schedule

October 30, 2011
Our Host: St. Boniface Episcopal Church
3906 Mequon Rd. Mequon, WI

December 11, 2011
Our Host: First Unitarian Society
1342 Astor St. Milwaukee, WI

March 25, 2012
Our Host: Islamic Society of Milwaukee
4707 S. 13th St. Milwaukee, WI

May 6, 2012
Our Host: Beth El Tamid Synagogue
2909 W. Mequon Rd. Mequon, WI

Figure 6.8: Flyer for the Youth Café events.

Shawnee Daniels-Sykes of Mount Mary University, and occasional participant in the women's dialogues, mentioned how she incorporates interfaith real-world issues into her classroom to help break the misconceptions that may make students resistant to dialogue. She explained, "My challenges revolve around education. There's a lot of religious prejudice out there. And it's always disheartening to me. So, those are my challenges and the fear is pervasive and I don't quite understand how such prejudice could be among young people. They are too young to be thinking like that."[62] She goes on to say, "What has helped me the most is to get under the fear of Islam. So, this semester as I teach, we talked about the travel ban. And the vetting process. . . . I wanted them to know that our fear, our Islamophobia, stems from a misunderstanding of ISIS, comparing that to what Islam represents."[63]

Figure 6.9: Youth Café event at the Quaker Meeting House in Milwaukee.

When asked if she had any advice for youth who want to start being involved with interfaith dialogue, Daniels-Sykes said, "Try to find a good advisor. Have the opportunity to talk. If there is someone in your class who is Muslim, ask [them] if that is a possibility. . . . See if someone who is interested in that kind of dialogue could maybe visit the Islamic center or a mosque."[64] Visiting other places of worship than one's own to forge a positive relationship is nothing new, but it is on the rise. There is something comforting about the hospitality in visiting someone's home that makes it easier to ask questions and become more active in participating within casual interfaith dialogue.

---

62. Daniels-Sykes, interview by Redick.

63. Ibid.

64. Ibid.

According to Liyakat Takim, "since September 2001, various Islamic centers have facilitated 'open house' events and have tried to become more 'people friendly' by encouraging their non-Muslim neighbors to visit the mosques."[65] While the mosques and Islamic Resource Center in the Milwaukee area had been giving tours to visitors since at least 2001, in 2013, the Milwaukee Muslim Women's Coalition and Islamic Society of Milwaukee also began a tradition of participating in an annual citywide event called "Open Doors Milwaukee," where visitors can come during designated hours without an appointment to get acquainted with the faith, the institution, and its history by interacting with community members. Arshad noted how an event like this became a great way for youth to interact with visitors and experience the value of dialogue. She cited how visitors felt more comfortable asking what they thought were "stupid" or basic questions to the youth, while they were often hesitant asking them with an adult.[66] This resulted in the mosque deciding to train many more youth, especially young women, to give tours and learn to be respectful participants in interacting across religious difference.[67]

The anonymous feedback from the event was often encouraging. One person stated, "very open and upfront. I always wanted to see what it was like and now I do understand about a few things, it was great. Thank you and the food was wonderful."[68] Another comment read, "I was impressed by how welcoming the people I interacted with were. I think ISM is a great contribution to the greater Milwaukee community."[69]

Najeeb recommends that youth and others interested in interfaith dialogue should, if possible, find an older, more experienced facilitator and start their own group of participants, rather than just join an established dialogue group.[70] She believes that it is time-consuming and even redundant to have the entire group in an established dialogue group to interrupt their progress every time a new member joins to bring him or her up to speed on the guidelines, goals, and basic information regarding the different traditions present. Instead, an experienced member or two should coordinate new dialogue groups where

---

65. Liyakat Takim, "From Conversion to Conversation: Interfaith Dialogue in Post 9-11 America," *The Muslim World* 94 (2004): 343–55.

66. Arshad, interview by Jaber and Redick.

67. Ibid.

68. Islamic Society of Milwaukee, website: www.ismonline.org.

69. Ibid.

70. Najeeb, interview by Jaber.

most attendees would be new.[71] Starting their own grassroots group would be a more rewarding experience because they would all begin the new journey together. This would, over time, increase local interfaith understanding exponentially as new groups of people form under the guidance of facilitators who are actively passing down the knowledge to new ears. By bringing these topics to the forefront of the community, we can see these women did their part to shift the meaning of interfaith dialogue from "a polite ecumenical dialogue between selected religious leaders"[72] and to use their unique voices as women from different religious backgrounds to strengthen the relations between Christians and Muslims in their locality through organizing events and discussions.

Challenges and Limitations

Some of the limitations I noticed in this research include the characteristics of access and status. Most of the women who participated in the dialogues had access to higher education and were generally from the middle and upper socioeconomic backgrounds. All but one of the participants mentioned here came from either a Caucasian or Middle Eastern background. In addition, the Sunni Muslim perspective was the dominant representation of all of the Muslim women and the content they focused on and/or presented in the dialogues. This is a problematic aspect because it shows an uneven learning of the other. Christians who were exposed to these Muslims had learned about a single denominational and, in this case, also a regional perspective. The broader Muslim perspective and the voices of Muslims from other regions or denominations were not part of the mix.

Najeeb mentioned how early on Christians of other denominations became frustrated with the Catholic members speaking on behalf of all Christians, which led to them feeling alienated during discussions and discontinuing participation in the dialogues.[73] At that point the title was adjusted from Christian–Muslim Dialogue to Catholic–Muslim Dialogue. While no Muslims of other denominations may have been present, the same issue essentially presented itself during the dialogues where Sunni Muslim women's interpretations of Islam were presented on behalf of all Muslim women and Islam as a whole.

A reason for the lack of diversity among the dialogue participants may stem from the fact that women from lower socioeconomic status and educational

---

71. Ibid.

72. Miroslav Volf, et al., "Loving God and Neighbor Together . . . ," in *A Common Word*, 55.

73. Najeeb, interview by Jaber.

levels were not explicitly invited or considered. The social privilege of the original participants of the dialogue may have played a role in who else would have access to the dialogues and who would set the agenda. Further, there may have also been an uneven distribution of institutional support and formal experience within interfaith organizing. It was mentioned that while most of the Catholic women who participated had the backing of their religious institutions, like Sister Jessine and Judi Longdin, the Muslim women did not have the mandate of a religious leader and worked independently of involvement or influence from a religious institution. However, Muslim women may have had more leeway in the content they chose for the dialogues and events and how they answered questions compared to the Catholic women. Inshirah mentioned that some of the Catholic women who did have the mandate to speak on behalf of their religious institution still had to consult authorities within the hierarchy of the Church for their opinions and approval.[74] They also had to document their interactions with the interfaith community as well, while the Muslim women did not do either.[75] This meant that the Muslim women did not have the opportunity to interact with institutional scholars. They also had no training or formal instruction regarding their own religion or interfaith dialogue per se.

Apart from the Healthcare Initiative, most of the Catholic–Muslim Women's Dialogue events did not cater to non-English-proficient community members, which included first-generation women or immigrants who would have benefitted from the interactions. In addition, there was not any specific programming developed for elementary- through middle school–aged children and their families. While their efforts to promote interfaith collaboration and understanding are valuable, it is essential to recognize the unique value women can have in passing down lessons in compassion and understanding in young children from all backgrounds and religious traditions.

It would have been beneficial if this group of women used their partnership to publicly advocate for issues that have a greater impact on women's and children's lives in Milwaukee and around the country, such as domestic abuse, rape, or human trafficking. The data suggest that every nine seconds a woman is assaulted or beaten in the United States.[76] It is an issue that impacts

---

74. Farhoud, interview by Rostollan and Jaber.

75. Ibid.

76. Ronet Bachman and Linda Saltzman, "Violence against Women: Estimates from the Redesigned Survey," National Crime Victimization Survey, Bureau of Justice Statistics, Special Report. US Department of Justice, August 1, 1995. Online source available at http://www.bjs.gov/content/pub/pdf/FEMVIED.PDF.

all women and men from all backgrounds and would have been a unique and substantial topic to address from an interfaith perspective. I can only speculate to say that maybe the topic was never pursued because it did not personally affect the women in the dialogue, or they felt it would be controversial for their specific audience, or that they feared it would "play into the stereotypes" of the "oppressed Muslim woman" imagery in media and public discourse—at the cost of addressing issues that impact millions of women and children.[77]

Figure 6.10: Naheed Arshad making a comment at one of the public events.

Conclusion

Milwaukee, Wisconsin, has seen some intense engagement in the form of a friendly and collaborative, often praxis-oriented Catholic–Muslim Women's Dialogue. It was a dialogue between the women of the two Abrahamic faith traditions who are rooted in their respective faith traditions and yet strove to reach out to a religious other. In the words of Ingrid Mattson, a noted scholar of Islam and interfaith dialogue in North America:

> Interfaith engagement has helped create meaningful relationships that are scripturally grounded and form the basis for our ethical action. These

---

77. Some women in the dialogue group routinely participate in public forums and push the boundaries of engagement to higher levels. Naheed Arshad is involved in all sorts of social justice issues independent of the dialogue group. See fig 6.10.

relationships are both a means for me personally to increase my mindfulness of God . . . [and] a means to engage in the good works which we are commanded to undertake. All of this furthers the cause of peace."[78]

Similarly, the participants of this dialogue exhibited the same zeal and found the same contentment in their interfaith relationships and the subsequent cooperative work for social justice and community peacebuilding.

One of the goals of this research is to remind all that more work needs to be done to be truly inclusive and to bring together the insights of both women and men for the betterment of society. As D'Souza and Edwards noted, when "women become full partners, the interreligious dialogue will change so much that what is now going on will be regarded as only an insufficient and misleading beginning."[79] The solution lies in "standing up to those whose God is too small, too mean, too tribal, and too male."[80] Male religious leaders and institutions, especially, should continue to encourage and make space for women to go into careers and to make their contributions more visible. It is also important to invest more time and energy into rereading religious texts from a more inclusive and compassionate point of view, while challenging patriarchal viewpoints and cultural practices that threaten equality at both the academic and community levels. Specific efforts should be made to include more women participants in dialogues and meetings, and this effort should be endorsed by both Christian and Muslim organizations, especially at the leadership level.

Bibliography

Bachman, Ronet, and Linda Saltzman. "Violence against Women: Estimates from the Redesigned Survey." *Bureau of Justice Statistics Special Report US Department of Justice Office of Justice Programs: National Crime Victimization Survey*, August 1, 1995.

Brown, Stuart. *Meeting in Faith: Twenty Years of Christian-Muslim Conversations Sponsored by the World Council of Churches*. Geneva: World Council of Churches, 1989.

---

78. Ingrid Mattson, "Of Fences and Neighbors: A Muslim Perspective on Interfaith Engagement for Peace," August 18, 2013.

79. Diane d'Souza and Danielle Edwards, "The Women's Interfaith Journey. A Report from the 1998–1999 Women's Interfaith Journey Conducted in India and Canada," quoted in Frederiks, "The Women's Interfaith Journey," 469.

80. Omid Safi, "Introduction: The Times They Are a Changing—A Muslim Quest for Justice, Gender Equality, and Pluralism," in *Muslim Progressive on Justice, Gender and Pluralism*, ed. Omid Safi (Oxford: Oneworld, 2003).

Columban Interreligious Dialogue. "Interreligious Dialogue." *Columban Interreligious Dialogue* (blog). 2015. http://columbanird.org/interreligious-dialogue/.

Davary, Bahar. "Mary in Islam: 'No Man Could Have Been Like This Woman.'" *New Theology Review* 23, no. 3 (2010): 26–34.

d'Souza, Diane. "Some Reflections on Women Doing Interfaith." *Jahrbuch für Kontextuelle Theologien* (2000): 101–109.

d'Souza, Diane, and Danielle Edwards, "The Women's Interfaith Journey. A Report from the 1998–1999 Women's Interfaith Journey Conducted in India and Canada." Hyderabad, India: Henry Martyn Institute, 1999.

Frederiks, Martha. "The Women's Interfaith Journey: Journeying as a Method in Interfaith Relations." *Missiology: An International Review* 40 (October 1, 2012): 467–79. https://doi.org/10.1177/009182961204000407.

Islamic Society of Milwaukee. "Islamic Society of Milwaukee." July 14, 2017. www.ismonline.org.

King, Ursula. "Gender and Interreligious Dialogue." *East Asian Pastoral Review* 44, no. 1 (2007). http://www.eapi.org.ph/resources/eapr/east-asian-pastoral-review-2007/volume-44-2007-number-1/gender-and-interreligious-dialogue/.

Marshall, Katherine, et al. *Women in Religious Peacebuilding*. Washington, DC: United States Institute of Peace, 2011. http://www.usip.org/publications/women-in-religious-peacebuilding.

Mattson, Ingrid. "Of Fences and Neighbors: A Muslim Perspective on Interfaith Engagement for Peace." October 26, 2013. http://ingridmattson.org/article/of-fences-and-neighbors/.

McCarthy, Kate. *Interfaith Encounters in America*. New Brunswick, NJ: Rutgers University Press, 2007. https://muse.jhu.edu/book/6100.

Merry, Jean. "18 Sisters Celebrate Jubilees of Profession." Sisters of St. Francis of Assisi. July 26, 2016. http://www.lakeosfs.org/news/18-sisters-celebrate-jubilees-of-profession/.

Milwaukee Muslim Women's Coalition (MMWC). "About Us." Milwaukee Muslim Women's Coalition (MMWC). 2018. www.mmwconline.org/.

Bin Muhammad, Ghazi. "On 'A Common Word Between Us and You.'" In *A Common Word: Muslims and Christians on Loving God and Neighbor*, edited by Miroslav Volf, Ghazi bin Muhammad, and Melissa Yarrington, 3–17. Grand Rapids, MI: Eerdmans, 2010.

Muslim–Catholic Women's Dialogue and Cardinal Stitch University. *Islam, Muslims and the Current Global Context: What US Catholics Need to Know*. Flyer, supplied by Judi Longdin.

Pickthall, M. M., trans. *The Meaning of the Glorious Qur'an*. Bethesda, MD: Amana Publications, 1996.

O'Neill, Maura. *Mending a Torn World: Women in Interreligious Dialogue*. Maryknoll, NY: Orbis Books, 2007.

Rudie, Scott. "Peacing Pioneers." *Stritch News*. October 8, 2012. https://www.stritch.edu/News/Stritch-Magazine/Sisters-of-St-Francis-ofAssisi/Peacing-Pioneers/.

Safi, Omid. "The Time They Are a Changing—A Muslim Quest for Justice, Gender Equality, and Pluralism." In *Muslim Progressive on Justice, Gender and Pluralism*, edited by Omid Safi, 1–29. Oxford: Oneworld, 2003.

Takim, Liyakat. "From Conversion to Conversation: Interfaith Dialogue in Post 9-11 America." *The Muslim World*, no. 94 (2004): 343–55.

Tetlow, Ruth. "The Missing Dimension: Women and Inter Faith Encounter in Birmingham." Ph.D. diss., University of Birmingham, 2004.

Volf, Miroslav et al. "Loving God and Neighbor Together: A Christian Response to 'A Common Word Between Us and You.'" In *A Common Word: Muslims and Christians on Loving God and Neighbor*, edited by Miroslav Volf, Ghazi bin Muhammad, and Melissa Yarrington, 51–75. Grand Rapids, MI: Eerdmans, 2010.

Winter, Miriam Thérèse. "Doing Effective Dialogue—and Loving It." *Journal of Ecumenical Studies* 43, no. 2 (2008): 25–34.

Interviews

1. Arshad, Naheed. Interview by Sundus Jaber and Caroline Redick. March 24, 2017.

2. Atta, Intisar. Interview by Dianne Rostollan, Sundus Jaber, and Caroline Redick. March 24, 2017.

3. Daniels-Sykes, Shawnee. Interview by Caroline Redick. May 16, 2017.

4. Farhoud, Inshirah. Interview by Dianne Marshall and Sundus Jaber. March 14, 2017.

5. Longdin, Judith. Interview by Sundus Jaber, Dianne Marshall, and Caroline Redick. March 14, 2017.

6. Najeeb, Janan. Interview by Sundus Jaber. April 18, 2017.

7. Reiss, Jessine. Interview by Irfan Omar and Caroline Redick. March 25, 2017.

8. Schmitt, John and Bobbie. Interview by Dianne Rostollan and Sundus Jaber. February 28, 2017.

2
PART

Interfaith Engagement in Milwaukee:

An Overview

The Role of Educational Institutions and Youth in the Milwaukee Interfaith Effort

Kaitlyn C. Daly

I n our efforts to understand the interfaith history and engagement in Milwaukee and take steps forward in a positive direction, it is essential to recognize the important role of universities in the greater Milwaukee area. The previous chapters in this book have pressed the beauty and necessity of creating and sustaining interfaith relationships in the community. An integral part of answering this resounding call for substantial interfaith relationships must include universities and their campus-wide engagement efforts toward the pursuit of such relationships. Colleges and universities have the potential to be influential advocates and partners in community interfaith engagement efforts. While the people at universities—students, faculty, staff, and leadership—are transient, the institution itself remains grounded in the city's geography and culture. This leads us to pose the question, how can we positively institutionalize the concept and practice of interfaith in the academic setting and experience? In this chapter, I explore this question on the basis of my belief that interfaith is important for the vitality of the institution itself and the people at its core, as well as for the wider Milwaukee community.[1]

To understand the intricacies of interfaith engagement in the university setting, I interviewed select university students, faculty, staff, and leadership from Cardinal Stritch University, Marquette University, and the University

---

1. There is a growing body of literature on the importance of interfaith on campus and in the lives of students. One prominent proponent of this is Eboo Patel. See, for example, Eboo Patel & Cassie Meyer, "Engaging Religious Diversity on Campus: The Role of Interfaith Leadership," *Journal of College and Character* 10, no. 7 (2009): 1–8.

of Wisconsin–Milwaukee about major interfaith cornerstones related to the university, including mission statements; interfaith activities; youth student participation and perspectives; leadership, faculty, and staff participation and perspectives; religious diversity as a key component to overall diversity; pedagogical learning; experiential opportunities; and implications for peace and world justice in campus, local, and global communities. To provide grounding for the purpose of this chapter and analysis, I have included pieces of my own personal interfaith experience and research, stories from my educational journey, and observations from the readings related to interfaith engagement.

To rephrase, this chapter explores the pedagogical and experiential role universities and individuals within these intuitions have played in interfaith engagement efforts. In doing so, it will highlight interfaith activities in classrooms, guest and house lectures, workshops, and conferences (pedagogical role); student organizations, campus ministries, and faculty and staff initiatives (experiential role—grassroots level); and university publications and leadership initiatives (experiential role—institutional level). The chapter includes a summary-analysis of the participation and perspectives of the students, leadership, faculty, and staff involved in such interfaith efforts to explore the impact of such efforts and how their respective institution supported such efforts. Based on the history accounted for, the chapter will end with an evaluation of the patterns that emerged from the student, faculty, and staff interviews; how the interfaith efforts relate to the university's mission statements; and the impact of such interfaith efforts for peace and world justice implications in campus, local, and global communities.

One limitation for this chapter is the imbalance in the information related to the source pool. When considering the material related to university students, faculty, staff, and leadership participation and perspectives presented in this chapter, it is important to take into account that quantitatively the most information was gathered from Marquette University, then the University of Wisconsin–Milwaukee, and then Cardinal Stritch University. This imbalance is due to the access and availability of personal connections, interview participants, and show-and-tell materials. Being a Marquette student at the time, I had greater access to Marquette students, faculty, staff, and leadership. Another reason for this imbalance may be that there is more to document on this topic at Marquette because of the dedication and commitment to the idea of interfaith by several of its faculty and staff members.[2] Nonetheless,

---

2. With respect to flyers and other show-and-tell items, I have cited many of these in footnotes because here they are used also as sources that provide critical information about the subjects covered.

dedicated, passionate, and informative students, faculty, staff, and leadership from the University of Wisconsin–Milwaukee and Cardinal Stritch University welcomed the opportunity to be interviewed for this project and made invaluable contributions in the form of sharing relevant stories, experiences, histories, materials, and responses.

Personal Experience

While Milwaukee has been recognized for its interfaith efforts city-wide,[3] Marquette University did not reflect the same positive climate for interfaith engagement and acceptance for which its greater surrounding urban community was recognized. This is where I started to see the great potential universities hold in the interfaith effort. Universities have the unique capability of tapping into the diversity of their students, faculty, staff, leadership, and communities around them to create a rich interfaith fabric on campus, or, as Father Thomas Michel. SJ, calls it, a "culture of dialogue,"[4] where interfaith is woven into everyday life. I realized this is a capability that must be turned into a reality at universities where our next leaders are educated. Universities must take an active role in cultivating interfaith engagement on their own campuses in order to foster peace in the local, national, and global community.

A more profound understanding of the importance of interfaith dialogue came during my time as an undergraduate student at Marquette University in Milwaukee, Wisconsin. My experience as a Lutheran at a Catholic university sparked my interest in interfaith engagement in the university setting. The structure of Marquette's Campus Ministry was Catholic-centered with "affiliated" ministries including Canterbury Fellowship, cru, InterVarsity, Hillel, Lutheran Campus Ministry, and the Orthodox Christian Fellowship.[5] A Muslim chaplain was added to the affiliated ministries housed in Campus Ministry in the 2017–2018 school year. Now, due to Marquette's foundation in the

---

3. See photo images of the letter addressed to Sister Lucille Walsh from the Secretariat of State via Monsignor G. B. Re Assessor, October 11, 1985, and another to Sister Jessine Reiss from Cardinal Francis Arinze, December 30, 1985, in the Introduction to this volume (figs. I.2 and I.3, respectively).

4. Thomas F. Michel, SJ, "Creating a Culture of Dialogue: Toward a Pedagogy of Religious Encounter," in *A Christian View of Islam: Essays on Dialogue by Thomas F. Michel, SJ*, ed. Irfan A. Omar (Maryknoll: Orbis Books, 2010), 21–22.

5. "Affiliated Ministries Staff & Religious Advisors," Marquette University, http://www.marquette.edu/cm/about/staff-affiliated-ministers.shtml.

Catholic Jesuit tradition, understandably there are some politics that may influence the structure of Campus Ministry. However, it was my expectation that a university campus ministry should encompass all religions, spiritualities, and worldviews of the people on its campus into one singular campus ministry without raising one up over the other, intentionally or indirectly, to allow for equal space, time, leadership, and presence. I directed my efforts as a student to cultivating necessary interfaith collaboration, acceptance, and visibility on campus to widen the scope of campus ministry efforts. The first step of this university interfaith pursuit was education in and out of the classroom to learn more about my own faith, the Jesuit tradition and Catholic faith, the Milwaukee community, and the interfaith efforts happening locally, nationally, and globally.[6]

In brief, experiential opportunities during my collegiate experience in which I have felt honored to partake in a tradition other than my own included volunteering with a Jewish Rabbinic chaplain at a Milwaukee hospital; experiencing diverse worship services, including a Jewish Shabbat, Jewish Passover Seder meal, Catholic mass, evening Islamic prayer, and a Tibetan Buddhist prayer service;[7] exploring a Hindu temple; attending cultural and religious dialogue dinners at the Turkish American Society of Wisconsin in Greenfield;[8] and presenting our interfaith research findings to the Milwaukee community. I have also attended two educational interfaith conferences in the United States with a Marquette student delegation: Iowa's Loras College River Crossing Interfaith Conference[9] in the winter of 2016 and Chicago's Interfaith Youth Core (IFYC) Interfaith Leadership Institute[10] in the summer of 2016.

---

6. In this venture, there were many people, places, and experiences that were invaluable to lifting and encouraging this worthy movement. To start, I met a handful of fellow Marquette students, faculty, and staff all interested in the same pursuit who became essential key players in Marquette's interfaith effort, namely, Bradley DeGarmo, Mary Sue Callan-Farley, Michelle Frederick, Dr. Irfan A. Omar, and Rev. Jessica Short. It is with endless gratitude that I thank them for encouraging me in all of my interfaith interests and activities.

7. "Deer Park Buddhist Center," Deer Park Buddhist Center, http://www.deerparkcenter.org.

8. "TASWI," Turkish American Society of Wisconsin, http://www.taswi.org.

9. Alan Garfield and Travis Carton, "River Crossing Storytelling Interfaith Conference, 2/20/2016," *YouTube*, last modified March 6, 2016, https://www.youtube.com/watch?v=CBq2zJVKV48&t=15s; Alan Garfield, "River Crossing Storytelling Interfaith Conference," *YouTube*, last modified February 20, 2016, https://www.youtube.com/watch?v=FrP-P-JoiAY.

10. "Interfaith Leadership Institutes," Interfaith Youth Core, https://www.ifyc.org/ili.

A monumental experience for Marquette University's interfaith efforts occurred at the Interfaith Youth Core's Interfaith Leadership Institute, where students, faculty, and staff representatives from colleges and universities across the United States gathered in Chicago, Illinois. A handful of interested Marquette students; the director of Marquette's Campus Ministry, Mary Sue Callan-Farley; and the Multicultural Ministry director, Bernardo Avila-Borunda attended as delegates of Marquette University. Relative to select schools sharing stories of changing their mission statements and creating campus interfaith centers to be more inclusive, Marquette had a long way to go. Challenged to reflect on ways our school was cultivating a positive environment for religious diversity, we recognized Marquette was in the beginning stages. On the last day of the conference, in the basement of the hosting hotel, our Marquette delegation gathered in an empty conference room around one round table to compile everything we had learned, process together, and create the next steps for Marquette moving forward. I remember pausing to pull back and look at the faces around the table, hearing the conversation lift in the empty room. It took my breath away and filled me with immense hope and gratitude. Here, in this basement, the Interfaith Coordinating Team was born, a team to be housed in Marquette's Campus Ministry with the goal to honor, facilitate, and celebrate the interfaith groups, peoples, and relationships on Marquette's campus.

Pedagogical interfaith experiences of my academic program included Dr. Irfan Omar's "Theology, Violence, and Nonviolence" course, exploring the implications of world religions working together for the common good of peacemaking. The course explored discussions and responses on violence, nonviolence, and peacemaking from scholars of Islam, Christianity, Judaism, Confucianism, Buddhism, Hinduism, and the American Indian religious tradition. Dr. Omar's "Survey of World Religions" course explored Hindu, Buddhist, Jewish, Christian, Muslim, Native American, and Marxist worldviews as well as the Israeli–Palestinian conflict, religious social teachings, liberation theologies, active nonviolence, and Just War Theory.[11]

In his courses, Dr. Omar consistently taught the idea of considering alternative versions of the "narrative" in order to realize that that no one narrative can contain the entire or even adequate truth about that subject, person, or the topic.[12] We are human beings: people of race, gender, ethnicity, religion

---

11. David Whitten Smith and Elizabeth Geraldine Burr, *Understanding World Religions: A Roadmap for Justice and Peace* (Lanham, MD: Rowman & Littlefield, 2015).

12. Irfan Omar, "Narratives" (class lectures, Survey of World Religions, Marquette University, Milwaukee, WI, July–August 2016).

and spirituality, heritage, sexuality, origin, geography, culture, and age. All of these individual narratives collectively shape our humanity, hold a story in our hearts, and create our all-encompassing larger narrative that makes us who we are. These narratives are not insignificant or independent. For the purpose of this chapter, I will recognize these pieces of one's narratives as "pieces" and the collection of these pieces as one's overall narrative. Our narratives are almost always incomplete and ever evolving. Pieces of our narrative are joyful and painful, autobiographical and biographical, lasting and fleeting. One's religion or worldview is only one of these pieces. It may be a significant and essential piece to one's narrative, or it may not be. It may be presented as significant when it is actually not, and vice versa. Interfaith dialogue and engagement allow us to discover "missing" pieces of one's narrative and understand their role, significance, and impact in the overall narrative. Further, Dr. Omar cautions the use of language such as "the other" and "us and them" when used to polarize the familiar from the unfamiliar and create false, incomplete, disconnected narratives that have the potential to turn into dangerous tales we tell about others, others tell about us, and we tell ourselves.[13] Chimamanda Ngozi Adichie, in her *TED Talk*, "The Danger of a Single Story," expresses that there is an imminent danger to the harmony of humanity when an individual has a limited framework of thinking.[14] Both Dr. Omar and Ngozi Adichie warn that many times we fail to recognize how we disfigure the other when we create our own narratives for them, based solely off of a single story of the other, which often reflect our prejudgments, distasteful encounters, or misguided or false information about others. We must widen the frame we are looking through to understand the bigger picture of ourselves, the people around us, and our world.

Pope Francis's recent *TED Talk*[15] expresses the message that we are all in existence for, with, and because of one another, together in this life, echoing Desmond Tutu's philosophy of "ubuntu"—I am because you are.[16] Pope Francis says, "The other has a face. The 'you' is always a real presence, a person to take

---

13. Ibid.

14. Chimamanda Ngozi Adichie. "The Danger of a Single Story," *TED Talk* video, filmed July 2009, https://www.ted.com/talks/chimamanda_adichie_the_danger_of_a_single_story.

15. Pope Francis, "Why the Only Future Worth Building Includes Everyone," *TED Talk* video, filmed April 2017, https://www.ted.com/talks/pope_francis_why_the_only_future_worth_building_includes_everyone?language=en.

16. This philosophy was shared to a group of students, including myself, while preparing for a Marquette immersion-service trip to Cape Town, South Africa.

care of."[17] In doing this, we express our love and tenderness for one another—an action described by Pope Francis as "the love that comes close and becomes real. It is a movement that starts from our heart and reaches the eyes, the ears, and the hands."[18] Sharing and celebrating together the expressions of our narratives reveals the very essence and origin of all humanity: our interconnectedness. A multitude of stories weave together to form the fabric of our hearts, the fabric of our narrative.

In a very beautiful way, all of these more formal interfaith interactions of going to conferences, attending workshops, and taking courses coexisted alongside the more informal interactions of conversations with students and friends on campus, patients in my nursing clinical experiences, and strangers on my trips to the local grocery store. Often, I felt my fellow students, family, friends, and colleagues perceive the practice of interfaith as a big, luminous project that required extensive amounts of time, attention, or formalities. Many times, interfaith does happen in this more formal way, taking shape in formal dialogues, events, and conferences. However, it is important to recognize the informal daily acts of interfaith engagement. These interfaith interactions occur every day on one's walk to class or work as they wave to a friend or smile at stranger, as one strikes up a conversation with a friendly local cashier at the store, or as one holds the door for the person coming behind them. In these informal interactions of our everyday existence and routine, we often are easily and kindly engaging with people without being privy to their religion or worldview. The former is what I consider to be "Capital 'I' Interfaith": the bigger, grander, more formal events. The latter are what I consider to be the "Lowercase 'i' interfaith": the everyday events of our lives with others. These actions, big or small, formal or informal, are interfaith at work and at its best between people of all faiths and worldviews meeting in moments of all kinds all over the world.

Interfaith education and encounter through pedagogy and experience in universities has a fundamental role in helping cities and other communities become a microcosm of the diversity and interfaith relations that exist around the globe. Milwaukee universities are paramount to advancing the interfaith movement in the city in both the "Capital 'I'" and Lowercase 'i'" ways. Students, faculty, staff, and leadership can be advocates for interfaith relationships and engagement, responding to the universal imperative to promote humanity's interconnectedness.

---

17. Pope Francis, "Why the Only Future Worth Building Includes Everyone."
18. Ibid.

Foundations for Interfaith Work

Father Thomas Michel, SJ, already mentioned, is a noted Jesuit scholar of Islam and Christian–Muslim relations. In one of his essays, "Creating a Culture of Dialogue," Father Michel speaks of "four facets of interreligious encounter: the dialogue of life, cooperation in social concerns, theological exchange, and the sharing of religious experience." Interreligious dialogue is multifaceted and "involves interaction at [all] levels of being (dialogue of life), doing (cooperation), studying (exchange of views), and reflecting on one's experience of the Divine (sharing religious experience)."[19] Dialogue, cooperation, exchange, and sharing are essential for interfaith engagement, and each manifests itself in everyday opportunities of being, doing, studying, and reflecting, especially in the university setting. Similarly, Smith and Burr outline the seven dimensions of a religion or worldview, giving us the ability to step into dialogue, cooperation, exchange, and sharing in our everyday reality:

1. *Experiential and emotional*—people gain experience of life; some people have life-changing experiences.

2. *Social and institutional*—they seek out others with similar experiences and form groups for support; gradually these groups grow in size and complexity.

3. *Narrative or mythic*—within the group, they pass on their experiences in the form of stories

4. *Doctrinal and philosophical*—as people ask questions about the experiences and the stories, they explain them rationally as best they can; some of the meaning cannot be expressed rationally, but must remain as expressed in the stories themselves.

5. *Practical and ritual*—if they understand their experiences to relate to powers or beings beyond visible, everyday experience, they work out concrete ways of relating to those powers or beings (for example, through liturgy or worship); they also work out formalized ways of relating to ordinary people and things (for example, social etiquette).

6. *Ethical and legal*—they decide what actions and way of life are appropriate to their experiences and their understanding of those experiences; they also develop laws to govern the communities they have formed.

---

19. Michel, "Creating a Culture of Dialogue," 19.

7. *Material and artistic*—in living out the preceding six dimensions, they produce material things (buildings like temples, songs like hymns, visual arts, literature like drama and poems) that are appropriate to their experiences and their understanding.[20]

In all these dimensions, we can seek to incorporate a "culture of dialogue" with outreach, cooperation, exchange, and sharing. While Smith and Burr do not present these dimensions with the explicit purpose of interfaith engagement, these seven listed dimensions of religions and worldviews offer anyone, specifically university folk for purposes of this chapter, a framework for one to engage with interfaith activities, interactions, and dialogues. These interfaith engagements take many forms (e.g., dialogues, service projects, friends talking to one another, services and memorials), build, and foster a positive social reality of religious pluralism on campus, interaction after interaction.

Interfaith activist Eboo Patel discusses IFYC's three parts to pluralism: respect for others, positive relationships, and common action.[21] Patel builds on this with three common measures for religious diversity: attitudes, relationships, and knowledge.[22] Patel explains, "If you know some (accurate and positive) things about a religion, and you know some people from that religion, you are far more likely to have positive attitudes toward that tradition and that community. The more favorable your attitude, the more open you will be to new relationships and additional appreciative knowledge."[23] Patel also warns this cycle can be harmful if experienced in reverse with negative attitudes and misguided or inaccurate information and representations or experiences.[24] He gives the example of Robert Putnam's "My Friend Al Principle," which illustrates the idea that personal relationships with people of different backgrounds positively affect one's attitude toward those who are different and make us more accepting and open.[25]

---

20. Smith and Burr, *Understanding World Religions*, 5–6.

21. Eboo Patel, *Sacred Ground* (Boston: Beacon Press, 2012), 71. IFYC stands for Interfaith Youth Core, the national nonprofit organization Patel founded in 2002.

22. Ibid., 77.

23. Ibid., 79.

24. Ibid., 80.

25. Ibid., 77–78. For more on "My Friend Al Principle," see Robert D. Putnam and David E. Campbell, *American Grace: How Religion Divides and Unites Us* (New York: Simon & Schuster, 2010). Putnam and Campbell contend that interfaith ties among friends and acquaintances help in maintaining a degree of tolerance for the religious other.

Tabitha Miller, a student at the University of Wisconsin-Milwaukee, shared a story of this principle in action. She talked in admiration of a friend she made in high school, a foreign exchange student who was Muslim and wore a hijab—the only one at their school to wear a hijab. Through their common interest in theater, Miller and the Muslim friend had the opportunity and interest to discuss their own religions together. Miller said, "I will never forget that conversation because that was my first time really, *really* understating it because I *met* somebody that practiced that religion."[26] This personal encounter with someone of a different cultural, geographical, and religious upbringing remained with Miller all the way to college, where she became strongly involved in interfaith activities. I reference all of this to say: social relationships are vital to our health, perception, learning, and community and world relations. Eboo Patel and his organization, IFYC, recognize that schools are among the most important places where these relationships can be fostered. Patel describes college as "the key space in our society where a choir of idealistic young people from a range of backgrounds come together to form their vocations, participate in a diverse community, and acquire a knowledge base that will help them be leaders in the world beyond."[27] He encourages, "though there are many sectors in our society where interfaith cooperation is relevant and necessary (houses of worship, neighborhoods, hospitals, and cities, to name a few), I believe college campuses play a uniquely powerful role."[28] Patel cites Eugenio Tironi, explaining that "the kind of society we seek is intimately connected to the type of education we offer."[29] Patel suggests we "make the teaching a practice of interfaith cooperation a priority on our nation's campuses."[30]

In September 2013, the US Department of Education published a project titled "The President's Interfaith and Community Service Campus Challenge Inaugural Report," which echoes Patel's message. The project was created by the White House Office of Faith-Based and Neighborhood Partnerships, calling for higher educational institutions to recognize, engage, and demonstrate the role they play in fostering the bond of interfaith engagement and community service among students, faculty, staff, leadership, and surrounding communities. Marquette University in Milwaukee—one of only three Wisconsin

---

26. Sean Heinritz and Tabitha Miller, interview by Kaitlyn Daly, February 28, 2017.

27. Patel, *Sacred Ground*, 102.

28. Ibid.

29. Ibid.

30. Ibid.

schools in the project (other two are Marian University in Fond du Lac and St. Norbert College in De Pere)—is featured in the inaugural report. Future research should explore how Marquette—and other Milwaukee or US universities and colleges—have continued their commitment to this cause beginning in 2013.[31] Patel poses important questions for colleges to ask themselves and students to question their colleges on such as, "what is their campus doing to advance an alternative narrative, teach an appreciative knowledge base, create spaces for meaningful relationships, offer opportunities for leadership, provide a model for the rest of the society *on interfaith issues?*"[32] And, especially for Marquette University and Cardinal Stritch University in Milwaukee, "how does a religiously affiliated college live out its heritage and identity in a world characterized by religious diversity, when even its student body comes from many different backgrounds?"[33] Patel explains, "The big question for interfaith cooperation in higher ed . . . is how to go from niche to norm, just like the multicultural movement . . . To go from niche to norm, you'd need everyone from presidents to professors to chaplains to students to view this work as a high priority, something to be not just talked about but also acted on, and to be not just done but also done well."[34] He further cautions, "Let's get something straight: just because you are not talking about religion in graduate schools does not mean that religion is not getting talked about. It just means you are forfeiting the conversation to someone else."[35]

I bring these points of Patel to light to give weight to the vital importance of pedagogy (classroom and textbook learning) and experiential learning (relationship building, dialogue facilitations, etc.). Universities across the nation offer a unique space for both of these essential components of interfaith engagement. However, it is important to assess whether these universities are utilizing this unique space to their advantage to further the growth and engagement of their students. One place to look for this commitment is in the mission statement of a university.

---

31. US Department of Education, "The President's Interfaith and Community Service Campus Challenge Inaugural Report," https://www.ifyc.org/sites/default/files/u4/campus-challenge-inaugural-years-report_small.pdf. This chapter can serve as an expansion or update to the efforts mentioned briefly in the report for Marquette, with the addition of qualitative data collected in recent years.

32. Ibid., 119.

33. Ibid., 127.

34. Ibid., 119.

35. Ibid., 126.

University Mission Statements and Their Pedagogical Impact

Below I will reproduce the mission statements of the three institutions of higher learning covered in this study. I will also discuss how interfaith is incorporated pedagogically in the classroom through undergraduate and graduate academic courses, guest and house lectures, workshops, and conferences in each of these universities.

Cardinal Stritch University

The mission statement for Cardinal Stritch, a private Franciscan Catholic university, states:

> Cardinal Stritch University, sponsored by the Sisters of St. Francis of Assisi and rooted in the liberal arts tradition, transforms lives and communities through servant leadership, learning, and service. The University is guided by the Catholic, Franciscan values of creating a caring community, peacemaking, showing compassion, and reverencing creation as we embrace and cultivate the diversity of all of God's creation.[36]

We see the call to positively influence and inspire communities and serve and learn from one another. Stritch's mission statement specifically calls for the expression of care and peace and the celebration of diversity. The mission is grounded in a God figure, which calls for openness to faith in general.

Stritch is a small, private university and fortunately has had several visionary leaders and faculty who paved the way for interfaith pedagogy on campus. We have already learned about the two sisters, cofounders of the original Christian–Muslim dialogue in 1980. Daniel Di Domizio, recently retired professor, now emeritus, has followed in the footsteps of Sister Lucille Walsh, OSF, and Sister Jessine Reiss, OSF, in maintaining the interest in important interfaith topics, discussions, and events into the campus setting.[37] Di Domizio is fully aware of their legacy and shares their passion for interfaith engagement. Di Domizio was only too happy to share Stritch's contribution

---

36. "Mission Statement," Cardinal Stritch University, https://www.stritch.edu/About/Mission-and-Vision/Mission-Statement/.

37. Sister Lucille and Sister Jessine are discussed in Redick's and several other chapters in this volume. They were both professors at Cardinal Stritch. They cofounded the first formal Islamic–Christian Dialogue in 1980. Daniel Di Domizio, *List of People of Interfaith Activity,* document; Daniel Di Domizio, *Info on Sr. Lucille,* document; Daniel Di Domizio, *Sr. Lucille CSU Award Intro,* document; Daniel Di Domizio, *Sr Lucille CSU Award Certificate,* document.

to the interfaith effort. One of these was the award certificate Stritch gave to Sister Lucille Walsh, the Saint Francis of Assisi Interfaith Dialogue Award. It was given in November 2012 for her interfaith service and commitment to the university's Franciscan values of Peacemaking and Respectful Dialogue (fig. 7.1).[38] To advance this pedagogy, Cardinal Stritch also offers an Interfaith Studies certificate and minor that requires courses on topics related to faith and film, faith and music, religions of the world, religious practices and texts, and religious movements.[39]

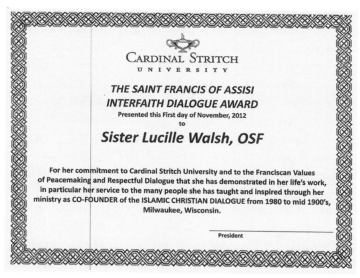

Figure 7.1: Cardinal Stritch awarded Sister Lucille Walsh the "Saint Francis of Assisi Interfaith Dialogue" Award for her interfaith service and commitment to the university and the Franciscan values of Peacemaking and Respectful Dialogue.

Marquette University

The mission statement of Marquette University, a Jesuit Catholic university, highlights the importance of a life of faith and the school's commitment to honoring and encouraging this life of faith:

> Marquette University is a Catholic, Jesuit university dedicated to serving God
> by serving our students and contributing to the advancement of knowledge.

---

38. Di Domizio, Sr. Lucille CSU Award Intro; Di Domizio, Sr. Lucille CSU Award Certificate.

39. Cardinal Stritch University, *CSU Interfaith Studies Certificate/Minor List*, document.

Our mission, therefore, is the search for truth, the discovery and sharing of knowledge, the fostering of personal and professional excellence, the promotion of a life of faith, and the development of leadership expressed in service to others. All this we pursue for the greater glory of God and the common benefit of the human community.[40]

It is important to recognize the university does not mention any specific faith. However, they do recognize the God figure. Marquette identifies with its Catholic Christian identity in the mission statement but keeps the meaning of "mission" open to interpretation, which may include respect for all faiths that subscribe to the greater good of all humanity. It is important to ask the question, does Marquette practice what they preach? Do all students of all faiths on campus feel they can take part in this mission? Do students of all faiths feel accepted and celebrated on campus? At a Jesuit-Catholic university, do students feel they are in the minority if they are not Christian or Catholic? Asking these questions and hearing the answers is vital to understanding the interfaith climate at Marquette University. Searching for truth, discovering and sharing knowledge, uplifting faithful lives, serving one another, and contributing to the well-being of the human community are all professed as the mission of Marquette and are all apropos to the mission of interfaith work.

Marquette University seeks to offer interreligious courses similar to others of its kind across the nation although expertise in this area is rather limited. Courses on world religions and those that may engender cross-religion discussions are on the books, however they are rarely offered due to lack of full-time staff who can teach these. This Jesuit-Catholic university requires all students to take a minimum of one theology course as part of their undergraduate education. Additionally, in the new core introduced in the fall of 2018, each student will need to take a "culminating experience" course that would include theological content. Many students also end up taking electives that have theology content. In the 2003–2004 academic year the first graduate seminar on interreligious dialogue, "Christians and Muslims in Dialogue," was introduced and was co-designed and team-taught by theology professors Bradford Hinze and Irfan Omar.[41] In 2006, a new undergraduate interdisciplinary course, "Islamic Theology and Philosophy," was team-taught by philosophy professor Richard C. Taylor and Irfan Omar.[42] In 2009, Richard Taylor, Irfan

---

40. "Our Mission," Marquette University, http://www.marquette.edu/about/mission.php.

41. Irfan A. Omar, *MU Interreligious Activities,* document.

42. Ibid.

Omar, and history professor Phillip Naylor applied for and received a Mellon grant to design a new course titled "Introduction to Islamic Studies," which they team-taught in 2010.[43] The College of Arts and Sciences and the chairs of the three departments were supportive of the effort. In 2011, Dr. Omar created and taught a new undergraduate second-level theology course, supported by the Center for Transnational Justice, titled, "Christian-Muslim Dialogue."[44] Since then, the topic has been offered at both the undergraduate and graduate levels on a regular basis. Other courses at Marquette include "Survey of World Religions" and "Theology, Violence, and Nonviolence," both with interfaith and religious diversity as their underlining themes. Dr. Omar makes it a point in his classrooms to invite guest speakers, such as local activists, scholars, and practitioners of dialogue, nonviolence, and peacemaking. Some of those who have visited his classrooms include Father Thomas F. Michel, SJ (Christian-Muslim studies), Richard Hanson (comparative theology), Jillian Holy-Skaja (yoga and Hinduism), and Marie Dennis (interreligious peacemaking and Pax Christi).

In addition to the course offerings that seek to highlight religious diversity, Professors Omar, Taylor, and Naylor have initiated and organized several conferences, symposia, and public lectures that Marquette University has hosted in the past 15 years (2004–2018). The topics addressed include the Abrahamic faiths in dialogue in areas featuring theology and philosophy, peacemaking and social movements for peace, interdisciplinary studies on Islam and Muslims, and interfaith relations.[45] Resect for other faiths is taught in nontheology courses, for example, Marquette's nursing program. The growing diversity of the community is reflected in the population of patients receiving health care every day. In Marquette's nursing program, students are taught to acknowledge, respect, and honor the faith or nonfaith of each individual. This is viewed as an essential component of the promise to provide holistic care of the mind, body, and spirit. In 2017, Dr. Louise Cainkar in the Social and Cultural Sciences department introduced an "interfaith immersion experience" for Marquette students and staff members, which has typically been a four-day trip to Dearborn and Hamtramck, Michigan, visiting Arab Muslim and Christian communities and their places of worship. The trip has been offered each year during spring break and is funded by the Center for Peacemaking.

---

43. Ibid.

44. Ibid.

45. See Irfan A. Omar, *MU Interreligious Activities,* document, for a comprehensive list.

University of Wisconsin–Milwaukee

The mission statement for the University of Wisconsin–Milwaukee, a public school, derives from the encompassing University of Wisconsin School System:

> The mission of this system is to develop human resources, to discover and disseminate knowledge, to extend knowledge and its application beyond the boundaries of its campuses, and to serve and stimulate society by developing in students heightened intellectual, cultural, and humane sensitivities; scientific, professional, and technological expertise; and a sense of purpose. Inherent in this mission are methods of instruction, research, extended education, and public service designed to educate people and improve the human condition. Basic to every purpose of the system is the search for truth.[46]

This mission statement has similar emphases to Marquette's in regard to the call for discovery, sharing, seeking of purpose and truth, and contributing positively to the human community and condition. This statement appears to have more openness to all faiths with no mention of God, although it is still important to ask the same questions of integrity and commitment to the mission to a public school as it is to ask to a private school. Again, these commitments reflect the possibilities of interfaith engagement. From private schools to public schools, interfaith should have a place in every setting.

The University of Wisconsin–Milwaukee (UWM) offers a Religious Studies degree program available for a major and minor.[47] They also offer several philosophy courses addressing interreligious concepts. In 2017, Sean Heinritz was a student at UWM pursuing the Religious Studies degree and is involved with building interfaith relations on campus. He defines interfaith as a way "to connect with those people that I definitely feel are my brothers and sisters spiritually, as well as the spiritual cousins of different faiths and different backgrounds."[48] He explains that being a religious studies student has allowed him to see connections between people of different faiths: "You can see that there is

---

46. "UWM's Vision, Values, and Mission Statements," University of Wisconsin–Milwaukee, http://uwm.edu/mission/.

47. "Religious Studies Program," University of Wisconsin–Milwaukee, https://uwm.edu/religiousstudies/.

48. Heinritz and Miller, interview by Kaitlyn Daly.

so much more, as far as interfaith is concerned, that we can do together, that we are already exposed to the same things just done in different ways."[49] Heinritz believes the goal of a Religious Studies student is to be cognizant and aware of all religions and their beliefs, practices, customs, culture, taboos, and reasoning. Heinritz connects this goal to the goal of interfaith student dialogue: connecting and understanding. Having students on campus with this training and education has the potential to facilitate further interfaith encounters. When pedagogical training is present and visible, experiential opportunities can grow and flourish. It is necessary to have students, such as Heinritz, taking these courses and sharing their acquired knowledge and passion to initiate and exemplify interfaith interaction on campuses across the nation.

Mission statements are like foundations for a university; they symbolize ideological roots from which all parts of the institution may grow. There are similarities and differences between the three examples offered here. There also is variance in how leadership, faculty, staff, and students all identify with the mission or use it as their source of inspiration and grounding. As it will become clear later in the chapter, the leadership, faculty, staff, and students I interviewed differed in varying degrees in how strongly they identified with the mission statement being their source of inspiration and grounding for interfaith work. For example, the work and words of former Marquette vice president of Mission and Ministry, Dr. Stephanie Russell, were very much grounded in Marquette's mission statement. However, for Dr. Omar, a professor in Theology, his interfaith efforts have been grounded in a more personal mission he has felt since his youth, which fuels his life and work. Regardless of one's strength of affiliation toward a university's mission, the mission has the potential to positively serve as motivation and immediate urgency for interfaith efforts on college campuses. However, a university's mission is just a statement. Without the support and actions of people who are in a position to make the mission a lived reality, it will not have any real impact.

Interfaith Events

How interfaith is incorporated experientially varies at both the grassroots level of student organizations, campus ministry, and initiatives by faculty and staff and the institutional level of university publications, initiatives by leadership, and institution support in the efforts. According to Father Michel, universities

---

49. Ibid.

must go beyond the classroom pedagogy and more fully embrace the lived personal encounter. Father Michel states,

> interfaith dialogue has a place in the education of youth. Interfaith dialogue is not only for the 'wise and wizened,' but also for those still in the process of preparing themselves for their life's work. It is not only for those who are intending to involve themselves in interfaith activities, but for all those believers whose worldly activities will bring them into direct or indirect contact with people of other faiths.[50]

To be effective, education for dialogue cannot remain limited to information that can be obtained from books and classroom presentations. Such formal introductions to the faith of others, while useful in providing basic information, remain on the surface level of concepts and lack the ability to touch the crucial "human" element. They remain "outside" the religious reality that is lived by people of faith. To change attitudes and perceptions, there is no substitute for personal encounter. No books or lectures can provide the deeper values of faith communicated through hospitality, body language, sharing jokes and conversation, and recounting personal histories. No amount of reading can take the place of observing directly how people of another faith approach the divine in worship. Opportunities for encountering people of other faiths must become an integral part of religious education if we hope to build what Father Michel refers to as a "culture of dialogue" within our own communities. Educational institutions are a prime location for this interactive education to occur. They are a training ground for cultivating intelligence, finding inspiration, and learning the value of intrigue. It is a place where young students discover opportunities for and seek interaction with their peers. Students, faculty, and staff should all take part in encouraging, creating, and fostering opportunities for this interaction and growth. University leadership, faculty, and staff should support students driven to change the culture of campus. Student-driven initiatives are powerful, but they need the opportunity and the support to be sustained. Universities are an ideal and essential place for this to occur with the immense potential of youth making changes that impact the university, the surrounding community, and the world. Especially in Milwaukee, the youth and university initiatives have the great responsibility to create symbiotic relationships with the Milwaukee community. To do this, it is essential for university

---

50. Thomas F. Michel, SJ, "A Variety of Approaches to Interfaith Dialogue," in *A Christian View of Islam*, 35.

persons to know and interact with the surrounding community and invite community leaders and activists to join efforts on campus.

In this section, I include a sampling of the kinds of events organized and/ or hosted by these educational institutions in recent years.

Cardinal Stritch University

At Cardinal Stritch University, Professor Daniel Di Domizio has been the key person to plan, organize, and coordinate interfaith events at the university. He is also deeply involved in the community as well as in interfaith circles, which helped make these events a great success. In 2011, a panel of Muslim students presented on "Diversity on Campus: Students in Dialogue" at a residence hall on campus sponsored by the JPICC, the Stritch Justice, Peace, Integrity of Creation Center, and the Milwaukee Muslim Women's Coalition (fig. 7.2).[51] The following year, in September 2012, Cardinal Stritch and the Milwaukee Muslim Women's Coalition (MMWC) also sponsored a Muslim–Christian Student Dialogue dinner in the university's union, which was open to all students, faculty, and staff (fig. 7.3).[52] The same year Stritch invited Eboo Patel for the "Bridging the Faith Divide" event, which included a student workshop, conversation, dinner, and a keynote speech, reception, and book signing (fig. 7.4).[53] The free event was open to students and advisors.

Figure 7.2: Flyer for a panel presentation on "Diversity on Campus: Students in Dialogue."

---

51. Cardinal Stritch University, *Student Dialogue Event Panel Flyer 1 and 2*, flyer.

52. Cardinal Stritch University, *Student Dialogue Event Flyer*, flyer.

53. Cardinal Stritch University, *Eboo Patel Talk Flyer,* flyer.

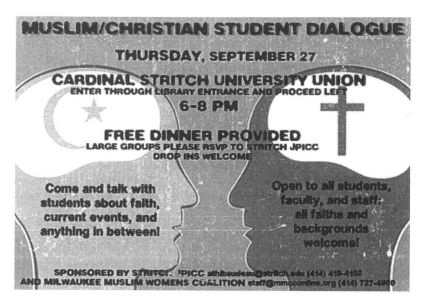

Figure 7.3: Flyer for the Muslim–Christian Student Dialogue dinner in the university's union, which was open to all students, faculty, and staff of all backgrounds.

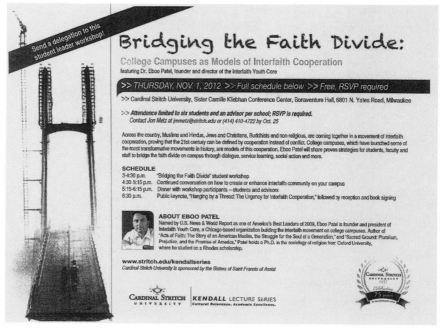

Figure 7.4: Flyer for the Eboo Patel lecture at Cardinal Stritch University.

Marquette University

At Marquette University (MU), there is a history of interfaith activities: new courses, conferences, and related events, often sponsored by the university's office of Mission and Ministry, various academic departments, and MU's prestigious Center for Peacemaking. Many of these programs were co-sponsored and partially funded by outside foundations and institutes. All of these events were often open to the public and were designed with Marquette students, faculty, and staff in mind.[54]

Figure 7.5: Poster for Marquette University's Interfaith Lecture Series on dialogue of the Abrahamic religions.

---

54. The documentation regarding Marquette's involvement in interfaith engagements was provided by Irfan Omar, Richard Taylor, and Kaitlyn Daly. More information on the events discussed below, including funding, sponsorship, and other details, can be found on the individual "show-and-tell" items saved in the project's archives.

In March and April 2004, Marquette University's Department of Theology offered an Interfaith Lecture Series focusing on the Abrahamic religions (fig. 7.5).[55] This was one of the first major events at the Marquette campus that explored interfaith themes. It was supported by various units of the university, but the main support came from the then-VP for Mission and Ministry, Dr. Stephanie Russell. She fully backed the efforts led by Dr. Bradford Hinze and Dr. Irfan Omar to engage in a conversation of interfaith matters.[56] The lectures, given by prominent scholars, were later compiled in a book, *Heirs of Abraham: The Future of Muslim, Jewish, and Christian Relations*.[57] The lectures were timed to be an extracurricular component of the new graduate seminar in Theology on "Christians & Muslims in Dialogue," team-taught by Hinze and Dr. Omar. In the fall of 2004, Dr. Omar organized a symposium titled, "Peace Service in the Abrahamic Traditions: An Interfaith Symposium," which was co-sponsored by a national peace organization Global Peace Services USA (based in Washington, DC) with representatives from each religion giving presentations, discussions, and responses (fig. 7.6).[58] Besides the individuals noted above who were personally and professionally committed to including interfaith into the pedagogical and the extracurricular, there were other units who believed in the necessity of using interfaith resources to educate the campus.

In September 2005, the Manresa Project, spearheaded by Dr. Susan Mountin, co-sponsored an international conference titled, "Justice and Mercy Will Kiss: A Conference on the Vocation of Peacemaking in a World of Many Faiths," showcasing over 40 presentations and workshops (fig. 7.7).[59] Many student organizations became involved in interfaith discussions and in April 2007, the Marquette Arab Student Association (ASA), the Manresa Project, several departments of the university, and the Office of Student Development (OSD) hosted a dialogue event on campus titled, "Jerusalem Women Speak: Three Women, Three Faiths, One Shared Vision," where a Muslim Palestinian,

---

55. Marquette University Department of Theology, *Interfaith Lecture Series*, flyer.

56. According to Omar, Stephanie Russell's support and encouragement opened new pathways and highlighted a need on campus that led to many more events in subsequent years. Omar, email message to author, June 22, 2017.

57. Bradford E. Hinze and Irfan A. Omar, eds., *Heirs of Abraham: The Future of Muslim, Jewish, and Christian Relations* (Maryknoll, NY: Orbis, 2005).

58. Marquette University and Global Peace Services USA, *Peace Service in the Abrahamic Traditions Interfaith Symposium*, program.

59. Marquette University and the Manresa Project, *Justice and Mercy Interfaith Peacemaking Conference*, poster, flyer, and call for papers.

a Jewish Israeli, and a Christian Palestinian came together to share their stories, fears, and hopes for peace (fig. 7.8).[60]

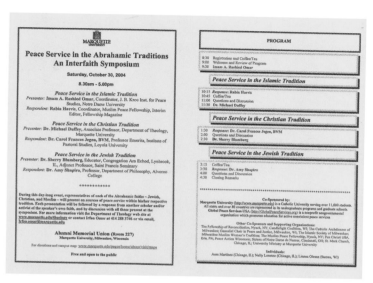

Figure.7.6: Flyer for the event on "Peace Service in the Abrahamic Traditions: An Interfaith Symposium" with representatives from each religion giving presentations, discussions, and responses.

Figure 7.7: Flyer for the Manresa Project conference titled, "Justice and Mercy Will Kiss: A Conference on the Vocation of Peacemaking in a World of Many Faiths."

60. Marquette University Arab Student Association, *Jerusalem Women Speak Panel*, flyer.

Figure 7.8: Flyer for the panel discussion on "Jerusalem Women Speak: Three Women, Three Faiths, One Shared Vision."

Events such as these drew people who were interested in political issues of the region as well as women's leadership roles in solutions to the conflict. Even though the event was dubbed as "interfaith," in fact, it was much more than that. It opened up space for conversation about peacemaking and conflict resolution as well as international cooperation and civilizational dialogue. The collaboration of various units of the university and student organizations showed that possibilities for organizing transformative events beneficial to so many demographics and revealing of many disciplinary perspectives.

A few faculty members who routinely teach or speak on interfaith issues from theological, philosophical, and historical perspectives continued to organize events in connection with their classes and scholarship/research. The momentum was building with several events having taken place in the span of three years since 2004. Some of the key Marquette persons who inspired, supported, sometimes participated, and promoted interfaith on campus at this time (besides the one's already noted above) were Father Eugene Merz, SJ, Sister Carol Ann Smith, SHCJ, Father Philip Rossi, SJ., Dr. Phillip Naylor, and Dr. Richard Taylor.[61]

In February–March 2007, through the efforts of Richard Taylor and Irfan Omar, Marquette University hosted a conference on philosophy and theology titled, "The Muslim, Christian, and Jewish Heritage: Philosophical and Theological Explorations in the Abrahamic Traditions" (fig. 7.9). The program was inaugurated with the keynote by Father Michel, titled, "Contemporary Muslim Peace Movements: A Dynamic Alternative to Violence." The conference considered issues that interests theologians and philosophers and that exist at the intersections of various religions. Father Michel's opening lecture set the tone of the conference: what do we know about collaboration between Jewish, Christian, and Muslim intellectuals and how did their efforts benefit the learning, especially in the medieval period?[62] As has been noted in earlier chapters, Father Michel was well informed about Milwaukee from his time as an official in the Vatican, and as an expert on Islam and interfaith dialogue. He was one of the people with whom the founders of the original CM dialogue communicated in the early 1980s seeking advice on official guidelines.

---

61. Information supplied by Irfan Omar.

62. Marquette University, *Muslim, Christian, Jewish Heritage Conference/Lecture Series*, flyer. See also the conference website: http://academic.mu.edu/taylorr/Abrahamic_Conference/Welcome.html.

The Muslim, Christian, and Jewish Heritage
Events in the week of Feb. 26 - March 2, 2007
Marquette University

1 pm Wednesday, February 28 – 6 pm Friday, March 2

"The Muslim, Christian, and Jewish Heritage: Philosophical and Theological Explorations in the Abrahamic Traditions"

A conference on philosophy and theology
Raynor Library Conference Center & Alumni Memorial Union

Advance Registration Limited to 75 persons: $25 (students $10)
On site registration: $35

For information, see
http://web.mac.com/mistertea/iWeb/Abrahamic%20Conference/Conference%20Registration%20Information.html

AND

"Contemporary Muslim Peace Movements: A Dynamic Alternative to Violence"

Rev. Thomas Michel, S. J.

Wednesday, February 28, 7:30-9:30 pm
Alumni Memorial Union Ballroom

Free and open to the public
Reception to follow

Funding and Sponsors:

The Helen Bader Foundation, the Departments of Philosophy, Theology and History, the Edward Simmons Religious Commitment Fund, the Marquette Excellence in Diversity Grant Fund, the Office of Mission and Identity, Manresa Project, Campus Ministry, and the Wade Chair Fund

Figure 7.9: Poster for the conference on philosophy and theology titled, "The Muslim, Christian, and Jewish Heritage: Philosophical and Theological Explorations in the Abrahamic Traditions."

The 2007 conference received support from various units in the university, but it was also supported by community organizations, including the Helen Bader Foundation of Milwaukee. This effort not only brought scholars from various places in the world to Marquette, but it also connected the university with community partners. In 2008, Taylor, Omar, and Naylor organized a conference exclusively for undergraduate students. Another philosophy colleague, Dr. Owen Goldin, joined the planning team, which was now truly Abrahamic, with faculty representing the Jewish, Catholic, Orthodox Christian, and Muslim religions. Marquette's departments of Theology, Philosophy, and History, Center for Peacemaking, Muslim Student Association, and Jewish Student Union co-sponsored, "Exploring the Abrahamic Heritage: A One-Day Undergraduate Student Conference on the Importance of Philosophical and Theological Developments in Medieval Islam, Christianity, and Judaism" (fig. 7.10). The theme was similar to 2007—the Abrahamic religions in dialogue. However, the focus was on mentoring and encouraging students in theology and philosophy to take up research on topics that offer opportunities for interfaith learning. Student representatives from Marquette University, Loyola University of Chicago, University of Wisconsin–Madison, and McGill University–Montreal delivered presentations.[63]

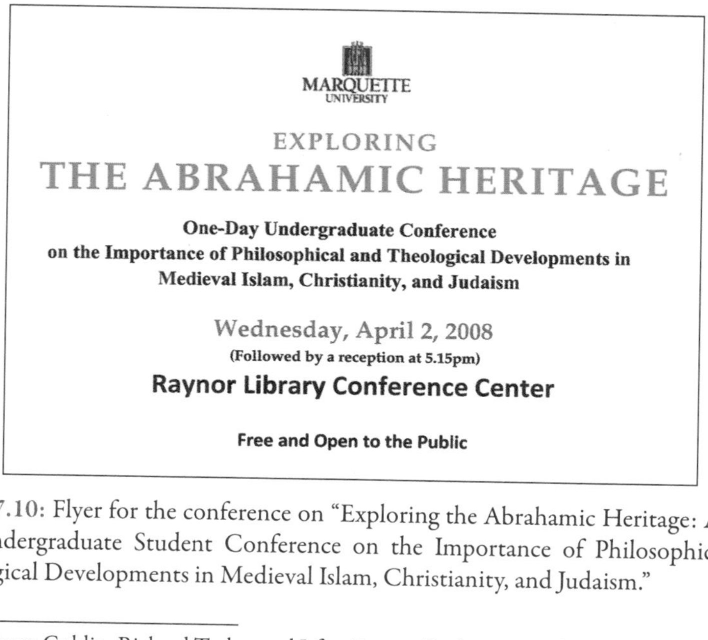

MARQUETTE
UNIVERSITY

EXPLORING
THE ABRAHAMIC HERITAGE

One-Day Undergraduate Conference
on the Importance of Philosophical and Theological Developments in
Medieval Islam, Christianity, and Judaism

Wednesday, April 2, 2008
(Followed by a reception at 5.15pm)
Raynor Library Conference Center

Free and Open to the Public

Figure 7.10: Flyer for the conference on "Exploring the Abrahamic Heritage: A One-Day Undergraduate Student Conference on the Importance of Philosophical and Theological Developments in Medieval Islam, Christianity, and Judaism."

---

63. Owen Goldin, Richard Taylor, and Irfan Omar, *Abrahamic Conference*, flyer.

In April 2009, Marquette's Department of Theology and the Office of International Education welcomed Professor Dr. Bärbel Beinhauer-Köhler of Johann Wolfgang Goethe-Universität in Germany to present on the "Visual Cultures of World Religions" (fig. 7.11).[64] This was an interfaith event made possible because of the faculty exchange program supported by Terry Miller, director of the Office of International Education (OIE).[65]

Tuesday, April 21, 2009

3.30 – 5.00 pm

Raynor Library Conference Center, Suite A

VISUAL CULTURES OF WORLD RELIGIONS

Since religious rituals and practices have been recognized to contain an aesthetic as well as an emotional dimension, visual experiences have become an important topic in religious studies. Perspectives of viewing (gaze) the divine differ between religions based on theological presumptions and rituals. For example, Hindus practice *darshan* which means an exchange of gazes between anthropomorphic and zoomorphic gods and believers, the Near Eastern monotheistic tradition in contrast displays many rules to represent God in a perceivable form that still hides the divine's true essence. Thus even though there is a difference in the modality of representation, many religions rely on visual aids in seeking the experience of the divine.

This presentation will guide us through some theoretical and methodological questions while showing relevant examples from the visual cultures in world religions.

Prof. Dr. Bärbel Beinhauer-Köhler
Johann Wolfgang Goethe-Universität
Frankfurt am Main, Germany

FREE AND OPEN TO THE PUBLIC

For more information, please contact Dr. Irfan Omar at 288-3746, or Irfan.Omar@Marquette.edu
Sponsored by the Department of Theology and the Office of International Education

---

Figure 7.11: Marquette's Department of Theology and the Office of International Education welcomed Professor Dr. Bärbel Beinhauer-Köhler of Johann Wolfgang Goethe-Universität in Germany to Marquette University to present on the "Visual Cultures of World Religions."

---

64. Irfan Omar, *Beinhauer-Kohler Visual Cultures of World Religions*, flyer.

65. OIE has supported and co-sponsored several other events involving international scholars and/or partnerships that included an interfaith and/or interdisciplinary aspect.

In September 2012, Father Michel returned to Marquette, this time as a visiting scholar and "Wade Chair" holder. He gave a public lecture at Marquette titled, "A Catholic Priest Among Muslims: What I Have Learned" (fig. 7.12).[66] Father Michel is a world-renowned scholar who worked with Pope John Paul II for many years as his advisor in matters related to Islam and Muslims. His command of the subject and his authenticity as a Catholic, Jesuit scholar is unquestioned. Thus, the event drew a standing-only crowd on campus. During that semester, Father Michel also visited and spoke at the Islamic Society of Milwaukee. He also met with several other dialogue actors including Imam Ronald Shaheed, the principal of the Clara Mohammed School, who has been leader in interfaith work in the African American community for several years, first in Chicago and then in Milwaukee (fig. 7.13).

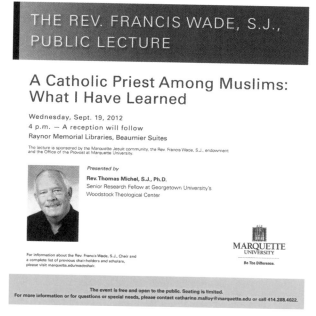

Figure 7.12: Poster for the "Rev. Francis Wade, S.J. Chair" public lecture given by Rev. Thomas Michel, SJ, at Marquette titled, "A Catholic Priest Among Muslims: What I Have Learned."

In his courses, Dr. Omar introduced several events as part of his pedagogical and research innovation. In October 2013, together with Dr. Michael Duffey, he organized a one-day symposium titled, "Peacemaking and Nonviolence

---

66. Marquette University, *Wade Chair Public Lecture on Christian–Muslim Relations*, flyer.

Figure 7.13: Father Thomas Michel, SJ (left) and Imam Ronald Shaheed in Milwaukee in 2012.

in World Religions," held at Marquette's campus with speakers representing and presenting on Buddhism, Christianity, Confucianism, Hinduism, Islam, Judaism, and the Native American tradition (fig. 7.14).[67] This was one of a handful of events that included a range of religious traditions. The theme was peacemaking and nonviolence. However, the interfaith framework was integral to the project. Each speaker gave a lecture on the theme in his own tradition followed by a response from two other scholars from different traditions. The symposium was planned as a public event and a book project on the theme from a world religions perspective. The book was later published as *Peacemaking and the Challenge of Violence in World Religions* and is now used as a textbook in courses on peacemaking and nonviolence at Marquette and at other universities.[68]

In the fall of 2015, Dr. Omar organized an "Amazing Faiths Dinner Dialogue" for his Christian–Muslim Dialogue class (figs. 7.15 & 7.16).[69] The Interfaith Conference of Greater Milwaukee sent trained facilitators to Marquette,

---

67. Marquette University, *Peacemaking and Nonviolence in World Religions*, program and flyer.

68. The event was co-sponsored by Dr. William Wellburn, executive director for the Office for Diversity and Inclusion, and Patrick Kennelly, director of the Center for Peacemaking. Both these offices and individuals have been staunch supporters of diversity and inclusion and are eager to support any event that invites conversation and dialogue across differences. The book was co-edited by Irfan A. Omar and Michael Duffey and published by Wiley Blackwell in 2015.

69. Omar, email message to author.

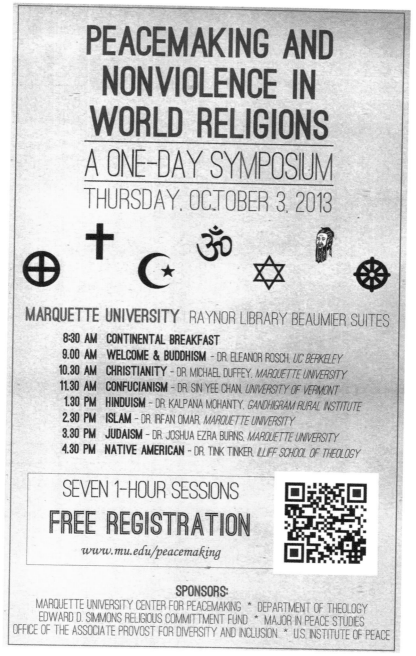

Figure 7.14: Flyer for a one-day symposium titled, "Peacemaking and Nonviolence in World Religions" on the campus of Marquette University.

and Campus Ministry provided funding for the dinner.[70] Students in this class also brainstormed and made suggestions as to the improvements Marquette can make to increase interfaith engagements on campus. These suggestions by students (numbering over 60 from two sections) were summarized in the form of a letter that the students signed voluntarily. The thought-provoking and action-calling memorandum (with the subject of "Strengthening the Culture of Interfaith Dialogue at Marquette") was sent by Dr. Omar to the then-VP for Mission and Ministry, Dr. Stephanie Russell. The letter included appreciation of the progress and commitment Marquette has made to engage a culture of interfaith on campus while highlighting further areas of need and development where Marquette's administration could improve working together with students, faculty, staff, and administration (fig. 7.17).[71]

Figures 7.15 & 7.16: An "Amazing Faiths Dinner Dialogue" event on Marquette campus attracted students from diverse backgrounds.

---

70. Ibid.

71. *Memorandum: Strengthening the Culture of Interfaith Dialogue at Marquette*, memorandum. Summary of student comments was made by class TA, Rev. Nathaniel Kidd.

MEMORANDUM

TO: **Dr. Stephanie Russell, Vice President of Mission and Ministry**

FROM: The students of THEO 2410 ("Christian-Muslim Dialogue") Fall 2015

DATE: 30 November 2015

SUBJECT: **Strengthening the Culture of Interfaith Dialogue at Marquette**

We are writing to you as students in the THEO 2410 "Christian-Muslim Dialogue" course to express our appreciation for the efforts and steps undertaken to strengthen the culture of interfaith dialogue on Marquette campus.

In this course, we have been studying and discussing the history, praxis, and issues of interreligious dialogue, particularly between Christians and Muslims. As one of our class activities, we visited the new Interfaith Meditation Room in the AMU. In light of our studies, it was exciting to see the tangible, practical steps that are being taken to create space for people of different religions to come together in faith and have the opportunity to engage and discuss subjects of common interest and create an organic "culture of dialogue." We were glad to discover and experience how the administration is investing in highlighting our interreligious diversity and making this a tangible priority for Marquette University.

As a part of our reflections on the visit to the Interfaith Meditation room, we spent some time as a class considering what more we could do as a community to promote and encourage interreligious interaction and sharing on campus. Recognizing that there are certain aspects of this project that are student-driven (such as taking advantage of and promoting the opportunities already available, developing student groups and initiatives, intentionally building relationships across traditions, etc), we also identified several ways in which the Marquette administration could extend its support for interfaith efforts on campus, and move towards a more robustly interfaith environment.

- It was observed that Marquette University already promotes a number of service activities and leadership opportunities that are already effectively "interfaith" on the basis of the students who participate. Without much difficulty, this "interfaith" aspect of service and leadership could be made explicit and intentional through specific training and facilitation for students talking about their faith backgrounds and deepest motivations.

- Many students lamented the fact that skills of interreligious dialogue were not a part of the regular theology requirement, and suggested that a course, seminar or module on the topic should be a regular offering, if not part of the core curriculum.

- Some of us noted that interfaith issues and opportunities could be specifically highlighted during freshman orientation, and immediate opportunities for students to become involved could be offered.

- Somewhat similar to the O-Fest, or Campus Ministry open houses, an event could be organized that would feature symbols and representatives from religious communities students are affiliated with, offering students the opportunity to "tour" the landscape of faiths at Marquette.

- Several of us thought that interfaith spaces might be expanded in size, number, and visibility.

- The role of sharing a meal together across religious and cultural boundaries has been a regular theme in our course, and not surprisingly, several students suggested that the university could open more opportunities and support for interreligious "dialogue dinners," perhaps even creating a space within the dining halls where there could be a regular, intentional exchange of cultures and faiths.

"Faith" is explicitly named as one of our core values at Marquette, yet because of the many different meanings people invest in the term and the many different expectations the word evokes, it can be tempting to reduce this value to the status of a rather vague sentiment. We hope that these thoughts and suggestions on the basis of our experience and reflection as a class will serve to encourage and challenge Marquette administration to deepen and further clarify its commitment to this value, just as we have been encouraged and challenged in this course to examine the self and other with respect to our general appreciation of faith.

Respectfully Yours,

Figure 7.17: Copy of the two-page letter summarizing the comments and suggestions from Dr. Omar's students.

Besides Dr. Omar's theology courses, Richard Taylor kept up the pace with his focus on Abrahamic philosophical dialogue through a global network of scholars under the "Aquinas and the Arabs" philosophy seminar. They hold meetings each year on themes that involved Christian, Jewish, and Muslim philosophical thinkers.[72] In March 2015, Sarah Pessin of the University of Denver and Richard Taylor organized "A Conversation on Philosophical and Religious Issues in the Work of Averroes and Maimonides" on Marquette's campus (fig. 7.18).[73]

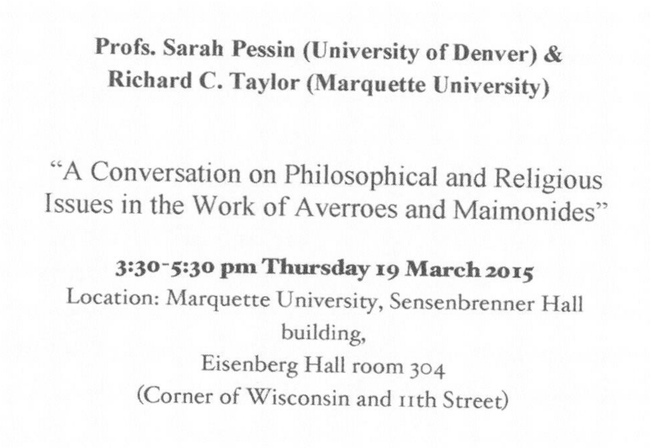

Profs. Sarah Pessin (University of Denver) &
Richard C. Taylor (Marquette University)

"A Conversation on Philosophical and Religious
Issues in the Work of Averroes and Maimonides"

3:30-5:30 pm Thursday 19 March 2015
Location: Marquette University, Sensenbrenner Hall
building,
Eisenberg Hall room 304
(Corner of Wisconsin and 11th Street)

Figure 7.18: Flyer for the seminar on "Philosophical and Religious Issues in the Work of Averroes and Maimonides," held on Marquette's campus.

Interfaith conversations and events continue to increase. In April 2015, Marquette University and the Milwaukee Jewish Federation, with support from the Isabel & Alfred Bader Fund, hosted a lecture by Father Patrick Desbois titled, "Holocaust by Bullets," a lecture about Holocaust education and genocide prevention, with echoes of the importance of interfaith relationships.[74] In November 2015, Marquette Muslim Student Association, Jewish Student Union, and Students for Justice in Palestine, among other co-sponsors,

---

72. For more on the history of this project, which extends beyond Marquette, visit its website at: http://academic.mu.edu/taylorr/Aquinas_and_the_Arabs/Aquinas_%26_the_Arabs.html.

73. Richard Taylor, *Philosophy and Religion Averroes Maimonides Seminar,* flyer.

74. President Michael R. Lovell (president, Marquette University), email interview by Kaitlyn Daly, May 20, 2017. Lovell also provided show-and-tell items to other events on campus about the Holocaust.

organized a "Pray for Paris Vigil" in response to the terrorist attacks in Paris. In their responses to my queries, Stephanie Russell and President Lovell also mentioned that Marquette's Mission Week celebrations often included interfaith themes and more recently also featured "dinner dialogues." There were also prayer services with interfaith themes including racial and environmental justice, charity, and the common good.

A recent major event on Marquette campus was held in March 2017 titled "Christian-Muslim Relations in America Today" (figs. 7.19 & 7.20), which included speakers from Marquette and other universities, academics, and community leaders. In attendance were students, faculty, and community leaders from Chicago and Milwaukee. Presentations focused on topics relevant to interfaith relations between Muslims and Christians in America today, including the history of local dialogue in Milwaukee. The two-day symposium was opened by President Michael Lovell and Dean of Arts and Sciences, Dr. Rick Holz. It was co-sponsored by various departments In his opening remarks, President Lovell quoted Pope Francis noting the emphasis on the need for dialogue between religions in order for us "to discover the profound truth . . . and, to contribute to building peace."[75]

Recently, travel-related interfaith opportunities have been offered through the Center for Peacemaking. Dr. Omar and Patrick Kennelly, director of the Center for Peacemaking, led a trip to India for the theology course, "Faith and the Role of Nonviolence: Religious Peacebuilding in India."[76] Also, as already noted, during a Spring Break immersion trip titled, "Engaging Muslims, Countering Islamophobia Immersion Trip," hosted by Dr. Louise Cainkar, students traveled to Dearborn and Hamtramck, Michigan, where some of the oldest Muslim communities reside. These cities are home to many cultural and religious sites related to the history of Muslims in the United States.[77]

In the school year of 2015–2016, a group of students interested in interfaith found one another through the director of Campus Ministry, Mary Sue Callan-Farley, a shared class, and connections through friends. In the summer of 2016, several of these students attended IFYC's Interfaith Leadership Institute in Chicago, Illinois. The group consisted of Farley; Bernardo Avila-Borunda,

---

75. Marquette University, "Christian-Muslim Relations in American Today: An Interdisciplinary Symposium," program pamphlet.

76. Marquette University Center for Peacemaking, *Travel Opportunities with the Center for Peacemaking Newsbrief*, flyer.

77. Ibid.

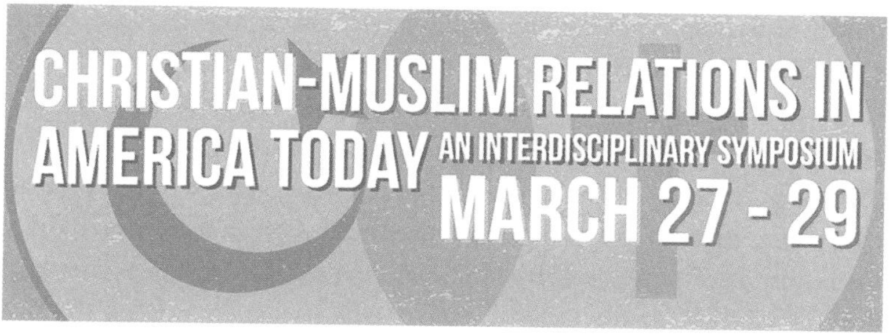

CHRISTIAN-MUSLIM RELATIONS IN AMERICA TODAY AN INTERDISCIPLINARY SYMPOSIUM MARCH 27 - 29

CHRISTIAN–MUSLIM RELATIONS IN AMERICA TODAY
AN INTERDISCIPLINARY SYMPOSIUM

MARQUETTE UNIVERSITY
27-29 MARCH 2017

> "Pope Francis calls on us to be in dialogue with religions, 'to discover the profound truth of their mission in the midst of humanity, and to contribute to building peace and a network of respect and fraternity'.... Our...Christian-Muslim Relations Symposium is an ideal way for us to live the Pope's words."
>
> Marquette President **Dr. Michael Lovell**

Monday, March 27, 2017
Alumni Memorial Union, Ballrooms AB

3.30-3.45p

Introduction: **Dr. Richard C. Taylor**, Professor, Department of Philosophy

Opening Remarks: **Dr. Michael Lovell**, President, Marquette University
Welcome: **Dr. Richard Holz**, Dean, Klingler College of Arts & Sciences

3.45-5.00
Dr. Ed Fallone, Marquette University Law School
"The Constitution and the Marketplace of Faith"

5.00-6.15
Dr. Risa Brooks, Marquette University Department of Political Science
"Extremism and Terrorist Violence in the United States Today"

6.15 Reception

1

Figures 7.19 & 7.20: Flyer and program of the symposium on "Christian-Muslim Relations in America Today" at Marquette.

assistant director for Multicultural Student Ministry; and five Marquette students: Kaitlyn Daly, Bradley DeGarmo, Michelle Frederick, Luiz Gabriel (LG) Dias Duarte Machado, and Anna Sisk (figs. 7.21 & 7.22). Students returned to campus ready to apply what they had learned and to see how interfaith could be better incorporated on Marquette's campus. During the 2016–2017 academic year, the group organized several small events to recruit and inform other students on campus. Their efforts have been partially successful because one of the main pieces for this to work is institutional support which, despite the rhetoric, is still missing.

With the help and guidance of Campus Ministry, the new Interfaith Coordinating Team (ICT) was created. This team was to serve as a liaison, resource, and advocate for interfaith relations on campus between students and religious student groups and organizations. An application was posted to invite passionate, collaborative leaders with an interest in interfaith and with the hopes to diversify the team. At the time of the institute, the majority of the Marquette delegation identified as Christian, specifically Catholic and Protestant. At the foundation of the Interfaith Coordinating Team in the fall of 2016, the team grew to seven students: Faezh Dalieh, Kaitlyn Daly, Bradley DeGarmo, Luiz Gabriel (LG) Dias Duarte Machado, Michelle Frederick, Nader Shammout, and Yuvraj (Yuvi) Sandhu, with advisors Mary Sue Callan-Farley and Bernardo Avila-Borunda.

 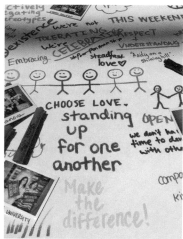

Figures 7.21 & 7.22: Several Marquette students attended IFYC's Interfaith Leadership Institute in Chicago, Illinois. Left to right: Luiz Gabriel (LG) Dias Duarte Machado, Kaitlyn Daly, Michelle Frederick, and Bradley DeGarmo.

Figures 7.23 & 7.24: The first interfaith group at Marquette University, Breaking Barriers and Building Bridges, or BB&BB for short, was established during the 2016–2017 school year.

This Interfaith Coordinating Team created Breaking Barriers and Building Bridges, or BB&BB for short. This was the first Marquette interfaith group formed to encourage students to participate in efforts that enrich the interfaith fabric at Marquette. There were discussions about starting an IFYC Better Together organization or registering BB&BB as a Marquette student organization. However, neither became a reality. As of today, both the Interfaith Coordinating Team and BB&BB are housed in Campus Ministry. In 2018–2019, despite their best efforts, Campus Ministry has struggled to find students to become part of the ICT.

Figures 7.25, 7.26, 7.27, & 7.28: The first event hosted by ICT and BB&BB was the September 11 memorial vigil in 2016; top left: standing in a circle for silent prayer; top right: sharing the light; bottom left and right: Kaitlyn Daly and Nader Shammout sharing a reflection.

The first event hosted by ICT and BB&BB was the September 11 memorial vigil in 2016 (figs. 7.25–7.28). Invitations were sent to Marquette leadership, including President Lovell, Vice President of Student Affairs, Dr. Xavier Cole, and, the then-VP of Mission and Ministry, Father Thomas Krettek, SJ (fig. 7.29).[78] A Facebook event and printed flyer were created to inform and invite students (fig. 7.30).[79] Interfaith Coordinating Team members led the crowd of about 20 students, faculty, and staff in reflection, guiding with interfaith intentions of respect, openness, sharing, listening, and silence. There was a time for participants to share reflections of their own, followed by a candle walk around the square outside the Alumni Memorial Union.

Dear President Lovell,

We hope this letter finds you refreshed from the summer months and excited for the new academic year ahead.

Today, we are writing to you as the new Interfaith Coordinating Team at Marquette University. We are a new team housed in Campus Ministry. We strive for the mission of working together, as a human family, to foster an environment that recognizes differences as our strength and to break down barriers and build bridges in the Marquette and greater Milwaukee communities.

As a team, we wanted to cordially invite you to our first interfaith event of the Fall 2016 semester. With the memorial of September 11, 2001 coming up, we wanted to honor all individuals, communities, and faiths touched by this tragic event. With heavy hearts, we hope to create a space for reflection, solidarity, and intention for our fellow Marquette students, faculty, and staff.

To do so, we will be hosting a memorial vigil on Monday, September 12, 2016 at 7:00-8:00p.m. in Westowne Square. The event will have various speakers, a candlelight solidarity walk, and end with an interfaith prayer for peace. Refreshments in the AMU will follow. We invite you to participate in this event as you feel called. Ways in which you can participate include: attending the event, spreading the word on social media and university news outlets, speaking at the event, and keeping the event in thought and prayer. Please contact Kaitlyn Daly at kaitlyn.daly@marquette.edu if you are interested in offering a prayer, reflection, or story at the vigil.

We also kindly ask that you please keep our team in your thoughts and prayers as we work with great effort and heart to enrich the interfaith fabric at Marquette University.

With peace and gratitude,

The Interfaith Coordinating Team
Marquette University

Kaitlyn Daly
Michelle Frederick
Nader Shammout
Luiz Gabriel Dias Duarte Machado
Bradley DeGarmo
J Bernardo Ávila-Borunda
Yuvi Sandhu
Mary Sue Callan-Farley
Faezh Dalieh

---

78. Marquette University Interfaith Coordinating Team, *9/11 Memorial Vigil*, flyer.

79. Marquette University Interfaith Coordinating Team, *9/11 Memorial Vigil Invitation*, flyer.

9/11 MEMORIAL VIGIL

TO HONOR ALL INDIVIDUALS, COMMUNITIES, AND FAITHS TOUCHED BY THIS TRAGIC EVENT. WITH HEAVY HEARTS, WE HOPE TO CREATE A SPACE FOR PERSONAL REFLECTIONS, SOLIDARITY, AND INTENTION FOR OUR FELLOW MARQUETTE STUDENTS, FACULTY, AND STAFF.

When: Monday, September 12, 2016

Time: 7:00 pm - 8:00 pm

Where: Marquette's Westowne square

Interfaith   www.mu.edu/cm

9/11 Memorial Vigil

Figures 7.29 & 7.30: Invitation and flyer on behalf of the Interfaith Coordinating Team for the 9/11 Memorial Vigil.

In January 2018, just before the start of the second semester, the Interfaith Coordinating Team created and organized the first on-campus half-day interfaith retreat titled, "You Change Your Life By Changing Your Heart" (fig. 7.31).[80]

Fig. 7.31: Flyer for the first on-campus half-day interfaith retreat titled, "You Change Your Life By Changing Your Heart."

80. Marquette University Interfaith Coordinating Team, *You Change Your Life By Changing Your Heart Interfaith Retreat*, flyer PDF.

The retreat had a great turnout, with nearly 20 participants attending the retreat, which included a panel discussion, reflections, and small and large group interactive activities.

Figures 7.32, 7.33, & 7.34: The retreat comprised of a panel discussion, reflections, and small and large group interactive activities for the participating students.

In February 2017, the group hosted interfaith dialogues in the Interfaith Meditation Room in Marquette's Memorial Union, a popular place for students to gather and pass through, centered on the theme of love (fig. 7.35).[81]

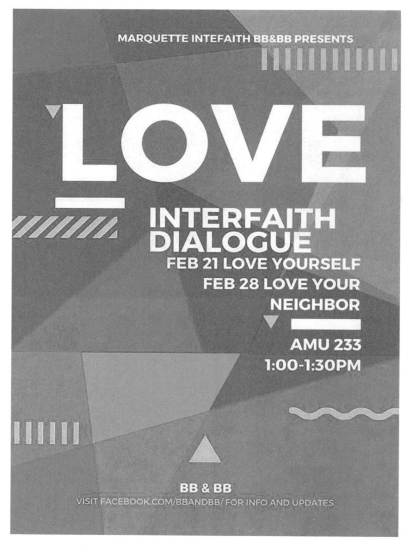

Figure 7.35: Flyer for the Interfaith Coordinating Team and BB&BB-sponsored interfaith dialogues in the Interfaith Meditation Room in Marquette's Memorial Union.

81. Marquette University Interfaith Coordinating Team, *Interfaith Dialogue February Love Yourself and Your Neighbor*, flyer and agenda.

Various religious student groups on campus have promoted and hosted interfaith events of their own. For several years, including 2017, the Jewish Student Union hosted an annual Passover Seder meal open to all students to come and learn about the Jewish tradition (fig. 7.36).[82] The group also advertised an Interfaith Shabbat Service and Dinner by Hillel Milwaukee (fig. 7.37).[83]

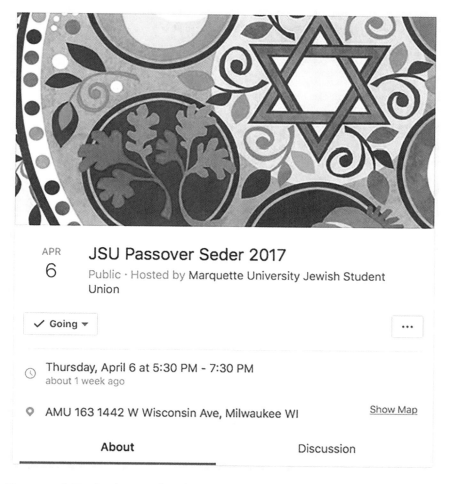

Figure 7.36: Facebook event flyer for a Passover Seder hosted by the Jewish Student Union.

---

82. Marquette University Jewish Student Union, *JSU Passover Seder Meal*, Facebook event and description.

83. Hillel Milwaukee, *Interfaith Shabbat Service and Dinner*, flyer and description.

Figure 7.37: In March 2017, the Jewish Student Union advertised an Interfaith Shabbat Service and Dinner by Hillel Milwaukee.

Figure 7.38: Photo taken on the Hijab Day, a well-attended event of the "Islam Awareness Week," organized by the Muslim Student Association.

The Muslim Student Association hosts an annual "Islam Awareness Week," which includes a variety of events, speakers, and service projects focused on expressing the values and traditions of the Islam and the many cultures where Islam is practiced. Hijab Day provides an opportunity for students to wear the hijab for a day as a sign of their solidarity with Muslim women (fig. 7.38). Muslim women students also share their unique personal reasons for wearing or not wearing the hijab. The event is followed by a reflection session to discuss the experience of those who chose to try on the hijab, including those who wear it for an entire day. I participated in this event in 2016 and 2017, and it was a moving experience for a variety of reasons. It made me connect deeply with the values and people for whom it is a daily practice. I learned what motivates them to commit to wearing religious symbols such as the hijab in public.

University of Wisconsin–Milwaukee

The University of Wisconsin–Milwaukee (UWM) offers several opportunities for spiritual and religious groups to organize themselves and plan events and activities that cater to students. According to their publicity literature these groups are known as SRCs or "spiritual and religious communities." There are 18 spiritual and religious communities and student organizations, and information about these can be found on UWM's student organizations website.[84] Some of these groups are also featured in the pamphlet on "Spiritual and Religious Communities at UWM" (figs. 7.39 & 7.40).[85] According to Thomas Dake, senior student services coordinator at Student Involvement at University of Wisconsin–Milwaukee, UW–Milwaukee has a few students, faculty, and staff members with interfaith ideas and hopes for them to become a reality. Interfaith on campus got a boost when the Lutheran Campus minister, Pastor Rachel Young Binter, became involved. She planned and sent students to the Interfaith Youth Core's Interfaith Leadership Institute in Chicago. Starting from that point on she was the "driving force and a true supporter" and a "tremendous ally.[86]

At a timely meeting for the Religious Centers on campus, Young Binter introduced the idea of engaging students in learning about interfaith. Dake had already been talking to his supervisor about his hopes to start an interfaith

---

84. Updated information on the spiritual and religious groups can be found on the webpage titled, "Spiritual and Religious Communities at UWM," University of Wisconsin-Milwaukee, https://uwm.edu/studentinvolvement/more/spiritual-religious/ministries/ (see figs. 7.39 and 7.40).

85. University of Wisconsin–Milwaukee, *Spiritual and Religious Communities at UWM*, pamphlet.

86. Dake, interview by Kaitlyn Daly, April 21, 2017.

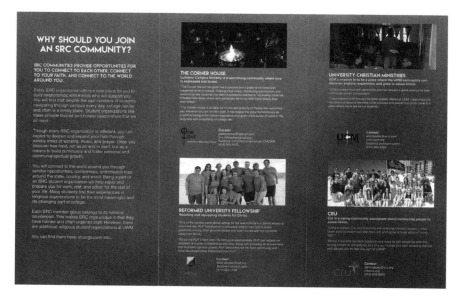

Figures 7.39 & 7.40: Pamphlet describing several of the eighteen spiritual and religious communities and student organizations offered at UWM.

group. He noted, "[interfaith has] been a hot topic in higher [education] for a number of years and the state institutions are the slowest to wake up on this one for reasons I think have to do with fear and lack of knowledge." These reasons further made it difficult for the university to allocate funds for any such event.[87]

In the early spring of 2014, a member of the UWM Muslim Student Association and a member of the Lutheran Campus Ministry Corner House collaborated in an interfaith event. Also, in the spring of 2014, sociocultural programming began plans to send students to the Interfaith Youth Core's Interfaith Leadership Institute in Chicago that coming summer. With the support of the Mitzvah fund—a fund that supports diversity, inclusion, social justice—the request to send a UWM delegation to the summer institute was approved. This made it possible for Dake, Young Binter, Miller, and other students to attend the IFYC's leadership institute in the summer of 2014. The following fall, a dedicated group of students created the first interfaith student group, "Better Together Interfaith,"[88] taking after the IFYC's "Better Together," which is a national organization for colleges and universities across the country (fig. 7.42).[89]

In her interview, Miller details that prior to 2013, sociocultural programming at UWM included events that discussed religious themes. Since Better Together was created in 2014, there have been interfaith events in select departments of the university and there is a student senator whose focus is interfaith.[90] Miller cites the Student Health Offices, LGBT Resource Center, Student Success Center, and Student Involvement as groups that strive to be inclusive of religious diversity.[91] Since 2014, the Interfaith Conference of Greater Milwaukee (ICGM) and Better Together have co-sponsored dialogue dinners. The Interfaith Conference has sent trained facilitators to lead small-group interfaith dialogues under their signature "Amazing Faiths" program.[92] The program consists of sharing ideas about questions that come from a variety of wisdom traditions. The group is usually diverse and meets in

---

87. Ibid.

88. Heinritz and Miller, interview by Kaitlyn Daly.

89. Interfaith Youth Core, *Better Together*, sticker. Provided by Thomas Dake.

90. Heinritz and Miller, interview by Kaitlyn Daly.

91. Ibid.

92. Dake, interview, interview by Kaitlyn Daly. The Amazing Faiths Dinner Dialogues Program originally began at Rice University in Dallas.

an intimate setting, such as in a home, and is facilitated by a trained person. Each participant receives a different question so their responses are unique and personalized.[93] Dake shared in his interview that he hopes the Interfaith Conference will train individuals on campus to create campus-based facilitators for these dialogue dinners.[94] At these dinners, Dake reports that participants came from various religious backgrounds, including a Sikh professor and Baha'i and Buddhist students.[95] Dake expressed hope by saying that as he saw the people engaged in a respectful discussion, he realized that "we are on our way."[96]

There were other events at the university. Eboo Patel visited the University of Wisconsin–Milwaukee campus in the fall of 2015 for its Distinguished Lecture Series.[97] In April 2016, faculty advisors for many different student groups, including the Jewish student group, Hillel, Muslim Student Association, and Desi Student Association visited the Interfaith Youth Core offices in Chicago. Dake and four other UWM students went with them. In April 2017, an Interfaith Youth Core representative came to campus to host a few interfaith workshops.[98] In recent years, Lutheran Minister Rachel Young Binter began hosting informal monthly interfaith talks.[99] There have been many memorable events; one that brought new students into the fold was when Pastor Rachel and Othman Atta, Muslim community leader, co-presented at an interfaith dinner hosted by the Muslim Student Association. The event attracted the attention of many students, including Christians from different denominations, Muslims, and others, sharing in a "wonderfully interactive evening."[100] In January 2017, the religious studies program brought a Coptic bishop to campus.[101] Similarly, the Hillel group invited a Muslim speaker and also hosted an interfaith Shabbat

---

93. Dake, interview by Kaitlyn Daly; more information on the Amazing Faiths Dinner Dialogues program in Milwaukee can be found on the Interfaith Conference of Greater Milwaukee's website at: http://interfaithconference.org/cms-view-page.php?page=amazing-faiths-dinners.

94. Dake, interview by Kaitlyn Daly.

95. Ibid.

96. Ibid.

97. "The Distinguished Lecture Series Presents an Evening with Eboo Patel," *University of Wisconsin-Milwaukee Student Involvement*, 2015, http://uwm.edu/studentinvolvement/event/the-distinguished-lecture-series-presents-an-evening-with-eboo-patel/.

98. Dake, interview by Kaitlyn Daly.

99. Heinritz and Miller, interview by Kaitlyn Daly.

100. Dake, interview by Kaitlyn Daly.

101. Ibid.

in March 2017.[102] Heinritz recalls a "March for Peace" recently around campus in which Muslims, Lutherans, Christians, and Jews participated, laughing and spending time together.[103]

Many of the activities and events noted above for each of the three universities covered in this study were at least partially funded by their respective institutions. The time and efforts made by the students, faculty, and staff are not always compensated adequately, but it is important to recognize that the institutions are at least taking small steps in making interfaith known. Apart from the educational institutions and various departments and offices within these, funding and support also came from various other outside groups and sources.[104]

Institutional Challenges

The interfaith events put on by students, especially at Marquette, are even more important in light of several recent events and reporting news publications that have surfaced, some detailing positive events, others revealing unfortunate news. Marquette University's journalistic channels have published several pieces relating to the religious climate and concerns of its campus and students. On February 2, 2012, an article, "Campus Muslims Seeking Larger Space for Prayer," was published on the *Marquette Wire*'s online site detailing the Muslim

---

102. Dake, interview by Kaitlyn Daly; Hillel Milwaukee, *Interfaith Shabbat Service and Dinner*, flyer and description.

103. Heinritz and Miller, interview by Kaitlyn Daly.

104. Past to present, in alphabetical order: the Arab Student Association; Edward D. Simmons Religious Commitment Fund; Global Peace Services USA; the Helen Bader Foundation; Innovation Grant/Strategic Innovation Fund program of Marquette Office of Research and Innovation; Isabel & Alfred Bader Fund; the Manresa Project; Marquette Campus Ministry; Marquette Center for Peacemaking; Marquette College of Education; Marquette Departments of English, Foreign Languages and Literatures, History, Philosophy, Political Science, Social and Cultural Sciences, Sociology, Theology; Marquette Excellence in Diversity Grant; Marquette Helen Way Klingler College of Arts and Sciences; Marquette Interfaith Coordinating Team; Marquette Jesuit community; Marquette Jewish Student Union; Marquette Major in Peace Studies; Marquette Muslim Student Association; Marquette Office of the Associate Provost for Diversity and Inclusion; Marquette Office of International Education; Marquette Office of the Provost; Marquette Office of Mission and Identity; Marquette Office of Mission and Ministry; Marquette Office of Student Development-Intercultural Programs; Marquette University Student Government; the Mellon Foundation; the Mellon Fund of the Marquette Klinger College of Arts and Sciences; Mellon Grant; Milwaukee Jewish Federation; the Niagara Foundation; Provost Office Grant; Rev. Francis Wade, SJ, endowment; US Institute of Peace; Wade Chair Fund; and, religious individuals and communities in the greater Milwaukee area.

Student Association's search for a more accommodating space for the needs of prayer, community gathering, and visibility on campus.[105]

On October 26, 2015, *Marquette Today Campus News and Events* mentioned the establishment of the Office of Institutional Diversity and Inclusion by the Provost's office in response to continued need for diversity and inclusion efforts at Marquette, as revealed in the Campus Climate Study (fig. 7.41).[106] On February 7, 2017, the *Marquette Wire* posted a story titled, "Story of a Personal Attack on Religious Clothing," describing a physical incident where an unidentified man "tugged" on one female student's hijab on campus while making aggressive verbal remarks.[107]

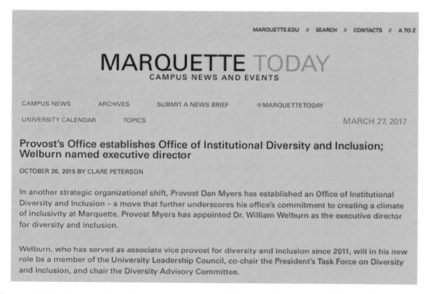

Figure 7.41: Screenshot of announcement of the establishment of the Office of Institutional Diversity and Inclusion on Marquette Today.

---

105. Simone Smith, "Campus Muslims Seeking Larger Space for Prayer," *Marquettewire. org*, February 2, 2012, accessed April 20, 2017, https://marquettewire.org/3805532/tribune/ tribune-news/campus-muslims-seeking-larger-space-for-prayer/.

106. Clare Peterson, "Provost's Office Establishes Office of Institutional Diversity and Inclusion; Welburn Named Executive Director," *Marquette Today*, October 26, 2015, accessed March 28, 2017, https://today.marquette.edu/2015/10/provosts-office-establishes-office-of-institutional-diversity-and-inclusion-welburn-named-executive-director/.

107. Clara Janzen, "Story of a Personal Attack on Religious Clothing," *Marquettewire. org*, February 7, 2017, accessed April 20, 2017, https://marquettewire.org/3965172/news/ saras-hijab/.

Figure 7.42: The sticker produced by the interfaith student group, "Better Together Interfaith."

Figure 7.43: On April 4, 2017, the Marquette Wire published a telling story, which also was the front-page cover story on the Marquette Tribune, titled, "Searching for Space."

On April 4, 2017, the *Marquette Wire* published a telling story, which also was the front-page cover story on the *Marquette Tribune*, titled, "Searching for Space" (fig. 7.43).[108] The article details the struggle minority religious groups on campus have with finding space and funding, especially Marquette's Lutheran Campus Ministry. Within the article, there is also a strong call for interfaith recognition and collaboration among all religious student groups on the predominately Catholic campus. Also included in the newspaper on this same date was an article titled, "Muslim Prayer Space Tarnished," also featured on the front page.[109] This story addressed two instances of hate speech and general harassment toward the Muslim students on campus and mentioned a few resolutions that were made. On April 11, 2017, another story appeared in *Marquette Wire* ("Take a Stroll in My Scarf") detailing the various responses to the Muslim Student Association's Hijab Day as part of Islam Awareness Week.[110] All of these recent publications point to the challenges Marquette's religious climate and interfaith efforts face. They all beg the question: What is Marquette actually doing about this?

Marquette publicly promotes a commitment to diversity on its campus, as seen in many statements and definitions that can be found on its website. The 2015 President's Task Force on Equity and Inclusion[111] framed its focus around diversity, equity, and inclusion, adopting their definition of inclusion from the Association of American Colleges and Universities.[112] However, Marquette's efforts have thus far been focused on ethnic diversity, although often the language used in official statements also highlights the need for opinion and viewpoint diversity as a valuable resource for dialogue and discussion. Marquette has not invested much to highlight the existing religious diversity on campus. The AACU definition of inclusion (below) prompts the necessity for recognition of religious diversity as well as investment in initiatives that encourage interfaith engagement on college and university campuses:

---

108. Alex Groth, "Searching for Space," *Marquette Tribune*, April 4, 2017, 1, 4–5.

109. Clara Janzen, "Muslim Prayer Space Tarnished," *Marquette Tribune*, April 4, 2017, 1–2.

110. Clara Janzen, "Take a Stroll in My Scarf," Marquettewire.org, April 11, 2017, https://marquettewire.org/3970701/news/take-a-stroll-in-my-scarf/.

111. "President's Task Force on Diversity and Inclusion," Marquette University, http://www.marquette.edu/diversity/presidents-task-force.php.

112. "Making Excellence Inclusive," Association of American Colleges and Universities, accessed September 4, 2017, https://www.aacu.org/making-excellence-inclusive as quoted in "President's Task Force on Equity and Inclusion," Marquette University, http://www.marquette.edu/diversity/presidents-task-force.php.

> The active, intentional and ongoing engagement with diversity—in the curriculum, in the co-curriculum, and in communities (intellectual, social, cultural, geographical) with which individuals might connect—in ways that increase awareness, content knowledge, cognitive sophistication, and emphatic understanding of the complex ways individuals interact within systems and institutions.[113]

This definition insists the interaction and appreciation of students of diverse backgrounds in pedagogical and experiential areas to engage further knowledge and understanding of other students and the world around them. Interfaith urges this same goal. Also, the University's Statement on Human Dignity and Diversity claims to embrace and celebrate the diversity of "age, culture, faith, ethnicity, race, gender, sexual orientation, language, and disability or social class" on its campus.[114] In this statement, as similar to the mission statement and many other public statements, faith is specifically mentioned.

In light of recent world events in early 2017, Marquette has been prompted to publish further public statements solidifying its support for diverse groups, especially undocumented and immigrant students. For example, in response to President Trump's travel ban executive order in January 2017, Marquette released several statements to all students, especially recognizing the international students and the global community at Marquette. These statements included: the January 30, 2017, *Marquette Today Campus News and Events*, "A Message from Marquette Leaders to the Campus Community;"[115] followed by the January 2017 Marquette Office of International Education, "A Message of Support and Solidarity from the Office of International Education";[116] the February 13, 2017, *Marquette Today Campus News and Events*, "A Message from Provost Myers and Xavier Cole Regarding Undocumented Students";[117] and

---

113. Ibid.

114. "Diversity and Inclusion – About," Marquette University, http://www.marquette.edu/diversity/about.php.

115. Marquette University, "A Message from Marquette Leaders to the Campus Community," *Marquette Today,* January 30, 2017, https://today.marquette.edu/2017/01/a-message-from-leadership-to-the-marquette-community/.

116. "A Message of Support and Solidarity from the Office of International Education," Marquette University Office of International Education, http://www.marquette.edu/oie/executiveorder.shtml.

117. Marquette University, "A Message from Provost Myers and Xavier Cole Regarding Undocumented Students," *Marquette Today,* February 13, 2017, https://today.marquette.edu/2017/02/a-message-from-provost-myers-and-xavier-cole-regarding-undocumented-students/.

the Marquette University Office of International Education's March 6, 2017, video, "You Are Welcome Here."[118] With these publications in the last five years and the publicly expressed commitments and statements by Marquette University leaders, we must ask ourselves the constant question: Is Marquette following up on what needs to be done? Are words enough? Or do they require positive changes and policy changes to match their statements? Is the university taking action toward making students feel safe seriously enough?

To my knowledge, there are people making this happen on a daily basis, but translation of grassroots, student-led interfaith efforts to the entire university-wide effort is slow. The university's Campus Ministry does have the Interfaith Student Leadership Council in place, which will have a representative from each religious student organization. As of 2017, participation was mandatory from religious student organizations but optional for affiliated ministry or nonstudent organizations. The council meets monthly, but attendance has proven to be inconsistent. A sustainable interfaith engagement, connection, and collaboration among all religious students, groups, and organizations on campus will take time at both the grassroots and institutional levels. It will require unwavering support and commitment by the leadership.

Finally, a major step was taken in the right direction with the hiring of a Muslim chaplain in 2017. Although the demand for a chaplain has been there for more than 10 years, it became a reality under the leadership of Rev. Thomas Krettek, SJ, as vice president of Mission and Ministry, and it happened around the time of the troubling incidents noted above. The part-time chaplain position was tenuous at first, but through the efforts of Campus Ministry director Mary Sue Callan-Farley, permanent funding has been secured for a 10-hour/week position starting in the fall of 2019.[119]

Participants and Perspectives

This section of the chapter will highlight the people involved in interfaith efforts, some of whom were mentioned previously. Apart from investigating the publicly promoted and supposedly lived institutional mission

118. Clare Peterson, "You Are Welcome Here: Office of International Education Shares New Video," *Marquette Today*, March 6, 2017, https://today.marquette.edu/2017/03/you-are-welcome-here-office-of-international-education-shares-new-video/.

119. In July 2019, per the information supplied by Irfan Omar, the hiring committee under the leadership of Mary Sue Callan-Farley hired Imam Sameer Ali as the new part-time Muslim chaplain.

statements, I interviewed select individuals who, in their view, have sought to promote interfaith values by offering courses, conferences, symposia, and lectures, both on and off campus. Students, faculty, and staff shared in detail their involvement in interfaith efforts, perceptions of the lasting impact of such efforts, and the unique perspectives on common goals toward building interfaith and inclusive communities. While the full summaries will not be reported, what I offer below are inspirations and summary version of their comments.

Faculty and staff involved in the interfaith effort at their universities include, but are not limited to: Dan Di Domizio, Sister Jessine Reiss, and Sister Lucille Walsh (d. 2013) as professors in World Literature and World Religions at Cardinal Stritch University; Irfan Omar and Richard Taylor as professors in Theology and Philosophy (respectively) at Marquette University; and Bernardo Avila-Borunda and Mary Sue Callan-Farley as Campus Ministry staff at Marquette University. Also, Dr. Stephanie Russell as the previous vice president of Mission and Ministry at Marquette University; President Lovell as the current president of Marquette University; and Pastor Jessica Short as the Lutheran Campus minister at Marquette; and Thomas Dake as Student Involvement staff and Rachel Young Binter as the Lutheran pastor at the University of Wisconsin–Milwaukee.

Students fueling change through their interfaith efforts on their respective campuses include, in school and alphabetical order: Monica Kling at Cardinal Stritch University; Faezh Dalieh, Bradley DeGarmo, Michelle Frederick, Luiz Gabriel "LG" Dias Duarte Machado, Sundus Jaber, Ruth Lied, Yuvraj "Yuvi" Sandhu, Nader Shammout, and Wyatt Meyer at Marquette University; and Sean Heinritz and Tabitha Miller at University of Wisconsin–Milwaukee. Of course, interfaith is a team effort, and there are a number of individuals not mentioned here who are interested and have been involved in learning and contributing to interfaith and starting or joining interfaith efforts. Their efforts, though not named or identified, are also greatly appreciated and deserve to be recognized.[120]

Based on my interviews, many of these individuals worked passionately and diligently to promote interfaith because of their professional and personal

---

120. Since I have interviewed students in 2017–2018, I am not able to provide a wholly comprehensive list of activities and people involved in the past. However, based on interviews and information supplied by the interviewees at the time, I am able to comment on the improved state of interfaith awareness among students on these campuses between 2007 and 2017.

commitment to what dialogue does to them and those around them. Dialogue helps build relationships and helps promote and celebrate religious diversity, inclusion, and collaboration. They may or may not be driven primarily by the mission statements of their respective universities, but they certainly have helped animate some of the same values. For example, Di Domizio is interested in walking in the footsteps of Sister Lucille Walsh and Sister Jessine Reiss in bringing interfaith matters into the classroom setting and supporting and attending interfaith activities on campus. Omar is interested in interfaith dialogue in both its academic and praxis dimensions. Richard Taylor is committed to increasing the knowledge base and awareness of centuries of interactions and discussions between Muslim, Jewish, and Christian philosophers, theologians, and other thinkers in the medieval period. Mary Sue Callan-Farley and Bernardo Avila-Borunda are actively engaged and seek to guide students who wish to do interfaith on campus. They are committed to enriching the acceptance, encounter, and celebration of all faiths on campus. However, they need help from the key players in the Marquette University administration who are in a position to set the tone and to offer resources necessary for meaningful interfaith engagement, including providing a listening ear, creating new initiatives, issuing public statements, and attending interfaith events on campus. Thomas Dake is the key point person when it comes to religious and spiritual organizations, groups, and activities on campus. The students named above have been the initiators of events that show religious diversity on their campus and by creating interfaith teams or organizations; attending local, regional, and national conferences and workshops; and being active in their student organizations to learn and promote dialogue on campus. They have tried to tailor the interfaith activism to fit their unique campuses.

Assessment and Analysis

Below I will summarize how the institutions of higher learning have treated the issue of interfaith in terms of both their word and deed, as it were. I will take into account the aforementioned university mission statements, human and other resources allocated for the activities deemed interfaith, and public statements by leaders, faculty, staff, and students. I will provide my own analysis of the patterns that emerged from the student, faculty, and staff interview and their perceptions on the pedagogical and experiential offerings at the aforementioned universities, based on the impact of such interfaith efforts. I will also evaluate how these pedagogical and experiential offerings relate to the university's mission and commitment to community engagement, based on the accounts of activities as documented above. I will end this section by commenting on the impact of such interfaith efforts for peace and justice awareness as well as for inclusion and diversity on campus, in Milwaukee, and the world.

Emerging Themes and Patterns from the Interviews

Father Thomas Michel, SJ, shares an insightful quote, which rings true in many of the comments in the interviews by students, faculty, and staff, alike. Father Michel states, "one does not build a culture of dialogue by decree. It is a slow process of study, planning . . . decisions and choices, communication . . . and, most of all, a question of changing attitudes" that requires patience and trust.[121] There were consistent themes woven through many of the interviews of university students and personnel, and even some that reflect Father Michel's quote above. The themes and patterns highlighted in this section certainly do not exhaust the list of thoughts, ideas, stories, and recommendations presented in each individual interview.

Common words defining interfaith included interdisciplinary and intersectional, dialogue, interaction, between faiths or worldviews, coming together, challenging, growing, unity, everyday, noble and sacred, and practice.

Common barriers to interfaith efforts mentioned by many interviewees included busy and conflicting schedules, fear of the other or the unknown, the problem of transient nature of students, the need for space, limited or no funding, inconsistent or lack of attendance, slow progress, state or religious affiliations, and fear of losing one's identity.

Common forms of support for interfaith efforts included outreach and efforts of the Interfaith Conference of Greater Milwaukee; dedicated professors, students, and other people in leadership roles at the university; campus ministries; Student Involvement or Student Affairs offices and organizations; university cultural centers; the mission and values of the university; and the diverse and engaged leaders in the surrounding Milwaukee community.

Common benefits of working with students on interfaith efforts included students' openness, energy, experience in a global context, and interest in interfaith and creativity. There were also common challenges mentioned, including students' impressionability, impulsiveness, lack of interest or mediocre interest, and busy schedules.

---

121. Michel, "Creating a Culture of Dialogue," *A Christian View of Islam*, 23.

Common goals of student interfaith dialogue included building relationships, community, understanding, awareness, sensitivity, education, acceptance, appreciation, pedagogical and experiential opportunities to engage, humanization of our neighbors, challenging misconceptions and misinformation, critical thinking, elimination of fear of the other, faith formation, human formation, discovering allies, and gaining new perspectives.

Common pieces of advice for starting interfaith on university campuses included do not give up, be persistent, expect a slow progress, make interfaith events attention grabbing, find your allies, and establish a reciprocal and symbiotic relationship with the surrounding urban community. It was also made clear in the interviews that students, faculty, and staff need to utilize each other more for the benefit of the communities in Milwaukee. Individuals at University of Wisconsin–Milwaukee, Marquette, and Cardinal Stritch University are all trying to do similar things in their own spheres. More needs to be done to encourage students, faculty, and staff to reach out beyond the campuses of their respective universities, connect with one another, help one another, support one another, and lead one another to the common goal we all share. In doing so, we will expand our spheres, knowledge, and make an impact to achieve desired goals on a wider, more comprehensive scale.

Another interesting idea that emerged from the interviews was about how one approaches interfaith dialogue. Does one have to be rooted in a faith to partake and contribute effectively to interfaith dialogue? Or, can interfaith dialogue serve as an avenue to help one explore the many religions and his or her path of commitment to one? Interfaith dialogue, when trying to explore grounds of commonality or agreement, tends to operate on the assumption that those involved in the dialogue are grounded in one tradition or another. However, informal settings of interfaith dialogue focus on the questions of life and the exploration of humanity. These questions may be more accessible to participants who wish to explore their faith and spirituality from a practical and not always dogmatic and/or theological perspectives. In thinking about student interfaith dialogue on campuses, I believe there are areas for both more formal and informal dialogues to take place that is welcoming of all students, faculty, and staff grounded in a faith tradition or seeking to discover their place in one of them or even those who fall in neither category. Regardless of either approach, what was evident through many of the interviews was that interfaith dialogue is a means to grow spiritually, emotionally, religiously, intellectually, and culturally together with others, forming stronger bonds with others.

Commitment and Challenges at the Institutional Level

Having a mission statement that states the importance of diversity is one thing but enacting that mission with adequate and accessible resources and intentional programming is quite another. That is where the true commitment to the espoused values becomes real. The university is the house where the mission is built and implemented. It is the people within these universities that serve as actors who will help animate the mission. Therefore, if the leadership interprets the mission too narrowly (either dogmatically or literally), it will remain oblivious to the needs that require the cultivation of interfaith spaces on campus.

CARDINAL STRITCH UNIVERSITY: For Cardinal Stritch University, Daniel Di Domizio and Monica Kling provided detailed evidence that there is a rich history of students, faculty, and staff at this university who are living out the university's commitment to "creating a caring community, peacemaking, showing compassion, and reverencing creation as we embrace and cultivate . . . diversity"[122] There was support in place at the university for students who identify with a religion other than Catholic. As Di Domizio notes, a lot of emphasis was placed on the Franciscan value of hospitality.[123] These commitments to embracing diversity include the newly developed prayer space on campus and courses that offer learning the tenets of other religions, not to mention the presence of staff and professors (like Di Domizio) who encourage interfaith conversation in the classroom. There is also the interfaith minor and certificate, and various events are held around campus to promote interfaith awareness amongst students, faculty, and staff at the university.

The university also provided an opportunity for students to attend the Interfaith Youth Core's conference in Atlanta, Georgia. Students created an interfaith group on campus. These are all important, positive contributions toward interfaith. However, are these efforts sustainable? Are there structures in place that will ensure the continuity of funding and human resources for the next generation? While it seems that the administration is open to the interfaith relationships and efforts, there is always more that the faculty, staff, and administration could do to maintain the presence of interfaith on campus.

---

122. "Mission Statement," Cardinal Stritch University, https://www.stritch.edu/About/Mission-and-Vision/Mission-Statement/.

123. Daniel Di Domizio, interview by Kaitlyn Daly, March 1, 2017.

MARQUETTE UNIVERSITY: For Marquette University, the Catholic identity is a difficult aspect to navigate. The interviews from Marquette faculty, staff, and students has helped illuminate the path they are currently walking, which may lead to a more enriched interfaith culture on campus. On the one hand, as many interviewees stated, Catholicism is inclusive and universal, welcoming and celebrating people of all faith traditions. However, the Catholic component may limit people of nonfaith traditions and worldviews from feeling connected. Also, Marquette is primarily Catholic, which while seeking to be universal and inclusive, can still be distant to students who do not identify with any religious tradition. This is where I believe the mission statement of the university can be a powerful bridge. There needs to be openness for diversity to be recognized in the mission. More inclusive language that names an alternate source of power or goodness other than God could be a positive addition to the mission statement.

The people and events detailed here seem to indicate that Marquette is doing okay in developing an interfaith awareness at the university in recent years, especially the work of Omar, Callan-Farley, Avila-Borunda, and on the student side, the Interfaith Coordinating Team. It is also uplifting to see the commitment to enhancing the lives of those in Marquette's education and employment system, as displayed by Russell. This shows, even though at the minimal level, a commitment to "the search for truth, the discovery and sharing of knowledge, personal and professional excellence, the promotion of a life of faith, and the development of leadership expressed in service to others" to the "common benefit of the human community."[124]

There are many other people and organizations on campus that strive each day to be bridge builders between the faces that walk Marquette. While I am unable to present the work of each of these, they make important contributions in classrooms as teachers, in decision making as administrators, and in the residence halls as students. While President Lovell acknowledged that the interfaith awareness is important and there is diversity of students on campus, it is time for the university to gather as a collective and take tangible steps to promote interfaith on campus and work toward bringing it to the forefront. There are support mechanisms available for student-led interfaith efforts, but more needs to be done from the top where the resources are controlled. This is vital if we wish to combat the challenges such as bigotry, violence, racism, and religious illiteracy, which are all too visible on campus despite the slogans to oppose them.

---

124. "Our Mission," Marquette University, http://www.marquette.edu/about/mission.php.

UNIVERSITY OF WISCONSIN–MILWAUKEE: For University of Wisconsin–Milwaukee, Dake, Heinritz, Miller, and Young Binter have been instrumental to the founding of interfaith on their campus. They have been the leaders in fulfilling the university's mission to "develop human resources, to discover and disseminate knowledge, to extend knowledge and its application beyond the boundaries of its campuses, and to serve and stimulate society by developing in students heightened intellectual, cultural, and humane sensitivities . . . and a sense of purpose" in order to "educate people and improve the human condition" while all being grounded in "the search for truth."[125] These words from the mission can be translated to mean interfaith work in its very core. Select students, faculty, and staff have stepped up in sharing the word that interfaith matters, engaging students in discussing these topics matters, and living with peace in our global world matters. The interfaith events have only been recent, but they have been impactful, even if just for a few. There is a momentum and, as we have learned from the comments of the interviewees, better results will take time. The intersection of state and religion at this university proves to be a unique challenge, but several people are committed to finding ways to bridge the two for the sake of peace and community building.

Conclusion

All of the three universities have taken steps toward cultivating interfaith activities on campus. Yet, no university has reached anywhere near what is necessary to create a culture of dialogue or even to increase basic awareness of the importance of interfaith. Father Thomas Michel describes this culture of dialogue as:

> when a group of believers has dialogue as an intrinsic part of their religious commitment, whereby a person's very participation in such a group includes an openness and willingness to engage in dialogue. . . . This is not something merely theoretical, but has effects in one's choice of activities, use of time and funds, and planning and projects for the future. It results in a community of believers where outsiders can presume that such a group will be open to efforts at dialogue, where one can point to concrete evidence of the group's involvement in dialogue. Dialogue becomes one of the characteristics that identify such communities and movements.[126]

---

125. "UWM's Vision, Values, and Mission Statements," University of Wisconsin–Milwaukee, http://uwm.edu/mission/.

126. Michel, "Creating a Culture of Dialogue," 21–22.

All three schools have shown a desire to develop this "concrete evidence" or interfaith engagement efforts, but none as of yet may be defined by these efforts. They exist, and that is wonderful. Their efforts are not adequate, and the existing efforts are not as well known, attended, or well supported as they could be. It will take the hard work of many more students, faculty, staff, and leadership administrators to create a culture of dialogue at the university. Russell, during her interview, noted the urgency to consider the implications of interfaith in today's world:

> This never really was . . . an optional issue for us, but now it's really not an optional issue. Interfaith dialogue, we're called to our moral core as a people right now. We need to do that in a way that's humble and connected and aware that there is someone bigger than us and so with a certain amount of mercy and care for each other. . . . I think that the work of scholars on interfaith issues has never been more important.[127]

This rings true as we live in world full of racial, geographical, political, ethnic, and religious diversity. We can no longer be complacent or be content with our preconceived notions and judgments. If interfaith is truly about faith and the common good, we can no longer rely on others, including world or religious leaders, to take the lead on building inclusion and compassion. Interfaith work helps resist attempts to spread misconceptions and false information about our neighbors of every race, gender, culture, and religion. Thinking critically for ourselves and for one another is part of the responsibility for anyone who identifies himself or herself as a person of faith or a person seeking truth. Getting involved and learning about the other is no longer an option. Father Michel embodies this idea of sharing all aspects of our lives together. When we do this, interfaith is exposed as a second—or first—nature:

> When people of various faiths live together—not simply cohabiting the same town but sharing life *together*—the questions of dialogue of proclamation doesn't arise. When they work, study, struggle, celebrate, and mourn together and face the universal crises of injustice, illness, and death as one, they don't spend most of their time talking about doctrine. Their focus is on immediate concerns of survival, on taking care of the sick and needy, on communicating cherished values to new generations, on resolving problems and tensions in productive rather than in destructive ways, on reconciling after conflicts,

---

127. Stephanie Russell, phone interview by Kaitlyn Daly, March 21, 2017.

on seeking to build more just, humane, and dignified societies. When believers are actively cooperating in such activities, at certain rare but privileged moments, they also express what is deepest in their lives and hearts, that is, their respective faiths, which are the source of strength and inspiration that forms the driving force that guides all their activities.[128]

Living up to our commitment to religious diversity, our overall diversity, and being open to the other person next to us or on the other side of the globe will allow us to more deeply see our humanity, learn about one another, and rediscover the foundations for peace that enrich life. Dr. Omar, in class and in conversation, has illustrated many times the idea of a person as a tree where he imagines one as being one: "the tree trunk is your core; it is the central structure like a spine which also grounds you or shows you are rooted somewhere. However, the branches represent the attempts to reach out and care for and interact with the other." Trees are built this way and so are human beings. For some people, religious and faith life play an essential role in the formation of this core, this central structure. For others, it may be humanism or something that brings value to their life and being that serve as the formational pieces of their core. One can recognize this core as a complex and indivisible base, with each facet of its formation bound up within the other. Everyone's tree trunk is unique to him or her and they have their own story to share.

As DeGarmo noted, interfaith helps you learn, discover, and grow your branches.[129] An openness to engaging with another individual or community from a different background or worldview than our own creates the invitation to them and to our own self to discover our "core" (who we really are) and our "branches" (what are really capable of when we connect and care for others). Dr. Omar elaborated on the analogy with branches noting that they often entangle with branches of other trees but are still connected with their own core and remain grounded through that connection. In nature, each tree has its own "identity," and yet it reaches out to its neighbor and shares the space, the sunlight, and the air between them as they grow and flourish using the very same resources. This applies equally to human beings. Interfaith is an avenue to discover how we are intertwined, interconnected, and interdependent. It will enable us to live peacefully, naturally, and harmoniously with others and with ourselves, echoing the rhythms and movements of the nature that surrounds us. Each person is grounded in a religious or humanistic tradition or in an idea that

---

128. Michel, "Creating a Culture of Dialogue," 21.

129. Bradley DeGarmo, interview by Kaitlyn Daly, June 24, 2017.

propels them to seek the truth. As they engage in dialogue, they are branching out to learn about the other. Through that process, they also learn about oneself, an important step for self-growth.

Bibliography

Academic Sources

Hinze, Bradford E., and Irfan A. Omar, eds. *Heirs of Abraham: The Future of Muslim, Jewish, and Christian Relations.* Maryknoll, NY: Orbis, 2005.

Michel, Thomas F. *A Christian View of Islam.* Edited by Irfan A. Omar. Maryknoll, NY: Orbis Books, 2011.

Omar, Irfan A., and Duffey, Michael K., eds. *Peacemaking and the Challenge of Violence in World Religions.* West Sussex: Wiley Blackwell, 2015.

Patel, Eboo. *Sacred Ground.* Boston: Beacon Press, 2012.

Patel, Eboo, and Cassie Meyer, "Engaging Religious Diversity on Campus: The Role of Interfaith Leadership." *Journal of College and Character* 10, no. 7 (2009): 1–8.

Putnam, Robert D., and David E. Campbell, *American Grace: How Religion Divides and Unites Us.* New York: Simon & Schuster, 2010.

Whitten Smith, David, and Elizabeth Geraldine Burr. *Understanding World Religions: A Roadmap for Justice and Peace.* Lanham, MD: Rowman & Littlefield, 2015.

United States Department of Education. "The President's Interfaith and Community Service Campus Challenge Inaugural Report," https://www.ifyc.org/sites/default/files/u4/campus-challenge-inaugural-years-report_small.pdf.

Video Sources

Garfield, Alan. "River Crossing Storytelling Interfaith Conference." *YouTube.* Last modified February 20, 2016. https://www.youtube.com/watch?v=FrP-P-JoiAY.

Garfield, Alan and Travis Carton. "River Crossing Storytelling Interfaith Conference, 2/20/2016." *YouTube.* Last modified March 6, 2016. https://www.youtube.com/watch?v=CBq2zJVKV48&t=15s.

Ngozi Adichie, Chimamanda. "The Danger of a Single Story." Filmed July 2009. TED video. https://www.ted.com/talks/chimamanda_adichie_the_danger_of_a_single_story.

Pope Francis. "Why the Only Future Worth Building Includes Everyone." Filmed Apr. 2017. TED video. https://www.ted.com/talks/pope_francis_why_the_only_future_worth_building_includes_everyone?language=en.

Institutional and Conference Sources (Flyers, Letters, Statements, Reports)

Arinze, Francis Cardinal. Letter to Sister Jessine Reiss, City of the Vatican, IT, December 30, 1985.

Association of American Colleges and Universities. "Making Excellence Inclusive." Accessed September 4, 2017. https://www.aacu.org/making-excellence-inclusive.

Cardinal Stritch University. *CSU Interfaith Studies Certificate/Minor List*. Document.

———. *Eboo Patel Talk Flyer*. Flyer.

———. "Mission Statement." Accessed May 3, 2017. https://www.stritch.edu/About/Mission-and-Vision/Mission-Statement/.

———. *Student Dialogue Event Flyer*. Flyer.

———. *Student Dialogue Event Panel Flyer 1 and 2*. Flyer.

Deer Park Buddhist Center. "Deer Park Buddhist Center." Accessed June 21, 2017. http://www.deerparkcenter.org.

Di Domizio, Daniel. *Info on Sr Lucille*. Document.

———. *List of People of Interfaith Activity*. Document.

———. *Sr Lucille CSU Award Certificate*. Document.

———. *Sr Lucille CSU Award Intro*. Document.

———. *Stritch Talks*. Document.

Goldin, Owen, Richard Taylor, and Irfan Omar. *Abrahamic Conference*. Flyer.

Groth, Alex. "Searching for Space." *Marquette Tribune*, April 4, 2017.

Hillel Milwaukee. *Interfaith Shabbat Service and Dinner*. flyer and description.

Interfaith Youth Core. *Better Together*. Sticker.

———. "Interfaith Leadership Institutes." Accessed December 1, 2019. https://www.ifyc.org/ili.

Janzen, Clara. "Muslim Prayer Space Tarnished." *Marquette Tribune*, April 4, 2017.

———. "Story of a Personal Attack on Religious Clothing." *Marquettewire.org*, February 7, 2017. Accessed Apr. 20, 2017. https://marquettewire.org/3965172/news/saras-hijab/.

———. "Take a Stroll in My Scarf." *Marquettewire.org,* Apr. 11, 2017. Accessed April 20, 2017. https://marquettewire.org/3970701/news/take-a-stroll-in-my-scarf/.

Marquette University. "Affiliated Ministries Staff & Religious Advisors." Accessed April 4, 2018. http://www.marquette.edu/cm/about/staff-affiliated-ministers.shtml.

———. "A Message from Marquette Leaders to the Campus Community." *Marquette Today*, January 30, 2017. Accessed September 5, 2017. https://today.marquette.edu/2017/01/a-message-from-leadership-to-the-marquette-community/.

———. "A Message from Provost Myers and Xavier Cole Regarding Undocumented Students." *Marquette Today*, February 13, 2017. Accessed September 5, 2017. https://today.marquette.edu/2017/02/a-message-from-provost-myers-and-xavier-cole-regarding-undocumented-students/.

———. *Christian-Muslim Relations in American Today: An Interdisciplinary Symposium*. Program pamphlet.

———. "Diversity and Inclusion – About." Accessed September 5, 2017. http://www.marquette.edu/diversity/about.php.

———. *Muslim, Christian, Jewish Heritage Conference/Lecture Series*. Flyer.

———. "Our Mission." Accessed May 3, 2017. http://www.marquette.edu/about/mission.php.

———. *Peacemaking and Nonviolence in World Religions*. Program and flyer.

———. "President's Task Force on Equity and Inclusion." Accessed September 5, 2017. http://www.marquette.edu/diversity/presidents-task-force.php.

———. *Wade Chair Public Lecture on Christian-Muslim Relations*. Flyer.

Marquette University Center for Peacemaking. *Travel Opportunities with the Center for Peacemaking Newsbrief*. Flyer.

Marquette University and Global Peace Services USA. *Peace Service in the Abrahamic Traditions Interfaith Symposium*. Program.

Marquette University and the Manresa Project. *Justice and Mercy Interfaith Peacemaking Conference*. Poster, flyer, and call for Papers.

Marquette University Arab Student Association. *Jerusalem Women Speak Panel*. Flyer.

Marquette University Department of Theology. *Interfaith Lecture Series*. Flyer.

Marquette University Interfaith Coordinating Team. *9/11 Memorial Vigil*. Flyer.

———. *9/11 Memorial Vigil Invitation*. Flyer.

———. *Interfaith Dialogue February Love Yourself and Your Neighbor*. Flyer and agenda.

———. *You Change Your Life By Changing Your Heart Interfaith Retreat*. Flyer.

Marquette University Jewish Student Union. *JSU Passover Seder Meal*. Facebook event and description.

Marquette University Office of International Education. "A Message of Support and Solidarity from the Office of International Education." Accessed September 5, 2017. http://www.marquette.edu/oie/executiveorder.shtml.

Omar, Irfan. "Beinhauer-Kohler Visual Cultures of World Religions." Flyer.

———. *MU Interreligious Activities*. Document.

———. "Narratives." Class lectures, Survey of World Religions, Marquette University, Milwaukee, WI, July–August 2016.

Peterson, Clare. "Provost's Office Establishes Office of Institutional Diversity and Inclusion; Welburn Named Executive Director." *Marquette Today*, October 26, 2015. Accessed March 28, 2017. https://today.marquette.edu/2015/10/provosts-office-establishes-office-of-institutional-diversity-and-inclusion-welburn-named-executive-director/.

———. "You Are Welcome Here: Office of International Education Shares New Video." *Marquette Today*, March 6, 2017. Accessed September 5, 2017. https://today.marquette.edu/2017/03/you-are-welcome-here-office-of-international-education-shares-new-video/.

Re, Monsignor G. B. Letter to Sister Lucille Walsh. Secretariat of State, City of the Vatican, IT, October 11, 1985.

Smith, Simone. "Campus Muslims Seeking Larger Space for Prayer." *Marquettewire.org*, February 2, 2012. Accessed April 20, 2017. https://marquettewire.org/3805532/tribune/tribune-news/campus-muslims-seeking-larger-space-for-prayer/.

Students of Christian-Muslim Dialogue Fall 2015 Course. *Memorandum to Dr. Stephanie Russell on Culture of Interfaith Dialogue*. Memorandum.

Taylor, Richard. *Philosophy and Religion Averroes Maimonides Seminar*. Flyer.

Turkish American Society of Wisconsin. "TASWI." Accessed June 21, 2017. http://taswi.org.

University of Wisconsin–Milwaukee. "Religious Studies Program." Accessed July 16, 2017. https://uwm.edu/religiousstudies/.

————. "Student Involvement – Student Organization Database." Accessed September 5, 2017, http://studentorgs.uwm.edu/uwmorgs.

————. "Spiritual and Religious Communities at UWM." Accessed December 1, 2019. https://uwm.edu/studentinvolvement/more/spiritual-religious/ministries/.

————. "The Distinguished Lecture Series presents an Evening with Eboo Patel." *University of Wisconsin–Milwaukee Student Involvement*. 2015. http://uwm.edu/studentinvolvement/event/the-distinguished-lecture-series-presents-an-evening-with-eboo-patel/.

————. "UWM's Vision, Values, and Mission Statements." Accessed May 3, 2017. http://uwm.edu/mission/.

INTERVIEWS

1. Callan-Farley, Mary Sue. Interview by Kaitlyn Daly. June 15, 2017.

2. Cole, Xavier. Interview by Kaitlyn Daly. March 29, 2017.

3. Dake, Thomas. Interview by Kaitlyn Daly. April 21, 2017.

4. DeGarmo, Bradley. Interview by Kaitlyn Daly. June 24, 2017.

5. Di Domizio, Daniel. Interview by Kaitlyn Daly. March 1, 2017.

6. Dias Duarte Machado, Luiz Gabriel. Interview by Kaitlyn Daly. March 15, 2017.

7. Heinritz, Sean and Miller, Tabetha. Interview by Kaitlyn Daly. February 28, 2017.

8. Jaber, Sundus. Interview by Kaitlyn Daly. March 7, 2017.

9. Kling, Monica. Email Message to Author. June 27, 2017.

10. ————. Email Message to Daniel Di Domizio. February 28, 2017.

11. Lovell, Michael. Interview by Kaitlyn Daly. May 20, 2017.

12. Omar, Irfan. Email message to author. June 22, 2017.

13. Pettee, Ben. Interview by Kaitlyn Daly. March 7, 2017.

14. Russell, Stephanie. Interview by Kaitlyn Daly. March 21, 2017.

15. Sandhu, Yuvraj. Interview by Kaitlyn Daly. March 6, 2017.

16. Taylor, Richard. Interview by Kaitlyn Daly and Irfan Omar. May 17, 2017.

An Overview of Interfaith Engagement in Milwaukee

Irfan A. Omar & Kaitlyn C. Daly

Interfaith dialogue is not new; what is new is our understanding of what it represents and how it can reshape the social and cultural fabric of our societies by inspiring civil and intercultural conversations in the service of peace and peacemaking. The Second Vatican Council in the mid-1960s opened a wider space for many Catholics and others for rethinking and reimagining relations across faith lines. In 1969, a Christian scholar defined dialogue in the then newly established *Journal of Ecumenical Studies*: "Dialogue means the reaching out of one person towards the other; it is the opening up to the other and his point of view."[1] Another, in 1970, noted that besides the scholarly and theoretical understandings, "dialogue is a practical exercise, a mode of experimental contact between persons whose inmost convictions differ."[2] Even though experts and theorists have been writing and publishing on formal dialogue since the late 1950s, the potential benefits of and the underlying need for dialogue has become more convincing only since the 1990s. What many are finding out through their study of and learning about world's religions is that even though convictions might differ in the dogmatic forms they are formulated, the ethical goals of these convictions converge across faith lines. Interfaith dialogue is increasingly being recognized as an important way to form relationships, discover areas of convergence, bridge differences, and celebrate the fact of diversity across faith lines.[3]

---

1. Peter Schreiner, "Roman Catholic Theology and Non-Christian Religion," *Journal of Ecumenical Studies* 6, no. 3 (1969): 394.

2. Eric J. Sharpe, "The Goals of Inter-religious Dialogue," in *Truth and Dialogue in World Religions*, ed. John Hick (Philadelphia, PA: Westminster Press, 1970), 78.

3. Much more can be said about relationships across faith lines but suffice it to say that they did not happen as a result of the rise of formal dialogues that began in middle of 20th century.

In Milwaukee, the 1980 Christian–Muslim (CM) dialogue inspired many in the community to see the value of dialogue. It helped the beginnings of a systematic effort to increase mutual understanding and collaboration for the greater good. Many Milwaukee interfaith leaders and community members have been impacted by the original CM dialogue. Chapters in part I discussed a few of these individuals along with their impact. The present chapter seeks to provide a brief history of what transpired around the time of the first Christian–Muslim dialogue. Here, we offer a sampling of the variety of interfaith efforts taking place in the Milwaukee area in the last four decades. In that respect, it is a summary version of the story of dialogue in Milwaukee. It is an accounting of the numerous events, initiatives, people, organizations, and institutions that have made Milwaukee a place where communities, religious or otherwise, have increasingly come together to interact, collaborate, and promote social justice and interreligious harmony.[4]

This chapter is more of a survey and less of a narrative; it contains only a sampling of organizations and people and offers only the basic information and analyses of these. It is not exhaustive. Based on our research findings, we believe an entire volume may be devoted just to the "overview" alone. The good news in all of this is that so much more can be said and reported on Milwaukee's interfaith story. This chapter is an attempt to highlight some of the key efforts made in the service of increasing mutual understanding, contributing to the cultivation of the interfaith fabric of the great city of Milwaukee and surrounding areas.

Key Organizations and Interfaith Actors

The chapter is organized around select organizations and people. These figures and groups become a window through which to witness a variety of interfaith activities that make Milwaukee unique among other cities of its size and demographics. In other words, the various pieces presented here are not

---

Interfaith relations existed long before the term *interfaith* was coined. In many societies, such relationships and friendships were (and continue to be) naturally formed between neighbors and colleagues of various faiths. As the Hindu filmmaker Laj Waghary noted, because she had experienced interfaith friendships growing up, for her participating in interfaith events today is not a starting point of a journey, it is more like coming home—a recurring experience of fulfilment. She continued: "It is natural to have and cultivate interfaith relationships." Laj believes her Hindu faith offers ample resources to support this. Laj Waghary, interview by Irfan Omar and Caroline Redick, May 24, 2017.

4. Many interfaith groups and people noted in this chapter do not appear to make a sharp distinction between social justice work and interfaith relationships. Some emphasize the former, while others see their primary identity as promoters of faith and, to some degree, interfaith culture and literacy.

chronological; they highlight the breadth and depth of interest in and history of interfaith outreach. A good number of recent interfaith activities, people, and relationships are noted as a demonstration of the emphasis that people and communities of faith continue to place on interfaith engagement along with key operating tropes such as social justice, dialogue and diplomacy, and diversity and inclusion. Interfaith activism in Milwaukee is growing largely due to the effort by religious institutions that are concerned with the rise in bigotry, violence, and misrepresentation of others, their religious beliefs, and practices.

The groups covered in this chapter are: Interfaith Conference of Greater Milwaukee (ICGM), Shir Hadash Reconstructionist Jewish Community (SH), Southeast Milwaukee Interfaith Covenant Community (SMICC), and the Turkish American Society of Wisconsin (TASWI). Several other groups and organizations are noted in passing, but the bulk of the chapter is built around the narratives based on interviews with dialogue actors belonging to various religious traditions, some of whom represent their respective faith organizations that support their interfaith work. These individuals include: Huda Alkaff (Interfaith Earth Network and Islamic Society of Milwaukee), Professor Swarnjit Arora (University of Wisconsin–Milwaukee and Sikh Community of Wisconsin), Pastor Lisa Bates-Froiland (Redeemer Lutheran Church in Milwaukee), Dr. Shawnee Daniels-Sykes (Mount Mary University), Rev. Reirin A. Gumbel (Milwaukee Zen Center), Elana Kahn (Jewish Community Relations Council), Rev. Ken Knippel (St. John Vianney Catholic Parish and Brookfield Elm Grove Interfaith Network, BEGIN), and Rev. Steve Lied (Peace Catalyst International and Brew City Church).

The types of dialogues noted in this chapter include: (a) Muslim–Christian, (b) Catholic–Jewish, (c) Muslim–Jewish, (d) multifaith, (e) environment-focused, and (f) youth-focused. The chapter also includes a sampling of what we believe are examples of the "dialogue of action," where the participants encounter the other through action for the common good and what they may consider to be faith-based action within an interfaith context. The concluding section contains a selection of the activities by the researchers' in this book recognizing their praxis in furthering the cause of dialogue.

Faith Groups and Interfaith Organizations

Strong interfaith groups and leaders are found within, across, and beyond the city limits of Milwaukee, Wisconsin. Interviews conducted with dialogue actors noted above demonstrate the new shape and meaning of interfaith in the city as a result of their efforts and impact. Blending of theology with other academic and career pursuits; pouring interfaith into educational efforts in higher education; rooting and expanding grassroots level interfaith efforts; rallying, supporting, and advocating the faith of one's own and others; and harmonizing the city's diverse religious population are all dreams these leaders have envisioned and enacted. Their interview narratives offer background, reflections, and advice grounded within their own personal interfaith pursuits. Some context is necessary to understand the existing landscape of interfaith engagement in Milwaukee. Therefore, we begin with a brief profile of one of the oldest organizations, the Interfaith Conference.[5]

Interfaith Conference of Greater Milwaukee

The establishment of the Interfaith Conference of Greater Milwaukee (ICGM) is undoubtedly one of Milwaukee's major interfaith accomplishments. With origins in the civil rights movement, the ICGM was founded in 1970, although it has gone through a few incarnations. It was first called the Greater Milwaukee Conference on Religion and Urban Affairs, which is indicative of its early emphasis on addressing social injustice and inequity. It adopted its current name in 1987, which was to signal the importance of being an interfaith organization while remaining engaged in social programs.[6] Over the years, ICGM has incorporated dialogue and membership from large and small faith communities. It has been in existence for 49 years and remains one of the major nonprofit organizations to serve as a platform for interfaith engagement and interaction. ICGM's legitimacy comes from the wide support and patronage it enjoys from its 20 member faiths and denominations.[7]

---

5. Interfaith Conference has been one of the prominent organizations in Milwaukee and perhaps in the world that sought to bring various communities under one umbrella to create an action-oriented institution aiming to address social injustice through interfaith action. ICGM has been profiled and mentioned by numerous studies; one that gives a succinct history can be found in Katy McCarthy, *Interfaith Encounters in America* (New Brunswick, NJ: Rutgers University Press, 2007), 103–115.

6. McCarthy, *Interfaith Encounters in America*, 104.

7. Interfaith Conference of Greater Milwaukee, "Ongoing Reports: Keeping Busy," http://interfaithconference.org/cms-view-page.php?page=year-in-review. As this book is being readied for press, ICGM announced the hiring of the new executive director, Pardeep Kaleka, as of July 1, 2019. It also added two new religious groups to its list of members, including the Hindu Temple of Wisconsin. See Sophie Carson, "Pardeep Singh Kaleka, Son of Oak Creek Sikh Temple Founder and Shooting Victim, Will Help Community Heal as Interfaith Leader," *Milwaukee Journal Sentinel*, July 27, 2019, https://www.jsonline.com/story/news/religion/2019/06/27/milwaukee-sikh-community-leader-kaleka-heads-interfaith-conference/1588372001/.

Tom Heinen, the outgoing executive director of ICGM, previously worked as a reporter of religion for the *Milwaukee Journal Sentinel.* Under his leadership, ICGM has become a champion of causes related to interfaith dialogue and action. Heinen believes interfaith dialogue is about acceptance, understanding, and respect. He believes, "if you have the truth, then others will perhaps perceive it when you interact with them. If you stay in a silo, isolated, then you will not have the opportunity to see what we have in common." Heinen described his involvement in interfaith as an opportunity to being challenged and to reflect and grow. He believes it is genuine learning when we meet people of different faiths sharing and enacting their beliefs and rituals during dialogue and interaction (fig. 8.1).[8] Heinen was a bridge builder even before he became the executive director of ICGM. As a journalist and staff writer for the *Journal Sentinel*, he routinely contributed to the work of peacemaking and to the "common quest for healing, justice and peace" in Milwaukee.[9] Heinen's efforts to showcase religion's resourcefulness and healing capacity through his reporting may have greatly helped strengthen interfaith bonds during the difficult and confusing times after the attacks of September 11, 2001.

Figure 8.1: Tom Heinen, then executive director of Interfaith Conference of Greater Milwaukee in the office premises in May 2018.

---

8. Tom Heinen, interview by Andrew Musgrave, November 14, 2017. Some content in this section comes from the narrative of this interview by Andrew Musgrave.

9. Tom Heinen, "Faithful Find Unity in Shattered World," *Milwaukee Journal Sentinel,* September 12, 2001. Online archive available at http://bahai-library.com/newspapers/2001/091301-1.html.

ICGM works in many areas related to community welfare. It is an interfaith organization, but it seeks to encompass all aspects that govern the community development.[10] One key theme that appears over and over in its activities is justice. ICGM's motto as it appears on its website is: "To uphold the dignity of every person and the solidarity of the human community," which guides all of its varied activities and affiliations. The following are some of the show-and-tell items regarding ICGM's leadership as well as the events hosted or sponsored by them.

Some of the major programs and committees of ICGM include: Amazing Faiths Dinner Dialogues, Committee for Interfaith Understanding, Interfaith Earth Network of Southeastern Wisconsin (IEN), Peace and International Issues Committee, Interfaith Restorative Practices Coalition, Annual Interfaith Conference Luncheon, and One Community. ICGM representatives sit on boards and commissions of major civic society and community organizations, including the City of Milwaukee's Board of Ethics.[11]

The Amazing Faiths Dinner Dialogues began in 2011 with a core objective of sharing stories (figs. 8.2 & 8.3). The program is described as:

People of all faiths and no faith, all spiritualities and philosophies gather(ing) in small groups to share a meal and participate in a moderated discussion using a proven model, evoking deep exchanges about lived experiences and the role of faith or spirituality in their lives. Through exploration and dialogue, participants learn about the beliefs and traditions of others within an atmosphere of respect and understanding and are empowered to stand as witnesses for tolerance.[12]

ICGM's main goals include creating and running programs that bring together people from the same faith as well as different faiths living in urban and suburban communities to inspire relationships and dialogue. They facilitate conversations on difficult topics and themes involving race, economic injustice, advocacy, and action. Various dialogues have been hosted at prominent Milwaukee venues, including the Medical College of Wisconsin, Milwaukee Repertory Theater, and Rockwell Automation.[13] ICGM routinely issues

---

10. ICGM was founded with an eye toward working for the welfare of communities in the Milwaukee area. In its first incarnation in 1970, it was called the Greater Milwaukee Conference on Religion and Urban Affairs.

11. Interfaith Conference of Greater Milwaukee, "Interfaith Conference Representatives," http://interfaithconference.org/cms-view-page.php?page=interfaith-conference-representatives.

12. Interfaith Conference of Greater Milwaukee, "Amazing Faiths Dinner Dialogues," http://www.interfaithconference.org/cms-view-page.php?page=amazing-faiths-dinners.

13. For a complete, up-to-date list of major events, programs, and highlights, visit ICGM's website at www.interfaithconference.org.

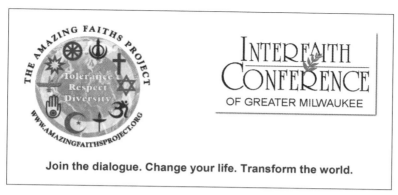

Figure 8.2: The logos for ICGM and The Amazing Faiths Project as displayed on their flyers.

Figure 8.3: Group photo from an Amazing Faiths Dinner Dialogue.

statements addressing social matters pertaining to the community, including statements against hate, mistreatment of refugees, and violence. In response to the Sikh Temple shooting in Oak Creek, Wisconsin, on August 5, 2012, ICGM quickly gathered together people of different faiths to address the tragedy and speak out against the violent act of terrorism.[14] The event "Know Your Neighbor" brought together Buddhist, Jewish, Muslim, and Sikh leaders/presenters in dialogue where they spoke about their faith and specifically its teachings against violence. At this event, the Sikh community was honored for their

---

14. *Milwaukee Journal Sentinel*, "Oak Creek Sikh Temple Shooting," http://archive.jsonline. com/news/crime/165082506.html.

compassion, forgiveness, and care for the first responders in the tragic events that impacted their community. Among the many such other statements and initiatives, ICGM recently helped the community by issuing an alert regarding a planned "security conference" in Waukesha, Wisconsin, which featured "a roster of speakers who are known to have repeatedly engaged in virulent hate speech against Muslims as a group."[15] This is part of ICGM's "Opposing Hate" campaign, which seeks to use all available resources to inform and advise communities and civic leaders of hate groups that seek to sow divisions based on race, religion, or ethnicity.[16] The 2017 annual luncheon event centered on the theme "Acting Against Hate," which brought together many community members and leaders who are not necessarily into interfaith but they are interested in how the interfaith work addresses issues related to the general welfare of the community (figs. 8.4–8.6).[17]

Figure 8.4: Invitation card cover for the 47th Annual ICGM Luncheon titled "Acting Against Hate."

---

15. Interfaith Conference of Greater Milwaukee, "Stand Against Hate in Waukesha County," May 13, 2019, http://interfaithconference.org/index.php.

16. ICGM, "Ongoing Reports."

17. Interfaith Conference of Greater Milwaukee, *Acting Against Hate: 47th Annual Luncheon,* flyer. ICGM's events are always packed with people; it attracts politicians, community leaders, and social activists as well as the those who are longtime dialogue partners. As noted previously, at this event, Judi Longdin, a longtime member of ICGM and a key member of the Christian–Muslim Women's Dialogue, was honored with the 2017 Frank Zeidler Award for her "exceptional service" in the interfaith community. The 2018 Zeidler award was received by Rev. Tonen O'Connor, resident priest emerita of the Milwaukee Zen Center.

Figure 8.5: Naheed Arshad and Swarnjit Arora at the ICGM's Annual award ceremony.

Figure 8.6: ICGM's Annual award luncheon.

Following the tragic September 11, 2001, attacks in New York City and Washington, DC, the ICGM hosted an Interfaith Prayer Service for Peace at the Central United Methodist Church in Milwaukee on September 12, 2001 (fig. 8.7). Participants came from various faith backgrounds, including Jewish, Lutheran, Muslim, Methodist, Baptists, Quaker, Hindu, Episcopal, Buddhist, Sikh, Church of God in Christ, Bahai, and Catholic. Since ICGM had been working to help communities and religious groups build trust and form close relationships for many years prior, they had the necessary resources as well as legitimacy to not only pull this event together in a time of crisis and confusion but also to offer a platform for a continuing discussion and collective healing.

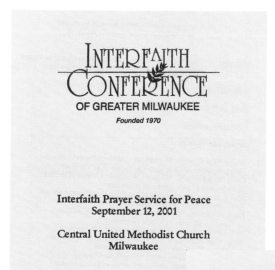

Figure 8.7: Following the September 11 attacks, ICGM hosted an "Interfaith Prayer Service for Peace" at the Central United Methodist Church in Milwaukee on September 12, 2001.[18]

18. Interfaith Conference of Greater Milwaukee, *Interfaith Prayer Service for Peace*, program.

Similarly, in 2012, when a gunman entered the Oak Creek Sikh Temple and shot and killed several community members preparing for the impending service, ICGM was one of the major organizations that facilitated, coordinated, and planned vigils and programs designed to heal the community. ICGM led the way in creating programs to educate the communities, civic leaders, political figures, and the public about the religion of Sikhism. In 2013, ICGM again led the charge in organizing a memorial service to mark the first anniversary of the tragic events but also to celebrate the coming together of thousands of people from all backgrounds and faith traditions (fig. 8.8). Interfaith events and programs have been happening with greater frequency since 9/11 bringing knowledge and greater understanding of community members and their faith perspectives. Unfortunately, some of it has been propelled by the rise in hate crimes and incidents of mass shootings around the country and around the world. And yet, interfaith actors and institutions in Milwaukee are quite determined to keep the momentum by organizing events that inform and educate on a regular basis (see figs. 8.9 & 8.10).

Figure 8.8: People from various faiths participating in the 2013 interfaith prayer and vigil commemorating the one-year anniversary of the mass shooting at the Sikh Temple of Wisconsin in Oak Creek.

Figure 8.9: Rabbi Steve Adams speaking at an event organized by the ICGM's Committee for Interfaith Understanding, held in Brookfield's Unitarian Universalist Church in 2015. The event included a dinner dialogue.

INTERFAITH
CONFERENCE
OF GREATER MILWAUKEE
Committee for Interfaith Understanding

Brookfield-Elm Grove
Interfaith Network
BEGIN

An Interfaith Experience
How does your faith inspire you to treat the stranger?

2 p.m. to 4:30 p.m. – January 25, 2015

Welcome: The Rev. Lori Hlaban, BEGIN representative and Assistant Minister,
Unitarian Universalist Church West, Brookfield

Rodney Sanchez, Chair, IFC Committee for Interfaith Understanding and
Milwaukee Buddhist Peace Fellowship representative on Interfaith Conference Cabinet

Background: Tom Heinen, Executive Director, Interfaith Conference of Greater Milwaukee

Emcee: Janan Najeeb, President, Milwaukee Muslim Women's Coalition and member of
Committee for Interfaith Understanding

Speakers: **Baha'i** – Dr. Mina Khorshidi, Brookfield Baha'i Community
Buddhism – Debbie Zarate, Shambhala Meditation Center of Milwaukee
Church of Jesus Christ of Latter-day Saints – John Heller, President,
Milwaukee North Stake
Evangelical Christianity – Karen Cumblad, Director, Elmbrook Church's James
Place outreach and service center in Waukesha
Hinduism – Dr. Lakshmi Bharadwaj, Director of Interfaith Relations & Community
Outreach, Hindu Temple of Wisconsin, Pewaukee
Islam – Ahmed Quereshi, President, Islamic Society of Milwaukee
Islamic Sufism – Dr. Saloumeh Bozorgzadeh, M.T.O. Shahmaghsoudi School of
Islamic Sufism, Franksville
Judaism – Rabbi Steven Adams, Congregation Emanu-El of Waukesha
Protestant Christianity – Rev. Karen Sundland, American Baptist minister
Roman Catholic Christianity – Judi Longdin, Director, Office of Ecumenical and
Interfaith Concerns, Archdiocese of Milwaukee
Sikhism – Dr. Swarnjit S. Arora, Brookfield and Oak Creek Sikh Temples
Unitarian Universalism – Rev. Lori Hlaban, Assistant Minister, Unitarian Universalist
Church West, Brookfield
Zoroastrianism – Toranj Marphetia, Zoroastrian resident of Brookfield and a moderator
for Interfaith Conference Amazing Faiths Dinner Dialogues

Break: There will be a 15-minute break. Refreshments are in the Community Room/foyer.
Please do not bring refreshments into the sanctuary.

Dialogue: Small-group dialoguing on prepared questions

Conclusion: Wrap-up in dialogue groups with final question: What other topics, themes or
activities would you like to see explored/offered?

Interfaith Conference of Greater Milwaukee
www.interfaithconference.org

Figure 8.10: Flyer and program for an Interfaith Experience event held at the Unitarian Universalist Church West in Brookfield, Wisconsin. Sponsored by ICGM and BEGIN (Brookfield Elm Grove Interfaith Network), the event included speakers across a variety of faith backgrounds.[19]

---

19. Wisconsin: Interfaith Conference of Greater Milwaukee and Brookfield Elm Grove Interfaith Network, *An Interfaith Experience: How does your faith inspire you to treat the stranger?*, flyer.

Figure 8.11: At a meeting convened by a local pastor in the fall of 2018, former executive directors of the ICGM, Marcus White (left), Tom Heinen (retired in 2019), and Jack Murtaugh (right) came together to offer suggestions and support for an interfaith student center initiative in the works.

Some of the challenges faced by the ICGM include being hospitable to and engaging with faith communities that are smaller in size, addressing language barriers for religious communities such as Hmong Christians to full participation, bridging historical differences such as those between white and black churches, recruiting individuals to serve and fundraise for the organization, and tending to controversial issues when appropriate. The evidence of growth of and community support for ICGM suggests that Heinen has been very successful in fostering the future of ICGM and its mission by improving the existing programs, addressing the disparities in Milwaukee (hate, fear, poverty), and increasing the resiliency of the organization by sharing its story and expanding its membership.

Shir Hadash Reconstructionist Jewish Community

Shir Hadash Reconstructionist Jewish (SH) community has been meeting regularly inside the Plymouth UCC Church of Milwaukee since 2013. SH was led by Rabbi David Brusin for 12 years; he retired after the move to Plymouth UCC. The current religious leader is Rabbi Michal Woll, who believes her congregation represents "progressive Judaism" (fig. 8.12).[20] Plymouth UCC, until recently (2019), has been led by Pastor Andrew Warner, who was

---

20. Rob Golub, "Signs of Change for Shir Hadash," *The Wisconsin Jewish Chronicle*, February 8, 2018, http://www.jewishchronicle.org/2018/02/08/signs-of-change-for-shir-hadash/.

a huge supporter of the SH–Plymouth UCC relationship. Under his leadership, the church community was happy to accommodate and welcome the Jewish congregation in their midst. Pastor Warner believed that it is "cool" to have this partnership; it is also in line with their (Plymouth UCC's) commitment to being inclusive.[21] This is a story of interfaith co-existence and even co-habitation that goes unnoticed for the most part. It is a story worth telling many times over.

Figure 8.12: Andrew Musgrave (left) with Pastor Andrew Warner and Rabbi Michal Woll.

After 20 years of meeting in a host Jewish community's synagogue in Mequon, Wisconsin, the SH community was challenged to find another synagogue. Given the smaller size of this branch of Judaism, their more liberal interpretations of their faith, and other factors, it is common for their synagogues to share space or to be hosted in Unitarian–Universalist houses of worship. By way of individual connections, Plymouth United Church of Christ (UCC) on the East side of Milwaukee opened its doors to host the SH group. The two groups recognize and cherish their common values, including openness, inclusivity, care for humanity, social justice, different but parallel journeys, leadership of women, acceptance and love for the LGBT community, and "playful" interpretations of scripture and rules. The group has shared in

21. Rabbi Michal Woll and Pastor Andrew Warner, interview by Irfan Omar and Andrew Musgrave, October 10, 2017. The information in this section is based on Andrew Musgrave's narrative of this interview.

various events together, including joint celebrations of holidays. One high-light shared was the celebration of Shavuot, a holiday connected to the Pentecost. Jody Hirsh, a renowned Jewish educator, spoke at the event, following dancing by both communities.

In this partnership, collaborations have included SH members joining the Plymouth UCC social justice committee. The mission statement of this committee included language about following Jesus. Rabbi Woll acknowledged that the way in which this statement is lived out by the Plymouth UCC members is in line with her own values. However, Pastor Warner did express compassion in his suggestion he might advocate for changing this line to make the mission statement more inclusive to the SH members on the committee. Ultimately, they kept the faith language referencing Jesus to help community members see the connection of the social justice work to their spirituality.[22] Anyone glancing at the notice board at the church premises would immediately realize that there is more to this church than what meets the eye (fig. 8.13).

Figure 8.13: Shir Hadash notice board displays some of the progressive causes they support.

According to Pastor Warner, one of the challenges faced by this community comes from the wider UCC church community, which has taken some

22. Pastor Andrew Warner, email correspondence to Andrew Musgrave, July 9, 2018.

strong "anti-Israel" positions. For the UCC general synod it was referred to as a "Just Peace in Israel/Palestine" position.[23] However, the two faith leaders and communities have not faced resistance or objections at local levels, such as from the episcopal office, on any of their programs. In fact, the largest problem addressed by both leaders is the lack of visibility and attention their relationship has received. While this relationship has evolved, the leaders recognize the need for these types of interfaith partnerships to be highlighted and shared in the face of our global "current reality of division competition, and fear."[24] This story represents one of the unique and inspiring possibilities of the kinds of relationships that religious communities may strive to foster: different traditions yet striving to live the shared values; different names for the sacred yet sharing the sacred spaces for their respective worship (fig. 8.14). The possibilities are endless.

Figure 8.14: A synagogue inside a church! Congregation Shir Hadash meeting location inside the UCC Plymouth Church.

---

23. In 2015, UCC General Synod adopted the resolution on "Just Peace in Israel/Palestine," which called for restrictions on companies that "profit from the Israeli occupation of Palestinian land and people." See Connie Larkman, "What the UCC General Synod Adopted on 'Just Peace in Israel/Palestine," *United Church of Christ News*, July 9, 2015, https://www.ucc.org/news_what_the_ucc_general_synod_adopted_on_just_peace_in_israel_palestine_07092015.

24. Rabbi Michal Woll and Pastor Andrew Warner, interview by Irfan Omar and Andrew Musgrave.

Southeast Milwaukee Interfaith Covenant Community

The Southeast Milwaukee Interfaith Covenant Community (SMICC)[25] is one of the first nationally recognized initiatives of 15 religious organizations of one city (14 Christian churches of Milwaukee's south side neighborhoods and one Islamic organization, the Islamic Society of Milwaukee) to create an ecumenical and interfaith covenant together.[26] In November 2000, there were 13 religious groups (12 Christian, one Muslim) who came together to join hands and form the first covenant of friendship and cooperation (fig. 8.15). The leaders of this courageous effort at the time were Imam Ziad Hamdan (Islamic Society of Milwaukee) and Pastor Lowell Bartel (Bay View United Methodist Church). The covenant discussions began in 1999 and were built upon the following promise, which is imprinted at the top of the covenant page itself, signed by representatives of member institutions.

> Within the unifying love of God, we commit ourselves and our communities to the exercise of understanding, cooperation, and growth in unity through faith. We, the following faith communities of southeastern Milwaukee, affirm our support and love for one another.[27]

The covenant encouraged ecumenical and interfaith "pulpit exchanges" between both faith leaders and members.[28] The first covenant was issued in 2000 and was renewed a year later with great enthusiasm following the tragic events of 9/11. The 2001 covenant singed on November 21, 2001, includes Baptist, Lutheran, Catholic, United Methodist, Presbyterian, Episcopal, and United Church of Christ denominations alongside the Islamic Society of Milwaukee. According to Rev. Karen Hagen of Tippecanoe Church and one of the founding members of the covenant, there are no Jewish organizations represented because there are no synagogues in Southeast Milwaukee.[29]

---

25. Sometimes also referred to as "South-East Milwaukee Faith Community Covenant."

26. Tom Heinen, "Interfaith Pledge Breaks Ground: Agreement by Mosque, 12 South Side Churches One of Nation's First," *Milwaukee Journal Sentinel*, November 22, 2000, p. 1B and 6B. See figures 17, 18, & 19.

27. *Southeast Milwaukee Faith Community Covenant*, signed November 21, 2001, copy supplied by Rev. Andy Oren.

28. Kim Poehlman, "Churches Find Common Ground through Religious Exchanges," *The Bay Viewer*, January 27, 2000. Article provided by Andy Oren.

29. Rev. Karen Hagen, interview by Irfan Omar, September 10, 2018.

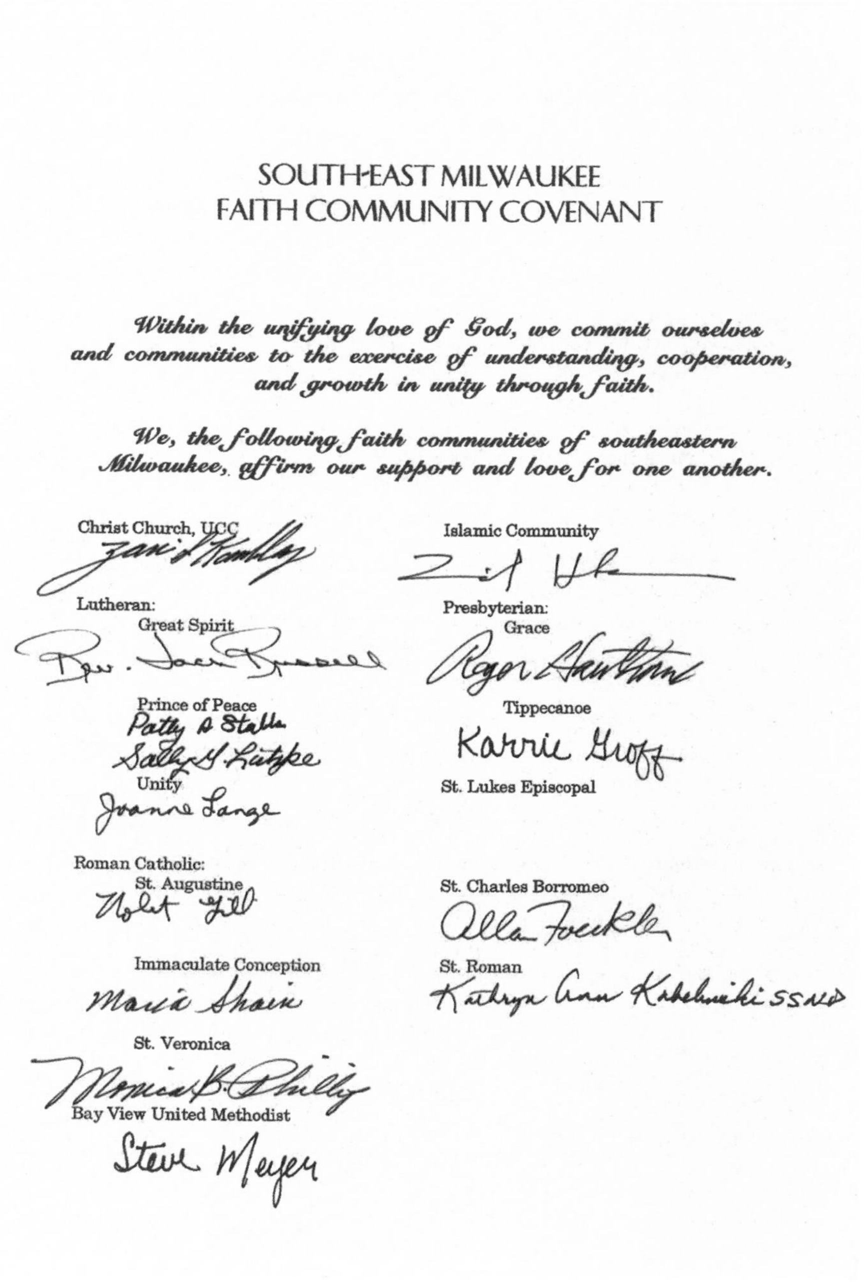

SOUTH-EAST MILWAUKEE
FAITH COMMUNITY COVENANT

*Within the unifying love of God, we commit ourselves
and communities to the exercise of understanding, cooperation,
and growth in unity through faith.*

*We, the following faith communities of southeastern
Milwaukee, affirm our support and love for one another.*

Christ Church, UCC

Lutheran:
Great Spirit

Prince of Peace

Unity

Roman Catholic:
St. Augustine

Immaculate Conception

St. Veronica

Bay View United Methodist

Islamic Community

Presbyterian:
Grace

Tippecanoe

St. Lukes Episcopal

St. Charles Borromeo

St. Roman

Figure 8.15: Copy of the "South-East Milwaukee Faith Community Covenant," first signed in 2000.

Figures 8.16, 8.17, & 8.18: Article reports from the Milwaukee Journal Sentinel on this historic covenant.

After 9/11, the covenant leaders became very active in educational programs aimed at healing and dialogue. They issued a document for immediate release for September 12, 2001, responding to the tragic events of September 11, 2001, and reaffirming the South-East Milwaukee Faith Community Covenant's commitment to the support, understanding, and cooperation without judgment or condemnation of the Christian and Muslim communities. The press release encouraged media and public life to follow suit.[30]

Already in 2000, the covenant signing and the faith communities partnership received some media publicity (figs. 8.16–8.18 & 8.21). With the events of 9/11, things began to change at a faster pace. Numerous programs and meetings were organized to build new relationships and renew existing ones (fig. 8.19). It may be argued that over the years, communities around Milwaukee remained united and resolved in the face of even major challenges because of the already established interfaith partnerships and a climate of trust and understanding.[31] Many years of engagement and dialogue, frequent meetings, and

---

30. South-East Milwaukee Interfaith Community Covenant, "14 Southeast Milwaukee Christian Churches and the Islamic Society of Milwaukee Stand in Solidarity," News release (September 12, 2001). Andy Oren, interview by Irfan Omar.

31. As McCarthy noted in her book *Interfaith Encounters in America* (87–88), community cohesion and resolve depend largely on the established structures that elevate interfaith partnerships allowing participants to see each other in relationship for the common good. In the aftermath of tragic, often violent and traumatic events, communities rely on the existing bonds to heal and move forward.

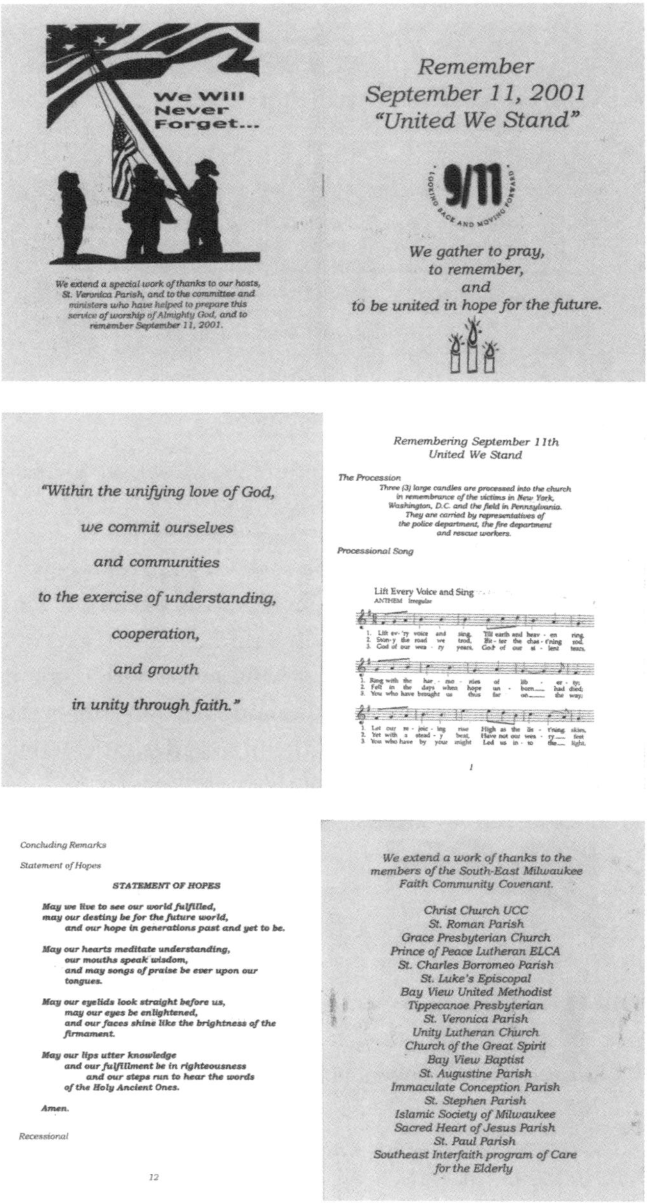

We Will Never Forget...

We extend a special work of thanks to our hosts, St. Veronica Parish, and to the committee and ministers who have helped to prepare this service of worship of Almighty God, and to remember September 11, 2001.

Remember
September 11, 2001
"United We Stand"

9/11
LOOKING BACK AND MOVING FORWARD

We gather to pray,
to remember,
and
to be united in hope for the future.

"Within the unifying love of God,
we commit ourselves
and communities
to the exercise of understanding,
cooperation,
and growth
in unity through faith."

Remembering September 11th
United We Stand

The Procession
Three (3) large candles are processed into the church
in remembrance of the victims in New York,
Washington, D.C. and the field in Pennsylvania.
They are carried by representatives of
the police department, the fire department
and rescue workers.

Processional Song

Lift Every Voice and Sing
ANTHEM Irregular

1. Lift ev - 'ry voice and sing, Till earth and heav - en ring,
2. Ston - y the road we trod, Bit - ter the chas - t'ning rod,
3. God of our wea - ry years, God of our si - lent tears,

1. Ring with the har - mo - nies of lib - er - ty;
2. Felt in the days when hope un - born had died;
3. You who have brought us thus far on the way;

1. Let our re - joic - ing rise High as the lis - t'ning skies,
2. Yet with a stead - y beat, Have not our wea - ry feet
3. You who have by your might Led us in - to the light,

1

Concluding Remarks

Statement of Hopes

STATEMENT OF HOPES

May we live to see our world fulfilled,
may our destiny be for the future world,
and our hope in generations past and yet to be.

May our hearts meditate understanding,
our mouths speak wisdom,
and may songs of praise be ever upon our tongues.

May our eyelids look straight before us,
may our eyes be enlightened,
and our faces shine like the brightness of the firmament.

May our lips utter knowledge
and our fulfillment be in righteousness
and our steps run to hear the words
of the Holy Ancient Ones.

Amen.

Recessional

12

We extend a work of thanks to the members of the South-East Milwaukee Faith Community Covenant.

Christ Church UCC
St. Roman Parish
Grace Presbyterian Church
Prince of Peace Lutheran ELCA
St. Charles Borromeo Parish
St. Luke's Episcopal
Bay View United Methodist
Tippecanoe Presbyterian
St. Veronica Parish
Unity Lutheran Church
Church of the Great Spirit
Bay View Baptist
St. Augustine Parish
Immaculate Conception Parish
St. Stephen Parish
Islamic Society of Milwaukee
Sacred Heart of Jesus Parish
St. Paul Parish
Southeast Interfaith program of Care for the Elderly

Figure 8.19: Pages from the program booklet for "Remember September 11, 2001 'United We Stand'" organized by the South-East Milwaukee Faith Community.[32]

32. Southeast Milwaukee Faith Community Covenant, *Remember September 11, 2001, "United We Stand,"* program.

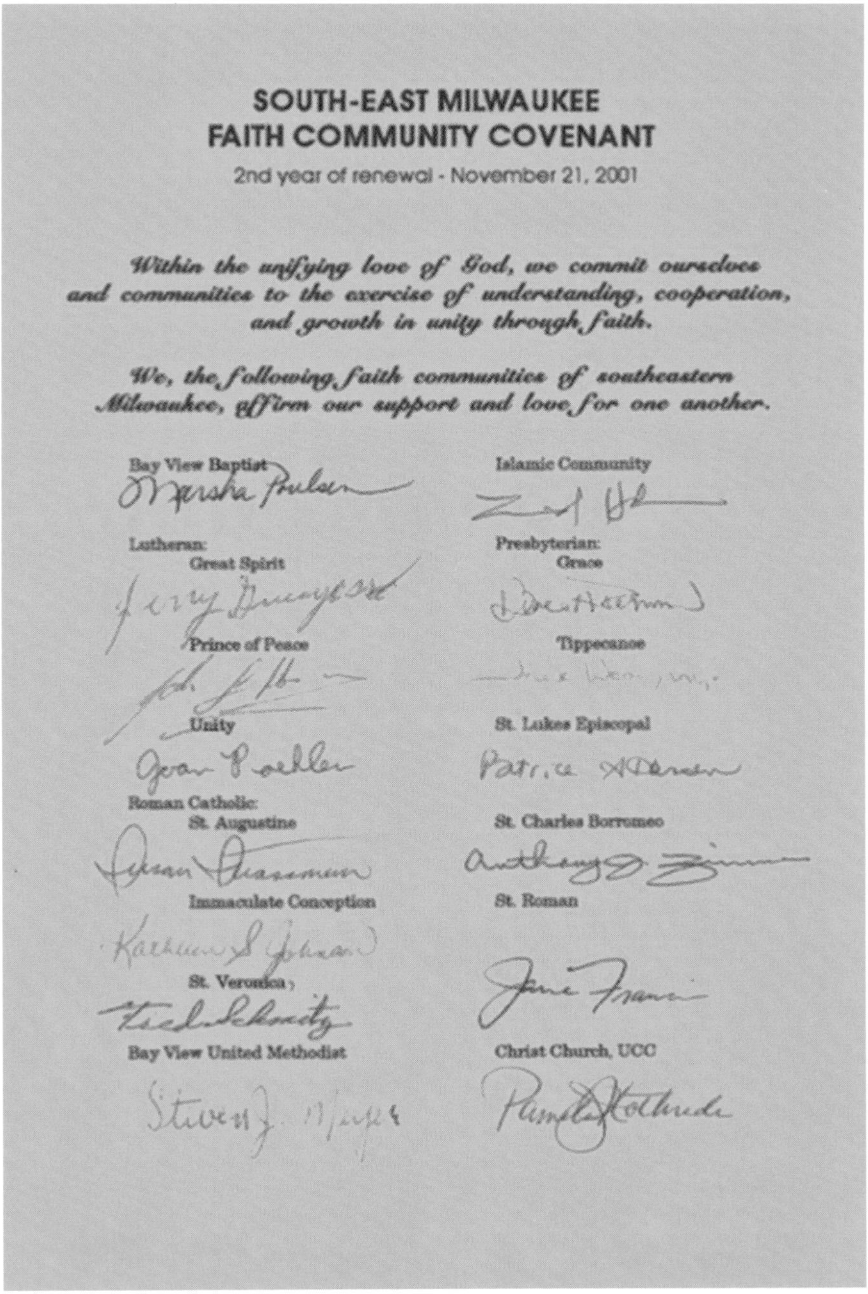

Figure 8.20: Copy of the "South-East Milwaukee Faith Community Covenant," which was renewed in November 2001.

cross-border friendships had opened pathways to forge institutional relationships that would become conduits for inviting, strenghtening, and enriching community members at large.

SOUTH-EAST MILWAUKEE
FAITH COMMUNITY COVENANT

Within the unifying love of God, we commit ourselves and communities to the exercise of understanding, cooperation, and growth in unity through faith.

We, the following faith communities of southeastern Milwaukee, affirm our support and love for one another.

Christ Church, UCC   Islamic Community

Lutheran: Presbyterian:
Great Spirit   Grace

Prince of Peace   Tippecanoe

Unity   St. Lukes Episcopal

Roman Catholic:
St. Augustine   St. Charles Borromeo

St. Roman   St. Veronica

Bay View United Methodist

Thanksgiving and Covenant Service

November 22, 2000
7:00 p.m

held at

Bay View United Methodist Church
2772 S. Kinnickinnic Ave
Milwaukee, WI 53207

ECUMENICAL THANKSGIVING
AND
COVENANT
SERVICE
                Southeast Milwaukee Faith Communities

GATHERING Music   Loretta Nalencz, Organist

WELCOME and Calling Together   Pastor Lowell Bartel,
                Bay View United Methodist Congregation

Loving God, each person is special to you. We have gathered in the spirit of this your created will.

As our traditions offer opportunity for the common gathering of our spirit, help us to seek the wonder of your being. In this season of thanksgiving we raise our common voice in gratitude.

+"For the Fruits of This Creation" No. 97

ISLAMIC Section of Worship Leadership
    Scripture - Surah 3:42-56 (see insert for translation)
    Reflection
    Music Offering

QUIET Moments

ROMAN Catholic Section of Worship Leadership
    Scripture - Luke 22:14-20   St. Charles Parish
    Reflection - St. Roman Parish
    Music Offering - St. Veronica Parish Adult Choir
                Lisa Malavsky, Directing

QUIET Moments

PROTESTANT Section of Worship Leadership
    Scripture - Micah 6:6-8 - Unity Lutheran Church
    Reflection - Tippecanoe Presbyterian Church
    Music Offering - Wesleyan Bells of Bay View UMC
                Mark Humphrey, Directing

QUIET Moments

COVENANT Service
    Looking at our world and all people, we confess our inadequacy in living up to the high calling as sons and daughters of God.
        O God, we know that we are a wayward people. Our footsteps falter as we seek to follow your way; our gaze is turned away from awareness of your will with preoccupation with our own needs and concerns; and even our love for one another is conditional. Let a new spirit be born among us.
    As we make our covenant with one another to seek and respond to the word and will of God as it comes to us, we propose to walk together in new ways. We will join in the mission of peace, striving for unity and justice. We will pray for the coming of the triumph of love and care. This we will do, with the help of Allah!

+"Many Gifts, One Spirit" No. 114

SIGNING the Covenant Document

COVENANTAL Choir   "Now Thank We All Our God"
                Pam Kathrade, Directing

+BLESSING   Fr. Tom Wittliff
                St. Agustine Parish

+DISMISSAL Music and Time of Fellowship

Figure 8.21: Pages from the program brochure for the event when the original covenant was signed at the "Thanksgiving and Covenant Service" on November 22, 2000, at Bay View United Methodist Church.[33]

---

33. South-East Milwaukee Faith Communities, *Thanksgiving and Covenant Service*, flyer.

The South-East Milwaukee Faith Communities began gathering for a community picnic prior to 9/11, but the event took on far more importance since then.[34] There has been media coverage of this and other interfaith programs. One particular event involving the youth from variety of religious communities, which became quite popular, was the Youth Café. Although it is no longer running, Imam Ziad noted that he appreciated this program because it was transformational for many youth and aimed at fostering future dialogue.[35]

Figure 8.22: A newspaper article announcing an ecumenical cooperation picnic in Grant Park of South Milwaukee and a memorial service in memory of the September 11, 2001, tragedy hosted by the Southeastern Milwaukee Faith Community Covenant at St. Veronica's Roman Catholic Church.[36]

According to Imam Hamdan, monthly meetings of the clergy belonging to the South-east Milwaukee Faith Covenant communities continues to draw

34. Apparently their first annual picnic was on September 8, 2001. See Taylor Bush, "Experiencing Diversity," *Interpreter Magazine*, July–August 2017, http://www.interpretermagazine. org/topics/friendship-bench-of-faith.

35. Imam Ziad Hamdan, interview by Irfan Omar, July 1, 2019.

36. Carrie O'Connor, "Muslims, Christians to Unite in Memory of Sept. 11 tragedy," *The Bay Viewer*, 2002.

Co-Sponsored by:

ISLAMIC SOCIETY OF MILWAUKEE

Islamic Society of
Milwaukee

Wisconsin Council
of Churches

and

Southeast
Milwaukee
Interfaith Covenant
Community

September 11th
Ten Years Later:
Our Commitment to
Peace and Justice

**A Workshop with Dr. Sam Richards and
Dr. Laurie Mulvey, Co-Directors,
World in Conversation Project
at Penn State University**

Saturday, September 10th, 2011

9 am – 3 pm

**Islamic Society of Milwaukee
Community Center**
815 West Layton Avenue, Milwaukee

How far have we come in our relationships since September 11th? And what are the challenges ahead of us? Join us for a one-day conversation as we reflect on the last decade and address the work that is ahead of us in Wisconsin to express our common commitment to peace and justice.

Lunch will be provided (suggested donation is $10).

Registration is free and open to the public. Advance registration forms and instructions are available online at:

www.wichurches.org/calendar/event-list/

or call (608) 837-3108

Figure 8.23: Program flyer for commemorating the 10-year anniversary of the September 11 tragedy, a collaboration of the SMICC, WCC, and ISM.

Celebrating Our 17ᵗʰ Year Of Interfaith Ministry Together...

The SE Milwaukee Interfaith Covenant Communities Call Us To Come Together!

Seeking Knowledge and Understanding: An Evening of Sharing As Interfaith Neighbors

Friday February 5ᵗʰ 6:30-8pm
Islamic Society of Milwaukee
13ᵗʰ and Layton Avenue

We come together as friends of faith to hear each other into speech, honoring the holy in our midst and ourselves as brothers and sisters.

Our evening will begin with a remembrance of our shared ministry over the years. Then, a holy time hearing invited members of our community share of their experience, concern, and hope during recent times of unrest...as thoughtfulness is tested by misinformation, anxiety and fear, projection, denial, and accusation. Included will be a time for those attending to take part using a peaceable participation technique we will learn together.

We conclude in quiet with lighting of candles. Each is invited to take home the "light of faith" as a remembrance of what is possible when we take time to hear each other and show care and concern for each other.

You are invited as able to stay after to join in ISM's Evening Prayer.

(Parking available in lot across from ISM on 13ᵗʰ. Child-Care provided.)

Questions? Please call your faith leader, or call Pastor Karen at Tippecanoe Church 414-481-4680

Figure 8.24: Flyer announcing the "17th Year of Interfaith Ministry" of the Southeast Milwaukee Faith Covenant Communities in 2016.[37]

37. Southeast Milwaukee Interfaith Covenant Communities, *The SE Milwaukee Interfaith Covenant Communities Call Us to Come Together!*, flyer.

between seven and 15 people. They come to renew friendships, participate in table fellowship, and exchange information about events relevant to faith and interfaith. They plan events together when needed and offer support for the common cause of building peace.[38] These friendships, cultivated for over two decades, now have the power to fight bigotry and extremism no matter what its source. The group often comes together to educate each other and everyone around them and to witness to the values of their resepctive faith traditions.[39] Apart from the formal discussions, the group has been hosting a community picnic each fall since 2000 (fig. 8.22).

Each year, events are organized to commemorate the past and celebrate the future (fig. 8.23 & 8.24). The Southeast Milwaukee Covenant Communities are hopeful that member communities and organizations will cultivate leaders to whom this exemplary legacy may be bestowed.

Turkish American Society of Wisconsin

The Turkish American Society of Wisconsin (TASWI) is a newcomer to Milwaukee, but it has made a name for itself in this short time as a hospitable group.

Figure 8.25: Niagara Foundation sponsored the Peace and Dialogue Award in 2014 in Milwaukee. The recipients included the then-chancellor of the University of Wisconsin–Milwaukee, Dr. Michael Lovell, who later that year joined Marquette University as its first lay president.

---

38. Hamdan, interview by Omar.

39. Wisconsin Conference of the United Methodist Church, "Milwaukee Interfaith Group Highlighted in Interpreter," July 20, 2017, https://www.wisconsinumc.org/connections/conference-news/hallelujah-moments/3453-milwaukee-interfaith-group-highlighted-interpreter.

They have been organizing programs that facilitate intercultural and interfaith interaction and friendships. According to Onur Asan, the former director of the Niagara Foundation–Wisconsin and TASWI, the aim of all of their events is to promote dialogue and celebrate interfaith engagement. In addition to TASWI, as executive director of Niagara Foundation, Asan organized civil society discussions as well as sponsored "Peace and Dialogue" awards, which brought people from different walks of life together to recognize leaders in the community (fig 8.25).[40]

The target audience for Niagara was different than for the TASWI programs. Each year since 2015, TASWI has hosted several interfaith dinners at the newly established center in Greenfield, Wisconsin, which attracts people from all backgrounds. Sometimes they have invited large groups to facilitate special bilateral interactions; such events included hosting special events for area Jewish congregations, the ICGM leadership and members, academics from colleges and universities, and Christian groups.[41] In addition, TASWI initiated a popular program called the "Abrahamic Tent," which involves hosting families at the home of a TASWI member. This is usually during the month of Ramadan, where visitors can have an experience of the rituals around fasting

Figure 8.26: An interfaith iftar (dinner) at TASWI in 2017, where Christians and Muslims gathered to learn about the Muslim practice of fasting. A few church leaders were specially invited, including from the Holy Communion Lutheran Church in Racine, Wisconsin.

---

40. Niagara Foundation Wisconsin is no longer active, but TASWI continues to thrive.

41. Onur Asan, interview by Irfan Omar, May 15, 2018. Prior to moving to Milwaukee, Asan was active in interfaith circles in the Madison, Wisconsin, area.

Figure 8.27: Turkish-style food served at the iftar.

and gather for the evening meal to break the fast.[42] Interfaith *iftar* dinners during Ramadan are also held at TASWI for large groups and are advertised via social media (fig. 8.26).

One of the more hopeful programs by TASWI is their ongoing dialogue with Brew City Church, a nondenominational protestant church community. They have been gathering over meals in restaurants and at homes with entire families on a monthly basis. In these "home discussion club" meetings, their aim is to have dinner over discussion of religious topics, such as love of God, mercy, and their respective faith journeys. They want to cultivate a deeper connection with one another as individuals and as families.[43] A key member of TASWI and a professor of religion at Carthage College, Prof. Fathi Harpci has led the dialogue and discussion from the Muslim side for several years. Harpci is a noted scholar and committed practitioner of interfaith dialogue, academically as well as in praxis; so, he is perfectly poised to be a leader in such a dialogue.[44]

TASWI has faced many challenges in recent years; some are related to the crises in Turkey where most of its members have friends and family members who are experiencing persecution and exclusion due to their supposed association with the Hizmet movement.[45] It is commendable that despite these and

---

42. Ibid. Onur Asan moved to New Jersey for employment reasons in early 2019, but some of these programs still take place with varying frequency.

43. Ibid.

44. *Wisconsin Muslim Journal*, "Muslims and Evangelicals hold Second Gathering to Breakdown Barriers and Build Trust," March 13, 2018. https://wisconsinmuslimjournal.org/muslims-and-evangelicals-hold-second-gathering-to-break-down-barriers-and-build-trust/.

45. The current Turkish government has targeted and imprisoned many Turkish citizens and journalists due to their (government's) opposition to the Hizmet movement. For more on this movement, see Martin E. Marty, ed. *Hizmet Means Service: Perspectives on an Alternative Path Within Islam* (Oakland, CA: University of California Press, 2015) and Mohammed Abu-Nimer and Timothy Seidel, eds. *The Hizmet and Peacebuilding: Global Cases* (Lanham, MI: Lexington Books, 2018).

other difficulties, TASWI members and volunteers have continued to live out their organization's mission of building intercultural and interfaith relations in the Milwaukee area. TASWI has become a well-known institution in a short time because of the dedication and commitment of the people behind it. Although the organization's leadership has changed several times in the last five years, its mission remains, and its activities continue to take place, although at not at the same pace as before.[46] TASWI members have routinely organized panels and round-table discussions in collaboration with churches and universities in the greater Milwaukee area. Their impact is already felt in the community and, as their participation and organizational initiatives continue to help bring different communities together in dialogue, their contribution as an interfaith player in Milwaukee will become even more crucial.

Interfaith Actors

Below are select individuals who have made and continue to make Milwaukee an interfaith city through their professional commitments and personal efforts. There are numerous examples to choose from; however, the individuals profiled below represent a diversity of arenas and directions where interfaith approaches are utilized in the pursuit of peace.

Huda Alkaff

Huda Alkaff is the founding director of Wisconsin Green Muslims and a founding member of the Interfaith Earth Network.[47] Since 2000, she has been involved in interfaith environmental justice and advocacy work. She views solar energy and water as resources that belong to all and as sacred gifts or trusts. She believes that her advocacy work allows her to exchange ideas, build relationships, and help create meaningful change in order to make a difference for better. Some of her personal goals include the promotion of the use of solar energy, strengthening interfaith relationships, and overcoming Islamophobia. In a recent talk at Marquette University, she noted that in her work these goals

---

46. One of the more recent and well-attended events was the "Turkish Fest," which, like all their events, was advertised through social media to attract people from all backgrounds. The 2019 festival took place on July 20. https://us12.campaign-archive.com/?u=429352e1b93d9d5 0f1415f049&id=c2bb61ff1c.

47. Huda Alkaff, interview by Andrew Musgrave, November 20, 2017. The information in this section is based on Andrew Musgrave's narrative of this interview.

are integrated and are mutually sustaining. Pursuing each of these goals contributes to others.

Alkaff's environmental efforts go back many years. Her first involvement was to educate and promote the Wisconsin Interfaith Climate and Energy Campaign (later it came under the name and national movement, Wisconsin Power & Light). In 2005, she started Wisconsin Green Muslims, a group that educates Muslims and the broader community about Islamic environmental teachings. The hope for this group was to form coalitions to work toward a just, healthy, peaceful, and sustainable future.[48] Alkaff saw working with water as spiritual, which has led to the Wisconsin Green Muslims receiving a Water Shield certificate, the first faith-based organization in Wisconsin to receive it. In 2015, Alkaff helped begin Faith & Solar (an interfaith initiative from Wisconsin Green Muslims), bringing faith communities together to improve their common home through solar energy efforts. This initiative facilitated conversations about the sacredness of light, peer learning circles, and financial support for solar assessments. Several groups that were part of this initiative have installed solar technology. In 2016, Alkaff was a part of Midwest Faith Climate Conversations Project, funded by a grant to sponsor interfaith climate conversations and action.

ENERGY STAR® CHANGE A LIGHT PLEDGE LEADER

The U.S. Department of Energy and
The U.S. Environmental Protection Agency congratulate

**Wisconsin Interfaith Climate & Earth Campaign
Islamic Environmental Group of Wisconsin**

for saving energy and helping reduce greenhouse gas emissions by
participating in the 2007 ENERGY STAR *Change a Light, Change the
World* Campaign.

Ann Bailey
U.S. Environmental Protection Agency
ENERGY STAR

Lari Macbee
U.S. Department of Energy
ENERGY STAR

Figure 8.28: Copy of the ENERGY STAR certificate awarded to the Islamic Environmental Group of Wisconsin by the US Environmental Protection Agency.

48. Kari Lydersen, "White House Honors Wisconsin Green Muslims Founder," *Energy News*, July 20, 2015. https://energynews.us/2015/07/20/midwest/white-house-honors-wisconsin-green-muslims-founder/.

In 2015, Alkaff was recognized by the White House with a "Champion of Change" award. She was one of only 12 faith leaders nationally to be selected for this award. The criteria for the award stated that it is given to those who "have demonstrated clear leadership across the United States and around the world through their grassroots efforts to green their communities and educate others on the moral and social justice implications of climate change."[49] Alkaff and her organization had previously won many other awards, including the USEPA 2007 Energy Star award (fig. 8.28). She is a well-known figure in the community and continues her work of advocacy and teaching on protecting natural resources through sustainable practices.

SWARNJIT ARORA

Dr. Swarnjit Arora is a professor emeritus at University of Wisconsin–Milwaukee, with an extensive teaching background in economics of 46 years.[50] Dr. Arora and his family are from the Punjab region in India. After receiving a mathematics degree and master's degree at University of Delhi, Dr. Arora and his family came to the United States, where he received his doctorate degree at State University of New York at Buffalo and a post-doctorate at the National Bureau of Economic Research.[51] Once in Milwaukee, a place Dr. Arora now considers a beloved home, he was presented with many challenges. Prior to his move to Milwaukee in 1972, Dr. Arora was warned about the discrimination in the city, and upon arrival, he was met with both extreme ignorance from those who lacked religious and cultural knowledge and warm welcome from those curious to learn. Dr. Arora is one of the founding members of the Sikh community organization in Milwaukee. In the 1970s, community members met in different homes to hold religious services on Sundays. Over time, the group moved their religious service to the basement of a local bank, which later became a gas station. The group moved again, first, to an older church building on the northside of Milwaukee, and finally to its existing location in Brookfield (in a former Christian church). Dr. Arora remembers the difficulties of negotiating to buy that property when they met with discrimination from owners who pointedly questioned their intentions, values, and beliefs, and at first

---

49. Ibid.

50. Swarnjit Arora, interview by Kaitlyn Daly and Irfan Omar, June 26, 2018, Wisconsin. The information and quotes in the following subsection are from this interview.

51. Marla Hyder, "Faculty/Staff Profile," *Myriad – A Publication of the Multicultural Student Center, UWM* (2008): 19.

refused to sell. They also had to face the legal battle of trying to build the Sikh temple, which lasted for about 10 years from 1991–2002.

Dr. Arora began his interfaith journey in 1975, three years after arriving in Milwaukee. His response to the prejudice he faced was with conversation and education about his faith and himself. Dr. Arora personally became involved in the Interfaith Conference in the 1980s, but the Sikh religious group gained institutional membership in 2015. The early years in Milwaukee had taught Dr. Arora to be ready to share information about his faith with kind and gentle manner. He now routinely gives presentations on faith and interfaith to a variety of groups locally and nationally. Dr. Arora has also been interviewed on national television, with appearances on NBC, CBC, and PBS to discuss

Figures 8.29 & 8.30: Dr. Arora received many awards for his academic and social work, including the "Lifetime Achievement Award" from the Sikh Religious Society of Wisconsin.

the Sikh temple tragedy in Milwaukee in 2012. He and his family have been serving the Milwaukee community for many years by preparing and providing an Indian meal at the Brookfield Sikh temple on most Sundays and at St. Ben's Parish near Marquette campus once a month. He is a valuable member of the Interfaith Conference of Greater Milwaukee and participates in the planning of many of their events. Dr. Arora has won numerous awards for his academic and social work, including the 2016 Lifetime Achievement Award from the Sikh Religious Society of WI (figs. 8.29 & 8.30).

another ISM facility off Carpenter Avenue that contains an elementary school and a community center.

"It could have been any one of us that was targeted," says Othman Atta, the tall, genial lawyer who serves as the society's director. Since Sept. 11, 2001, community groups and Christian churches have peppered the society with requests for guest presenters, and this is often Atta, who's learned to set aside most of the time allotted for questions. "I make it very clear that the only bad question is a question that isn't asked," he says.

Those that arise include whether Islam supports violence, and he says no. People also ask if the women wearing Muslim dress are oppressed. "No one is forcing anyone to wear or not to wear," he says. "According to the religion, women and

50 Milwaukee Magazine

ECONOMICS PROFESSOR Swarnjit Arora has become an ambassador for Sikhs in the city.

ple shooter, Wade Michael Page. "We had actually had Page on our radar for about a dozen years," Cohen said, adding that three months before the shooting, the center released a police training video, "Understanding the Threat: Racist Skinheads," which singled out Page as an example.

Cohen also read the names of the six Sikhs killed Aug. 5, 2012, as a table ringed with Sikh men wearing suits and turbans looked on. One of those in attendance, Kanwarjit Singh Bajwa, helped to shepherd the construction of the Oak Creek temple in 2007, along with Satwant Singh Kaleka, the temple president who died trying to stop Page's attack. Before immigrating to the U.S., Bajwa supervised the installation of sewers as a captain in the Indian Army Corps of Engineers, and

Figure 8.31: Dr. Swarnjit Arora was featured in *Milwaukee Magazine* in April 2013 in an article, "The New Faith."[52]

As member of the UW–Milwaukee community, Dr. Arora has contributed to the intercultural and interfaith activities on campus and has advised student organizations for many years. He stated that his aim is to "bring students together from different religions" on various occasions sacred to Hindus, Muslims, Christians, and others. He has also volunteered with UWM students at the Hunger Task Force. Dr. Arora explains his views on interfaith saying, "if we want to bring peace in a country, we have to have peace among religions. The

---

52. Matt Hrodey, "The New Faith," *Milwaukee Magazine*, April 2013, 50–51. Access to the online article provided by Brock E. Kaplan at *Milwaukee Magazine* on September 28, 2018.

only way you can get peace among religions is by give and take . . . if I have no desire of learning about [other faiths], how do I anticipate that they will have any desire to learn about me?"[53] Through his numerous activities at UWM, the Sikh Temple, and Interfaith Conference, Dr. Arora, along with his fellow interfaith activists and change agents, has left a lasting impact on the Milwaukee community. Remembering his first years in Milwaukee, he remarked: "I do not see that level of ignorance. Now, Milwaukee has changed . . . [people] are a lot more understanding." This is indeed a hopeful sign, thanks to Dr. Arora and others like him, who have and continue to work tirelessly to create a culture of tolerance through dialogue.

LISA BATES-FROILAND

Rev. Dr. Lisa Bates-Froiland is the head pastor at Redeemer Lutheran Church and former first executive director the Zeidler Center in downtown Milwaukee.[54] Prior to attending seminary, Pastor Lisa came to ministry with an extensive academic background completing her undergraduate degree in political science and communication–speech theatre at St. Olaf College and graduate degrees (MA and PhD) in speech communication with a specialization in 20th century American political rhetoric at Indiana University.

Pastor Lisa shares that she struggled with the exclusivism of being brought up in a fundamentalist branch of the Lutheran church. This upbringing caused her to reflect on the meaning behind Christian values which motivated her to become involved in interfaith effort. Pastor Lisa's introductory engagement with interfaith began in the classroom as an undergraduate student at St. Olaf College. In graduate school at Indiana University, she engaged with interfaith on a more relational level, starting to meet and create relationships and friendships with people of differing faith commitments, such as Jewish, Muslim, and others. Pastor Lisa believes this casual encounter via relationship building "spawns a lot of great conversation." When she began her pastoral work in Milwaukee, she was invited to participate in interfaith panels. Redeemer also has been a host site for dialogue between Muslim and Jewish students, with facilitation from the Zeidler Center and Redeemer church members. Now, seeing space, opportunity, and an energetic congregation at Redeemer, Pastor Lisa has been encouraged to pursue a new breath for Redeemer by starting to imagine

---

53. Arora, interview by Kaitlyn Daly and Irfan Omar.

54. Pastor Dr. Lisa Bates-Froiland, interview by Kaitlyn Daly, March 27, 2018.

interfaith collaborations and actions on its premises. She mentioned that her congregation is "incredibly curious about other world religions and many of them have family systems that are populated by people of many different faiths."[55] The divisive political events also prompted Pastor Lisa to act upon her vision to take a stand for equality, justice, and unity in her community. Pastor Lisa has visions of long-term interfaith engagement and impact. When responding to questions regarding next steps, Pastor Lisa noted:

> On one hand there is tremendous value in the first time you ever engage someone of a different faith tradition . . . there is that kind of warming and that eye-opening of having a first-time engagement. And then, those first several dialogues as you learn more and more are incredible. But then, where does it go? When you've had that experience and you've matured into some real relationships with people?"[56]

Pastor Lisa hopes ongoing, side-by-side, and consistent engagement and interaction through interfaith service, events, and experiences between people of various faith traditions will transform "the doing, the experiencing, and the sharing" into the "new normal." She wants to be a "convener and facilitator of what's possible here." She believes finding well-fitted partnerships is key in interfaith efforts, and her role as pastor allows her to help align the gifts and talents of people around her into such efforts. She foresees the potential challenges of structure, territory, and energy, giving examples such as community relationships, use of space, design to accommodate all visions, financial responsibilities, accommodating all groups that want to be involved, sustaining participation and energy, maintaining motivation, and deciding how to engage in dialogue those who are considered not committed to a specific religion, nonbelievers, or spiritual-but-not-religious. However, Pastor Lisa remains optimistic as she gathers with others who share a similar vision, researching, dreaming and visualizing, collecting resources, creating a culture and getting to know one another, and building on progress. Pastor Lisa expands upon this idea of resistance to religion and cooperation:

> It is personal to me because I have chosen to stake my career, my energy, my love, my devotion—and I know a lot of people are fleeing organized religion—but I am going to hang in there. And I do it because I have a hope

---

55. Ibid.
56. Ibid.

that younger generations will find and do what's necessary for organized religions to again be relevant, be welcoming, be gracious, because I think it's...a low point right now. I feel like a steward . . . who is just trying to keep the lights on and the flame going until it is [clear] what needs to be next.

Pastor Lisa is hopeful that a long-term interfaith engagement can positively transform youth to lead communities into the next decade. Her advice to those starting anew or are in the beginning stages of involvement with interfaith is to be prepared for more "listening than speaking."[57]

Shawnee Daniels-Sykes

Dr. Shawnee Daniels-Sykes is an associate professor of theology and ethics at Mount Mary University in Milwaukee, Wisconsin. Dr. Daniels-Sykes received her bachelor's degrees in biology and biochemistry and nursing and then went on to complete a master's degree in pastoral studies and theology at St. Francis Seminary and a doctoral degree in religious studies at Marquette University. Dr. Daniels-Sykes identifies with the Catholic and Christian faith tradition.[58] She first got involved with interfaith during her time in prison ministry, where volunteers and inmates came from a variety of religious traditions and would want to have conversations together on diverse topics. In the 1990s, Dr. Daniels-Sykes worked in the Black Catholic Ministry office at the Archdiocese of Milwaukee where she began to form relationships with Jewish, Muslim, and Christian denominations. Through this office, interfaith dialogues were conducted, and Dr. Daniels-Sykes would often be asked to present on panels, especially to offer her expertise in health care bioethics. She was also invited to participate in events at colleges and churches, one of which included an event at Plymouth UCC Church on "Reviving Peace," where she presented alongside a Muslim community leader, Dr. Mushir Hassan. She noted that people attending such events often come away with a desire to know more (fig. 8.32).

Dr. Daniels-Sykes also brings interfaith programing to the Mount Mary campus. Pedagogically, she enhances her classes, such as "Faith and Community" and world religions, with discussion on topics relevant to world events, such as the recent "Muslim" travel ban, immigration issues and policies and the politics behind them, and terrorist groups like ISIS and their problematic claims about the religion of Islam. Dr. Daniels-Sykes encourages dialogue when

---

57. Ibid.

58. Dr. Shawnee Daniels-Sykes, interview by Caroline Redick, May 23, 2017.

Figure 8.32: Shawnee Daniels-Sykes speaking at the Plymouth UCC Church conference on "Reviving Peace."

speaking about faith and values, religious prejudice, and misrepresentation of others in order to get to the bottom of why someone might harbor views that they do. She explained that she encourages her students to "bring in" their traditions to class and not be shy about being who they are. She has helped many student groups, including Muslims students, to set up space for prayer on campus. Dr. Daniels-Sykes has also been involved in helping students find interfaith dialogue partners and mentors so they can practice and learn how to facilitate dialogue. She introduced students to other interfaith actors in the Milwaukee area and with people of different faiths. Dr. Daniels-Sykes noted that it is important for those becoming involved in interfaith to learn and share why an individual or group would care to engage in these efforts. What might motivate one to pursue dialogue?[59]

Reirin A. Gumbel

Rev. Reirin Alheidis Gumbel is the resident Buddhist priest and guiding teacher at the Milwaukee Zen Center on Milwaukee's lower-east side. Rev. Gumbel is a member of the Interfaith Conference of Greater Milwaukee cabinet. She is not new to interfaith; she has previous experience in California as a Buddhist priest participating in meetings with those of different faiths.[60] She believes meeting

---

59. Ibid.

60. Rev. Reirin Gumbel, interview by Kaitlyn Daly, April 3, 2018.

Figure 8.33: The 45th Annual Interfaith Conference of Greater Milwaukee Luncheon in 2015 honored new member faiths, including the Buddhist Peace Fellowship Milwaukee. Rev. Gumbel believes BPF can serve not just area Buddhists but all communities.[61]

---

61. Interfaith Conference of Greater Milwaukee, *Working for Justice*, flyer.

The Mirror 湖鏡庵

volume 32, no. 1

February 2018

milwaukee zen center

MZC provides a place for meditation, study and reflection, leading to inner awakening and mindful, compassionate action through traditional Soto Zen Practice.

How Rare the Dharma

By Reirin Gumbel,
Resident priest

*The unsurpassed, profound and wondrous Dharma is rarely met with, even in a hundred thousand million kalpas. Now we can see and hear it, accept and maintain it. May we unfold the meaning of the Tathagata's truth.*1*

A bird flies over a mountain once every one hundred years, swiping the top with its wing. When the mountain is completely worn down, one kalpa has passed. Even one kalpa is unimaginable: How much more so a hundred thousand million!

The universe is unfathomably vast, and time is beyond concepts. How amazing that we find ourselves here on the Earth, in Shakyamuni's saha world, where we are able to meet the Dharma! Humans are born into the world of samsara, ignorant of reality. Actions are followed by consciousness, name and form appear, and quickly we are caught in habits of grasping and clinging. Greed develops, because we feel we may not have enough; hatred arises for others who may be threatening our wellbeing; and existential fear rules our lives.

At some point, there may be a voice that says: Stop! Suddenly we can see and hear the truth of impermanence and interconnectedness, and the links of the chain are shattered. There is nothing to hold onto, nothing to cling to, no others to be afraid of -- we are free!

The price of the ticket for the train to freedom is suffering. Only in the world of endurance (saha) is transformation possible. A deep look into the self is required in order to see its true nature. Eihei Dogen instructs the practitioner to "learn the backward step that turns your light inward to illuminate your self." *2

James Baldwin urges the artist in us to do the same:"The conquest of the physical world is not man's only duty. He is also enjoined to conquer the great wilderness of himself. The precise role of the artist, then, is to illuminate that darkness, blaze roads through that vast forest, so that we will not, in all our doing, lose sight of its purpose, which is, after all, to make the world a more human dwelling place." *3

山 時
Mountain Time

Shakyamuni Buddha's mission was to free sentient beings from suffering, and bring peace and joy to the world. Luckily, we are now in the position to see and hear the Dharma. Let us accept it and maintain it, so we may unfold the Tathagata's truth!

*1 Kaikyo-ge (Sutra-Opening Verse) from Soto School Scripture for Daily Practice

*2 Fukanzazengi of Eihei Dogen

*3 James Baldwin, The Creative Process, in: The Price of the Ticket, Collected Nonfiction 1948-1985

On Sewing the Rakusu

By Anne Johnson

Great robe of liberation
Field far beyond form and emptiness
Wearing the Tathagata's teaching
Saving all beings

(continued)

Figure 8.34: Front page of a recent issue of the Milwaukee Zen Center newsletter.[62]

62. Milwaukee Zen Center, *The Mirror* 32 (February 2018).

with other people is imperative in order to create the realities desired by religious traditions. Rev. Gumbel emphasizes that coming together in discussion, life, and openness will allow us to realize that our differences that separate us may not be as deep or as real as once thought or felt.

Rev. Gumbel believes there is openness and awareness in Milwaukee around interfaith matters. While she is aware that bringing people to interfaith events is not an easy task, she is hopeful that conversations between the faithful will continue: "It is not necessarily conservative or liberal, it's people across the board [who] want peace in this city."[63] No one person or group can achieve it alone. Rev. Gumbel acknowledges that the shared human bond, openness to learning, and love of religion has allowed her to encounter strangers with whom she became friends. She equates and appreciates the variation and connectedness of world religions to the variations and connections present in Buddhism.

Rev. Gumbel mentioned a social activist project with which she is involved called the Community Coalition for Quality Policing as an example of working with other groups for the benefit of everyone and for social justice. With this project, the Community Coalition and the Milwaukee Police Department aim to bridge the gap between community and police in the city. As an integral part of the ICGM, Rev. Gumbel works closely with other members and faith leaders in Milwaukee on a variety of programs. One of her major tasks is to host students from the Milwaukee area who visit the Zen Center. Meeting these young people keeps her motivated. She believes that visiting places of worship other than your own compels us to step outside of our comfort zone and helps us explore new ideas.

ELANA KAHN

Elana Kahn, director of the Jewish Community Relations Council (JCRC), has been involved in the Interfaith Conference of Greater Milwaukee since 2010. She is now part of the executive board and its current chair for 2018–2019. She believes that interfaith interactions and dialogue has helped strengthen her connection to Judaism.[64] Kahn is rooted in her community and faith tradition and yet is committed to relations with others with a common cause.

Kahn speaks of the achievements made through dialogue over the years. There have been numerous events to celebrate Jewish–Catholic dialogue in Milwaukee. More recently, they include the conference commemorating 40

---

63. Ibid.

64. Elana Kahn, interview by Irfan Omar and Caroline Redick, May 24, 2017. Most of the information and quotes in the following subsection are from this interview.

years of *Nostra Aetate*, which was also the occasion to reflect on the maturity of this relationship between Jews and Catholics. The key concerns for Jews in dialogue revolve around humanistic issues. The theological dialogue is important. Some are interested in it as well, but for "most Jews . . . interfaith dialogue is more about belonging than believing."[65] Some Jews come to dialogue because they are still concerned about the sense of their safety and security. Knowing and collaborating with others becomes an imperative for these social reasons.

Kahn coordinates with others in managing the many bilateral dialogues

Figure 8.35: Group photo at a recent gathering of Milwaukee Jewish and Muslim religious leaders.

with other groups such as Presbyterian–Jewish dialogue and the Latino–Jewish alliance. For a time, there was a nascent Jewish–Muslim dialogue around 2009 between religious scholars, but it has not been active for several years. However, a new Muslim–Jewish dialogue initiative began in 2017, which remains promising. According to Kahn, "the Palestinian issue has been a source of great sadness and total frustration" and has made it difficult to initiate dialogue. The impact of this renewed effort can be great as communities need each other combat the challenges faced by everyone.[66] Among her interfaith activities, Kahn also coordinates the monthly

65. Kahn, interview by Irfan Omar and Caroline Redick.

66. These challenges include the recent rise in violence against places of worship. To address these concerns, ICGM in partnership with other religious groups organized a security conference with 250 faith leaders in attendance. Jack McCordick, "'If It Can Happen There, Maybe It Can Happen Here,' Faith Leaders Gather Over Rising Threats to Places of Worship," *Milwaukee Journal Sentinel*, June 11, 2019, https://www.jsonline.com/story/news/local/milwaukee/2019/06/11/milwaukee-religious-leaders-gather-over-threats-places-worship/1420777001/.

Figure 8.36: The religious leaders monthly breakfast meeting, in February 2017, hosted by Archbishop Listecki. From left to right: Rabbi Jessica Barolsky, president of the Wisconsin Council of Rabbis; Ms. Elana Kahn, executive director of JCRC; Bishop Miller of the Episcopal Diocese; Mr. Isa Sadlon, former executive director of the Islamic Society of Milwaukee; Archbishop Jerome Listecki; Bishop Richard Sklba; Rabbi Marc Berkson; Rev. Marie Onwubuariri, American Baptist; Rev. Franz Rigert, United Church of Christ; Mr. Ahmed Quereshi, former president of the Islamic Society of Milwaukee; and Rev. Keith Cogburn, Layton Avenue Baptist Church (Southern Baptist).

Figure 8.37: The May 2017 religious leaders breakfast brought members from the Jewish, Catholic, Protestant, and Muslim communities.

breakfast gathering with select religious leaders in Milwaukee, which is separate from the Interfaith Conference.[67] Various denominational heads

---

67. According to Tom Henein, the outgoing executive director of the ICGM, most who attend the breakfast meeting are either members or affiliates of the ICGM. The reasons for holding the breakfast meeting independent from ICGM has to do with the disagreement over an issue involving an interfaith trip to Israel/Palestine some years ago.

take turns hosting the breakfast meeting. Both Archbishop Jerome Listecki (Roman Catholic) and Bishop Steven Miller (Episcopal) have hosted the group in the past (figs. 36 & 37).

Ken Knippel

Rev. Ken Knippel has served as a priest at St. John Vianney Parish Center in Brookfield, Wisconsin, for over a decade. Rev. Knippel joined the Brookfield/Elm Grove Interfaith Network (BEGIN), an active, voluntary interfaith religious leaders' group that meets monthly to discuss prevalent local and global issues concerning religious leaders and congregations. As a Catholic, Knippel sees his involvement in interfaith as rooted in the messages from the Second Vatican Council calling the Catholic Church to recognize and not "discard" other faith traditions.[68] The active traditions and/or congregations (at time of interview) include: Baha'i Faith (Prospect Drive, Brookfield, WI); Immanuel Baptist Church (North 137th Street, Brookfield, WI); Shambhala Meditation Center of Milwaukee (Buddhist; North Oakland Avenue, Milwaukee, WI); St. Anthony's on the Lake Parish (Catholic; Prospect Avenue, Pewaukee, WI); St. John Vianney Parish (Catholic; North Calhoun Road, Brookfield, WI); St. Luke's Parish (Catholic; West Greenfield Avenue, Brookfield, WI); Church of Jesus Christ of Latter-day Saints (Mormon; Woelfel Road, Brookfield, WI); Congregation Emanu-El of Waukesha (Jewish Reform, West Moreland Boulevard, Waukesha, WI); Brookfield Lutheran Church (Lutheran Church-Missouri Synod; West Burleigh Road, Brookfield, WI); Calvary Lutheran Church (North American Lutheran Church; Calhoun Road, Brookfield, WI); Christ the King Evangelical Lutheran Church (ELCA; North Pilgrim Road, Brookfield, WI); Unity Lutheran Church (ELCA; West North Avenue, Brookfield, WI); Peace United Methodist Church (North Brookfield Road and West North Avenue, Brookfield, WI); Community United Methodist Church (Watertown Plank Road, Elm Grove, WI); Islamic Society of Milwaukee West (Pheasant Drive, Brookfield, WI); Living Hope Presbyterian Church (Pilgrim Road, Menomonee Falls, WI); Sikh Religious Society Gurudwara (North Calhoun Road, Brookfield, WI); Unitarian Universalist Church West (West North Avenue, Brookfield, WI); and Brookfield Congregational United Church of Christ (Gebhardt Road, Brookfield, WI).

---

68. Rev. Kenneth Knippel, interview by Kaitlyn Daly and Jashive Quintas, March 16, 2018.

Figure 8.38: St. John Vianney Parish Center in Brookfield, Wisconsin.

The activities hosted by BEGIN include various youth and adult projects, holiday services, dinner dialogues, and educational sessions. The participating faith communities take turns organizing a prayer service, presentation, lecture, or dinner for all congregations in attendance. Some communities allow attendees to observe a worship or prayer service of that particular religion, if comfortable. In November 2016, for the Thanksgiving gathering at St. John Vianney Catholic Parish, Rev. Knippel delicately crafted a prayer service with words inclusive for all faiths, which is not an insignificant thing given the position of many other Catholic priests and leaders who are not as open.[69] About 200 people attended this prayer service, including youth and their parents. BEGIN's Youth Delegates created a video, "Gratitude Unites Us," to show at the service. The video included a slideshow of photos of youth members holding a sign with the writing, "I'm (insert religious affiliation)/I'm thankful for (insert answer)" with inspirational music in the background.[70] Similarly, in 2011, the group organized a memorial service to mark the 10th anniversary of 9/11, called *Weaving Hope: A Litany in Remembrance for the Tenth Anniversary of 9-11*.[71] According to Rev. Knippel, such events make us gain a new perspective

69. Shaykh Noman Hussain (Imam and religious leader at ISM West), email correspondences to Kaitlyn Daly, March 29, 2018, and May 7, 2018.

70. BEGIN Youth Delegates, *Gratitude Unites Us* (Milwaukee, WI: 2016), video. Video provided by Noman Hussain in March 29, 2018. Email correspondence to Kaitlyn Daly.

71. BEGIN, *Weaving Hope: A Litany in Remembrance for the Tenth Anniversary of 9-11*, flyer.

on how to see events and ideologies that divide us as human beings. It offers a moment to reflect on the humanity of the other who is just like me.

Under the auspices of BEGIN, there are also bilateral meetings and events. For example, Brookfield Islamic Society and the Congregation Emanu-El of Waukesha members maintain regular interaction by arranging joint dinners and lectures several times a year (fig. 8.39). They visit each other's places to become familiar with the other, so as to make them less "other" in thought and feeling.

Figure 8.39: Shaykh Noman Hussain and Cantor Deborah Martin at the Jewish–Muslim dialogue event at the Brookfield Islamic Center.

Rev. Knippel noted that the mission statement of the group is centered on common and essential themes of interfaith dialogue such as respect, advocacy, and humanity. These values shine through in their various meetings and activities. Rev. Knippel stated,

> [religious differences] [are] fine and that's what inspires each of us in our world. But what happens as a result of that is what's important. And that's where we can come together...over an issue or we come together to bring our youth together in peace, or we talk about gun violence or we talk about safety in schools. . . . [Then] there's no denominational difference [between us].[72]

---

72. Rev. Ken Knippel, interview by Daly and Quintas.

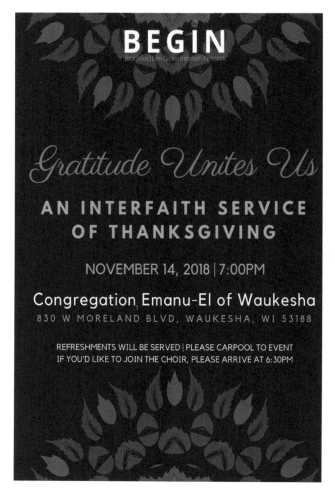

Figure 8.40: BEGIN's Thanksgiving interfaith service flyer in collaboration with the host Congregation Emanu-El of Waukesha.

STEVE LIED

Rev. Steve Lied is the Southeast Wisconsin regional representative of Peace Catalyst International, an organization centered around the mission to "catalyze multi-dimensional peace," founded by Rick Love.[73] The organization mainly targets millennials, young adults, and their families. Rev. Lied himself first became involved in Muslim–Christian dialogue when in Macedonia. In

---

73. Steve Lied, interview by Caroline Redick, May 26, 2017.

2011, at the time of a growing divide between Albanian Muslims and Christians, he collaborated on a symposium funded by the American Embassy regarding love of God and neighbor, which featured internationally known speakers such as Miroslav Volf. In Milwaukee, working with the Peace Catalyst International, Rev. Lied facilitates learning and engagement between evangelical Christians and Muslims. He creates opportunities of interaction between the two communities at Brew City Church, households of interested members, and across the community, such as tours to Muslim-owned restaurants and mosques (including the Islamic Society of Milwaukee). He believes in employing innovative methods of such dinner discussions[74] and what he calls "quick to listen" sessions in churches with a focus on topics like love of neighbor, refugee, enemy, and so on. The aim for such events is to make space for relationships and mutual enrichment of the people involved.

Rev. Lied cites a few challenges that he has faced, including skepticism from leaders of some churches, nationalism and parochialism, and grand assumptions about evangelical Christianity. Rev. Lied himself has gone through a "personal conversion" of re-defining the meaning of evangelism to include mutual learning and understanding of the other. He believes that evangelicals and Muslims have an important role and responsibility to work toward Shalom on earth. Rev. Lied explained the tribalism he has to confront: the challenge of extending love to our neighbors beyond our own faith tradition is Christian love, whereas if one only has love others in the same group, that is not Christian. That is "not doing the will of God." He continued, saying that the true "measure of our faith is how much we love the person outside of our faith."[75]

Rev. Lied's advice for establishing dialogue, especially for newcomers, is to first determine the purpose of the dialogue. Activities should focus on relationship building and grounding it in the principles of faith, which invite us to become peacebuilders. He cites several scripture passages and stories throughout his interview to support the need for and give voice to the call for interfaith work in the Christian evangelical tradition. He continues to warn of the challenges ahead and to forgo the desire to seek quick results. Dialogue requires patience and struggle; one should not "be afraid to swim upstream" or "lose heart."[76]

---

74. Example of an innovative event is the "Peace Fest" or dinner discussion in order to cultivate relationships between Christian and Muslim neighbors. The event was held at Holy Land Deli, whose owners are Palestinian Muslims. Steve Lied email correspondence to Caroline Redick on June 3, 2017 (see fig. 8.44).

75. Ibid.

76. Ibid.

Peace Feast

On **Saturday, March 29** we'll feast at **Holy Land Deli.** The deli can accommodate 30 people. Owner Ali from Palestine is ready to warmly greet us. His hummus is amazing!

Saturday March 29 at 6pm

Holy Land Deli
2755 W. Ramsey Ave
Greenfield, WI 53221

The Peace Feast concept is about introducing Christians to their Muslim neighbors through a low key gathering over a meal. The purpose is to break down walls of fear and mistrust so that personal connections of trust and respect can be established, resulting in on-going relationship and cooperation for the common good. Any follower of Jesus the Messiah who has a heart to love their Muslim neighbor is invited.

Meal and cultural presentation.

Menu is ala carte.

Prices start at $5 for a sandwich, or hummus or falafel.

RSVP by March 25.

RSVP by March 25

steve.lied@peace-catalyst.net

Invite others who are committed to respect and love their neighbor.

Steve & Karen Lied

PCI Program Coordinators in Wisconsin

Wisconsin

Figure 8.41: Informational flyer for Peace Feast coordinated by Steve and Karen Lied in 2014.[77]

---

77. Peace Catalyst International of Wisconsin, *Peace Feast*, flyer.

Types of Interfaith Engagement

Muslim–Christian Engagement

Formal Muslim–Christian dialogue in Milwaukee began in November 1980, initiated by two Franciscan sisters and professors at Cardinal Stritch and a Muslim professor from UW–Milwaukee. Their stories and other forms of Christian–Muslim engagement are discussed in Part I. In this section, we want to briefly note its key features for the sake of appreciating the typology of dialogue.

The first group of interfaith activists and initiators included Sister Lucille Walsh, OSF, Sister Jessine Reiss, OSF, Dr. Abbas Hamdani, Zubeda Hamdani, Mahmoud Atta, Intisar Atta, Rev. Elliot Bush, Rev. Humphrey Walz, and a few others.[78] Their dialogue was exemplary in that it inspired and educated many individuals and community groups with the programs they organized as well as through personal relationships built over two decades. Theirs was an "official" dialogue, approved by community and religious leaders on both sides. Many of the early attendees of this dialogue are no longer active; some have passed away. Through the 1990s and certainly after 9/11, their legacy continued with the emergence of the younger generation of leaders (see Part I in this volume for more on these individuals and their contributions).

Figure 8.42: Photo of Sister Jessine and Intisar Atta, long-time partners in dialogue.

---

78. Dr. Abbas Hamdani email correspondence to Irfan A. Omar on April 23, 2017.

```
                            MINUTES

         SECOND MEETING OF THE ISLAMIC-CHRISTIAN DIALOGUE

                Memorial Library -- Marquette University
                Saturday, January 17, 1981 - 1:30 p.m.


Present:  Dr. Abbas Hamdani
          Mr. Vali Kiaie
          Dr. Martin Kretzmann
          Rev. Robert Lambeck
          Rev. Melvin Michalski
          S. Jessine Reiss
          S. Lucille Walsh (chairperson)
          S. Maureen Hopkins (ex officio member)

Excused:  Rev. L. Humphrey Walz

S. Lucille Walsh, chairperson, opened the meeting with a short re-
flective prayer.

Minutes of the previous meeting were corrected as follows:  the spell-
ing of "Craig" (#3, par. 2) should be changed to "Cragg" (Bishop Kenneth
Cragg).  The minutes were then approved as corrected.

The chairperson then introduced new members of the dialogue:

          Dr. Martin Kretzmann -- member of the Association
                of Evangelical Lutheran Churches; former mis-
                sionary to India for 33 years; co-chairman of
                the 6th National Workshop on Christian-Jewish
                Relations

          S. Jessine Reiss -- associate professor of Middle
                Eastern Literature at Cardinal Stritch College;
                member of the Ecumenical & Interfaith Commission
                of the Milwaukee Archdiocese

          S. Maureen Hopkins -- director of the Ecumenical &
                Interfaith Commission of the Milwaukee Archdio-
                cese; ex officio member of various interfaith
                dialogues in the Archdiocese and ex officio
                member of this dialogue

BUSINESS


1.  S. Walsh displayed the news clippings which appeared in The Milwaukee
    Journal and the Catholic Herald Citizen, announcing the formation of
    this group.  Rev. Michalski indicated that an article also appeared
    in The Milwaukee Sentinel.  Members were asked to bring any articles
    carrying news about the group to the chairperson who will keep them
    on file.
```

Figure 8.43: Minutes from the second meeting of the Islamic–Christian Dialogue which took place on January 17, 1981.

African American Muslim groups often held dialogue meetings that reflected an entirely different agenda than the ones that involved Caucasian Christians and immigrant-heavy Muslim groups. One of the major national movements among Black Muslims was led by Imam Warith Deen Mohammed

Figure 8.44: Imam Warith Deen Mohammed at UW-Milwaukee being introduced by Milwaukee City Councilman Marvin Pratt in 1997.

Figure 8.45: Midwest Focolare group leaders Bill Neu (left) and Paola Santastefano (third from left) with Clara Mohammed School principal, Basimah Abdullah (second from left) and Imam Ronald Shaheed (right) at Washington Park Senior Center in 1998.

(d. 2008), which had centers in almost every major city in the United States. Imam Mohammed was deeply interested in and actively involved with inter-community and intercultural dialogues that were by default also interfaith. The Milwaukee followers of the Imam were fairly energetic and regularly engaged with different Christian groups including members of the Focolare movement. During the 1990s they frequently met either in Milwaukee or in Chicago (fig. 8.45).[79]

Another initiative of dialogue, as noted briefly in Redick's chapter, was organized under the auspices of the Archdiocese of Milwaukee's (now retired) Auxiliary Bishop, Richard Sklba, who has been involved in interfaith dialogue for many decades.[80] In 2011, he convened a "theological" dialogue between select Muslim and Catholic religious and community leaders that met regularly for many years. Their meetings discontinued in 2017, although the commitment to resume discussion remains.[81]

Over the years, other forms of Christian–Muslim interaction have surfaced in Milwaukee. The Muslim youth group MA'RUF has taken the lead in organizing events that seem to depart from the normative understanding of dialogue in that they appear to be driven by social justice work. They are a nonprofit group seeking to cater to the youth from nonaffluent communities. These religious and ethnic cross-border interactions would be best character-ized as "dialogue of action" since they are often rooted in action on behalf of one's faith collaborating with others in serving those in need. MA'RUF volun-teers organize many programs in underserved areas of Milwaukee. One recent such event was called the "Taco Truck Iftar," inviting Latino community mem-bers of all faiths or no faith (fig. 8.46) to partake in Muslim breaking of the fast ritual. MA'RUF's Facebook page described the event in the following words:

> As minority groups in this country, Muslims and Latinos have more in com-mon than we think, especially with the new political climate. Join us as we continue to build bridges with our Latino Community Members and talk family, life and politics. EVERYONE is welcome!"[82]

---

79. Imam Ronald Shaheed, interview by Irfan Omar, June 17, 2019.

80. Bishop Richard J. Sklba, "Breaking Bread for the Kingdom of God," *Herald of Hope*, March 6, 2014.

81. Bishop Sklba, personal communication with Irfan Omar, April 2018.

82. MA'RUF, ISM, Voces de la Frontera, *Feliz Ramadan: Taco Truck Iftar*, Facebook event. https://www.facebook.com/marufmilwaukee/photos/a.253152964730547.61077.208799 862499191/1477736238938874/?type=3&theater.

Figure 8.46: Flyer for a food dialogue event organized by MA'RUF for Muslims and Latinos (many of whom were Christian) in June 2017.

This is not a typical dialogue, but it serves some of the same purposes. It brings people together to experience the other through food and learn about what is important to them. In this event, Latinos, Muslims, and Latino-Muslims were able to see possibilities of working together in solidarity for the challenges they face as minority groups.[83]

Another example of dialogue (of action, mostly) can be seen in the unwritten contract between Bay View Methodist Church and Islamic Society of Milwaukee, where members of the latter serve at the soup kitchen every Easter Sunday. This is more of a partnership and dialogue between individuals than institutions (fig. 8.49). Among the Muslims who regularly volunteer to serve the guests at the meals program at this church (and other churches at different times) is Inshirah Farhoud. Each year, Farhoud has brought in different people from the Muslim community depending on who is available, including teenagers. This helped relieve church members who would be otherwise occupied on this important holiday for Christians.

The reputation of Milwaukee's history of Muslim–Christian relations has reached far and wide to the point that it has attracted the attention of national groups. Milwaukee's legacy of dialogue compelled the Catholic and Muslim leaders of the Midwest Catholic–Muslim Dialogue to hold its annual meeting here for two years in a row, in 2009 and 2010 (see fig. 4.4 in chapter 4 by Najeeb).

The Amazing Faiths Dinner Dialogue (AFDD) has already been noted previously. Their gatherings are often multifaith and diverse. Everyone is

Figure 8.47: Members of the Islamic Society of Milwaukee visiting First Congregational Church of Wauwatosa for a large group dinner dialogue.

---

83. MA'RUF has expanded tremendously in recent years. It now runs a Center for Youth Innovation in the northside of Milwaukee to help the youth from underserved communities in among other things, tutoring, counseling, and training for martial arts. https://www.marufcenter.com/.

Figures 8.48 & 8.49: Bay View Methodist Church front view (top). Mary (Methodist) and Inshirah (Muslim) have been teaming up for several years to serve homeless guests on Easter Sunday.

invited regardless of affiliation with faith community or institution. On occasions, AFDD has organized special events where opportunity for bilateral dialogue becomes possible. In October 2018, the First Congregational Church of Wauwatosa invited Muslims from the Islamic Society of Milwaukee to eat and dialogue. This was sponsored and facilitated by the ICGM (fig. 8.47).

Jewish-Catholic Engagement

In Milwaukee, before the 1980 "original Christian–Muslim dialogue," the Catholics and Jews had begun to meet with the establishment of the Catholic–Jewish Conference. One of the outcomes of the early dialogue between Catholics and Jews was the building of mutual trust between members, mostly leaders in these communities. As they interacted with others, the idea of interreligious relations continued to expand to other communities, mostly Christian, but in time it included Muslim, Hindus, Sikhs, and Buddhists. Although initially the interfaith landscape did not include all of the varieties of religious and cultural communities, it nevertheless was an important step along the way to where we are today in terms of our interfaith realities.

The Jewish–Catholic dialogue is exemplary in the sense that it has continued for over 40 years since 1975. There were times that may be looked upon as moments of harvest, as in harvesting the results of a sustained dialogue. One such moment was when Archbishop Rembert Weakland attended the Catholic–Jewish Conference's jubilee celebrations. While there, he surprised many by reading a statement accepting the Catholic Church's role in the Holocaust, offering a sincerely apology for the suffering of Jews at the hands of Catholics in the past.[84] The Catholic–Jewish Conference have held several events recently related to the anniversary of *Nostra Aetate*. According the mission statement adopted in 1985, 10 years after the establishment of the Catholic–Jewish Conference, the purpose of the conference was to work for mutual understanding and respect between the two communities. Here is the passage from a brief history of the Catholic–Jewish Conference:

> The Catholic-Jewish Conference, founded in 1975, is dedicated to the premise that understanding is the bedrock of mutual respect. Faithful to the spirit of commitments promulgated by the Second Vatican Council on the Jewish people in "Nostra Aetate," it underscores the proposition that the journey to God can take many paths and that each person has an inviolable right to his or her religious convictions. It subscribes to the philosophy that open-mindedness for the views of others lies at the core of any successful dialogue.
>
> The consensus of this organization is that both Jews and Catholics be assured of reinforcing support when the faith or concerns of one or the other is challenged, thus helping to build a bulwark against such catastrophic events that have occurred in our time and in the past. It is our belief that the dignity of humankind stands in proportion to its obligations as well as its rights.[85]

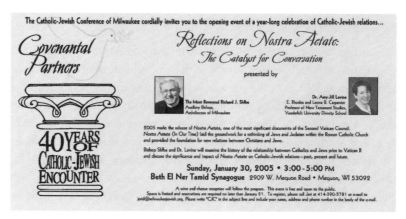

Figure 8.50: Flyer for the 40th anniversary of Nostra Aetate celebrated by the Catholic–Jewish Conference of Milwaukee in 2005.[86]

---

84. Kahn, interview by Omar and Redick.

85. Catholic–Jewish Conference, *Mission Statement,* document. Provided by Elana Kahn; attributed to Kathy Heilbronner, former executive director of the JCRC.

86. The Catholic–Jewish Conference of Milwaukee, *On Turning Forty: Visions for a New Generation,* flyer.

The Catholic–Jewish Conference offers a successful model as to how two faiths can come together to address issues that threaten safety, freedom, and, to use Kahn's word, "belonging."[87] After the 2017 bomb threats received by the Jewish Community Center, the community collaborated with the Catholic-Jewish Conference on solutions to address this issue. Similar consultations have occurred to address the increase in anti-Semitic incidents.[88]

Figure 8.51: The Catholic–Jewish Conference offered various programs to celebrate Catholic–Jewish relations in light of the 50th Anniversary of the Vatican Council II document Nostra Aetate.

Jewish–Muslim Dialogue

Jewish–Muslim relations were formally established in 2006, but in recent years, a concerted effort has been made to meet more regularly. Several challenges to their relationship remain (e.g., Israeli–Palestinian conflict), but a handful of leaders in Milwaukee are coming together to ally. Elana Kahn, director of JCRC, has also been encouraged that organic relationships have sprouted between Imams and Rabbis, as people are "hungry for it" because of "this moment of minority groups being particularly vulnerable." This vulnerability has served as the foundation for such relationships that seek common cause.[89] The following events are examples of Jewish–Muslim engagements in Milwaukee.

---

87. Kahn, interview by Omar and Redick.

88. Kahn, interview by Omar and Redick.

89. Kahn, interview by Omar and Redick.

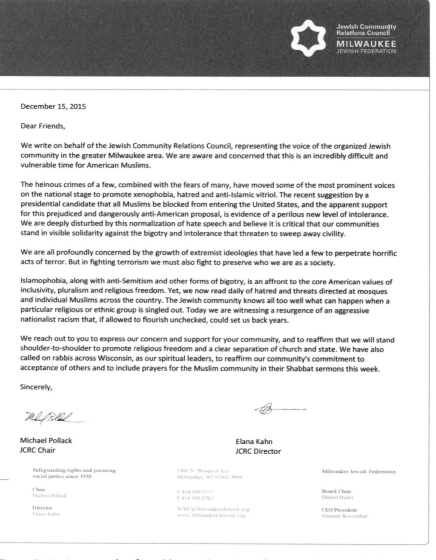

Figure 8.52: An example of a public proclamation of unity and support by the Jewish Community Relations Council.[90]

90. Jewish Community Relations Council and Milwaukee Jewish Federation, letter to friends, December 15, 2015.

Figure 8.53: Turkish Muslim group hosted an iftar for the Jewish community on June 8, 2017, at TASWI in Greenfield, Wisconsin.

One form of Jewish–Muslim dialogue includes the support given by communities to each other, especially in times where they see common cause. One beautiful example of a public proclamation of unity and support by JCRC toward the American Muslim community can be seen in the letter it issued in December 2015 in response to hate crimes and hate speech promoting xenophobia, Islamophobia, and anti-Semitism (fig. 8.53).

Multifaith Dialogue

A variety of dialogues have been taking place in Milwaukee. It is not possible to even list all of the events and foci that use the interfaith platform to pursue their respective agendas. Below are a few examples of interfaith cross-border conversations and actions.

Environment

The environment is an area of common interest for people of different faith backgrounds. Throughout the city, programs have been established and maintained to bring together interfaith and environmental goals. It is important to recognize these local interfaith events that speak to one of the central issues in the world today (e.g., our care for the earth and its resources). The following are examples of environment-related interfaith events (figs. 8.54 & 8.55).

Earth Speaks

Water, a Sacred Gift of Life: Sustaining It For All

An Interfaith Conversation

Sunday October 16 and Monday October 17, 2011
Siena Retreat Center
5635 Erie Street, Racine, WI

As people of faith, what are our responsibilities to ensure the sustainability of water? What are the forces that are stopping access? What can we do locally, regionally and globally? Join us for this two-day interfaith conversation about water and the challenges we face.

In addition to our keynote presenters, we will be joined by an interfaith panel of respondents:

- Huda Alkaff, (Muslim perspective), Founder and Director of the Islamic Environmental Group of Wisconsin.
- Dr. Daniel N. Weber, (Jewish perspective), is Senior Scientist at the Children's Environmental Health Sciences Core Center and the Great Lakes Water Institute, University of Wisconsin-Milwaukee.
- Dr. Jame Schaefer, (Roman Catholic perspective), systematic theologian and ethicist, teaches Religious Foundations for Ecological Ethics at Marquette University.

The conference begins with a light supper at 5:30 pm on Sunday, October 16th and concludes on Monday, October 17th at 4 pm. A variety of workshops will be offered on Monday afternoon. Cost is $100 per person, which includes overnight accommodations (single room) at the Siena Center, three meals and all conference materials. Commuter fee for the conference (includes 3 meals w/o sleeping room) is $70. Sunday evening registration for the keynote presentation and discussion (not including supper) is $25.

REGISTRATION
Earth Speaks - Water, A Sacred Gift of Life: Sustaining It For All

Name(s): _____

Street: _____ City: _____ State: ____ Zip: _____

Phone (___) _____ Email Address _____ @ _____

Denomination/Faith Tradition (optional) _____

Early Bird Registration (fees listed are prior to October 1st) After October 1st add $10 for each category.

_____ Number of Registrations (single rooms) x $100
_____ Number of Commuter Registrations x $70 (includes 3 meals)
_____ Number of Reservations Sunday Evening Only (does not include supper) x $25

I/we want: __Vegetarian Meals; __Kosher Meals; __Halal Meals; __Other dietary needs: _____

Mail your registration with a check payable to "WCC" to the address at the left. Online registration with payment by check or credit card is available at: www.wichurches.org under List of Events.

The Rev. Dr. Clare Butterfield

As Faith in Place's executive director and a Unitarian Universalist minister, Rev. Dr. Clare Butterfield has a life-long interest in environmental matters and preaches and teaches regularly at congregations throughout Illinois, while coordinating programmatic and organizational development. She started as Faith in Place's original organizer and developed the organization into a regional voice for people of faith to understand that ecology and economic topics are important social justice issues for people of faith.

Dr. Peter B. McIntyre

Dr. McIntyre is Assistant Professor, Center for Limnology, UW Madison and an expert on global lakes and rivers, fish diversity, fisheries, the Great Lakes, and water resource management issues. He will address the scientific issues implicit in the global threats to water.

Wisconsin Council of Churches
750 Windsor Street #301
Sun Prairie, WI 53590
(608) 837-3108
www.wichurches.org

Figure 8.54: The Earth Speaks events in 2011 in Racine, Wisconsin, engaged interfaith discussion on the conservation responsibilities of our planet's water. Keynote presenters included a Muslim, Jewish, and Roman Catholic perspective. The event was organized by the Wisconsin Council of Churches.[91]

91. Wisconsin Council of Churches, *Earth Speaks*, flyer.

Environmental Justice: A Human Rights Issue

Save the Date

Sunday
December 11, 2011
2:00 - 4:30 pm
Islamic Society of Milwaukee
4707 S. 13th St., Milwaukee

Sponsored by:

Islamic Environmental Group of Wisconsin

Eco-Justice Center

Midwest Environmental Advocates

Islamic Society of Milwaukee

Wisconsin Interfaith Power & Light

Interfaith Earth Network of Milwaukee

An Interfaith Educational Free Event

✴ Interfaith Panel:
Jewish, Christian and Muslim
✴ Presentation:
Making Environmental Justice A Reality
by Kimberlee Wright
Executive Director, Midwest
Environmental Advocates
✴ Cleaner Valley Coalition Panel
✴ Exhibits & Networking

———————————————

Please RSVP by Friday, December 2, 2011
Contact interfaith.earth@yahoo.com
Go to
http://islamicenvironmentalgroup.org/events/

Figure 8.55: The Islamic Environmental Group of Wisconsin, Eco-Justice Center, Midwest Environmental Advocates, Islamic Society of Milwaukee, Wisconsin Interfaith Power & Light, and Interfaith Earth Network of Milwaukee hosted a free educational collaboration with faith speakers, presentations, exhibits, and networking in 2011.[92]

92. Islamic Environmental Group of Wisconsin, Eco-Justice Center, Midwest Environmental Advocates, Islamic Society of Milwaukee, Wisconsin Interfaith Power & Light, and Interfaith Earth Network of Milwaukee, *Environmental Justice: A Human Rights Issue*, flyer.

Among the numerous events, St. Sebastian Catholic Church in Milwaukee hosted an event titled, "Renegotiating Our Relationship With the Earth: A Conversation on Democracy, Sustainability, and the Role of the Faithful" in May 2014.[93] This was part of a series of interfaith conversations regarding faith and the environment and were open to the public. The event was organized and jointly sponsored by Milwaukee Muslim Women's Coalition (MMWC), Interfaith Earth Network (IEN) of Southeastern Wisconsin, Interfaith Conference of Greater Milwaukee (ICGM). Other supporters included the Islamic Environmental Group of Wisconsin, the Islamic Society of Milwaukee, and Wisconsin Interfaith Power & Light.

The Urban Ecology Center in Milwaukee and the Interfaith Earth Network of Southeastern Wisconsin hosted a faith and ecology seminar series in 2015 and 2016, featuring monthly conversations for six months. The focus of these conversations was captured by the apt title: "Water: Faith and Ecology Conversation Series: Reflecting on Faith Traditions' Statements on Care for Our Home."[94]

Through the efforts of Prof. Jame Schaefer and under her guidance, numerous events, both academic and praxis oriented, occurred on Marquette University campus in the last 15 years. Among these has been the influential Capstone Seminar for the Interdisciplinary Minor in Environmental Ethics (INEE 4997). In May 2017, capstone students collected and presented research on the environment, including how we can better call upon religious communities to spark change in improving the use and care of our environmental resources.[95] These students presented their work to representatives of the Archdiocese of Milwaukee, parishes, the City of Milwaukee, nongovernmental organizations, project consultants, and INEE faculty. According to Jame Schaefer, INEE director at Marquette University, the Priests Council for Social Justice recommended uploading the tool kit to the Archdiocesan website for wider dissemination of this resource.

93. Islamic Environmental Group of Wisconsin, Eco-Justice Center, Midwest Environmental Advocates, Islamic Society of Milwaukee, Wisconsin Interfaith Power & Light, and Interfaith Earth Network of Milwaukee, *Renegotiating Our Relationship With the Earth: A Conversation on Democracy, Sustainability and the Role of the Faithful*, flyer.

94. Interfaith Earth Network, *Water: Faith and Ecology Conversation Series: Reflecting on Faith Traditions' Statements on Care for Our Home*, flyer.

95. Alyx Birmingham, Eleni Eisenhart, Heidi Golembiewski, Lydia Melland, Tony Peacoc, and Wyatt Meyer, "Flipping the Default Toolkit: Renewable Energies, Fossil Fuels" (Capstone project, Marquette University, 2017.) Provided by Jame Schaefer, PhD, INEE director. In email to Irfan A. Omar, May 17, 2017.

YOUTH

There is a rise in initiatives from the youth in local communities that involve interfaith conversations and activities. The following are a few examples of youth-related interfaith events.

In 2008, the South East Milwaukee Interfaith Community Youth Ministries hosted their third annual Youth Interfaith Service Retreat. Christian and Muslim members from several area churches and the Islamic Society of Milwaukee served residents of Milwaukee completing simple task chores, while participating in ice-breakers and mealtimes together (fig. 8.56).[96]

YOUTH INTERFAITH SERVICE RETREAT... 'YISR'

On Saturday April 26th, the Muslim community along with several churches came together to build bridges in the Milwaukee community. The event was not an unfamiliar one. Being in its third consecutive year, the South East Milwaukee Interfaith Community Youth Ministries pulled together another successful event. All over Milwaukee, groups of students donning bright orange t-shirts bearing the label "Youth Interfaith Service Retreat", volunteered their time and energy to help the community. The program began Friday April 25th, with the youth and adult organizers meeting at

Tippecanoe Presbyterian Church for snacks and ice-breaker games. The youth were able to get to know each other in order to break the ice for the next day. That night, the boys slept at Tippecanoe Church while the girls slept at the Islamic Center. At 8:00 the next morning, the boys met back at the Islamic Center and everyone enjoyed breakfast provided by the ISM. Everyone packed bag lunches and were divided into groups of about seven or eight students with two adult drivers setting out to their assigned homes. Each group went to three or four homes and attended to tasks such as

window-washing, garden work, exterior painting, and backyard cleaning. Most residents were elderly people having difficulty performing the tasks themselves. After the groups were finished, they met back at the Islamic Center or went to the Unity Lutheran Church to await the Spaghetti Dinner at 5:00. Several of the people who benefited from the volunteers also attended the dinner, which began with a slide-show of this year's and last year's retreat. Everyone enjoyed dinner and headed home afterwards. "The retreat was such a good way to make da'wa and learn

about other faiths at the same time," said Dalal Ahmad, one of the youth who participated, "I hope to see more events like this in the future." This seemed to echo the feedback given by the majority of youth who attended. Most found the event fun and worthwhile. As a senior in high school, I easily see the importance of events like this. To have Muslim students helping the greater community without compensation is fundamental in challenging negative perceptions of the Islamic community. Inshallah this will continue to be an annual event for the Islamic Community.

-Besma Jaber

Figure 8.56: Report of the third annual Youth Interfaith Service retreat published in the Islamic Society of Milwaukee newsletter.

In 2015, Milwaukee Muslim Women's Coalition (MMWC) and Interfaith Conference of Greater Milwaukee (ICGM) sponsored a five-month workshop, called "I-You Interfaith Youth," where high school students met once a month for unique interfaith activities hosted at various faith communities in the greater Milwaukee area.[97]

The Brookfield Islamic Center hosts interfaith *iftar* for youth and adults separately each year during Ramadan. Due to the strong interfaith bonds built through BEGIN, this event is very popular and attracts people from a variety of denominations and religions in the area (fig. 8.57).

---

96. Besma Jaber, "Youth Interfaith Service Retreat," *Al Kawthar*, ISM newsletter, June 2008, 3.

97. Milwaukee Muslim Women's Coalition and Interfaith Conference of Greater Milwaukee, *Interfaith Youth: Explore, Expand, Engage*, flyer; Tom Heinen, interview by Andrew Musgrave.

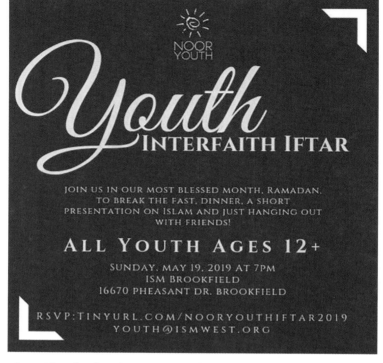

Figure 8.57: Flyer for the Islamic Society of Milwaukee Brookfield's Youth Interfaith Iftar (dinner) in 2019.[98]

Community Relations and Outreach

For several years now the M.T.O. School of Islamic Sufism in Franksville (a Milwaukee suburb) has opened its doors to people from all backgrounds and faiths for education and learning about Islam and Sufism. In addition, each Ramadan, they host an interfaith dinner that also includes a talk and demonstration of *zikr* (remembrance of God) in the style particular to this branch of Sufism (figs. 8.58–62).

The Islamic Society of Milwaukee has hosted community outreach events on a regular basis for many years. Individually, Muslims have also regularly participated in the AFDD. Here is a recent example of the dinner dialogue at Inshirah Farhoud's house featured in the Islamic Society of Milwaukee newsletter (fig. 8.64).

---

98. Islamic Society of Milwaukee Brookfield, *Interfaith Iftar*, flyer.

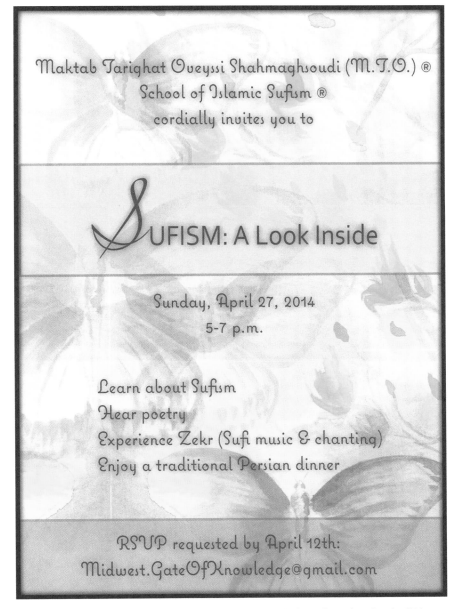

Maktab Tarighat Oveyssi Shahmaghsoudi (M.T.O.) ®
School of Islamic Sufism ®
cordially invites you to

$\mathcal{S}$UFISM: A Look Inside

Sunday, April 27, 2014
5-7 p.m.

Learn about Sufism
Hear poetry
Experience Zekr (Sufi music & chanting)
Enjoy a traditional Persian dinner

RSVP requested by April 12th:
Midwest.GateOfKnowledge@gmail.com

Figure 8.58: The Milwaukee branch of the M.T.O. Shahmaghsoudi School of Islamic Sufism hosted an educational event on Sufism in 2014.[99]

99. M.T.O Shahmaghsoudi School of Islamic Sufism and Midwest Gate of Knowledge, *Sufism: A Look Inside*, flyer.

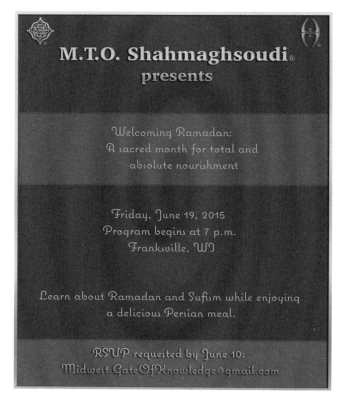

Figure 8.59: The School of Islamic Sufism in Franksville hosted a Ramadan dinner that included a brief introduction to Sufism in 2015.[100]

Figures 8.60 & 8.61: Ramadan interfaith dinner at the M.T.O. Shahmaghsoudi School of Sufism in 2017.

---

100. M.T.O Shahmaghsoudi School of Islamic Sufism and Midwest Gate of Knowledge, *Welcoming Ramadan: A Sacred Month for Total and Absolute Nourishment*, flyer.

Figure 8.62: Ms. Khouri (left), spiritual director at the MTO Shahmaghsoudi School of Sufism, hosted the Ramadan interfaith dinner in 2017.

Guests get a tour of the MTO School of Islamic Sufism in Franksville prior to a dinner dialogue hosted by the Students of Islamic Sufism. One of the highlights was authentic Persian cuisine. On the menu: Persian pomegranate soup, lentil rice, and rice pudding. (Click the links for recipes!)

Figure 8.63: Guests of one of the dinner dialogues pose for a group photo at the MTO School of Sufism.

VOLUME I   ISSUE 2

Outreach to the Community

The above picture was taken by a Journal Sentinel photographer who covered an Amazing Faith Dinner that was hosted by members of the Islamic Society of Milwaukee. The Journal Sentinel also carried an article about this particular dinner, in their Sunday edition. The participants in the above dinner included Sr. Inshirah Farhoud, Sr. Bayan and Br. Nabil Salous, Sr. Jill Ochoa, members of several Christian denominations, a Jewish couple and others. A link to this article can be found here:

http://www.jsonline.com/news/milwaukee/milwaukee-area-group-hopes-simple-meals-lead-to-religions-tolerance-b99107336z1-225670301.html

NEEDED
Big Sisters and Big Brothers for NEW Muslims

Please contact Sr. Inshirah for more details
414.313.1595

The Amazing Faith Dinner Projects

I would like to invite our community members to participate in The Amazing Faith Dinner Projects.

The Amazing Faith Dinner Project is a program that is sponsored by the Interfaith Conference of Greater Milwaukee. This program brings people of various faiths together so that all may learn about the beliefs and faith traditions of others through exploration and dialogue. These events take place in an atmosphere of mutual respect and enable everyone involved to stand as witness for tolerance and understanding.

The format: a group of 8 - 10 people gather in one of the participants' homes over a very light meal. One of the participants is a moderator who will facilitate the discussion.

Please contact Inshirah Farhoud if you are interested in participating in one of the dinner projects.

Inshirahf@aol.com or 414-313-1595.

ISM TODAY

Figure 8.64: A page from the newsletter of the Islamic Society of Milwaukee promoting the Amazing Faiths Dinner Dialogue Project. The photo in the newsletter is of a recent dinner dialogue hosted by Inshirah Farhoud.

The Episcopal Diocese of Milwaukee in collaboration with ICGM organized an event commemorating the legacy of Dr. Martin Luther King, Jr. This was an interfaith gathering with speakers from Muslim, Jewish, and Christian communities as well as from the ICGM (fig. 8.65).

Figure 8.65: Interfaith event to honor the legacy of Dr. King in 2018, which included speakers from ICGM and three faith communities.[101]

101. All Saints' Cathedral Episcopal Diocese of Milwaukee and Interfaith Conference of Greater Milwaukee, *Continuing Dr. King's Call: An Interfaith Gathering*, flyer.

Figure 8.66: The dean of All Saints Episcopal Cathedral, Rev. Kevin Carroll, offering welcoming remarks at the event "Continuing Dr. King's Call: An Interfaith Gathering."

In 2016, the United Methodist Church under the leadership of Bishop Hee-Soo Jung began a summer program for UMC's community, which is also open to other Christian denominations. The program, "Bishop Jung's Interfaith Bus Tour and Retreat" has been running for three years and attracts those interested in learning about faith communities in Milwaukee area but also to see how to be faithful in a multifaith world (figs. 8.67–8.71). The interfaith tour is sponsored by the Wisconsin Conference Commission on Christian Unity and Interreligious Relationships, part of the United Methodist Church. Bishop Jung has vast experience in the areas of intercultural and interreligious engagement, and he offers this tour in the hope of creating more spaces for dialogue between people who will otherwise not have a chance to encounter one another. The Milwaukee and Wisconsin leaders of the United Methodist Church have been key players in inspiring and organizing interfaith programs for over two decades. One of the early members and activists in the Southeast Milwaukee Interfaith Covenant Community, Rev. Andy Oren, was part of Bishop Jung's organizing team.

Figure 8.67: Flyer for the August 2018 Interfaith Bus Tour and Retreat organized and led by Bishop Hee-Soo Jung.[102]

Figure 8.68: Dr. Swarnjit Arora and Bishop Hee-Soo Jung at one of the dialogue sessions during the Interfaith Bus Tour in 2018.

---

102. Wisconsin Conference United Methodist Church, Commission on Christian Unity and Interreligious Relationships, *Join Bishop Jung's Interfaith Bus Tour and Retreat*, flyer.

PARTICIPATION GOALS

Registration is limited to 52 persons. Laity and clergy are both invited. The schedule begins in the evening Friday and ends before dinner on Sunday.

PROCESS

Bishop Hee-Soo Jung will speak to us during our travel time Saturday in a comfortable motor coach with restrooms. Comfortable accommodations, space for informal conversation, meeting rooms, and worship settings in the DeKoven Retreat Center will provide the environment for this inspiring retreat.

PREPARATION

All registrants will receive a packet by email containing important information, including directions about attire and principles of interfaith dialog.

SPONSORSHIP

Bishop Hee-Soo Jung and the Commission on Christian Unity and Interreligious Relationships have planned this event with the assistance of various religious leaders from greater Milwaukee.

OVERNIGHT ACCOMMODATIONS

Overnight accommodations are available for up to 80% of our group at the retreat site, The DeKoven Center, 600 21st Street, Racine, WI. Overnight accommodations include the costs of breakfast on Saturday and Sunday. If you desire a room, you may register for this online when you sign up for the event. Single rooms are $85/night. Double rooms are $75/night.

REGISTER ONLINE

https://www.etouches.com/bustour2018

COSTS

The registration fee for this event is $120 per person. This includes all meals. It is important to register as soon as possible. In the prior years, registration lists have filled up; and we have had to turn away some applicants.

QUESTIONS?
Call Andy Oren 414-744-3927.

FRIDAY SCHEDULE August 17	
5:30 p.m.	Gathering at Congregation Sinai 8223 N. Port Washington Road Milwaukee, WI
6:00 p.m.	Shabbat Worship Service and Discussion
8:15 p.m.	Car Caravan for Overnight Guests of DeKoven Retreat Center

SATURDAY SCHEDULE August 18	
8:30 a.m.	Boarding the Bus at DeKoven Retreat Center 600 21st St. Racine, WI
9:00 a.m.	The Basilica of St. Josaphat Milwaukee, WI
11:00 a.m.	St. Sava Serbian Orthodox Church Milwaukee, WI
12:15 p.m.	Lunch at Serb Hall
2:30 p.m.	Islamic Society of Milwaukee West Brookfield, WI
5:15 p.m.	Bus Returns to the DeKoven Retreat Center for Dinner
6:30 p.m.	Discussion with Bishop Jung and Holy Communion

SUNDAY SCHEDULE August 19	
10:00 a.m.	MTO Shahmaghsoudi School of Islamic Sufism Franksville, WI
12:00 p.m.	Lunch at the DeKoven Center
12:30 p.m.	Interfaith Dialogue with Dr. Swarnjit S. Arora, Sikh Presenter
1:30 p.m.	Interfaith Dialogue with Bushra Zaibak, Muslim Presenter
2:40 p.m.	Interfaith Prayer Service

Figure 8.69: The Interfaith Bus Tour program consisted of Friday evening and Saturday and Sunday events including visits to places of worship in the greater Milwaukee area. In 2018, the group visited the Brookfield Islamic Center and mosque, Congregation Sinai synagogue, as well as the Basilica of St. Josaphat.[103]

---

103. Wisconsin Conference United Methodist Church, Commission on Christian Unity and Interreligious Relationships, *Interfaith Bus Tour*, program.

Figure 8.70: Bishop Hee-Soo Jung speaking on the final evening of the two-day inter-faith event in August 2018.

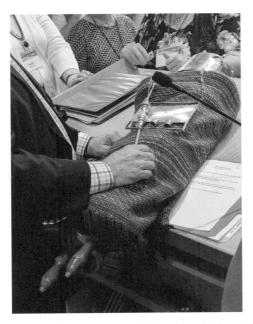

Figure 8.71: Congregation Sinai was one of the places Bishop Hee-Soo Jung took the group in 2018, where among other things they witnessed how the Torah scroll is treated and handled.

Under the auspices of religious charity Worldwide Hunger Relief, Inc. and Helping Hand for Relief and Development, several food-packing events have been organized around the city, often hosted by places of worship. One such event took place at the Islamic Society of Milwaukee Community Center/Salam school premises in 2017, where people from all backgrounds and of all ages came together to prepare rice packets to be sent to Jordan to benefit the growing Syrian refugee population. Many participants, clergy and lay members, came from the Islamic Center and area churches, including St. John's in Brookfield and King of Glory Lutheran Church in Greenfield (figs. 8.72–8.75).

Figure 8.72: The Islamic Society of Milwaukee, Worldwide Hunger Relief, Inc., and Helping Hand for Relief and Development collaborated to host a Food Pack Event and clothing drive for the Syrian refugees in Jordan. The resident imam of the Islamic Center, Shaykh Ziad Hamdan (right), volunteering alongside volunteers from a nearby Christian congregation.

Figures 8.73 & 8.74: Volunteers at the food pack event from the Islamic Society of Milwaukee, St. John's in Brookfield, and King of Glory Lutheran Church in Greenfield.

PLEASE JOIN THE ISLAMIC SOCIETY OF MILWAUKEE, WORLDWIDE HUNGER RELIEF, INC. AND HELPING HAND FOR RELIEF AND DEVELOPMENT FOR A...

Food Pack Event

BENEFITING SYRIAN REFUGEES IN JORDAN

When:

Saturday, April 22, 2017
5 shifts (8:30 - 10:00, 10:00 - 11:30, 11:30am - 1:00pm, 1:00 - 2:30, 2:30 - 4:00)

Where:

ISM Community Center - 815 W. Layton Ave. Milwaukee, WI

Who Can Help:

- Anyone 7 years and older.
- People from all faiths and backgrounds are welcome.
- Need to sit or stand for a 90-minute shift.

Cost:

None. $20 suggested donation to cover food and shipping costs.

How Can I Sign Up?

We highly recommend signing up to guarantee your spot. There are 160 spots available per 90 minute shift. Reserve your spot at:
tinyurl.com/FoodPack2017

We will also be holding a clothing drive to be sent with the food.
Please consider donating new/gently used clothing.

Please contact the Islamic Society of Milwaukee at ismoffice@ismonline.org or 414-282-1812 for any questions.

Figure 8.75: Flyer of the food pack event at ISM Community Center.[104]

---

104. Islamic Society of Milwaukee, Worldwide Hunger Relief, Inc., and Helping Hand for Relief and Development, *Food Pack Event*, flyer.

Researchers in Action

The following illustrates some of the work the researchers of this project have undertaken and completed. Their efforts resulted in the gathering of the materials and telling the story of dialogue in Milwaukee. In 2017, the team presented at two venues. The first presentation was at a panel on dialogue as part of the interdisciplinary symposium on "Christian-Muslim Relations in America Today" held at Marquette University in March (figs. 8.76 & 8.77). The second presentation took place at one of the monthly community forums organized by TASWI (fig. 8.78).

CHRISTIAN–MUSLIM RELATIONS
IN AMERICA TODAY
AN INTERDISCIPLINARY SYMPOSIUM

MARQUETTE UNIVERSITY
27-29 MARCH 2017

3.30-5.00   **Prof. Irfan A. Omar**, Department of Theology
"Christian-Muslim Relations in Milwaukee"

Kaitlyn Daly, Undergraduate, Nursing and Theology
"Interfaith Activities of the Educational Institutions in the Milwaukee Area and Youth Participation and Perspectives

Sundus Jaber, Undergraduate, Speech Pathology & Psychology
"Catholic Muslim Women's Dialogue in Milwaukee: A Brief History"

Dianne Marshall, MACD, Department of Theology
"Catholic Muslim Women's Dialogue in Milwaukee: Themes and Participants"

Caroline Redick, Graduate Student, Department of Theology
"Milwaukee Christian-Muslim Dialogue: History, Purpose, and Future"

Figures 8.76 & 8.77: The research team presented its findings on a panel at the Marquette University symposium on "Christian-Muslims Relations in America Today."

The research team worked on various aspects of the project for six months, interviewing, documenting, revising their drafts and coordinating with each other on how to connect the dots in a volume that maintains the integrity of the various themes covered. Below we offer a sampling of the kinds of activities undertaken by team members (figs. 8.79–85).

Figure 8.78: Research team member Dianne Rostollan (Marshall) presenting on Women's Dialogue at a TASWI event in 2017.

Figure 8.79: Kaitlyn Daly interviewing Dr. Swarnjit Arora at his office at the University of Wisconsin–Milwaukee.

Figure 8.80: Researchers Caroline Redick and Sundus Jaber with Naheed Arshad.

Christians, Muslims engage in discussion

Interfaith dialogue breaks barriers, forms relationships

By Grace Connatser
sarah.connatser@marquette.edu

Two students shared their findings on interfaith dialogue between Christians and Muslims in the Milwaukee area at the annual Interfaith Symposium Monday.

Kaitlyn Daly, Nursing '17, and Caroline Redick, a Ph.D. candidate in theology, worked on a year-long research project with three other students examining different aspects of interfaith dialogue between Christians and Muslims in Milwaukee. Irfan Omar, a professor of theology and world religions, helped facilitate the research project.

Daly, Redick and the three other students were in Omar's interfaith graduate class in spring 2017. Their final project evolved beyond the classroom and grew into an academic publication.

Daly focused on the role of institutions like Marquette, University of Wisconsin-Milwaukee and Cardinal Stritch University in furthering interfaith dialogue efforts. Redick created an in-depth timeline

of how formal interfaith dialogue began in the area.

"People think that religions are not supposed to mix or contact each other because they have exclusive claims," Omar said. "On the contrary, what we find out is that the exclusive claims made by people of religious traditions are only a minority."

Omar said he noticed an increase of people from different religions saying that interfaith dialogue is mandatory.

Daly said she hoped to increase awareness and encourage more interfaith activities at Marquette through her research.

"I noticed that there was a little bit of a lack of interfaith opportunities at Marquette," Daly said. "Amongst other students ... a handful of us wanted to go forth and pursue more interfaith efforts on campus."

There had been no academic research done on the insurgence of Christian-Muslim relations in Milwaukee before Daly and her peers began researching the issue. A book compiling all five students' research will be published sometime in fall 2018, titled "Bridging the Religious Divide: 36 Years of Christian-Muslim Dialogue in Milwaukee."

Daly found that many barriers to

interfaith dialogue still hinder students and community members from being a part of the dialogue, such as conflicting schedules and fear of the unknown. She also mentioned several people she interviewed in her research were scared of being converted to a different religion.

Daly said the solution to breaking down these barriers is creating relationships.

"The overall dialogue and coming together can look a lot of different ways, but it welcomes all ... regardless of being grounded in a faith tradition or to discover one," Daly said. "It invites them all to grow spiritually, religiously, intellectually, together in one spot."

Redick said nine mosques serve 15,000 Muslims in the Milwaukee area. That number was much smaller in 1980 when two nuns from Cardinal Stritch University, Sr. Lucille Walsh and Sr. Jessine Reiss, began an interfaith effort with Abbas Hamdani, a professor emeritus of Islamic studies at UW-Milwaukee. The three continued to create a conversation between faiths until 2000.

While the formal dialogues ended, Redick said the annual Interfaith Conference of Greater Milwaukee and the Milwaukee Muslim-Catholic Healthcare Initiative,

among other efforts, have spurred further collaboration between Christians and Muslims.

Redick said loving one's neighbor is one of the most important aspects of the Christian and Muslim faiths. She said the power of that love should not be underestimated.

"The dialogue's not just about academically understanding this religion, and it's also asking how we can work together to do this project," Redick said.

"The end is love and saying, 'How do I love the other?'"

Redick said she believes challenging one's identity also strengthens it by increasing knowledge of others.

"I get to understand ideas and things that I held because now I'm conversing with someone else about them," Redick said. "They have questions about it, and I didn't think about those questions."

Daly (left) and Redick (right) pose at the symposium Monday, April 30.
Photo by Helen Dudley helen.dudley@marquette.edu

Figure 8.81: Marquette Tribune article by Grace Connatser highlighting the April 2018 Interfaith Symposium at Marquette University featuring two researchers, Kaitlyn Daly (left) and Caroline Redick (right).[105]

---

105. Grace Connatser, "Christians, Muslims Engage in Discussion: Interfaith Dialogue Breaks Barriers, Forms Relationships," *Marquette Tribune*, May 1, 2018.

Figure 8.82: Research team member Sundus Jaber interviewing Ms. Kirsten Shead, former program leader of the Interfaith Earth Network.

Figure 8.83: Research team member Caroline Redick interviewing filmmaker Laj Waghray.

her fellowship, Abigail worked with youth on projects that addressed self-esteem, bullying, violence, and team-building.

"There were so many fun things that happened during my fellowships that helped me grow. It helped me learn and it helped me plan for my future career. I know I want to work with kids now and I know that that's what I'm good at. My fellowship helped me take what I'm learning in the classroom—take my passions that I know I have—and combine them and turn them into a career that I never imagined I would have the ability to do before this... It was the best thing that could have happened to me."

Following her fellowship, Abigail worked as a Nonviolence Educator with the Center's Peace Works program. Throughout her senior year, she co-facilitated weekly lessons with fifth grade students at Messmer Catholic Schools. The lessons covered skills such as empathy, gratitude, and forgiveness.

All of these experiences led Abigail to accept a position with Equinox RTC in North Carolina to work with youth in mental health treatment centers. •

Student researchers turn class project into a book on interfaith dialogue in Milwaukee

When Dr. Irfan Omar assigned his graduate level theology class a research project on interfaith dialogue in Milwaukee, he knew there was a wide range of possible outcomes. It didn't take long for him to see that his students felt a sense of purpose while working on the research. In fact, it became more than just a research project: Dr. Omar and his students came to see this project as important for historical memory, community relations, and for students at Marquette.

Dr. Irfan Omar (left) with a few of his student researchers (from left to right: Kaitlyn Daly, Dianne Marshall, Sundus Jaber, and Caroline Redick) after a meeting with interfaith leaders in Milwaukee.

The students started by conducting interviews and compiling articles, documents, and photos. They didn't have to look far to uncover a rich history of interfaith relations in Milwaukee. In 1980, two Catholic nuns, professors at Cardinal Stritch University, and a Muslim professor from UW-Milwaukee, formed an "official" Christian-Muslim dialogue group with the support of the Archbishop of Milwaukee. It was the first time in Milwaukee's history a group brought attention to the city's religious diversity which included Muslim communities and highlighted the need for dialogue.

The story became even more compelling to the students when they learned that this group of pastors and priests, professionals, nuns, professors and others met on a regular basis for nearly 20 years.

In addition to their monthly meetings where they discussed issues of common interest, they organized public events and brought notable Christian and Muslim scholars and leaders to Milwaukee. The group was diverse and included Christian and Muslim men and women from a variety of denominational and cultural backgrounds. In addition to learning from each other, this group focused on building trust and friendships, some of which have

Figure 8.84: The Summer 2018 Prints of Peace Newsletter published by Marquette University Center for Peacemaking reported on the progress of the interfaith dialogue project.[106]

---

106. Marquette University Center for Peacemaking, "Student Researchers Turn Class Project into a Book on Interfaith Dialogue in Milwaukee," *Prints of Peace*, Summer 2018, 3–4.

Figure 8.85: Andrew Musgrave (left) interviewed Tom Heinen in 2018.

Conclusion

Milwaukee has been a hidden gem of interfaith dialogue and action. This chapter has highlighted the fervent grassroots efforts in the community that shows the interreligious fabric of Milwaukee. We hold these pioneers of interfaith action with the sincerest gratitude, respect, and honor, and encourage the newcomers in this effort to seek wisdom in the stories before us. While this chapter is only a brief sample, the reality of interfaith collaboration in Milwaukee is evolving and growing strong. Previously recognized by the Vatican in the 1980s for its interfaith efforts, leaders of past and present have continued to fulfill the city's promise of bridging faith relations across the Milwaukee area. They stand as a global model for interfaith efforts. While this chapter has described and illustrated interfaith events and encounters that have resulted in improved relations, deeper understanding, and opened pathways for infinite collaborations, there have also been times when opportunities were missed. As can be imagined, much more needs to be done to take full advantage of the resources at the disposal of the religious institutions in Milwaukee. They have the power to make religion relevant and beneficial to all by reaching out and by living the values that are central to faith, namely, building peace that truly benefits every member of the creation of God.

Bibliography

Abu-Nimer, Mohammed, and Timothy Seidel, eds. *The Hizmet and Peacebuilding: Global Cases.* Lanham, MI: Lexington Books, 2018.

Birmingham, Alyx, Eleni Eisenhart, Heidi Golembiewski, Lydia Melland, Tony Peacoc, and Wyatt Meyer. "Flipping the Default Toolkit: Renewable Energies, Fossil Fuels." Capstone project, Marquette University, 2017.

Bush, Taylor. "Experiencing Diversity." *Interpreter Magazine*, July–August 2017, http://www.interpretermagazine.org/topics/friendship-bench-of-faith.

Carson, Sophie. "Pardeep Singh Kaleka, Son of Oak Creek Sikh Temple Founder and Shooting Victim, Will Help Community Heal as Interfaith Leader." *Milwaukee Journal Sentinel*, July 27, 2019, https://www.jsonline.com/story/news/religion/2019/06/27/milwaukee-sikh-community-leader-kaleka-heads-interfaith-conference/1588372001/.

Connatser, Grace. "Christians, Muslims Engage in Discussion: Interfaith Dialogue Breaks Barriers, Forms Relationships." *Marquette Tribune*, May 1, 2018.

Golub, Rob. "Signs of Change for Shir Hadash." *The Wisconsin Jewish Chronicle*, February 8, 2018, http://www.jewishchronicle.org/2018/02/08/signs-of-change-for-shir-hadash/.

Heinen, Tom. "Faithful Find Unity in Shattered World." *Milwaukee Journal Sentinel*, September 12, 2001.

————. "Interfaith Pledge Breaks Ground: Agreement by Mosque, 12 South Side Churches One of Nation's First." *Milwaukee Journal Sentinel*, November 22, 2000.

Hrodey, Matt. "The New Faith." *Milwaukee Magazine*, April 2013.

Hyder, Marla. "Faculty/Staff Profile." *Myriad – A Publication of the Multicultural Student Center, UWM* (2008): 19.

Interfaith Conference of Greater Milwaukee. "Amazing Faiths Dinner Dialogues." http://www.interfaithconference.org/cms-view-page.php?page=amazing-faiths-dinners.

————. "Interfaith Conference Representatives." http://interfaithconference.org/cms-view-page.php?page=interfaith-conference-representatives.

————. "Ongoing Reports: Keeping Busy." http://interfaithconference.org/cms-view-page.php?page=year-in-review.

————. "Stand Against Hate in Waukesha County." May 13, 2019. http://interfaith-conference.org/index.php.

Jaber, Besma. "Youth Interfaith Service Retreat." *Al Kawthar*, ISM newsletter, June 2008.

Jewish Community Relations Council and Milwaukee Jewish Federation. Letter to friends, December 15, 2015.

Larkman, Connie. "What the UCC General Synod Adopted on 'Just Peace in Israel/Palestine." *United Church of Christ News,* July 9, 2015, https://www.ucc.org/news_what_the_ucc_general_synod_adopted_on_just_peace_in_israel_palestine_07092015.

Lydersen, Kari. "White House Honors Wisconsin Green Muslims Founder." *Energy News*, July 20, 2015, https://energynews.us/2015/07/20/midwest/white-house-honors-wisconsin-green-muslims-founder/.

Marquette University Center for Peacemaking. "Student Researchers Turn Class Project into a Book on Interfaith Dialogue in Milwaukee." *Prints of Peace*, Summer 2018, 3–4.

Marty, Martin E., ed. *Hizmet Means Service: Perspectives on an Alternative Path Within Islam.* Oakland: University of California Press, 2015.

McCarthy, Katy. *Interfaith Encounters in America.* New Brunswick, NJ: Rutgers University Press, 2007.

McCordick, Jack. "'If It Can Happen There, Maybe It Can Happen Here,' Faith Leaders Gather over Rising Threats to Places of Worship." *Milwaukee Journal Sentinel*, June 11, 2019, https://www.jsonline.com/story/news/local/milwaukee/2019/06/11/milwaukee-religious-leaders-gather-over-threats-places-worship/1420777001/.

Milwaukee Journal Sentinel. "Oak Creek Sikh Temple Shooting." http://archive.jsonline.com/news/crime/165082506.html.

Milwaukee Zen Center. *The Mirror* 32 (February 2018). Provided by Reirin Gumbel.

O'Connor, Carrie. "Muslims, Christians to Unite in Memory of Sept. 11 Tragedy." *The Bay Viewer*, 2002.

Poehlman, Kim. "Churches Find Common Ground through Religious Exchanges." *The Bay Viewer*, January 27, 2001.

Schreiner, Peter. "Roman Catholic Theology and Non-Christian Religion." *Journal of Ecumenical Studies* 6, no. 3 (1969): 376–99.

Sharpe, Eric J. "The Goals of Inter-religious Dialogue." In *Truth and Dialogue in World Religions*, edited by John Hick, 77–95. Philadelphia, PA: The Westminster Press, 1970.

Sklba, Richard J. "Breaking Bread for the Kingdom of God." *Herald of Hope*, March 6, 2014.

Southeast Milwaukee Interfaith Covenant Community. "14 Southeast Milwaukee Christian Churches and the Islamic Society of Milwaukee Stand in Solidarity," News release, Wisconsin: September 12, 2001.

Wisconsin Conference of the United Methodist Church. "Milwaukee Interfaith Group Highlighted in Interpreter." July 20, 2017, https://www.wisconsinumc. org/connections/conference-news/hallelujah-moments/3453-milwaukee-inter faith-group-highlighted-interpreter.

Wisconsin Muslim Journal. "Muslims and Evangelicals hold Second Gathering to Break Down Barriers and Build Trust, March 13, 2018. https://wisconsinmuslimjournal. org/muslims-and-evangelicals-hold-second-gathering-to-break-down-barriers-and-build-trust/.

Institutional and Organizational Sources

(Flyers, Program brochures, Documents)

All Saints' Cathedral Episcopal Diocese of Milwaukee and Interfaith Conference of Greater Milwaukee. *Continuing Dr. King's Call: An Interfaith Gathering.* Flyer.

BEGIN Youth Delegates. *Gratitude Unites Us.* Recorded 2016. Milwaukee, WI.

BEGIN. *Weaving Hope: A Litany in Remembrance for the Tenth Anniversary of 9-11.* Flyer.

Catholic-Jewish Conference. *Mission Statement.* Document.

Feliz Ramadan: Taco Truck Iftar. Wisconsin: MA'RUF, ISM, Voces de la Frontera, 2017, https://www.facebook.com/marufmilwaukee/photos/a.2531529647305 47.61077.208799862499191/1477736238938874/?type=3&theater.

Interfaith Conference of Greater Milwaukee and Brookfield Elm Grove Interfaith Network. *An Interfaith Experience: How does your faith inspire you to treat the stranger?* Flyer.

Interfaith Conference of Greater Milwaukee. *Acting Against Hate: 47th Annual Luncheon.* Flyer.

———. *Interfaith Prayer Service for Peace.* Program.

———. *Working for Justice.* Flyer.

Interfaith Earth Network. *Water: Faith and Ecology Conversation Series: Reflecting on Faith Traditions' Statements on Care for Our Home.* Flyer.

Islamic Environmental Group of Wisconsin, Eco-Justice Center, Midwest Environmental Advocates, Islamic Society of Milwaukee, Wisconsin Interfaith Power & Light, Interfaith Earth Network of Milwaukee. *Environmental Justice: A Human Rights Issue.* Flyer.

Islamic Society of Milwaukee Brookfield. *Interfaith Iftar*. Flyer.

Islamic Society of Milwaukee, Worldwide Hunger Relief, Inc., and Helping Hand for Relief and Development for A… *Food Pack Event*. Flyer.

M.T.O. School of Islamic Sufism and Midwest Gate of Knowledge, *Sufism: A Look Inside*. Flyer.

———. *Welcoming Ramadan: A Sacred Month for Total and Absolute Nourishment*. Flyer.

Milwaukee Muslim Women's Coalition and Interfaith Conference of Greater Milwaukee. *Interfaith Youth: Explore, Expand, Engage*. Flyer.

Milwaukee Muslim Women's Coalition, Interfaith Conference of Greater Milwaukee, Interfaith Earth Network, Islamic Environmental Group of Wisconsin, Islamic Society of Milwaukee, Wisconsin Interfaith Power & Light, *Renegotiating Our Relationship with The Earth: A Conversation on Democracy, Sustainability, and the Role of the Faithful*. Flyer.

Peace Catalyst International of Wisconsin, *Peace Feast*. Flyer.

Southeast Milwaukee Faith Communities. *Thanksgiving and Covenant Service*. Flyer.

Southeast Milwaukee Faith Community Covenant. *Remember September 11, 2001 "United We Stand."* Program.

Southeast Milwaukee Faith Community Covenant. Signed November 21, 2001

Southeast Milwaukee Interfaith Covenant Communities. *The SE Milwaukee Interfaith Covenant Communities Call Us to Come Together!* Flyer.

The Catholic-Jewish Conference of Milwaukee. *On Turning Forty: Visions for a New Generation*. Flyer.

Wisconsin Conference United Methodist Church, Commission on Christian Unity and Interreligious Relationships. *Interfaith Bus Tour*. Program.

———. *Join Bishop Jung's Interfaith Bus Tour and Retreat*. Flyer.

Wisconsin Council of Churches. *Earth Speaks*.

Interviews

1. Alkaff, Huda. Interview by Andrew Musgrave. November 20, 2017.

2. Arora, Dr. Swarnjit. Interview by Kaitlyn Daly and Irfan Omar. June 26, 2018.

3. Asan, Dr. Onur. Interview by Irfan Omar. May 5, 2018.

4. Bates-Froiland, Pastor Lisa. Interview by Kaitlyn Daly. March 27, 2018.

5. Daniels-Sykes, Dr. Shawnee. Interview by Caroline Redick. May 23, 2017.

6. Gumbel, Rev. Reirin. Interview by Kaitlyn Daly. April 3, 2018.

7. Hagen, Rev. Karen. Interview by Irfan Omar. September 10, 2018.

8. Hamdan, Shaykh Ziad. Interview by Irfan Omar. July 1, 2019.

9. Hamdani, Dr. Abbas. Interview (via email) by Irfan Omar and Caroline Redick. April 23, 2017.

10. Heinen, Tom. Interview by Andrew Musgrave. November 14, 2017.

11. Kahn, Elana. Interview by Irfan Omar and Caroline Redick. May 24, 2017.

12. Knippel, Rev. Kenneth. Interview by Kaitlyn Daly and Jashive Quintas. March 16, 2018.

13. Lied, Rev. Steve. Interview by Caroline Redick. May 26, 2017.

14. Oren, Rev. Andy. Interview by Irfan Omar. August 16, 2018.

15. Shaheed, Imam Ronald. Interview by Irfan Omar, June 17, 2019.

16. Waghary, Laj. Interview by Irfan Omar and Caroline Redick. May 24, 2017.

17. Woll, Rabbi Michal and Pastor Andrew Warner. Interview by Irfan Omar and Andrew Musgrave. October 10, 2017.

Personal Correspondence

Hamdani, Dr. Abbas. Email correspondence to Irfan Omar. April 23, 2017.

Hussain, Imam Noman. Email correspondence to Kaitlyn Daly. March 29, 2018 and May 7, 2018.

Lied, Rev. Steve. Email correspondence to Caroline Redick. June 3, 2017 and June 6, 2017.

Sklba, Bishop Richard J. Personal communication with Irfan Omar. April 2018.

Warner, Pastor Andrew. Email correspondence to Andrew Musgrave. July 9, 2018.

EPILOGUE

Kaitlyn C. Daly

This book is a small attempt to gather and share the intricate details of various dimensions and efforts of the original Christian–Muslim dialogue in Milwaukee. While this chronology is by no means exhaustive of the numerous perspectives and experiences procured during the decades since the first formal dialogue, it is a genuine attempt to congratulate these dialogue actors as well as to seek inspiration from them who made every honest effort to bring together individuals and communities from across the ideological and religious divide. Presented in this book are rich stories of interfaith experiences that have been woven into the city's history, passed on through generations, and lived anew in this very day.

The recounting began with an explanation of the rationale and the need for interfaith dialogue. A brief intro to interfaith dialogue is provided for those who may need it. The chapters that follow in part 1 offer a window into the first-hand accounts of the communities' grassroots efforts in dialogue based on the words and worlds of the people involved. The two chapters in part 2 serve more like a catalogue of events with accompanying albeit brief narratives. These concluding chapters include individual perspectives embedded in Milwaukee's interfaith history. The interfaith activists showcased here have been leading the way in making dialogue integral to the task of maintaining civic society relations and institutions. In the process, they have broadened the scope for all future interfaith work in Milwaukee.

Milwaukee has been and remains a vibrant city where civic society institutions are actively working to address problems that plague today's America, such as violence, racial inequities, political discord and the like (figs. E.1 & E.2). Interfaith dialogue and interaction are considered by many to be one of the most effective methods to deal with these issues. Milwaukee-area religious leaders and community activists have shown what can be possible when people come together in the spirit of compassion and empathy—two of the fundamental ethical precepts found in all the faith and spiritual traditions.

As this book comes to a close, the interfaith actors across Milwaukee continue to inspire and engage in dialogue with one another. Various individuals and groups in the city are planning future events related to issues of our shared human experience—engaging religious, political, socioeconomic, and other forms of diversity. They are reaching out and embracing the other, whether he or she is a refugee, a victim of trauma, a neighbor with a different faith, or a racialized other; or, someone within their own faith tradition who disagrees on matters of doctrine. The faces, types, and settings of dialogue are limitless; the invitation is open for all to participate in building intentional relationships for the sake of peace in local and global communities. Indeed, dialogue has many dimensions and levels; this book has only covered a sliver of these.

Figure E.1: In response to the mass shootings in El-Paso, Texas, and Dayton, Ohio, the Milwaukee community leaders organized a vigil on August 5, 2019, that attracted a large number of people from all backgrounds and representing many religious and secular groups.

Figure E.2: Mayor Tom Barrett and Congresswoman Gwen Moore were among those who attended the vigil. The new executive director of the Interfaith Conference, Pardeep Kaleka (center), was one of the coordinators of the event.

The guiding questions for this research were simple. First, the researchers wanted to know what were the various kinds of activities in the genesis of early dialogues in the area of Christian–Muslim relations. Second, the researchers sought to identify how the early efforts in dialogue provided an impetus and a model for the next set of dialogue leaders, and in what new directions did these leaders moved the dialogue forward. Third, the researchers aimed to explore some of the immediate and long-term benefits to the individuals and communities to which the dialogue interlocutors belonged. This book has documented some of the tangible results and the impact of the years of engagement across the religious divide. It has attempted to answer these questions within the parameters and scope of this work. However, there are many more stories of engagement that are left out and numerous dialogue actors—past and present—whose exemplary efforts need to be shared. Thus, this is just a beginning.

Appendices

Members of Various Dialogue Groups

Members who attended the formal Islamic–Christian dialogue (1980–1991)

Dr. Waheed Ahmed, Milwaukee, WI

Mr. George Allam, Milwaukee, WI

Mr. and Mrs. Reid D. Allen, Milwaukee, WI

Dr. Omar M. Amin, Kenosha, WI

Dr. Robert Ashmore Jr., Mequon, WI

Ms. Greta Assaly, Milwaukee, WI

Mr. Mahmoud Atta and Mrs. Intisar Atta, Milwaukee, WI

Mr. Hassan Baalbaki, Milwaukee, WI

Mr. Ahmad Bader, Milwaukee, WI

Mr. Radwan Baytiyeh, Milwaukee, WI

Rev. Elliot Bush and Mrs. Trudy Bush, Milwaukee, WI

Dr. Mohammed Aslam Cheema, Elm Grove, WI

Robbie Coles, Madison, WI

Rev. and Mrs. Roy Denning, Janesville, WI

Rev. Paul Esser, Milwaukee, WI

Mahmoud Hafeez, New Berlin, WI

Dr. Abbas Hamdani and Zubeda Hamdani, Milwaukee, WI

Dr. Moustafa Hassan, New Berlin, WI

Scott Hill, Milwaukee, WI

Faruk Khair, Milwaukee, WI

Dr. Akbar Komijani, Milwaukee, WI

Rev. Robert Lambeck, S.J., Milwaukee, WI

Gloria Lueneberg, Milwaukee, WI

Joseph Makhlouf, New Berlin, WI

Fahed Masalkhi, Milwaukee, WI

Walter Neevel, Milwaukee, WI

Rev. Joseph Perry, Milwaukee, WI

Rev. Thomas Pexton, Shorewood, WI

Fahed Ra'ad, Milwaukee, WI

Rev. Paul Rogers, Waupun, WI

Mohammad Saleem, Greendale, WI

Dr. John Schmitt, Wauwatosa, WI

Loretta Ropella, Milwaukee, WI

Mohsin and Tracy Said, Elm Grove, WI

Mohammed and Tayibah Sethi, Brookfield, WI

Dr. Richard Taylor, Brookfield, WI

Nancy Theoharis, Milwaukee, WI

Gamil Tourky, Milwaukee, WI

Rev. Jim Tully, Franklin, WI

Glenn Van Haitsma, Waukesha, WI

Rev. Humphrey Walz, Janesville, WI

Dr. Andreas and Denise Wesserle, Milwaukee, WI

Key Members of Muslim–Catholic Women's Dialogue (1996–2016)

Inshirah Farhoud

Judith Longdin

Janan Najeeb

Bobbie Schmitt

Invited Members of the Muslim–Catholic "Theological" Dialogue (2011–2017)

Othman Atta

Dr. Barbara J. Freres

Judith Longdin

Janan Najeeb

Dr. Waleed Najeeb

Ahmed Quereshi

Father Philip Reifenberg

Dr. Zulfiqar Ali Shah

Bishop Richard Sklba (convener)

List of Interviews

Alkaff, Huda (Founder and director of Wisconsin Green Muslims; founding member of Interfaith Earth Network). Interview by Andrew Musgrave. November 20, 2017.

Arora, Dr. Swarnjit (Professor Emeritus at University of Wisconsin–Milwaukee). Interview by Irfan Omar and Kaitlyn Daly. June 26, 2018.

Arshad, Naheed (Community Activist and Muslim Dialogue partner). Interview by Sundus Jaber and Caroline Redick. May 24, 2017.

Atta, Intisar (Early member of the Islamic-Christian dialogue). Interview by Andrew Musgrave. Circa November 2007.

Atta, Intisar. Interview by Irfan Omar, Dianne Marshall, Sundus Jaber, and Caroline Redick. March 24, 2017.

Atta, Othman (Executive Director of Islamic Society of Milwaukee). Interview by Irfan Omar, Dianne Marshall, Sundus Jaber, and Caroline Redick. March 24, 2017.

Bates-Froiland, Pastor Lisa (Pastor of Redeemer Lutheran Church). Interview by Kaitlyn Daly and Jashive Quintas. March 27, 2018.

Callan-Farley, Mary Sue (Director of Campus Ministry at Marquette University). Interview by Kaitlyn Daly. June 15, 2017.

Cole, Dr. Xavier (Vice President of Student Affairs at Marquette University). Interview by Kaitlyn Daly. March 29, 2017.

Dake, Thomas (Senior Student Services Coordinator at Student Involvement at University of Wisconsin-Milwaukee). Interview by Kaitlyn Daly. April 21, 2017.

Daniels-Sykes, Dr. Shawnee (Professor at Mount Mary University). Interview by Caroline Redick. May 16, 2017.

DeGarmo, Bradley (Undergraduate student at Marquette University). Interview by Kaitlyn Daly. June 24, 2017.

Dubey, Rahul and Dimple (Interfaith activists and members of the Sikh Temple of WI). Interview by Sundus Jaber and Caroline Redick. April 19, 2017.

Di Domizio, Dr. Daniel (Professor Emeritus at Cardinal Stritch University). Interview by Kaitlyn Daly, Milwaukee. March 1, 2017.

Farhoud, Inshirah (Community Activist and Vice President of the Milwaukee Muslim Women's Coalition). Interview by Dianne Marshall and Sundus Jaber. March 14, 2017.

Gabriel Dias Duarte Machado, Luiz (Undergraduate student at Marquette University). Interview by Kaitlyn Daly. March 16, 2017.

Gumbel, Rev. Reirin (Resident Priest at Milwaukee Zen Center). Interview by Kaitlyn Daly. April 3, 2018.

Hagen, Rev. Karen (Pastor at Tippecanoe Church and Founding member of the Southeast Milwaukee Interfaith Covenant Community). Interview by Irfan Omar. September 10, 2018.

Hamdan, Imam Ziad (Imam at the Islamic Society of Milwaukee and member of the Southeast Milwaukee Interfaith Covenant Community). Interview by Irfan Omar. July 1, 2019.

Hamdani, Dr. Abbas (Retired Professor of History and founding member of the Islamic-Christian dialogue. Interview by Andrew Musgrave. Circa October 2007.

Hamdani, Dr. Abbas. Interview (via email) by Irfan Omar and Caroline Redick. April 23, 2017.

Heinen, Tom (Executive Director, Interfaith Conference of Greater Milwaukee, 2009–2019). Interview by Andrew Musgrave. November 4, 2017.

Heinritz, Sean (Graduate student, University of Wisconsin-Milwaukee). Interview by Kaitlyn Daly. February 28, 2017.

Jaber, Sundus (Undergraduate student at Marquette University). Interview by Kaitlyn Daly. March 7, 2017.

Jacobs, Rev. Alexander (Sandy) (Lutheran Pastor and community leader). Interview by Irfan Omar. May 23, 2017.

Jung, Bishop Hee-Soo (Resident Bishop in the Wisconsin Annual Conference, United Methodist Church). Interview by Irfan Omar. August 18, 2018.

Kahn, Elana (Director of Jewish Community Relations Council). Interview by Irfan Omar and Caroline Redick. May 24, 2017.

Knippel, Rev. Ken (Pastor of St. John Vianney Parish). Interview by Kaitlyn Daly and Jashive Quintas. March 16, 2018.

Lied, Rev. Steve (Peace Catalyst International). Interview by Irfan Omar and Caroline Redick. May 26, 2017.

Longdin, Judith (Former Director of Archdiocese of Milwaukee Ecumenical and Interfaith Commission). Interview by Sundus Jaber, Dianne Marshall, and Caroline Redick. March 14, 2017.

Lovell, Dr. Michael R. (President of Marquette University). Interview (via email) by Kaitlyn Daly.

Miller, Tabetha (Tabby) (Undergraduate student at University of Wisconsin–Milwaukee). Interview by Kaitlyn Daly. February 28, 2017.

Najeeb, Janan (Community leader and founding president of the Milwaukee Muslim Women's Coalition). Interview by Andrew Musgrave. Circa November 2007.

Najeeb, Janan. Interview by Sundus Jaber. April 18, 2017.

Oren, Rev. Andy (Former Pastor of the Bay View United Methodist Church). Interview by Irfan Omar. August 14, 2018.

Pettee, Benjamin (Undergraduate student at Marquette University). Interview by Kaitlyn Daly. March 7, 2017.

Quereshi, Ahmed. (Board member of ICGM, former president of the Islamic Society of Milwaukee). Interview by Irfan Omar. August 6, 2019.

Reiss, Sister Jessine OSF (Franciscan Sister and the founding member of the Islamic-Christian dialogue). Interview by Andrew Musgrave. Circa October 2007.

Reiss, Sister Jessine OSF. Interview by Irfan Omar and Caroline Redick. March 25, 2017.

Russell, Dr. Stephanie (Former Vice President of Mission and Ministry at Marquette University). Interview (via phone) by Kaitlyn Daly. March 21, 2017.

Sandhu, Yuvraj (Yuvi) (Undergraduate student at Marquette University). Interview by Kaitlyn Daly. March 6, 2017.

Schmitt, Dr. John and Bobbie (Dialogue participants). Interview by Dianne Marshall and Sundus Jaber. February 28, 2017.

Shaheed, Imam Ronald (Former Principal of Sister Clara Muhammad School). Interview by Irfan Omar. June 17, 2019.

Sklba, Bishop Richard (Retired Auxiliary Bishop of Milwaukee). Interview by Caroline Redick. February 17, 2017.

Taylor, Dr. Richard C. (Professor of Philosophy at Marquette University). Interview by Irfan Omar and Kaitlyn Daly. May 17, 2017.

Waghary, Laj (Milwaukee filmmaker, social activist). Interview by Irfan Omar and Caroline Redick. May 24, 2017.

Walsh, Sister Lucille, OSF (Franciscan Sister and the founding member of the Islamic-Christian dialogue). Interview by Andrew Musgrave. Circa October 2007.

Warner, Pastor Andrew (Retired pastor of the Plymouth UCC). Interview by Irfan Omar and Andrew Musgrave. October 10, 2017.

Woll, Rabbi Michal (Religious leader at the Reconstructionist Jewish Community). Interview by Irfan Omar and Andrew Musgrave. October 10, 2017.

Interview Questions

I. General Questions

1. What is your own faith background (briefly)? (e.g., denomination)
2. How do you define "interfaith"? What does this mean to you? What images, experiences, thoughts, words come to mind when you think of "interfaith"?
3. How are you involved in interfaith engagement in your daily life?
4. When did your involvement with (organization/dialogue) begin?
5. How long have you been engaged in interfaith outreach?
6. What first motivated you to become involved with this work?
7. Who were your main interlocutors and partners in dialogue?
8. Which communities/religious groups (parishes/churches/synagogues/temples, etc.) are you most engaged with?
9. What are some of your best memories of dialogue? Why are they important?
10. Did you run into any challenges in initiating/sustaining the dialogue?
11. In your capacity as (role), what are some of the challenges in advancing the interfaith agenda?
12. How do you deal with those within your community that are against interfaith dialogue?
13. What are some of your goals of interfaith outreach? What do you hope to achieve?
14. What do you think was the impact of the dialogue in which you were involved?
15. Are you still involved in this dialogue or organization? If not, has it continued? Do you know who is currently involved?
16. If you were to start it all over again, would you have done it differently?
17. What advice do you have to someone who is in college right now, wanting to start interfaith dialogue in a new place?
18. Is there anything additional you would like to add to this interview (comments, questions, feedback, etc.)?
19. Do you have any "show and tell," such as pictures, articles, published reports, etc., to share?

20. Who else should we be contacting regarding the dialogue? Are there other people in the Milwaukee area that you would recommend we interview for the book?

21. Can we include this interview, pictures, or other show-and-tell items in a future publication?

II. Additional Questions Specific to Category

   a. University Leadership, Faculty, and Staff:

     1. What is your role as (position title)? In your own words, what do you do on campus?

     2. How do you see faith playing a role at your university?

     3. As (position title) at the university, what role do you play in interfaith work on campus?

     4. What interfaith activities or groups are currently engaging in interfaith work at your university? Have you had the opportunity to attend any of these activities or group meetings while serving as (position title)?

     5. What are the supports and barriers to interfaith work at your university (i.e., personal, political, structural)?

     6. What value is your university to interfaith work? What value is interfaith work to your university?

     7. How is your university a value to the greater Milwaukee community in regard to interfaith work? How is the greater Milwaukee community a value to your university in regard to interfaith work?

     8. What is the value that university can bring to interfaith efforts in Milwaukee? How does Milwaukee community and Milwaukee interfaith efforts have a positive effect on the university?

     9. What are the benefits and challenges of working with young adult university students as well as leadership, faculty, and staff for interfaith efforts?

    10. Have there been any other key figures, whether in leadership/faculty/staff, specifically, or throughout campus or among students who have been influential to your experience with "interfaith" at the university?

    11. Interfaith dialogue can take many different forms among the various genders, religions, and roles (i.e., women's dialogue; Muslim–Christian dialogue; student dialogue). What is the goal of student interfaith dialogue? What hopes do you have going forward?

    12. The university's mission statement encourages "XYZ." How do you see the mission having an impact on students' faiths lives whether the students are Christian, Jewish, Muslim, Buddhist, Sikh, or of any other religious or nonreligious tradition? Do you see that the mission

encompasses all individuals as a whole, or is it more directed toward a certain religious group of students?

13. In your experience, what is the leadership's attitude toward interfaith efforts? Among leadership, is there a common commitment to interfaith engagement and awareness on campus? Is there acceptance or resistance toward such efforts?

14. Officially delivered messages on (date) regarding important topics (listed). How can these messages and initiatives improve interfaith efforts at the university to benefit and enrich the interfaith fabric on campus and in Milwaukee?

15. Students are transient. They go somewhere after graduation. However, the university remains. What is the university's role in promoting and maintaining interfaith engagement at the university and Milwaukee?

b. University Students:

1. What has been the history of interfaith work at your university?

2. At your (university), who are your peers and are they interested in interfaith?

3. What are the changes you would like to see (at the university) with regard to interfaith efforts?

4. Do you have any ideas for best approaches to engaging students?

5. What role do you play in interfaith work on campus?

6. What value does your university bring to interfaith work? What value does interfaith work bring to your university?

7. What are the supports and barriers to interfaith work at your university (i.e., personal, political, structural)?

8. What are the benefits and challenges of working with students and young adults?

9. What is the goal of student interfaith dialogue?

10. How is your university a value to the greater Milwaukee community with respect to interfaith work?

11. How is the greater Milwaukee community a value to your university with respect to interfaith work?

12. What was your interfaith retreat experience?

13. What advice do you have for someone who is in college right now and wants to start interfaith dialogue in a new place, or to initiate or participate in existing interfaith activities?

Sample Letter

Dear [Mr./Dr./Ms._____],

My name is [researcher's name], and I am currently enrolled in the [name of program] at Marquette University. I received your name from Dr. Irfan Omar at Marquette, who teaches a doctoral seminar on Muslim–Christian dialogue. He recommended you as someone who has been involved in interfaith dialogue in Milwaukee. I am wondering if you might be willing to set up an informational interview at your convenience.

I am hoping to interview persons who have been active in or have interest in interfaith and/or Muslim–Christian dialogue in Milwaukee. This information is collected as part of a research project to chart the history of interfaith dialogue in this city. We are working to document the efforts and history of dialogue, especially Christian–Muslim dialogue, in Milwaukee in a research-based publication, supplemented by quantitative data. I would be happy to meet with you in person, or interview by phone, if that would be more convenient for you.

I am particularly interested in how you became involved in interfaith dialogue and your memories of the dialogue. In addition, we are interested in any "show-and-tell" items you may want to share, such as pictures, flyers, and other related items.

Here is a sample of some of the questions I would ask:

1. When did your involvement with this organization or dialogue begin?
2. What first motivated you to become involved with this work?
3. Who were your main interlocutors and partners in dialogue?
4. What are some of your best memories of dialogue? Why?
5. What do you think was the impact of the dialogue in which you were involved?

Thank you for your time and consideration. If you are interested in participating in our project, or have further questions, please email me at [researcher's email].

Sincerely,

[Name of the researcher]

Images Acknowledgments and Credits

Figure I.1: copy supplied by Jessine Reiss.

Figure I.2: copy supplied by Jessine Reiss.

Figure I.3: copy supplied by Jessine Reiss.

Figure I.4: copy supplied by Jessine Reiss.

Figure P.1: copy supplied by Irfan A. Omar.

Figure P.2: copy supplied by Irfan A. Omar.

Figure 1.1: copy supplied by Jessine Reiss.

Figure 1.2: photo supplied by Jessine Reiss.

Figure 1.3: photo supplied by Jessine Reiss.

Figure 1.4: photo supplied by Jessine Reiss.

Figure 1.5: photo supplied by Jessine Reiss.

Figure 1.6: copy supplied by Jessine Reiss.

Figure 1.7: photo supplied by Steve Lied.

Figure 1.8: photo by Irfan A. Omar.

Figure 2.1: courtesy of the *Milwaukee Journal*; copy supplied by Jessine Reiss.

Figure 2.2: courtesy of the *Catholic Herald*, copy supplied by Jessine Reiss.

Figure 2.3: copy supplied by Jessine Reiss.

Figure 2.4: photo supplied by Jessine Reiss.

Figure 2.5: courtesy of R. Marston Speight, copy supplied by Jessine Reiss.

Figure 2.6: photo supplied by Tom Heinen.

Figure 3.1: photo by Sundus Jaber.

Figure 3.2: courtesy of the Islamic Society of Milwaukee.

Figure 3.3: flyer supplied by Bobbie Schmitt.

Figures 3.4 and 3.5: courtesy of the *Mount Mary Magazine*, copy supplied by Inshirah Farhoud.

Figure 3.6: photo by Sundus Jaber.

Figure 4.1: photo supplied by Jessine Reiss.

Figure 4.2: photo supplied by Jessine Reiss.

Figure 4.3: flyer supplied by Steve Lied.

Figure 4.4: photo by Irfan A. Omar.

Figure 4.5: courtesy of *Wisconsin Muslim Journal*.

Figure 5.1: flyer supplied by Kirsten Shead.

Figure 5.2: flyer supplied by Kirsten Shead.

Figure 5.3: courtesy of National Catholic Muslim Dialogue and Anthony Cirelli.

Figures 5.4 and 5.5: courtesy of Bobbie and John Schmitt.

Figures 5.6 & 5.7: photo and text supplied by Tom Heinen.

Figure 6.1: copy supplied by Judi Longdin.

Figure 6.2: flyer supplied by Janan Najeeb.

Figure 6.3: copy supplied by Judi Longdin.

Figure 6.4: flyer supplied by Janan Najeeb.

Figure 6.5: flyer supplied by Janan Najeeb.

Figure 6.6: copy supplied by Judi Longdin.

Figure 6.7: flyer supplied by Janan Najeeb.

Figure 6.8: flyer supplied by Judi Longdin.

Figure 6.9: photo supplied by Judi Longdin.

Figure 6.10: photo supplied by Naheed Arshad.

Figure 7.1: copy supplied by Dan Di Domizio.

Figure 7.2: flyer supplied by Dan Di Domizio.

Figure 7.3: flyer supplied by Dan Di Domizio.

Figure 7.4: flyer supplied by Dan Di Domizio.

Figure 7.5: flyer supplied by Irfan A. Omar.

Figure.7.6: flyer supplied by Irfan A. Omar.

Figure 7.7: courtesy of Susan Mountin.

Figure 7.8: flyer supplied by Enaya Othman.

Figure 7.9: flyer supplied by Irfan A. Omar.

Figure 7.10: flyer supplied by Irfan A. Omar.

Figure 7.11: flyer supplied by Irfan A. Omar.

Figure 7.12: flyer supplied by Irfan A. Omar.

Figure 7.13: photo by Irfan A. Omar.

Figure 7.14: flyer designed by Chris Jeske and the staff at the Marquette University Center for Peacemaking.

Figures 7.15 & 7.16: photos by Irfan A. Omar.

Figure 7.17: copy supplied by Irfan A. Omar.

Figure 7.18: flyer supplied by Richard C. Taylor.

Figures 7.19 & 7.20: flyer supplied by Irfan A. Omar.

Figures 7.21 & 7.22: photos supplied by Kaitlyn Daly.

Figures 7.23 & 7.24: images supplied by Kaitlyn Daly.

Figures 7.25, 7.26, 7.27, & 7.28: photos by Michael Carpenter.

Figures 7.29 & 7.30: courtesy of the Interfaith Coordinating Team (ICT) at Marquette University.

Figure 7.31: courtesy of the Interfaith Coordinating Team.

Figures 7.32, 7.33, & 7.34: photos by Luiz Gabriel Dias Duarte Machado.

Figure 7.35: flyer courtesy of the Interfaith Coordinating Team.

Figure 7.36: courtesy of the Jewish Student Union (JSU) at Marquette University.

Figure 7.37: courtesy of Hillel Milwaukee.

Figure 7.38: photo supplied by Kaitlyn Daly.

Figures 7.39 & 7.40: courtesy of the Student Union at University Wisconsin-Milwaukee.

Figure 7.41: courtesy of Marquette University Department of Marketing and Communications.

Figure 7.42: courtesy of Interfaith Youth Core (IFYC)

Figure 7.43: courtesy of *Marquette Tribune*.

Figure 8.1: photo by Irfan A. Omar.

Figure 8.2: courtesy of the Interfaith Conference of Greater Milwaukee (ICGM).

Figure 8.3: courtesy of ICGM.

Figure 8.4: courtesy of ICGM.

Figure 8.5: photo by Irfan A. Omar.

Figure 8.6: courtesy of ICGM.

Figure 8.7: courtesy of ICGM.

Figure 8.8: photo supplied by Tom Heinen.

Figure 8.9: photo supplied by Elana Kahn.

Figure 8.10: courtesy of ICGM and the Brookfield, Elm Grove Interfaith Network (BEGIN).

Figure 8.11: photo by Jashive Quintas.

Figure 8.12: photo by Irfan A. Omar.

Figure 8.13: photo by Andrew Musgrave.

Figure 8.14: photo by Andrew Musgrave.

Figure 8.15: supplied by Andy Oren.

Figures 8.16, 8.17, & 8.18: copies supplied by Andy Oren.

Figure 8.19: supplied by Andy Oren.

Figure 8.20: copy supplied by Andy Oren.

Figure 8.21: copies supplied by Andy Oren.

Figure 8.22: copies supplied by Andy Oren.

Figure 8.23: flyer supplied by Andy Oren.

Figure 8.24: flyer supplied by Andy Oren.

Figure 8.25: photo supplied by Onur Asan.

Figure 8.26: photo by Laura Hermanns.

Figure 8.27: photo by Laura Hermanns.

Figure 8.28: copy supplied by Huda Alkaff.

Figures 8.29 & 8.30: photos by Irfan A. Omar.

Figure 8.31: courtesy of *Milwaukee Magazine*, photo by Adam Ryan Morris.

Figure 8.32: photo by Sue Vliet.

Figure 8.33: supplied by Reirin Gumbel.

Figure 8.34: supplied by Reirin Gumbel.

Figure 8.35: photo supplied by Orusa Hassan.

Figure 8.36: photo supplied by Elana Kahn.

Figure 8.37: photo supplied by Elana Kahn.

Figure 8.38: St. photo by Kaitlyn Daly.

Figure 8.39: photo by Irfan A. Omar.

Figure 8.40: courtesy of the Islamic Society of Milwaukee.

Figure 8.41: flyer supplied by Steve Lied.

Figure 8.42: photo supplied by Jessine Reiss.

Figure 8.43: copy supplied by Jessine Reiss.

Figure 8.44: photo supplied by Ronald Shaheed.

Figure 8.45: photo supplied by Ronald Shaheed.

Figure 8.46: courtesy of Ma'ruf, Milwaukee.

Figure 8.47: photo supplied by Tom Heinen.

Figures 8.48 & 8.49: photos by Irfan A. Omar.

Figure 8.50: flyer supplied by Elana Kahn.

Figure 8.51: flyer supplied by Elana Kahn.

Figure 8.52: courtesy of the Jewish Community Relations Council (JCRC), Milwaukee.

Figure 8.53: photo supplied by Elana Kahn.

Figure 8.54: supplied by Jame Schaefer.

Figure 8.55: flyer supplied by Kirsten Shead.

Figure 8.56: copy supplied by Othman Atta.

Figure 8.57: courtesy of the Islamic Society of Milwaukee, Brookfield.

Figure 8.58: courtesy of the MTO School of Sufism, flyer supplied by Nooshin Nekooei.

Figure 8.59: courtesy of the MTO School of Sufism, flyer supplied by Nooshin Nekooei.

Figures 8.60 & 8.61: photo by Irfan A. Omar.

Figure 8.62: photo by Irfan A. Omar.

Figure 8.63: courtesy of ICGM.

Figure 8.64: courtesy of the Islamic Society of Milwaukee and Othman Atta.

Figure 8.65: courtesy of ICGM.

Figure 8.66: photo by Irfan A. Omar.

Figure 8.67: courtesy of the Wisconsin Conference United Methodist Church and Andy Oren.

Figure 8.68: photo by Ben Cruz.

Figure 8.69: courtesy of the Wisconsin Conference United Methodist Church and Andy Oren.

Figure 8.70: photo by Irfan A. Omar.

Figure 8.71: photo by Ben Cruz.

Figure 8.72: photo by Irfan A. Omar.

Figures 8.73 & 8.74: photo by Irfan A. Omar.

Figure 8.75: courtesy of the Islamic Society of Milwaukee

Figures 8.76 & 8.77: flyer supplied by Irfan A. Omar

Figure 8.78: photo by Onur Asan.

Figure 8.79: photo by Irfan A. Omar.

Figure 8.80: photo by Irfan A. Omar.

Figure 8.81: courtesy of *Marquette Tribune*.

Figure 8.82: photo by Irfan A. Omar.

Figure 8.83: photo by Irfan A. Omar.

Figure 8.84: courtesy of the Marquette University Center for Peacemaking.

Figure 8.85: photo supplied by Andrew Musgrave.

Figure E.1: photo by Irfan A. Omar.

Figure E.2: photo by Irfan A. Omar.

Further Reading

DIALOGUE IN MILWAUKEE

Bush, Trudy, and Elliott Bush, "Muslims and Christians: Sharing Faith and Life." *The Christian Century* (May–June 1991): 9–11.

> This short article is written by the couple from Wisconsin who were part of the Islamic Christian Dialogue of the 1980s and 1990s. It showcases the Milwaukee dialogue and presents the facts of what has happened and its impact. It is written for a lay Christian audience.

Hinze, Bradford. "Jewish, Christian, Muslim Trialogue: An Introductory Survey." *Heirs of Abraham: The Future of Muslim, Jewish, and Christian, Relations,* 1–19. Eds. Bradford Hinze and Irfan A. Omar. Maryknoll, NY: Orbis, 2005.

> Hinze notes that "this particular project builds on many efforts being made by religious communities throughout the Milwaukee metropolitan area." He outlines the history of Muslim–Christian dialogues globally, as well as trialogues between Christians, Jews, and Muslims.

Islamic Society of Milwaukee. "Muslims in Milwaukee: A Brief History." In *Islamic Society of Milwaukee: 25 Years of Service* (2007).

> This pamphlet, written and published by the Islamic Society of Milwaukee for its anniversary, gives a detailed history of Muslims in Milwaukee, including Nation of Islam, the first Arab migrants to Milwaukee, and the origins of the Islamic society. The information appears to be well researched and the best source available for the history of Muslims in the area.

McCarthy, Kate. *Interfaith Encounters in America*. New Brunswick, NJ: Rutgers University Press, 2007.

> This groundbreaking book explores the activism related to interfaith dialogue in the form of case studies. It delves deeper into documenting the experiences of dialogue actors in select communities across America. McCarthy engages with people at a variety of levels to understand how dialogue is understood and how it is evolving based on the emerging relationships across individuals and institutions. Milwaukee is one of the five case studies discussed in this book.

Midwest Dialogue of Catholics and Muslims. "Revelation: Catholic and Muslim Perspectives." Washington, DC: United States Conference of Catholic Bishops, 2006, 1–49.

> There is a helpful section on "the Midwest Dialogue of Catholics and Muslims." The document was sponsored by the Islamic Society of North America and the United States Conference of Catholic Bishops. Representatives of the Islamic Society of Milwaukee and the Archdiocese of Milwaukee have participated in the dialogue since 2003.

Renard, John. *101 Questions and Answers on Islam*. New York: Paulist Press, 1998.

Under the question heading "could you give an example of successful Christian-Muslim dialogue? What do people talk about in dialogue groups and what lessons have their members learned thus far?" Renard presents Milwaukee as an example of successful dialogue. He mentions the 1980 dialogue in Milwaukee but does not further specify the organization or participants. The paragraph is an example of Milwaukee's reputation in Muslim–Christian relations.

Sklba, Richard J. "A Local Tribute to Muslim/Catholic Cooperation." *Herald of Hope*, July 23, 2015.

In this article for the *Catholic Herald*, Bishop Sklba describes the work of a small group (nine people) of Catholics and Muslims that meet monthly to explore each other's religious beliefs and practices. The article points out current misconceptions of Islam in the United States, such as the portrayal of radical groups as normative for Islam. The group believes that it is a religious duty to be ambassadors for one another, speaking truth, and working together for the common good.

Speight, R. Marston. *God Is One: The Way of Islam*. 2nd edition. New York: Friendship Press, 2001.

In the section on dialogue, it includes text boxes about Lucille Walsh and Abbas Hamdani about their work in Milwaukee. Pages 106–11 are relevant to Wisconsin dialogues.

Sweas, Megan. "Won't You Be My Neighbor?" *US Catholic*, February 2007, 24–27.

This article highlights the success of different Christian–Muslim dialogues in the United States and includes a section on the Milwaukee Muslim–Catholic Women's Dialogue.

Wisconsin Council of Churches. "Loving Our Neighbors: A Statement of the Wisconsin Council of Churches on Interfaith Relations." November 17, 2014.

The document notes religious diversity in Wisconsin and various interfaith initiatives. It takes the commandments of love of God and love of neighbor as paradigmatic for interfaith relations. From these commandments, the document argues that love of God is a free act of conscience and occludes coercive persuasion. Second, Christians are commanded to love their neighbor—even in disagreement. It then recommends dialogical virtues such as humble listening, prophetic witness, and compassionate collaboration.

Responses to "A Common Word"

"A Common Word between Us and You." Amman, Jordan: The Royal Aal al-Bayt Institute for Islamic Thought, 2012.

A letter from Muslim scholars to the Christian world, seeking common theological ground, since the peace of the world depends on harmonious relations between members of these two religious traditions. The document has had global as well as local impact.

El-Ansary, Waleed, and D. Linnan, eds. *Muslim and Christian Understanding: Theory and Application of 'A Common Word.'* New York: Palgrave MacMillan, 2010.

This work seeks to expand "A Common Word between Us and You" through a comparative study of "theology, mysticism and metaphysics," as well as law and governance (4). Scholars and religious leaders from various traditions offer perspectives on the "vertical" (theological) and "horizontal" (praxis) dimensions of "A Common Word."

Markiewicz, Sarah. *World Peace through Christian-Muslim Understanding.* Göttingen: V&R Unipress, 2016.

This scholarly work contextualizes "A Common Word between Us and You," noting the intent and context of its authors, the context of the Regensburg address, and the impact of the letter.

Volf, Miroslav, Ghazi bin Muhammad, and Melissa Yarrington. *A Common Word: Muslims and Christians on Loving God and Neighbor.* Grand Rapids, MI: Eerdmans, 2010.

This volume contains the original "A Common Word" document along with responses and reflections. "A Common Word between Us and You" (2007) is a foundational document calling for cooperation based on the values and ethics shared by these two faiths.

WOMEN'S PERSPECTIVES ON DIALOGUE

Cornille, Catherine, and Jillian Maxey. *Women and Interreligious Dialogue.* Interreligious Dialogue Series 5. Eugene, OR: Cascade Books, 2013.

Fletcher, Jeannine Hill. *Motherhood as a Metaphor: Engendering Interreligious Dialogue.* New York: Fordham University Press, 2013.

Frederiks, Martha. "The Women's Interfaith Journey: Journeying as a Method in Interfaith Relations." *Missiology: An International Review* 4 (October 2012): 467–79.

McGarvey, Kathleen. *Muslim and Christian Women in Dialogue: The Case of Northern Nigeria.* New York: Peter Lang, 2008.

Mollenkott, Virginia Ramey, ed. *Women of Faith in Dialogue.* New York: Crossroad Publishing, 1990.

O'Neill, Maura. *Women Speaking, Women Listening: Women in Interreligious Dialogue.* Maryknoll, NY: Orbis Books, 1990.

Schlumpf, Heidi. "Women Leaders Under the Cross and Crescent." *National Catholic Reporter,* April 25, 2003.

Thomas, Marie-Claude. *Women in Lebanon: Living with Christianity, Islam, and Multiculturalism.* New York: Palgrave MacMillan, 2013.

Islam & Christian–Muslim Dialogue

Aasi, Ghulam-Haider. "Christian-Muslim Dialogue in the United States: A Muslim Perspective." *Currents in Theology and Mission* 33.3 (2006): 213–22.

Alexander, Scott. "We go way back." *U.S. Catholic* magazine (June 2008): 1–13.

Ayoub, Mahmoud. *A Muslim View of Christianity: Essays on Dialogue*. Edited by Irfan A. Omar. Maryknoll, NY: Orbis Books, 2007.

Benedict XVI. "Address to the Catholic-Muslim Forum." Speech, Vatican's Clementine Hall. November 6, 2006.

Benedict XVI. "Need for Dialogue between Christians and Muslims." September 25, 2006. https://www.catholicculture.org/culture/library/view.cfm?recnum=7177.

Borrmans, Maurice. *Guidelines for Dialogue between Christians and Muslims*. Translated from the French by R. Marston Speight. Mahwah, NJ: Paulist Press, 1990.

Curtis, Edward E. *Muslims in America: A Short History*. Oxford: Oxford University Press, 2009.

Dardess, George, and Marvin L. Krier Mich. *In the Spirit of St. Francis & the Sultan: Catholics and Muslims Working Together for the Common Good*. Maryknoll, NY: Orbis Books, 2011.

Esposito, John. *What Everyone Needs to Know About Islam*. New York: Oxford University Press, 2002.

George-Tvrtković, Rita. *Christians, Muslims, and Mary: A History*. Mahwah, NJ: Paulist Press, 2018.

Goddard, Hugh. *Christians and Muslims: From Double Standards to Mutual Understanding*. Surrey: Cruzon Press, 1995.

Gülen, Fethullah. *The Necessity of Interfaith Dialogue: A Muslim Perspective*. Somerset, NJ: The Light, 2004.

Hedges, Paul, ed. *Contemporary Muslim-Christian Encounters: Developments, Diversity and Dialogues*. London: Bloomsbury, 2015.

Hussain, Amir. *Muslims and the Making of America*. Waco, TX: Baylor University Press, 2016.

Ipgrave, Michael, ed. *Building Better Bridges: Muslims, Christians and the Common Good*. Washington, DC: Georgetown University Press, 2008.

Michel, Thomas F. *A Christian View of Islam: Essays on Dialogue*. Edited by Irfan A. Omar. Maryknoll: NY: Orbis Books, 2010.

Midwest Dialogue of Catholics and Muslims. "Revelation: Catholic and Muslim Perspectives."

Washington, DC: United States Conference of Catholic Bishops, 2006.

Miss Understanding: Two Faiths, One Friendship. http://www.missunderstanding.com.

Mohammed, Ovey. *Muslim-Christian Relations: Past, Present, Future.* Maryknoll, NY: Orbis Books, 1999.

O'Mahony, Anthony, and Emma Loosley, eds. *Christian Responses to Islam: Muslim-Christian Relations in the Modern World.* Manchester: Manchester University Press, 2008.

Phipps, William E. *Muhammad and Jesus: A Comparison of the Prophets and their Teachings.* New York: Continuum, 1999.

Pignedoli, Cardinal Sergio. "The Catholic Church and the Jewish and Muslim Faiths: Trialogue of the Three Abrahamic Faiths." *Trialogue of the Abrahamic Faiths*, 1–12. Edited by Isma'il Raji al-Faruqi. Herdon, VA: International Institute of Islamic Thought, 1986.

Pontifical Council for Interreligious Dialogue. *Recognize the Spiritual Bonds Which Unite Us: 16 Years of Christian-Muslim Dialogue.* Vatican City: Pontifical Council for Interreligious Dialogue, 1994.

Pratt, Douglas. *Christian Engagement with Islam: Ecumenical Journeys since 1910.* Leiden: Brill, 2017.

Pratt, Douglas. "The Vatican in Dialogue with Islam: Inclusion and Engagement." *Islam and Christian-Muslim Relations* 21.3 (2010): 245–62.

The Shoulder-to-Shoulder Campaign. http://www.shouldertoshouldercampaign.org.

World Council of Churches. "Issues in Christian-Muslim Relations: Ecumenical Considerations." World Council of Churches, January 1, 1992.

Wright, Timothy. *No Peace without Prayer: Encouraging Muslims and Christians to Pray Together, a Benedictine Approach.* Collegeville, MN: Liturgical Press, 2013.

INTERRELIGIOUS DIALOGUE

Aspen Institute Justice & Society Program. *Interfaith Engagement in West Michigan: A Brief History and Analysis.* Edited by Charles Honey. Washington, DC: Aspen Institute, 2015.

Aspen Institute Justice & Society Program: Inclusive America Project. *Principled Pluralism: Report of the Inclusive America Project.* Washington, DC: Aspen Institute, 2013.

Borelli, John, and Michael Fitzgerald. *Interfaith Dialogue: A Catholic View.* Maryknoll, NY: Orbis Books, 2005.

Cornille, Catherine, ed. *The Wiley Companion to Interreligious Dialogue.* Hoboken, NJ: Wiley-Blackwell, 2013.

The Evangelical Interfaith Resource Center. http://evangelicalinterfaith.org.

Hinze, Bradford. *Practices of Dialogue in the Roman Catholic Church: Aims and Obstacles, Lessons and Laments.* New York: Continuum, 2006.

Knitter, Paul F. *No Other Name?: A Critical Survey of Christian Attitudes toward the World Religions.* Maryknoll, NY: Orbis Books, 1985.

Moyaert, Marianne. *Fragile Identities: Towards a Theology of Interreligious Hospitality*. Translated by Henry Jansen. Amsterdam: Rodopi, 2011.

Nolan, Ann Michele. *A Privileged Moment: Dialogue in the Language of the Second Vatican Council, 1962–1965*. New York: P. Lang, 2006.

Phan, Peter. *Being Religious Interreligiously: An Asian Perspective on Dialogue*. Maryknoll, NY: Orbis Books, 2004.

Sacks, Jonathan. *The Dignity of Difference: How to Avoid the Clash of Civilizations*. London: Continuum, 2002.

Sherwin, Byron L., and Harold Kasimow, eds. *John Paul II and Interreligious Dialogue*. Maryknoll, NY: Orbis Books, 1999.

World Council of Churches Pontifical Council for Interreligious Dialogue World Evangelical Alliance. "Recommendations for Conduct." Christian Witness in a Multi-Religious World, 2011.

Rossi, Philip J., ed. *Seekers and Dwellers: Plurality and Wholeness in a Time of Secularity*. Washington DC: Council for Research in Values and Philosophy, 2016.

Contributors

Kaitlyn C. Daly is a graduate of Marquette University (2017) with a Bachelor of Science in Nursing (BSN) degree with double majors in Nursing and Theology & Religion. Throughout her time at Marquette, as a Lutheran coming to a Catholic campus, Kaitlyn pursued interfaith-related activities, including courses, campus events, and conferences. She became one of the founding members of Marquette's first Interfaith Coordinating Team (ICT) and interfaith group, Breaking Barriers & Building Bridges (BB&BB). In her final year at Marquette she took a graduate-level course on Muslim–Christian dialogue, which allowed her to explore the roles played by Milwaukee educational institutions and the persons within them in the overall interfaith effort in Milwaukee and beyond. Kaitlyn plans to continue to pursue her passion of studying and promoting interfaith education and engagement even as she pursues her doctoral studies in Nursing at Duke University. Her goal is to explore the intersection of spirituality, theology, and health.

Sundus Jaber is currently pursuing her Master of Divinity (M. Div.) at Bayan-Claremont School of Theology in Islamic chaplaincy. She also serves as the Muslim Life Fellow at the Claremont University Consortium in Claremont, California. Sundus was born and raised in Milwaukee, Wisconsin, and where she studied at Marquette University, graduating in 2017 with a Bachelor of Science (BS) in speech pathology and audiology, and a minor in psychology. At Marquette, she was a student leader responsible for organizing events on peacemaking, interreligious dialogue, and Muslim spirituality. During her time at Marquette, Sundus was a Mellon research fellow at the local non-for-profit organization *Arab and Muslim Women's Research and Resource Institute* (AMWRRI) and a staff member at Milwaukee Muslim Women's Coalition (MMWC). Her research work on the history of Muslim–Catholic dialogue has been transformative; she has developed a passion for interdisciplinary approaches to interreligious dialogue, peacemaking, pastoral care, and counseling.

Judith Longdin served as director of the Office of Ecumenical and Interfaith Concerns for the Archdiocese of Milwaukee from 1993 until her retirement in January 2018. In that capacity she worked to promote ecumenical and interfaith relations throughout the archdiocese, providing support for parishes and Catholic institutions, and for various dialogues sponsored by the diocese. She also represented the archdiocese on the statewide, regional, and national levels. She served on the Unity and Relations Committee of the Wisconsin Council of Churches. She also served on the Midwest Muslim/Catholic Dialogue and the National Muslim–Catholic Dialogue sponsored by the US Catholic Conference of Bishops, the Islamic Society of North America, and other national Muslim organizations. She was privileged to participate in national Sikh–Catholic conversations in 2014 and 2016. Judith has also participated in national Evangelical–Catholic and Buddhist–Catholic conversations. As a member of the Catholic Association of Diocesan Ecumenical and Interreligious Officers, she served on its Faiths in the World Committee, most recently serving as chair. In 2011 and 2015 she co-facilitated the Interreligious Institute for CADEIO members. Locally, she co-founded the Milwaukee Muslim–Catholic Women's Dialogue and participated in the local Muslim–Catholic Dialogue. Judith has worked closely with the Interfaith Conference of Greater Milwaukee (ICGM), serving on various committees including the Cabinet and the executive committee. She co-chaired the Milwaukee Catholic–Jewish Conference, and, is a founding member of the Lux Center for Catholic–Jewish Relations at Sacred Heart Seminary and School of Theology.

Andrew Musgrave is a graduate of Marquette University (2008) with an MA in public service and nonprofit leadership. Prior to that he attended the University of Notre Dame where he received a BA in theology (2003) with a focus on comparative religion, peace studies, and Middle Eastern studies. Andrew has many years of experience working in the nonprofit and faith sectors; he currently serves as the director of the Catholic Social Action office for the Archdiocese of Cincinnati. He is passionate about working to justly address issues regarding racism, immigration, climate change, and hunger.

Janan Atta Najeeb is the founding member and the current president of the Milwaukee Muslim Women's Coalition (MMWC). She has been a spokesperson for Milwaukee's Muslim community to media outlets, government officials, interfaith leaders, academic institutions, hospitals, and a wide range of community groups. A microbiologist by profession (UW–Milwaukee), Janan left her career because of the need to bridge the gap between the erroneous perception of Islam and Muslims in society and the actual beliefs and practices of the vast majority of the world's Muslims. She is active in many social justice organizations locally and nationally and has been an adjunct professor at Cardinal Stritch University in Milwaukee. She is the founding director of the Islamic Resource Center (IRC), located on the south side of Milwaukee. In 2015,

Janan founded the Milwaukee Muslim Film Festival, and in 2016 she became the first Muslim in Wisconsin to open the floor of the State Legislature with a prayer. Janan is the recipient of numerous awards and recognitions, including the International Institute of Wisconsin's "World Citizen Award," The Wisconsin Community Fund's "Grantee of the Year Award," CAIR's (Council on American Islamic Relations) national award for activism, and the ACLU's "Special Recognition Award." She was also named by Wisconsin's *Women Magazine* as a "Leader Making a Difference."

Irfan A. Omar is associate professor of theology at Marquette University in Milwaukee, where he teaches courses in Islamic and interfaith studies as well as a course on religion and nonviolence. He is also an affiliated faculty member with the Center for South Asia at the University of Wisconsin–Madison. He has published several book chapters, journal articles, and book reviews, and has edited and co-edited seven books, including *Peacemaking and the Challenge of Violence in World Religions* (2015), *The Judeo-Christian-Islamic Heritage: Philosophical and Theological Perspectives* (2012), *A Christian View of Islam: Essays on Dialogue by Thomas F. Michel, S.J.* (2010). He currently serves on the editorial boards of the *Journal of Ecumenical Studies* and the *Journal of Race, Ethnicity, and Religion.*

Caroline Redick is currently a doctoral candidate in theological ethics at Marquette University in Milwaukee, Wisconsin. Her main research focus is Pentecostal ethics and moral sources for solidarity. Caroline has published articles in scholarly journals *Pneuma* and the *International Journal of Public Theology*. She became interested in ecumenical and interfaith dialogue after taking a graduate course on Christian–Muslim dialogue, which allowed her to explore the theme of solidarity from an interreligious perspective.

Dianne Rostollan (Marshall) graduated from Marquette University in 2018 with a master's degree in Christian doctrine (MACD). Dianne has been the director of youth ministry for the Northside Sheboygan Catholic Parishes in Sheboygan, Wisconsin. She is currently serving as the director of youth ministry at St. Mary Immaculate Parish in Plainfield, Illinois. She works with teenagers from diverse schools and is passionate about teaching the need for dialogue as a way of living the Catholic faith today.

Index